From Historical to Critical Post-Colonial Theology

african christian studies series (africs)

This series will make available significant works in the field of African Christian studies, taking into account the many forms of Christianity across the whole continent of Africa. African Christian studies is defined here as any scholarship that relates to themes and issues on the history, nature, identity, character, and place of African Christianity in world Christianity. It also refers to topics that address the continuing search for abundant life for Africans through multiple appeals to African religions and African Christianity in a challenging social context. The books in this series are expected to make significant contributions in historicizing trends in African Christian studies, while shifting the contemporary discourse in these areas from narrow theological concerns to a broader inter-disciplinary engagement with African religio-cultural traditions and Africa's challenging social context.

The series will cater to scholarly and educational texts in the areas of religious studies, theology, mission studies, biblical studies, philosophy, social justice, and other diverse issues current in African Christianity. We define these studies broadly and specifically as primarily focused on new voices, fresh perspectives, new approaches, and historical and cultural analyses that are emerging because of the significant place of African Christianity and African religio-cultural traditions in world Christianity. The series intends to continually fill a gap in African scholarship, especially in the areas of social analysis in African Christian studies, African philosophies, new biblical and narrative hermeneutical approaches to African theologies, and the challenges facing African women in today's Africa and within African Christianity. Other diverse themes in African Traditional Religions; African ecology; African ecclesiology; inter-cultural, inter-ethnic, and inter-religious dialogue; ecumenism; creative inculturation; African theologies of development, reconciliation, globalization, and poverty reduction will also be covered in this series.

SERIES EDITORS

Dr. Stan Chu Ilo (St. Michael's College, University of Toronto)
Dr. Philomena Njeri Mwaura (Kenyatta University, Nairobi, Kenya)
Dr. Afe Adogame (University of Edinburgh)

From Historical to Critical Post-Colonial Theology

The Contribution of John S. Mbiti
and Jesse N. K. Mugambi

ROBERT S. HEANEY

Foreword by Christopher Rowland

☙PICKWICK *Publications* · Eugene, Oregon

FROM HISTORICAL TO CRITICAL POST-COLONIAL THEOLOGY
The Contribution of John S. Mbiti and Jesse N. K. Mugambi

African Christian Studies Series 9

Copyright © 2015 Robert S. Heaney. All rights reserved. Except for brief quotations in critical publications or reviews, no part of this book may be reproduced in any manner without prior written permission from the publisher. Write: Permissions, Wipf and Stock Publishers, 199 W. 8th Ave., Suite 3, Eugene, OR 97401.

Pickwick Publications
An Imprint of Wipf and Stock Publishers
199 W. 8th Ave., Suite 3
Eugene, OR 97401

www.wipfandstock.com

ISBN 13: 978-1-62564-781-8

Cataloguing-in-Publication Data

Heaney, Robert S.

    From historical to critical post-colonial theology : the contribution of John S. Mbiti and Jesse N. K. Mugambi / Robert S. Heaney.

African Christian Studies Series 9

    xvi + 262 p. ; 23 cm. Includes bibliographical references and index.

    ISBN 13: 978-1-62564-781-8

    1. Postcolonialism. 2. Postcolonial theology. 3. Mbiti, John S. 4. Mugambi, J. N. Kanyua (Jesse Ndwiga Kanyuga). 5. Africa—Religion. I. Series. II. Title.

BT124.5 H214 2015

Manufactured in the U.S.A.   11/05/2015

To Sharon and Sam

Contents

Foreword by Christopher Rowland | ix
Acknowledgments | xiii
Abbreviations | xv

Introduction | 1
1. Post-Colonialism | 11
2. The Critique of Mission Christianity in the Theological Writings of Mbiti and Mugambi | 31
3. Eschatological Issues and Context: Mbiti and the Akamba | 62
4. The Theological Significance of African Traditional Religions: Engaging the Religio-Cultural Experience of Africa | 94
5. Christ and Symbol in African Community | 126
6. Coloniality and Mugambi's Theology of Reconstruction | 149
7. Comparing the Writings of Mbiti and Mugambi with Post-Colonial Theology | 182

Conclusion | 200

Bibliography | 219
Index | 259

Foreword

ROBERT HEANEY WAS UNIQUE among my graduate students. During his doctorate he took time out to teach at St. John's University, in Dodoma in Tanzania. His experience of African theology, therefore, is not primarily from books but from his students, their struggles to find the resources to do their study and life that he, Sharon, and Sam made with people in Tanzania. It is no surprise, therefore, that he wants theologians and others in "the North" to attend to a theology which may have resonances with, but speaks from beyond, their context with words of wisdom and challenge. As Robert says, to listen is to be open to God's grace as well as to a judgment on our presumption and the narrowness of our perspective. He sets his task to take very seriously the work of two pioneering African theologians, John S. Mbiti and Jesse N. K. Mugambi. His work challenges the hegemonic discourse of so-called Western theologians and postcolonial theologians and their much cherished vaunting of critical thought which is at risk of overlooking engagement with the work of those from the World Church. Robert Heaney's work was revealing to me in the way in which it unfolded the evolution of different forms of contextual theology. I had come across Mbiti as his work had been drawn to my attention fifty years ago by one of my teachers, Charlie Moule, who was Lady Margaret Professor at the University of Cambridge for many years. The thesis of Mbiti's first book is illuminated by the variegated cultural context of its genesis and gestation. Robert Heaney identifies a methodological shift that begins in Mbiti, is present in Mugambi and remains a chronic issue for all theologians. He offers both a sympathetically insightful reading of Mbiti and Mugambi's writings, as well as framing the reading within a post-colonial approach to theology. Thus he broadens our perspectives beyond any binary presentations of Europe and Africa, and offers the possibility of a postcolonial

FOREWORD

theology nourished by the insight of Africa. Robert Heaney explores the contextualization of African theology, stressing the experience of particular people in a particular context as the point of theological departure. The ministry of Jesus is seen to correlate more closely with African traditional practice than with imported practice. Also, such contextualization is seen in the emphasis on symbol and praxis when considering the person of Christ, speaking from *within* African traditional religion as the one who is co-equal with a marginalized humanity. All this is complemented by a practical understanding of the analysis of power. Robert Heaney points out that there are ongoing theological, missiological, and pedagogical implications arising from listening to World Christianity, and listening to African theology in particular. Participationist, kenotic, and grassroots mission challenge overweening power and marginalization. Such theological themes are as important as the desire for cogency based on coherence. Teaching that begins with such counter-cultural discourse offer a different frame to Christian pedagogy.

In his conclusion Robert succinctly expresses his aim in this book when he writes:

> . . . with the continued justifications of Euro-American Christian expansionism by missiologists, mission historians, and foreign missionaries, there remains much work to be done uncovering how imperialism and colonialism has often influenced Western theology. As is already seen, the existence of this lacuna undermines the ongoing claim that the pedagogy of the traditional colonial centres is, in practice, critical. In practical terms, responding to coloniality and contributing to a decolonizing critique will therefore mean, at the very least, an engagement with marginalized theology and theologians. For marginalized voices to interrupt or intervene in Eurocentric theology already redefines the discipline. For, as has been seen, no longer can coherency be a chief aim of the theological task. Instead, some sort of liberative or transformative practice will be the end goal for theology. Such reflections underline the concern that some within the movement have that abstract and abstruse theorizing, while important and potentially transformative, can too easily lead the field away from the concrete, historical, practical theologizing that has been going on in particular contexts and particular experiences for many years. It is hoped that a critical engagement with the writings of Mbiti and Mugambi, taking into account both weaknesses and

possible constructive moves which their work evokes, begins to disrupt such abstractionism and abstruseness.

Amen to that. Liberative and transformative practice must be the end goal for theology too, for it too must be part of the messianic lifestyle which is the characteristic of the gospel of Jesus who came to preach good news to the poor.

Christopher Rowland
Dean Ireland's Professor of Exegesis of Holy Scripture
University of Oxford
Advent 2014

Acknowledgments

THE HOSPITALITY, WELCOME, AND kind assistance of various institutions and bodies in Africa and beyond which aided me in finding rather obscure sources and/or provided me with stimulating conversation on the subject of this book include Cambridge University (UK); Carlile College, Nairobi (Kenya); Centre for World Christianity, Edinburgh (UK); Crowther Centre for Mission Education, Oxford (UK); Ecumenical Institute, Bossey (Switzerland); Gordon College Postcolonial Roundtable (American Academy of Religion San Francisco 2011 and Chicago 2012); Hekima College, Nairobi (Kenya); Henry Martyn Centre, Cambridge (UK); Kampala Evangelical School of Theology (Uganda); Oxford Centre for Christianity and Culture (UK); Oxford Centre for Mission Studies, Oxford (UK); Regent's Park College, Oxford (UK); Postcolonial Theology Networks; Rhodes House, Oxford (UK); St. John's University of Tanzania, Dodoma (Tanzania); St.. Paul's University, Limuru (Kenya); Uganda Christian University, Mukono (Uganda); University of Nairobi (Kenya); and Wheaton College (USA).

I have already benefited from the insight, friendship, and fellowship of Phillip Baji, Patrick Bendera, Timothy Chiboti, Timothy Chimeledya, George Chiteto, Hilda Kabia, Moses Matonya, David Mdabuko, John Midelo, Peter Mkengi, Phanuel Mung'ong'o, Francis Ntiruka, George Okoth, George Otieno, Joshua Rutere, and Alfred Sebahene. These voices, along with others like Rosie Mbaraya and Seba Twiga which will not be heard by the world beyond Africa, have shaped my thinking and practice in ways they, nor I, will ever fully realize.

J. N. K. Mugambi kindly took time to correspond with me at various stages of my work and life. His critical and frank feedback was gratefully received. It was my great pleasure to meet with John S. Mbiti and his family.

ACKNOWLEDGMENTS

Professor Mbiti was most generous in his hospitality by inviting me to stay with him in his home. He was most patient in spending time with me and discussing many theological and philosophical issues from within and without Africa. He too was generous in allowing me access to his materials and archives. I am indebted to him and to his wife, Verena.

This book began as an Oxford University thesis and Professor Christopher Rowland deserves special thanks. I have learned much by virtue of his critical acumen, guidance, and patience. I am indebted to him for his insight and I am indebted to him for the example he has set me on what it means to practise Christian scholarship. I am honored and humbled that he wrote the foreword to this book. Thanks are due to Pickwick Publications for supporting this work and to Stan Chu Ilo for his penetrating reading of the text and gracious guidance towards publication. I am thankful to Kyle Martindale and James Stambaugh who helped prepare the text and proved to be careful proof readers. James also prepared the index for which I am most grateful.

Dear friends Melissa Jackson and Brian Hill have provided humor, help, and hope to me during my time in Oxford and in East Africa. Craig and Dana Doerksen have been a constant and blessed presence in my life from across the world. My family continue, both metaphorically and literally, to journey with me. I give thanks to God for Sharon and for Sam. I give thanks that it is through them I continue to know what grace looks like and feels like everyday. Thank you.

Abbreviations

ACT	*African Christian Theology* (Mugambi)
AIM/ABGC	Collection 81, The Records of the Africa Inland Mission, International / Archives of the Billy Graham Center, Wheaton College, Illinois, USA
AIC	Africa Inland Church
AICs	African Initiated Churches
AIM	Africa Inland Mission
ARAP	*African Religions and Philosophy* (Mbiti)
ARH	African Religious Heritage
ATR(s)	African Traditional Religion(s)
BATAC	*The Bible and Theology in African Christianity* (Mbiti)
BBE	*The Biblical Basis for Evangelization* (Mugambi)
CCAL	*Critiques of Christianity in African Literature* (Mugambi)
CMA	*Crisis of Mission in Africa* (Mbiti)
CMS	Church Missionary Society
COGA	*Concepts of God in Africa* (Mbiti)
CTAC	*Contextual Theology Across Cultures* (Mugambi and Guy)
CTSR	*Christian Theology and Social Reconstruction* (Mugambi)
EATWOT	Ecumenical Association of Third World Theologians.
FLTR	*From Liberation to Reconstruction* (Mugambi)
GHN	*God, Humanity and Nature in Relation to Justice and Peace* (Mugambi)
LAMA	*Love and Marriage in Africa* (Mbiti)

ABBREVIATIONS

NTEAB	*New Testament Eschatology in an African Background* (Mbiti)
RSCR	*Religion and Social Construction of Reality* (Mugambi)
TL	Typewritten letter
TMs	Typed manuscript
TAHCC	*The African Heritage and Contemporary Christianity* (Mugambi)
UMCA	Universities Mission to Central Africa
WCC	World Council of Churches
WSCF	World Student Christian Federation

Introduction

AFRICAN THEOLOGIES AND THEOLOGIANS and those who hear the voice of God's judgment and grace through African theologizing are beginning to engage with post-colonial theory and theology.[1] However, just as Christian theology in Africa and beyond Africa begins to experience the transformative potential of disturbance and disruption brought by post-colonial theologizing, there lurk old dangers at the dawn of a purported new theological movement. For in a desire to unveil colonialisms and imperialisms, earlier theological works emerging from historic situations of colonialism can be marginalized. This book, in part, is an appeal to those writing contemporary critical post-colonial theologies not to write off those who have gone before. It will be argued that thought and practice emerging from historical situations of formal colonialism prior to the emergence of the discipline of post-colonial theory and theology must always be a central part of whatever becomes of post-colonial theology. One would hope that such an argument in relation to African Initiated Churches (AICs) and their attendant theologies could be made with some ease. A more difficult task would be to argue for the post-colonial significance of theology that emerges from within a Church long associated with British expansionism and imperialism. That, however, is precisely the task of the present book. I begin by arguing for a

---

1. Lartey, *Postcolonializing God*; Ezigbo and Williams, "Converting a Colonialist Christ," 88–101. In terms of the broader development of post- or anti-colonialist African thought, Ngũgĩ wa Thiong'o charts its rise as beginning with the foundational moment of Haitian independence (1804), the 1900 Pan-African Congress in London, the foundation of the African National Congress (1912), Garvey's Universal Negro Improvement Association (1914), the Manchester Conference (1945), and other political parties and philosophies for independence and nationalism always in fruitful exchange between the African diaspora and Africa herself. See wa Thiong'o, *Something Torn*, 72–98. See wa Thiong'o, *Decolonising the Mind*; Kenyatta, *Facing Mount Kenya*; Nkrumah, *Speak of Freedom;* Nkrumah, *Neo-Colonialism*; Fanon, *Wretched of the Earth*; Nyerere, *Ujamaa*; Cabral, *Revolution in Guinea*; Césaire, *Discourse on Colonialism*; Eze, *Postcolonial African*; Young, R., *Postcolonialism: Historical Intro*, 217–92.

clear definition and task for post-colonial theology. In light of this definition, major themes in the writings of Kenyan Anglican theologians John S. Mbiti and Jesse N. K. Mugambi are identified towards assessing to what extent their work can be considered critically post-colonial or a source for critically post-colonial theology.

Practical Post-Colonial Theology

Critical post-colonial theologians and theologies, often indebted to postmodern deconstructionism, can tend toward levels of abstraction that make their work less accessible. However, such apparent abstraction and acontextualism may evidence a pluriformity of reflection that is too often mistaken for abstruseness. Post-colonial theology refers not simply to theology emerging from post-independence contexts. It refers to a critical way of doing theology. Such theologizing, at its best, begins with experiences of colonial or proto-colonial subjugation, identifies how such subjugation impacts theological disciples and doctrines, and seeks to move toward a more just (decolonized) practice of theology.[2] That is to say, a postcolonial theology is a practical theology. The present study emerges from particular experiences in East Africa. It emerges from conversations with scholars and community leaders on the nature of contextual African theology and its relation to colonial history, enduring colonial influences, and national aspirations. Such conversations and theologizing by these Christians evidence a commitment to Jesus Christ and reverence for African cultures and traditions, but criticism towards the modern missionary movement and disdain for the colonial past and its ongoing subjugating effects. Amidst these discussions, it remained unclear how such experiences, strong feelings, and reflections might be related and considered theologically significant. This is the primary motivation for the present work as a study of theology which seeks an African contextualism beyond so-called Western theology and beyond experiences of oppression and suppression. This book seeks to answer the question: what is the ongoing significance of the work developed by first generation African theologians, emerging from experiences of colonialism and coloniality?

As already noted, a very obvious place to investigate African contextualism and its attendant critique of foreign subjugation is amongst AICs. However, AICs represent but a small part of the African Christian

---

2. See chapter 7 of the present book and Heaney, "Coloniality and Theological Method," 55–65.

experience.[3] To neglect theological developments within the historical or mission churches can result in an oversimplified dichotomy. On the one hand, African Christians belonging to mission churches, such as Anglicanism, are then depicted as acquiescent to European domination. On the other hand, Africans without mission Christianity are depicted as independent in both ecclesiastical and theological terms. The present study will present a more complex situation through a consideration of the writings of Kenya's most innovative Anglican theologians. As a result, it will be argued that the theological contextualizing of Mbiti and Mugambi has significance hitherto unrecognized. It will further be submitted that such fresh perspective does indeed provide theological significance to the experiences, strong feelings, and reflections of those who continue to practice contextual theologies in the face of ongoing marginalization.

A study of the writings of Mbiti and Mugambi is not only undertaken because they are theologians who dominated the conversations the present writer had in Kenya and subsequently in other East African contexts. Nor is an examination of their writings undertaken simply because a comparative and thematic approach such as this has yet to be done. The contribution and significance of Mbiti's and Mugambi's work, emerging from the same context, is worthy of study in its own right.

Mbiti and Mugambi

John Samuel Mbiti, born in 1931, is at times regarded as the father of modern African (Anglophone) theology.[4] He is described as being in the "vanguard of intellectual innovation" when he brought "aspects of African thought into the global stadium of ideas."[5] Emerging in a post-independent Africa, Adrian Hastings adjudged Mbiti to be "the leading African theologian."[6] While his writing may not now seem particularly distinct or contentious, it is important to note that in the 1960s and 1970s, the idea of African theology remained vague, ambiguous, and even controversial.[7] Mbiti is a leading innovator amongst the first generation of African theologians and continues to be a significant figure in the field of African theology. For example, his work on African eschatology and African traditional understandings

---

3. Spear, "Towards the History," 3.

4. For the emergence of Francophone African theology, see, for example, Clark, "Against Invisibility," 71–92; Abble, *Prêtres Noirs*. See also Kinkupu, et al., *Prêtres Noirs*.

5. Mazrui, "Cultural (Re)Construction," 130.

6. Hastings, *History of African Christianity*, 232. See Ray, *African Religions*, xi–xii.

7. Mugambi, *ACT*, iv.

of God is still considered inventive and foundational to African Christian theology. Little work on African Christianity or African theology can be done without reference to him. However, Mbiti is not just a theologian with experience of the Kenyan context. His scholarship emerges also from studies and experiences outside Kenya. In the 1950s and early 1960s, he studied at Makerere University (Uganda), Barrington College (Rhode Island, USA), and Cambridge University (UK). As well as parish ministry in the UK and in Switzerland, Mbiti has significant research and teaching experience. After completing his PhD he joined Makerere University, where he stayed for ten years rising to the rank of professor. In 1974, he left Uganda to work at the World Council of Churches Ecumenical Institute in Bossey (Switzerland) where he eventually became its Director. He has had visiting professorships at Union Theological Seminary (USA), Harvard University (USA), several Swiss universities, the University of Bayreuth (Germany), and the University of Hamburg (Germany).[8]

Both Mbiti and Mugambi are Kenyans and Anglicans. Mbiti was born, educated, and taught for some time in Kenya. Mugambi, like Mbiti, is Kenyan born, but unlike Mbiti he has remained in Kenya. Some see him as the Kenyan scholar most obviously continuing and building on the work of Mbiti.[9] Jesse Ndwiga Kanyua Mugambi, born in 1947, is considered a "major African voice" credited with introducing a new (reconstructionist) paradigm to African theology.[10] In the mid 1960s, he attended the Machakos Teachers' College and Kenyatta College before, in the late 1960s, travelling to the UK for studies at Westhill College of Education in Birmingham (1969–70). In 1971, he joined the University of Nairobi as a student and eventually rose to the rank of Professor of Religious Studies in 1993. He remains proud of the fact that his BA, MA, and PhD were all gained in Kenya. Though gaining his PhD only in 1984, he associates the genesis of his formal theological work with Mbiti. For in 1968, Mbiti invited him to submit a paper on the African heritage in a publication of the Department of Religious Studies at Makerere.[11]

As well as being a Professor at the University of Nairobi, he has been a visiting professor at the University of South Africa; Emmanuel College,

---

8. See Olupona, "Biographical Sketch," 6–9; Pobee, "African Theology Revisited," 133–43; Kinney, "Theology of Mbiti," 65–68, Aguilar, "Postcolonial African," 303. Both Mbiti and Mugambi attended the first exploratory consultation between African and African American theologians at Union Theological Seminary, New York. See Mugambi, *ACT*, v; Hopkins, "Transatlantic Comparison," 103–9.

9. See Mwase, "Critical Evaluation," 1.

10. Mwase, Review of *FLTR*, 909–11. See Mwase, "Critical Evaluation," 46–48.

11. Mugambi, "Traditional Religion," 1–58.

Toronto (Canada); University of Copenhagen (Denmark); and Rice University, Texas (USA). He is a founding member of the Ecumenical Association of Third World Theologians (EATWOT). As well as working for the All Africa Conference of Churches, he has served the cause of worldwide ecumenism particularly through the World Council of Churches (WCC).[12] Mugambi was on the staff of the World Student Christian Federation (WSCF) as the Theology Secretary for Africa (1974–76), spent ten years as a member of the Faith and Order Commission of the WCC (1974–84), was a member of the WCC Sub-Unit of Church and Society (1984–94), was Senior Consultant for Development and Research at the All Africa Conference of Churches (Nairobi, 1994–97), and since 1994, he has been a member of the WCC Working Group on Climate Change.[13]

As has been seen, in the 1960s and 1970s, African theology was a term which sounded awkward and offensive to some. Yet, Mbiti sees his writing and theologizing emerging from his Christian upbringing and Christian commitment. He does not consider his theological scholarship as "something completely new upon which I . . . embark[ed]."[14] In the 1970s, Mugambi's task as Theology Secretary of the WSCF Africa Region was to "stimulate discussion and reflection" on African theology and "highlight the significant features of African Christian theological reflection in distinction from other brands of Christian theologizing."[15] Mugambi's early theologizing begins self-consciously within a context where, along with thinkers like Mbiti, Harry Sawyerr (Sierra Leone), E. B. Idowu (Nigeria), Charles Nyamiti (Tanzania), C. G. Baeta (Ghana), and theological conferences at Kampala (1972) and Accra (1974), he contributes to the first wave of African theology.[16] In sum, the writings of Mbiti and Mugambi together provide a resource for African theology and, it will be argued, a much broader field of post-colonial theology, which spans at least five decades.

---

12. See Mugambi and Guy, *CTAC*, 41–42.

13. See Dedji, *Reconstruction and Renewal*, 88 f.n. 1; Mwase, "Critical Evaluation," 37–57; Mugambi, *RSCR*, 2–4.

14. Mbiti, Interview by Heaney, April 7.

15. Mugambi, *ACT*, iv.

16. Mugambi, "Some Perspectives," 174–98; Mugambi, *ACT*, 11. He specifically refers to Sawyerr, "Basis of a Theology for Africa," 266–78; Idowu, *Towards an Indigenous Church*; Mbiti, *ARAP*; Mbiti, *NTEAB*. See also Nyamiti, *African Theology*; Nyamiti, *Scope of African Theology*. For the conferences in Kampala (1972) on "African Theology and Church Life" and the Accra Consultation on African and Black Theology (1974), see, for example, Wilmore, *Pragmatic Spirituality*, 214–22; Hopkins, "Transatlantic Comparison," 103–9; Fasholé-Luke, "Quest for an African Theology," 259–69.

A Fresh Perspective

This book argues for a fresh perspective on the writings of Mbiti and Mugambi, which will provide both opportunity for demonstrating the ongoing significance of their work and opportunity to further build on their innovative contributions. Despite the importance of both scholars in the field of African theology, engagement with the writings of Mbiti and Mugambi remain inadequate.[17] This is the case for at least four reasons. First, scholarly work on both Mbiti and Mugambi has failed to provide a significant study of their work together. This is despite the fact that, for example, both scholars belong to the same Kenyan context, both are Anglicans, both have worked for the World Council of Churches, both have contributed to East African institutions of higher learning, both have submitted innovations in African theology, and Mugambi is seen as continuing the work begun by Mbiti.

Second, no study has yet identified what amounts to a methodological shift in the work of Mbiti subsequent to his Cambridge PhD. A discernible shift is here identified as a move from the particular to a more generalized understanding of African theology. This shift takes his theologizing away from the particular as the locus for African theology in favor of a more generalized understanding of African tradition. Because of Mbiti's influence, this shift may well have repercussions for African theology more broadly. For the purposes of this study, its repercussions are certainly evident in the writing of Mugambi.

Third, Mugambi's theology of reconstruction is innovative. This innovation has been received critically and the present study will not be uncritical of it. However, the literature fails to recognize, because of a lack of comparative work between the two theologians, that this is but the culmination of a methodological shift instigated by Mbiti thirty years prior. It is only as a result of taking the work of the two theologians together that such an insight becomes apparent, thus creating space not only for an emphasis on its shortcomings but also in recognizing its contribution to theology.

Fourth, both the writings of Mbiti and Mugambi emerge from a context of colonialism. The recent emergence of post-colonial theology, at its

---

17. Scholarly engagement with both Mbiti and Mugambi is seen in numerous works referenced throughout this book and include p'Bitek, *African Religions*; Kato, "Theological Trends"; Kato, *Theological Pitfalls*; Kato, "Black Theology"; Kinney, "Theology of John Mbiti"; Olupona and Sulayman, *Religious Plurality*; Mwase, "Critical Evaluation"; Ritchie, "African Theology"; Musopole, *Being Human*; Farisani, "Theology of Reconstruction"; Dedji, *Reconstruction and Renewal*; Farisani, "Use of Ezra-Nehemiah"; Gathogo, *Liberation and Reconstruction*; Mwase and Kamaara, *Theologies of Liberation*.

best, brings to the theological fore such experience and seeks some sort of theological decolonization. Despite the fact that Mbiti's and Mugambi's theologizing emerges from a context of brutal colonialism and despite the fact that, in recent times, a stream of theological work has emerged addressing just these issues, no attempt has been made to engage their writings with the emergence of post-colonial theology. This study will redress that situation, beginning with a clear definition of post-colonial theology in chapter 1.

The writings of Mbiti and Mugambi signify an exercise in contextual theology. That is to say, they seek to understand the revelation of God in conversation with specific and explicitly stated African settings and questions. The Kenyan context they begin their theologizing in is dominated by mission Christianity. It might appear that this is the point of departure for their theology (chapter 2). It will be argued, however, that a gradual shift away from the particular is evident in their work. Though not recognized until now, a comparison between Mbiti's PhD dissertation with subsequent published work evidences a methodological shift. The locus for African theology becomes not the particularism of an African context, but the more generalized concept of African tradition (chapter 4). It is the discovery of this methodological shift, which can be seen as the unifying factor, or heuristic lens, for the present study. Thus, the subsequent chapters are structured in such a way as to illustrate this gradual move away from the particularism of context (chapter 3—eschatological issues and context), experience (chapter 4—religio-cultural experience), community (chapter 5—christ & symbol in African community), and coloniality (chapter 6—coloniality and reconstruction).

In response to such trends away from the particular, a series of constructive moves will be proposed. Such constructive moves, it will be argued, counter the unintended acontextuality in their work, weaken the most serious criticisms of their work, and begin to point to the ongoing significance of their work. The constructive moves, evoked by the writings of Mbiti and Mugambi, are fourfold. First, it is argued that Mbiti's eschatology be read according to his own initial method (chapter 3). Second, experiential dialogue is proposed resulting in criticism of African theology also (chapter 4). Third, a christology that integrates the importance of symbol and christopraxis is envisaged (chapter 5). Fourth, the need for power analysis is established (chapter 6) and the means to power analysis is identified through a thoroughgoing comparison of Mbiti's and Mugambi's work with post-colonial theology (chapter 7).

Conspectus

The writings of Mbiti and Mugambi emerge from experiences of a British colony (Kenya) and a British (Anglican) church. Indeed, Mbiti's PhD is completed in the year that Kenya gains her independence. In historical terms, their work is post-colonial. To what extent it is critically post-colonial is at the heart of the present work. Chapter 1 defines post-colonial theology as emerging from experiences of subjugation (coloniality), contending for marginalized agency, theologically hybridizing, and resisting hegemony. The experience of coloniality[18] in Kenya cannot be considered independent of mission Christianity.[19] Chapter 2 examines the ways in which they react to Christian mission and seek to articulate a theology which they believe more authentically relates to their context.

Chapter 3 examines how Mbiti moves away from the specificity of context in his examination of African temporality and eschatology.[20] It will be argued that reading Mbiti according to his own initial method will counter a move toward a more generalized, and therefore less contextualized, understanding of African theology. Such a reading recovers the innovative contextualism of his work while, at the same time, disarming much of the criticism of his eschatology. It foregrounds the subjugation at work in the specific context that his PhD thesis examines, thereby opening up space for a more thorough comparison of this African theologizing with the more recently emerging post-colonial theology, which also begins with contexts of subjugation or coloniality.

The move away from the specificity of context seems clear in Mbiti's work on eschatology. In chapters 4 and 5, this tendency is seen to be at work further in Mugambi's work as well as Mbiti's other work. It will be found that a shift to African Traditional Religions (ATRs) as the locus for the ongoing emergence for African theology creates tensions for the christology of Mbiti and Mugambi. They move away from the primacy of experience

---

18. *Coloniality* can be understood as a process subjugating culture and/or agency by incursive cultural and, in this case, theological discourse. For a fuller treatment of the term and its potential significance for theology see Heaney, "Conversion to Coloniality."

19. See Mugambi, "History of the Church"; Ng'eny, *Rabai to Mumias*, 29; Temu, *British Protestant*; Strayer, *Making Mission*, 10–11, 87; Oliver, *Missionary Factor*; Reed, *Founded in Faith*; Anderson, W., *Church in East Africa*; Reed, *Pastors, Partners*. Mbiti grew up in the African Inland Mission. For its history, see, for example, Mbiti, "Christian Eschatology," 37–40; Morad and Arensen, "The Spreading Tree." Strong, *Anglicanism and British Empire*, 108–10, 135–97, 217–23, 263, 283–94. See Frere, *Eastern Africa*, 120–21.

20. See Mbiti, *ARAP*, 21.

by defining the God of ATRs in reference to metaphysical categories such as omniscience, omnipresence, omnipotence, transcendence, immutability, and immanence. What I will call "experiential dialogue" is proposed as one way of countering such a shift. It will be argued that experiential dialogue is a distinct move, but one which is in continuity with the thought of Mbiti and Mugambi. That is to say, an approach is anticipated that proposes reading Christian tradition and text within the experience of traditional practice.

In chapter 5, the not uncommon assumption that African christology is "latent" because of a preoccupation with what I will call theistic contextualization, is noted.[21] It will be argued that the supposed latent nature of African christology oversimplifies the issues. For there is no inherent theological necessity that Mbiti and Mugambi develop a systematic christology. However, even in their more practical and communitarian intent, the approach evidences a move away from the particularisms of both traditional and Christian faith communities in Kenya. For while they seek to establish a relationship between traditional experience and theism, this is not extended to christology, and their hesitancy over further engagement and development on ontological issues is not congruent with a Kenyan church that displays much less hesitancy in this regard. A further constructive move is proposed by identifying the contextual potency of a symbolic approach to christology and the identification of christopraxis. A symbolic approach to christology will move their work back towards the practice of African traditional religionists. Christopraxis will move their work back towards the Christian faith community in a practical christologizing, which does not need to eschew or avoid questions about the nature of Christ.

Chapter 6 deals with Mugambi's most recent attempt at theologically addressing coloniality. He does this with the innovation of a theology of reconstruction. It appears that this reappraisal of the context might result in a theology that moves back to the immediate context and, therefore, remedies the continued shift away from the particular towards generalized understandings of African theology identified in this study. This, unfortunately, is not the case. Rather, beyond movement away from context (chapter 3), experience (chapter 4), and community (chapter 5), his intimations toward a reconstructionist theology constitutes a movement away from coloniality. A constructive move that can provide a means to analyze power relations within theological discourse, therefore, becomes urgent. This constructive step is recognized as necessary in chapter 6 and developed in chapter 7.

In chapter 7, it is argued that within a critically post-colonial framework, the work of Mbiti and Mugambi demonstrates post-colonial

21. See Stinton, *Jesus of Africa*, 4–9, 16–18.

characteristics. From this comparison of the writings of both scholars with post-colonial theology, a means to power analysis emerges. However, just as the work of Mbiti and Mugambi can be compared positively to post-colonial theology, it can also be contrasted with post-colonial theology. This contrast must not be avoided.

A Fresh Appreciation

Despite the criticisms that a post-colonial perspective might bring to the work of Mbiti and Mugambi, and the criticisms that they would in turn undoubtedly have of post-colonial theology, such dialogue exemplifies post-colonial discourse. Consequently, it will be argued that their work should be considered part of a broad body of post-colonial literature. Their work should no longer be marginalized by post-colonial theologians. Rather, in bringing their writings into the discourses on post-colonialism, through critical and constructive responses, a new appreciation for their work emerges. Even if it may be claiming too much to say that they anticipated later post-colonial theology, it is not claiming too much to argue that they should now be considered part of the antecedents of post-colonial theology. This is a new way of reading their work, which provides fresh significance for their contribution and a means to practice power analysis in the particularism of context, experience, community, and coloniality. Contextualism is more than inter-cultural relatedness. It is a means to decolonization. To what extent such conclusions can be sustained is the task of the remainder of this study.

1

Post-Colonialism

THE WRITINGS OF MBITI and Mugambi emerge from an historical situation of colonialism. Any assessment of the extent to which their work is critically post-colonial is predicated upon a clear definition of what it means for theology to be post-colonial. This chapter, against the backdrop of the broad field of post-colonial studies, defines post-colonial theology as responding to coloniality, promoting the theological agency of marginalized peoples, developing hybridized forms of theology, and resisting theological hegemony culminating in some form of decolonization. This is the ground upon which a comparison with major themes in the writings of Mbiti and Mugambi will be subsequently made. The present chapter, therefore, sets this study within a larger context of current and emerging theological discourses relating to the nature of theology and the exercise of power as it especially relates to historical colonialisms and colonialities.

Stephen Slemon acknowledges that to define post-colonialism is problematic. For the studies which labor under that heading are so very disparate. He acknowledges that a comprehensive and coherent study of such a large field would be almost unattainable.[1] While primarily arising from cultural studies, post-colonial scholars draw their conceptual vocabulary from a variety of sources. They borrow from anthropology, feminism, history, human geography, Marxism, philosophy, poststructuralism, psychoanalysis and sociology, using each for their own end.[2] This borrowing is both the strength and weakness of post-colonialism. In borrowing it can analyze

---

1. Slemon, "Post-colonial Critical Theories," 178–79. See Young, R., "Ideologies of the Postcolonial"; Eagleton, "Postcolonialism and 'postcolonialism.'"

2. Young, R., *Postcolonialism: Historical Intro*, 67.

the suffering of colonial subjects from more than one perspective. However, such pluriformity has tended toward a post-colonialism dominated by deconstructionist approaches and abstract discourses.³ Worse, such influences may result in the proliferation of literature at the expense of liberative practice.⁴ Such problems are mitigated somewhat when it is recognized that those initially involved in post-colonial studies did not intend to create any type of grand theory. Rather, works such as *The Empire Writes Back* seek to analyze how colonized peoples strategically engaged with imperial discourse and how these strategies compared to strategies adopted elsewhere.⁵ R. S. Sugirtharajah's insight is, therefore, useful when he defines post-colonialism not as theory but as criticism. It is not so much about applying theoretical principles to a plurality of contexts. It is the adoption of a critical stance in favor of those suppressed in colonial and post-colonial circumstances.⁶ The purpose of the criticism is to demonstrate how "counterdiscursive practices" seek to correct and undo Western power and hegemony.⁷ Such power analyses and counter-practices, arising from post-colonial literature, I argue, have five priorities that may begin to define how post-colonial criticism might function. As will be seen presently, these priorities relate to coloniality, agency, hybridization, hegemony, and decolonization.

Post-Colonialism is Responding to Coloniality

For Bill Ashcroft, Gareth Griffiths, and Helen Tiffin, texts which are post-colonial emerged "out of the experience of colonization and asserted themselves by foregrounding the tension with the imperial power, and by emphasizing their differences from the assumptions of the imperial centre."⁸ The best of post-colonial critique begins and holds in view the experience of the subjugated. For, whether explicitly acknowledged or not, the historical phenomenon of colonialism is "the determining condition" of post-colonial

---

3. See Keller, et al., *Postcolonial Theologies*, 8–9; Kwok, *Postcolonial Imagination*, 36–37; Shohat, "Notes on the Postcolonial"; Young, R., *Colonial Desire*, 159–65, 389–410; Joh, *Heart of the Cross*, 54.

4. Taylor, M. L., "Spirit and Liberation," 46. See Keller, et al., *Postcolonial Theologies*, 8–9. Sugirtharajah, with some justification, is skeptical of the influence of postmodernism as another example of the Eurocentric colonization of the field. See Sugirtharajah, *Postcolonial Reconfigurations*, 37–50.

5. Ashcroft, *Post-Colonial Transformation*, 7.

6. See Sugirtharajah, *Postcolonial Reconfigurations*, 13–16.

7. Gugelberger and Brydon, "Postcolonial Culture," 757.

8. Ashcroft, et al., *Empire Writes Back*, 2.

criticism.⁹ For this reason the present study retains the hyphenated use of post-colonial. For whatever the "post" might include it is important that it does not exclude the specificity of historical and existential subjugation.¹⁰

> . . . the hyphen is a statement about the particularity, the historically and culturally grounded nature of the experience it represents. Grounded in the practice of critics concerned with the writings of colonized people themselves, it came to stand for a theory which was oriented towards the historical and cultural experience of colonized peoples, a concern with textual production, rather than towards the fetishization of theory itself . . . In this respect the hyphen distinguishes the term from . . . unlocated, abstract and poststructuralist theorizing . . .¹¹

Post-colonialism is not a chronological marker so much as an oppositional movement towards decolonization. Therefore, I argue, the particularity, historicity, and existential nature of post-colonial struggles should not be occluded.

As an oppositional movement, Ania Loomba begins by defining what it is that post-colonialism opposes. Imperialism or neo-imperialism is a process that begins in the metropolis towards the domination and control of others. The result of such imperialism is colonialism or neo-colonialism.¹² However, it should be noted that this causal link from imperialism to colonialism is not inevitable. For example, some colonies on the east coast of North America were established to escape oppression from the metropolitan center. They were not created by imperial mandate. Equally, not a few white settlers in Kenya left Britain to escape societal factors that they felt restricted their lifestyle or future prospects. It is not difficult, therefore, to envisage an inversion of Loomba's causality: imperialism arises from colonialism. While such distinctions make little difference to those experiencing imperialisms and colonialisms it does indicate the complexity of the issues at stake. Indeed, colonialism as an analytic category is not nearly as potent in explanatory power as might be expected. On the one hand, Mbiti and

---

9. See Introduction to Part 1 in Ashcroft, et al., *Post-Colonial Studies Reader*, 9; Ashcroft, et al., *Empire Writes Back*, 197–98.

10. See Ashcroft, et al., *Empire Writes Back*, 198; Ashcroft, *Post-Colonial Transformation*, 8–10.

11. Ashcroft, *Post-Colonial Transformation*, 10; Shohat, "Notes on the Postcolonial." Shohat is concerned with the acontextualism and universalizing at work in post-colonial theory. With McClintock, Shohat argues for post-colonial critiques to be grounded in specific contexts. See McClintock, "Angel of Progress."

12. Loomba, *Colonialism/Postcolonialism*, 11–12. See Slemon, "Post-colonial Critical Theories," 180.

Mugambi recognize that missionaries were not straightforwardly colonialist agents.[13] On the other hand, there are beliefs evident in the assumptions and practices of many missionaries that could be described as proto-colonialist as well as colonialist.[14] Colonialisms experienced by those beyond Europe also included cultural belittling of indigenous tradition and history, loss of agency to act freely and to represent oneself, and a struggle to find meaning in a hegemonic system.[15] In short, the colonialisms often countered by post-colonial literature are on the border between the immaterial and the material. The concern is with the representation of the colonizing (or missionary) project and the colonized (or evangelized) and how that serves to legitimize certain practices of subjugation. It is because of the recognition of a more complex exercise of power in colonial situations (beyond, for example, land grabbing) that *coloniality* will be preferred in this study over colonialism. I submit, as an initial definition of coloniality the following definition: a process subjugating culture and/or agency by incursive cultural and, in this case, theological discourse.[16] In critique, counter-discourses, and resistance there is an attempt to get beyond such oppression. There is an attempt to be post-colonial.[17] In doing so, resistance is not only directed toward the material domination involved in (direct and indirect) foreign incursion, it is directed also against discourses of coloniality through the agency and actions of the marginalized.[18]

13. See Mbiti, "When the Right Hand," 10–11; Mugambi, "Religion and Social Reconstruction," 18.

14. For example, see Temu, *British Protestant*; Strayer, *Making Mission*. See also Stanley, *Missions, Nationalism*; Bosch, *Transforming Mission*, 220–30, 302–13; Etherington, *Missions and Empire*.

15. While Mbiti's and Mugambi's writing emerge from a British colonial situation, it should not be assumed that the practice of colonialism is monolithic. See Young, R., *Postcolonialism: Historical Intro*.

16. *Discourse* here refers to how particular knowledge comes to be seen as legitimate by the practice and networking of, in this case, particular missionaries, scholars, and institutions. See Kim, U., *Decolonizing Josiah*, 20–21; Young, R., *Postcolonialism: Historical Intro*, 385–410; Nandy, *Intimate Enemy*, 1; See wa Thiong'o, *Barrel of a Pen*, 90–100.

17. See Introduction in Ashcroft, et al., *Post-Colonial Studies*, 11; Temu and Swai, *Historians and Africanist History*, 25.

18. This notion of *discourse* is adopted and adapted, problematically, in post-colonialism from Foucault. See Young, R., *Postcolonialism: Historical Intro*, 385–410. It should not be assumed that the concept used by Foucault and Said correlates. Indeed, Young observes that Said uses it in an almost opposite manner (p. 405). For example, Hulme, *Colonial Encounters*; Young, R., *White Mythologies*; Lowe, *Critical Terrains*; Ahmad, *In Theory*; Bhabha, *Location of Culture*; McClintock, *Imperial Leather*; Yeğenoğlu, *Colonial Fantasies*; all are founded on critiques and/or developments of

Post-Colonialism is Agency for the Marginalized

Robert Young defines post-colonialism as a critical stance and language that gives voice to the marginalized. This agency results in a critical stance towards the relationships and cultural domination between Europe and its colonies. More positively, post-colonialism seeks to disrupt such relationships of domination by developing new forms of internationalist understanding and communication.[19] The "post-" in post-colonial is concerned with going beyond coloniality as an "ethical intention and direction."[20] Young argues that this critical stance and language emerges from such international (tri-continental) struggles against historic colonialisms and imperialisms.[21] Indeed, some of the most influential theorists, such as Edward Said, Homi Bhabha, and Gayatri Spivak, are those who are not from the metropolitan center but have placed themselves in it and have influenced the development of post-colonialism.[22] Post-colonialism is, therefore, a "dialectical product" of interaction between so-called Western and non-Western thought and practice.[23]

> Postcolonial critique marks the moment where the political and cultural experience of the marginalized periphery developed into a more general theoretical position that could be set against western politics, intellectual and academic hegemony and its protocols of objective knowledge.[24]

> Theory... gives [indigenous people] space to plan, to strategize, to take greater control over our resistances.[25]

It is not surprising, therefore, that post-colonialism emerges from the particularities of the 1970s as post-war immigrants from Latin America, Africa, and Asia begin to bring radically different perspectives into the universities of the North Atlantic. It is equally unsurprising that it is in literature

Saidian arguments.

19. Young, R., "What is the Postcolonial," 3. See Bhabha, *Location of Culture*, 345–46.

20. Keller, et al., Introduction to *Postcolonial Theologies*, 6.

21. Young, R., *Postcolonialism: Historical Intro*, 4–24, 57–69.

22. Said, *Orientalism*; Said, *Culture and Imperialism*; Bhabha, *Location of Culture*; Spivak, *Critique of Postcolonial Reason*. See Young, R., *Postcolonialism: Historical Intro*, 61–63, 412–26. See Bhabha, *Location of Culture*, 2.

23. Young, R., *Postcolonialism: Historical Intro*, 68.

24. Ibid., 65.

25. Smith, L., *Decolonizing Methodologies*, loc. 1018.

departments, with an openness to "subjective" and "experiential" knowledge, where such critique and voice was heard first.[26] Thus, eventually, the Northern academies become affected by African experience and reflection on colonization.[27] However, even a history that seeks to take account of African perspectives and experiences may not appreciate that such perspective is fundamentally met not only in historical fact and counterfactual, but also in an intense complexity and subjectivity.[28] Any post-colonial analysis must take care not to simply outline the effect of the colonialist's action on the colonized but also take account of the agency of the marginalized. This is an agency which, by definition, struggles for realization under oppression and is often practiced in the subversive tactics of mimicry and hybridization.[29] In hybridization, a concept and practice exists that draws attention to the agency of the colonized over against the hegemonic desire and strategies of the colonizers. Hybridizing is engendered not simply from unforeseen contingencies but from intentional resistance. If seen as the result of colonial interactions, it creates interpretative and creative space for resistance and undermines the very intention of the colonialists.[30]

Post-Colonialism is Hybridization

There is both an *organic* hybridizing and an *intentional* hybridizing.[31] The former results in linguistic fusions and mixing with the result, sometimes,

26. Young, R., *Postcolonialism: Historical Intro*, 61–66. See Temu and Swai, *Historians and Africanist History*, 12; Tiffin, "Plato's Cave," 160; Gugelberger and Brydon, "Postcolonial Cultural Studies," 757. See Ashcroft, et al., *Empire Writes Back*, 2. See Kwok, "Legacy of Cultural Hegemony," 47–70.

27. See Davidson, "African Resistance"; Boahen, *African Perspectives*; Neale, *Writing "Independent"*; Boahen, "Africa and the Colonial"; Lonsdale, "States and Social"; Lonsdale, "European Scramble"; Ranger, "Connexions: Part 1"; Ranger, "Connexions: Part 2."

28. Cooper, "Conflict and Connection," 1520–22. Cooper argues that the first generation of African scholars, specifically historians, after independence tended to stress notions of African sovereignty in the pre-independence era and evidence of indigenous "progress" toward a modernity not dissimilar to European nation-statehood. For an analysis of the same era that focuses more on the dissimilarities and internal tensions within African societies before independence, see Lonsdale, "European Scramble," 680–766. See also Temu and Swai, *Historians and Africanist History*, 153–69.

29. Bhabha, *Location of Culture*, 112. See Moore-Gilbert, "Spivak and Bhabha."

30. This is often overlooked when too narrow a focus is given to political or military resistance to colonization. See Boahen, *African Perspectives*, 39–57.

31. Young, R., *Colonial Desire*, 21. See Bakhtin, *Dialogic Imagination*, 358–59.

Post-Colonialism is Resistance to Hegemony

Hybridizing, at least from a theological perspective, does not necessarily have inherent worth.[41] It is doubtful if the playful bricolage of postmodernism will evoke liberative (decolonizing) practice. An emphasis on hybridity can, therefore, disempower attempts at decolonizing practice if oppositional stances are seen as comprised of people and circumstances that are a hybrid of both good and bad. Colonizer hybridity is a possibility.[42] The decolonizing practices of hybridization in view here are, therefore, set within the struggles that exist because of differentials of power. It is because of the differentials of power that the potentially revolutionary and decolonizing effects of hybridization exist. Hybridizing will have a decolonizing effect when it is resistance against powers and practices that are pushing for the erasure of local differences in favor of some kind of cultural and/or theological uniformity.[43]

> Liberation theologies dramatically challenged the hierarchies built on those binaries. But inasmuch as they content themselves with exalting a single, liberatory identity such as the poor, or the people, blacks or women, they remain, we have suggested, more or less within the same modern paradigm.[44]

In contrast to such binaries of identity as pure/impure and rational/chaotic, post-colonial theory seeks to unveil the "ethico-political agenda that drives

---

41. Taylor sees this clearly. He sees the concept and practice of hybridity as standing in the way of resistance and transformation. For this reason, despite the post-colonial affirmations and practices of power analysis, agency, and hybridity, he wants to maintain a "necessary binary" of colonizer and colonized. This is well meaning. However, it is a mistake. For the dualisms and binary opposites problematized by post-colonial thinkers is not simply a rhetorical or theoretical option to be adopted or rejected by post-colonial theologians. Rather, it gets to the very heart of the matter. That identities are hard to fix in situations of coloniality is central to a post-colonial theology. For example, those involved in attaining independence in Kenya could quickly become those who land-grabbed and excluded others. More seriously, however, is the post-colonial insight that a binary such as colonizer/colonized actually veils the subjugation of the most oppressed. This is particularly the case for the experiences of women. Taylor is correct, writing from an American context, to be wary of the influence of a "(playful) postmodernism" on post-colonial practice. But this need not be the nature or purpose of post-colonial hybridity, which attends to context, historicity, and the existential dimensions of coloniality. See Taylor, M. L., "Spirit and Liberation," 46–47; Rieger, *Christ and Empire*, 146.

42. Tinker, *Spirit and Resistance*, 753, 693.

43. Rieger, *Globalization and Theology*, 31.

44. Keller, et al., *Postcolonial Theologies*, 11.

the differentiation between the two."[45] In simple terms, it examines the processes and relations of power and history that make, for example, "Third World" theology.

In *Orientalism* (1978) Said draws attention to the exercise of power not only in colonialist land grabbing but also in the production of "knowledge" about, in his case, the so-called Orient. Colonization is both physical and epistemic violence. At the heart of Said's argument is a rejection of the autonomy and objectivity of academic knowledge. Academic knowledge is also part of the structure of western power. The will to knowledge is also the will to power. Consequently, Orientalism is a "kind of Western projection onto and will to govern over the Orient."[46] In order to examine the "cultural forms" of imperialism and colonialism the concept of "discourse" is employed.[47] Colonial discourse, for Said, operates through texts which engage, reflect, and construct the Orient.[48] Through, for example, literature, debates and university courses the Orient is created by reflection on the non-European other. This discourse becomes authoritative in terms of its reflexivity (that is to say, for its seeming ability to describe what lies beyond Europe and while doing so giving greater definition to what it is to be European) and production of apparent knowledge of non-European cultures and subjectivity. Always however, argues the post-colonial critic, there is the exercise of power towards domination in such discourses. Post-colonial criticism and theory seeks to identify such power relations, generate a "liberating perspective"[49] and achieve decolonization.[50]

Post-Colonialism is Decolonization

The purpose of post-colonial criticism is to identify practices of coloniality and to seek to practice decolonization. Kwame Appiah depicts "post-coloniality" as a "space-clearing gesture" that attempts, in cultural life, to transcend or go beyond colonialism[51] For Georg Gugelberger the term post-colonial refers to reading practices, as well as writing practices, which take account of experiences occurring outside Europe but as a consequence

---

45. Ibid., 11.
46. Said, *Orientalism*, 95.
47. As has been seen, this notion of discourse is adopted and adapted, problematically, from Foucault. See Young, R., *Postcolonialism: Historical Intro*, 385–410.
48. Ibid., 383–89; Said, *Orientalism*, 3, 12.
49. wa Thiong'o, *Decolonising the Mind*, 87.
50. Said, *Orientalism*, 95.
51. Appiah, *In My Father's House*, 149.

of European expansion and exploitation. A fundamental purpose of such "counterdiscursive practices" toward a decolonized end is to examine work which seeks to, as has already been seen, correct or undo Western hegemony.[52] Such literature, as Ashcroft, Griffiths, and Tiffin rightly acknowledge, includes texts that are not explicitly produced to gain the appellation "post-colonial." It is the engagement with colonial power, as it affects contexts socially, culturally, politically (and theologically), which ultimately defines the "post-colonial" even if authors of such material like Mbiti and Mugambi do not see themselves in such terms.[53] There may be danger in generalizing what such decolonized ends will be. For not all experiences of coloniality are the same and the exercise of agency, hybridity, and critique will be shaped by specific contexts. However, if post-colonialism is to be a field of study or, more importantly, an international movement for liberative practice then I argue some decolonizing commonalities should be discernible and should be important.

To decolonize is to unveil coloniality. It is to disrupt discourses and knowledge created in traditional colonial centers by and through the agency of those who experience and resist coloniality. It is to identify and participate in hybridizing processes that have been realized in the face of hegemonic agenda and practice. It is to recognize the importance of exercises of power in cultural and academic, as well as social and political, interfaces and to struggle towards the decentering and displacing of "Western" knowledge.[54] For Fanon decolonization is changing the order of the world.[55] For Young, who might unwittingly reference Acts 17:6, the essence of post-colonialism is to turn the world upside down.[56] He argues that so-called Western knowledge is organized philosophically through "binary oppositions," which result in the "demonizing or denigrating" of the other. Consequently, post-colonialism seeks to develop a "third space" where master/slave, man/woman, civilized/uncivilized, colonizer/colonized, the West and the rest are "no longer starkly oppositional or exclusively singular but defined by their intricate and mutual relations with others." In illustrating this, Young refers to Ashish Nandy's famous phrase in describing the relationships between colonizers and colonized as "intimate enemies." But even more is at stake.

---

52. Gugelberger and Brydon, "Postcolonial Cultural Studies," 757.
53. Ashcroft, et al., *Empire Writes Back*, 197.
54. See Young, R., "What is the Postcolonial," 3–4.
55. Fanon, *Wretched of the Earth*, 27.
56. Young, R., *Postcolonialism: Very Short Intro*, 2. See Gutiérrez, *Theology of Liberation*, 23–25.

> ... the postcolonial project seeks the introduction not just of knowledge *of* other cultures, but of different kinds of knowledge, new epistemologies, *from* other cultures.
>
> Postcolonialism, therefore, begins from its own knowledges, the diversity of its own cultural experiences, and starts from the premise that those in the West, both within and outside the academy, should relinquish their monopoly on knowledge, and take other knowledges, other perspectives, as seriously as those of the West. Postcolonialism, or tricontinentalism as I have also called it, that is the discourse of the three continents of the South—Africa, Asia, and Latin America—represents a general name for these insurgent knowledges, particularly those that originate with the subaltern, the dispossessed, and seek to change the terms and values under which we all live. It's about learning to challenge and think outside the norms of Western assumptions. You can learn it anywhere if you want to. The only qualification you need to start is to make sure that you are looking at the world not from above, but from below, not from the north, but the south, not from the inside, but from the outside, not from the centre, but from the margin's forgotten edge. It's the world turned upside down. It's the language of the South challenging the dominant perspectives of the North.[57]

This, therefore, is the broad vision from which post-colonial theologies emerge.

The Emergence of Post-Colonial Theologies

Young, acknowledging the role of religious resistance toward colonial dominance, submits that post-colonial critics are only beginning to take seriously the role of religious movements in contexts dominated by colonial structures. He concedes that post-colonial studies are "distinguished by an unmediated secularism." It seems post-colonial scholars are committed to excluding religious (and theological) attempts to provide alternative value-systems to those of the so-called West.[58] In other words, the importance or

---

57. Young, R., "What is the Postcolonial," 3–4. While Young sums up the nature of post-colonialism well here, there is, nonetheless, a danger in the assumption that a scholar from the North Atlantic can simply take on the perspective of people "from below." See Heaney, "Conversion to Coloniality."

58. Young, R., *Postcolonialism: Historical Intro*, 338. See Sugirtharajah, *Postcolonial Reconfigurations*, 156–58.

possibility of theological decolonization has not been pursued in the wider field of post-colonial studies.

> . . . an absolute division between the material and the spiritual operates within postcolonial studies, emphasizing the degree to which the field is distinguished by an unmediated secularism, opposed to and consistently excluding the religions that have taken on the political identity of providing alternative value-systems to those of the west . . . Postcolonial theory, despite its espousal of subaltern resistance, scarcely values subaltern resistance that does not operate according to its own secular terms.[59]

Young has Islam and Hinduism in mind here. However, African theology too expressly seeks to offer an "alternative value-system" to that brought to Africa by foreign missionaries. Young submits that a "spiritual" approach to decolonization may emphasize individual self-rule, duty over rights, non-violent resistance and a critique of the Western obsession with materiality.[60] Whether or not these are the themes of a Christian theological decolonization in Africa, or elsewhere, remains largely to be seen. Suffice it to say, at this juncture, if post-colonial critics are guilty of excluding the religious from the post-colonial debate then theologians are often equally guilty of excluding the post-colonial debate from their theologizing. Sugirtharajah rightly notes, it is not uncommon for theologians to systematize with the Reformation, the Counter-reformation, the Enlightenment, modernity, the Holocaust, or postmodernity in view. However, there has been "remarkable unwillingness" to theologize with the effects of imperialism and colonialism in view.[61]

> Precisely in the 1960s when the process of decolonization was taking place, Western theologians spent their creative energies addressing issues such as secularization and its impact on Christian faith. They were eloquent in their silence when it came to assessing the role of the West in the colonial domination . . .[62]

---

59. Young, R., *Postcolonialism: Historical Intro*, 338. Recently, Young has addressed more directly issues of theology and post-colonialism at a fringe meeting, organized by the Postcolonial Theology Network, at the Lambeth Conference in 2008. Because post-colonialism seeks to intervene in the established ways of thinking and acting in North Atlantic academies and is committed to voices from "elsewhere" it can be seen to share an "area of sympathy with the commitments of Christianity." See Young, R., "What is the Postcolonial," 1–8.

60. Young, R., *Postcolonialism: Historical Intro*, 338.

61. Sugirtharajah, *Postcolonial Criticism*, 25, 28.

62. Ibid., 26.

Joseph Duggan, reflecting on the significance of what appears to be the first post-colonial theology conference in Britain (2008), sees three stages of development in (published) post-colonial theology.[63] First, post-colonial criticism is practiced in biblical studies. Scholars, including R. S. Sugirtharajah, Musa Dube, and Fernando Segovia, have been doing exegesis from a post-colonial perspective for at least ten years.[64] For Sugirtharajah post-colonialism is:

> An active interrogation of the hegemonic systems of thought, textual codes, and symbolic practices which the West constructed in its domination of colonial subjects. In other words, postcolonialism is concerned with the question of cultural and discursive domination. It is a discursive resistance to imperialism, imperial ideologies, and imperial attitudes and to their continual reincarnations in such wide fields as politics, economics, history, and theological and biblical studies.[65]

Second, the work of Kwok Pui-lan and Catherine Keller introduces a post-colonial critique from a feminist perspective.[66] For Kwok, postcolonialism is:

> . . . a reading strategy and discursive practice that seeks to unmask colonial epistemological frameworks, unravel Eurocentric logics, and interrogate stereotypical cultural representations . . . I am interested in exploring the steps necessary for a postcolonial intellectual to dislodge herself from habitual ways of thinking, established forms of inquiry, and the reward system vigilantly guarded by the neoliberal academy . . . I hope to create a little space to imagine that an alternative world and a different system of knowing are possible.[67]

Third, the 2008 conference at Manchester University entitled, "Church Identity/ies and Postcolonialism" sought to provide post-colonial theological

---

63. The proceedings of the conference were published in a special edition of the *Journal of Anglican Studies* 7:1 (2009). Since then, further conferences have taken place in Bangalore (2010), Melbourne (2012), and Nairobi (2014). The present author was involved in the inaugural conference.

64. See Duggan, "'I Found Space,'" 6; Sugirtharajah, *Postcolonial Reconfigurations*; Dube, *Postcolonial Feminist*; Segovia, *Interpreting Beyond Borders*.

65. Sugirtharajah, *Asian Biblical Hermeneutics*, 17.

66. See Kwok, *Postcolonial Imagination*; Keller, et al., *Postcolonial Theologies*. These are, according to Duggan, among the first post-colonial theology books written. See also, Douglas and Kwok, *Beyond Colonial*.

67. Kwok, *Postcolonial Imagination*, 2–3.

critiques of theological and ecclesiological questions of identity and mission.[68] Manchester did raise unconventional questions in a British theological context. However, care must be taken in overstating the significance of such gatherings and care must be taken not to succumb to a progressivist chronology when outlining the development of any theological movement. For a central focus of the present study is to examine the possibility that theological reflection and theological texts produced by Africans scholars since the 1960s might already be theologically post-colonial (see chapter 7). Furthermore, biblical scholars also make theological contributions. To make too stark of a distinction between "theology" and "biblical studies" will only serve to mask that contribution. Lastly, any tendency toward progressivist chronologies can result in an exclusive relationship between post-colonialism and formal post-colonial academic work. Young especially establishes the antecedence of post-colonialism in movements before the existence of post-colonial studies in the academy. Indeed, as seen in the previous section, one of the functions of post-colonialism is to challenge the rejection of experiential knowledge.[69] Nonetheless, Duggan's encapsulation of the nature of the theologies being crystallized at this conference as "a decolonizing theological critique" is instructive for understanding emerging post-colonial theologies.[70]

While anti-colonialism may have a long history, as has been seen, post-colonial criticism emerges only in the late 1970s. The history of published and self-identifying post-colonial theology has an even shorter history. It arises first in biblical studies and has only recently emerged in theological studies. Its potential significance for African theology has not yet been widely recognized.[71] Its potential significance for first generation African theologians and the writings of Mbiti and Mugambi has not been recognized at all. I would argue that this may be the case for a least three reasons. Firstly, thinkers who have influenced the development of post-colonialism within Africa are often antagonistic towards Christianity and, therefore, not obvious sources of theology. For example, wa Thiong'o argues:

> . . . imperialist pretences to free the African from superstition, ignorance and awe of nature often resulted in deepening his ignorance, increasing his superstitions and multiplying his awe

---

68. Duggan, "'I Found Space,'" 6.

69. Young, R., *Postcolonialism: Historical Intro*. See also Loomba, *Colonialism/Postcolonialism*, 1–5; Shohat, "Notes on the Postcolonial," 99–113; Althaus-Reid, *Indecent Theology*, 148–51.

70. Duggan, "'I Found Space,'" 7.

71. See Kwok, *Postcolonial Imagination*, 126; Kwok, "Mercy Amba."

of the new whip-and-gun-wielding master. An African, particularly one who had gone through a colonial school, would more readily relate to the bible with its fantastic explanation of the origins of the universe, its 'divine' revelations about the second coming and its horrifying pictures of hell and damnation for those sinning against imperialist order . . .[72]

Secondly, related to this is the widespread assumption that African Christianity, especially in its mainline manifestation, is a part of the perpetuation of colonialism and neocolonialism. This is especially seen over against the rise of African Initiated Churches (AICs) that are depicted as movements for "spiritual decolonization."[73] Thirdly, within African Christian theology itself there is some resistance to a perceived politicization of theology. This is seen particularly clearly in Mbiti's thought who is wary of the Gospel being co-opted for ideological or political ends whether from within or without Africa. As with liberation theology, he would be equally suspicious of post-colonial theology doing just that.

This book will argue that the writings of Mbiti and Mugambi should be examined within a post-colonial frame not only for the purposes of a fresh perspective on their work but also for the benefit of the developing field of post-colonial theology. That is not to say that post-colonial theologians would be uncritical of their writing, nor is it to say that Mbiti and Mugambi would be uncritical of post-colonial theology. However, it is to say that their work should now be considered part of the broad field of post-colonialism and as important precursors for the development of post-colonial theology. I will therefore outline the development of post-colonial theology not only as the most recent context for the ongoing work of African theology but also as a means of comparison with major themes in Mbiti and Mugambi's writings. In light of this, chapter 7 will assess to what extent their writings might be considered critically post-colonial.

Characteristics of Post-Colonial Theologies

The emergence of post-colonial theology reflects and develops the agenda both of post-colonial biblical studies and post-colonialism more generally. At least four characteristics emerge from an overview of the literature.

---

72. wa Thiong'o, *Decolonising the Mind*, 67. See also p'Bitek, *African Religions*, 52–69, 80–120.

73. Etherington, Introduction in *Missions and Empire*, 4. See Hastings, *African Christianity*, 24–25.

First, in opposition to imperial theologies and coloniality there is a contending for marginalized *agency*. Central to Douglas and Kwok's collection is the contention that those beyond the North Atlantic are not missiological objects but theological subjects.[74] Keller, Nausner, and Rivera see post-colonial theology as continuous with liberation theology and set it within the matrix of eschatological promise. Post-colonial theology is, therefore, an engaged and hopeful work committed to the realization of "a time, a space, and earth" beyond the colonizing powers of "every imperialism, every supremacism."[75] For Kwok, agency begins with imagination. Imagining, as part of a decolonizing of the mind, is necessary because without envisaging a different reality it will be impossible to struggle or live such a reality. Consequently, "stepping outside" Eurocentrism will be achieved by historical (hearing, for example, the voices of marginalized women), dialogical (problematizing the liberal notion of diversity and recognizing asymmetrical power relations), and diasporic (undermining the assumptions that Christianity is normatively Western) imagining.[76] Rivera replaces an imperial understanding of transcendence with a metaphorical relational practice of transcendence. Divine transcendence is to be understood in panentheistic terms.[77] Rieger seeks to discover "christological surplus" within apparently thoroughgoing imperialist images of Christ. Abraham, identifying space for the metaphysical in post-colonial theory, argues for a dialogic model between post-colonial theory and theology. Such a model will expand the analytic and constructive potency of both theology and theory as they address issues of subjectivity, gender, and violence.[78] Althaus-Reid contends for a theological agency that comes from the margins and is "indecent."[79] An indecent theology affirms theologies and images of God which belong not only to the economically marginalized, but to the sexually marginalized.[80]

Second, the agency struggled for in post-colonialism is not an idea but a practice in situations of coloniality. Consequently, this (theological) agency is neither consistent nor always apparent. Things are more complex than this. Sometimes the colonizers can act for decolonization and sometimes the colonized can be guilty of internal colonization. *Hybridization*

---

74. Introduction in Douglas and Kwok, *Beyond Colonial*, 11.
75. Keller, et al., *Postcolonial Theologies*, xi. See 16, 58–132.
76. Kwok, *Postcolonial Imagination*, 22, 29–51.
77. See Rivera, *Touch of Transcendence*, 127–40.
78. Abraham, *Identity, Ethics, and Nonviolence*, 1–50, 105–206.
79. See Althaus-Reid, *Indecent Theology*, 11–46.
80. Ibid., 168–73.

signifies this and can be seen to arise in the interstices emerging in situations of colonial incursion.[81] In contrast, modern thought, it is argued, is largely predicated on and organized according to "discrete and mutually exclusive categories," which include same/other, spirit/matter, religion/politics, subject/object, inside/outside, pure/impure, rational/chaotic, civilized/primitive, Christian/pagan, transcendence/immanence, sacred/profane, native/alien, white/black, male/female, rich/poor, whole/disabled. These discrete and mutually exclusive categories create, or reveal, a relationship to the other that emerges in contrast to the self or some universal standard. They imply superiority/inferiority and thus inspire and legitimize subjugation. For they are inscribed on others with the assumption that the other can be appropriated and apprehended. They also imply contestation and thus inform both colonial policies and revolutions. Post-colonialism, however, recognizes that these oppositional identities are not secure. It draws attention to the experiences of colonialists (and missionaries) and colonized (and converts) that problematize, hybridize, and undermine such polar distinctions. It seeks to identify the underlying subjugating agenda that sustains such differences.[82] More constructively, post-colonial theologies identify and affirm the apparent hybridities present in Christian theology that will serve a multilingual, multiracial, multicultural world better. Consequently, Christianity itself emerges as a "great hybrid," intermixing metaphysics, philosophies, and identities at the "urban crossroads of the Roman Empire."[83] That hybridity continues to provide opportunity for creative and constructive post-colonial theologizing. For example, Wonhee Anne Joh proposes a post-colonial hybridization of Christology from an Asian/Korean American perspective. Such a hybridizing emerges in theological reflection on the cross through the Korean practices of *han* (suffering/abjection) and *jeong* (love/relationality). The cross signifies both *han* and *jeong* and therefore, Joh seems to argue, is itself a moment of redemptive hybridity. The cross refuses to conceive of love as the resignation of agency and power. Rather, it recognizes the complexity of "hybrid realities and relationalities."[84]

Third, despite the struggle for marginalized theological agency and the contention for theological expression through hybridization, much theology

81. See Young, R., *Colonial Desire*, 22–23; Nandy, *Intimate Enemy*, xv.

82. Introduction in Keller, et al., *Postcolonial Theologies*, 11. See Spivak, *Critique of Postcolonial Reason*, 332; Bhabha, *Location of Culture*, 2–12; Rivera, *Touch of Transcendence*, 5–13, 61–75, 93, 108, 129–40; Young, R., *Colonial Desire*, 22; Rieger, *Christ and Empire*, 45–67; Heaney, "Conversion to Coloniality," 65–77.

83. Introduction in Keller, et al., *Postcolonial Theologies*, 13–14.

84. Joh, "Transgressive Power," 162–63. See Joh, *Heart of the Cross*, xiii–xxvi, 19–48, 53–55.

continues to be produced and published in dominant cultures. *Resistance*, therefore, plays a key role in post-colonial theologizing. For example, Douglas and Kwok bring together a collection of essays on Anglicanism and its colonial legacy (philosophical, cultural, social and political) and the implications of globalization. Contributors seek to identify misuses of power in subjugating peoples from beyond the metropole in terms of hegemony, violence, suffering, ecology, debt, sexuality, urbanization, scripture, education, episcopacy, and communion.[85] Keller, Nausner, and Rivera begin with the lived experience of plural identities and mislocation, which contradicts the imposed singular identities of colonialism and neo-colonialism (black, white, oppressed, oppressor). Kwok identifies the ongoing subjugation and Eurocentrism in theology, which marginalizes the experience of women and, most severely, the experience of colonized women. Rivera recognizes that understandings of divine transcendence are often forged in imperial contexts. It becomes associated with spatial and temporal beyondness. God is removed from the mundane. God condescends.[86] Rieger explores the role of imperialism in the construction of orthodox and European christologies. Althaus-Reid is critical of theologians for excluding the sexed realities of poverty and for not overturning the (hetero)sexual assumptions "built into" theology.[87] Abraham probes Rahner's theology of freedom and argues that its limitations are conditioned by ecclesial and academic institutions. She also accuses post-colonial theorists of being guilty of similar reductionism by excluding the religious.[88] There is then a need for ongoing processes of decolonization.

Fourth, the goal of post-colonial theology is theological *decolonization*. This is both the culmination and summation of what post-colonial theologizing is and does. Political decolonization did not end colonial subjugation. This is seen both in the terms of independence agreed between former colonizers and colonies and by the reality of "internal colonialism" after independence. Coloniality too can continue for churches and scholars in countries with flag independence (see chapter 6).[89] As has already been seen, when identifying the nature of post-colonialism more generally, a process of decolonization is a movement that involves unveiling coloniality, disrupting dominant discourses, participating in hybridity, and decentering so-called Western knowledge. Processes of theological decolonization seek

---

85. See Introduction in Douglas and Kwok, *Beyond Colonial*, 14–20.
86. Rivera, *Touch of Transcendence*, 5–15, 45.
87. Althaus-Reid, *Indecent Theology*, 4–7.
88. See Abraham, *Identity, Ethics, and Nonviolence*, 195–96.
89. See Taylor, M. L., "Spirit and Liberation," 43.

to unveil oppression and suppression in theological discourses and theologies. They seek to disrupt dominant perspectives or the perspectives of the dominant in terms, for example, of biblical readings, doctrinal formulations, and church practices. They foreground the hybrid nature of Christianity and readings of Christian doctrines, traditions, and histories. In providing such counter-discourses theological decolonization decenters the "authority" or "normality" of so-called Western assumptions and discourses.

Conclusion

Post-colonial theologies respond to coloniality, promote the theological agency of marginalized peoples, develop hybridized forms of theology, and resist theological hegemony culminating in some form of decolonization. *Prima facie* the motivation and content of the writings of Mbiti and Mugambi seem to compare favorably with such a definition of post-colonial theology. The task of subsequent chapters will be test to what extent this initial impression can be justified *via* detailed study of major themes in their work beginning with how they critique mission Christianity especially as it relates to coloniality.

2

The Critique of Mission Christianity in the Theological Writings of Mbiti and Mugambi

IT WILL BE ARGUED presently that Mbiti and Mugambi depict mission Christianity, in relation to colonialism, as transcending it, serving similar purposes to it, and justifying it. In relation to cultural subjugation, mission Christianity practiced acculturation, denigrated traditional practice, imported denominationalism, and superimposed foreign categories of thought and action onto the emerging African church. In light of such critique, the chapter will conclude with a short section on the more constructive task of how Mbiti and Mugambi seek to define African theology. I will propose that their understanding of African theology can be encapsulated in the four characteristics of African reflection, African sources, African universalism, and African agency.

Mission Christianity and Empire

Mbiti and Mugambi are clear that colonial and foreign mission expansion are related and that the former infected the latter. It is argued that mission intersected with the interests of British colonialism and that missionaries provided theological justification for colonialism. However, it would be misleading to deny that they also identify positive contributions made by the modern missionary movement.

Foreign missionaries could transcend colonial interests. Mbiti recognizes that missionaries were at times opposed not only by African peoples but by colonial authorities too. As part of the humanitarian lobby they protested, with debatable effectiveness, against colonial policies that were disadvantageous to Africans.[1] Despite facing difficulties, they persevered in response to their understanding of Christ's command to evangelize all peoples.[2] Mbiti has "personal admiration and appreciation" for the achievements of missionaries and the support given to them by their home churches. Most are "highly dedicated people" working in difficult circumstances.[3] Provided missionaries are aware of the part they played in past injustices, where they remained largely "silent or muted" in colonial times, and are alert to the ongoing need for justice in Africa they continue to have a contribution to make.[4] Mugambi's writing is, on the whole, less conciliatory toward foreign missionaries. However, like Mbiti, it would be unfair to characterize it as outright condemnation.[5] For he does recognize that, despite their limitations, missionaries did lobby for the sake of Africans and against the ambitions of white settlers. Indeed, Mugambi depicts foreign missionaries as a "buffer" between "rulers and citizens."[6] While Mugambi identifies the provision of health care as the most significant and long lasting contribution missionaries have made in Africa, he also recognizes that some missionaries, such as John V. Taylor (1914–2001) and Lesslie Newbigin (1909–98), are people "open and willing to recognize that the Spirit of God cannot be contained, controlled, or directed by any man or woman."[7]

Both Mbiti and Mugambi identify Taylor, and especially his book *The Primal Vision*, as the exemplar of foreign mission theologizing. Indeed, Mugambi wrote the introduction to the 2001 SCM edition of Taylor's work.[8] Unlike Mbiti, Mugambi goes as far as to say that the genesis of modern African Theology is initiated, in part, by missionaries like Taylor.[9] Taylor's *Primal Vision* is, for Mugambi, a critical reflection on the effects of the modern missionary movement on the African cultural and religious heritage. It

1. Mbiti, "When the Right Hand," 10–11. See Maxon, "Colonial and Foreign," 36.

2. Mbiti, "Future of Christianity" (*CC*), 389.

3. Ibid. See also Mbiti, "When the Right Hand," 1–21.

4. Mbiti, "When the Right Hand," 20; Mugambi, *FLTR*, 73–77.

5. Isaac Mwase comes close to doing just that. See Mwase, "Critical Evaluation," 145–46.

6. Mugambi, "Religion and Social Reconstruction," 18.

7. Mugambi, *BBE*, 59. See Mbiti, "When the Right Hand," 20; Mugambi, *FLTR*, 144–46. See also Wood, N., *Faiths and Faithfulness*; Wainwright, *Lesslie Newbigin*; Wood, D., *Bishop John V. Taylor*.

8. Taylor, J., *Primal Vision*, xi–xxxv. See Mugambi, "Vision of the African Church."

9. Mugambi, *BBE*, 17. Cites conclusion to Taylor, J., *The Growth of the Church in Buganda*, as evidence for this view on the genesis of African theology. See Mugambi, Introduction in Taylor, J., *Primal Vision*, xxii–xxiii, xxvii.

demonstrates the thought and practice of a foreign missionary who while acknowledging that he is a guest is nonetheless, "at home" in Africa. It is full of empathy not sympathy and it illustrates the idea that missionaries need conversion too. The stress on "presence," for Mugambi, is "the core of the gospel."[10] Taylor's method is inductive. It avoids the "cool detachment" and "objectivity" characterizing much missionary writing. The role of the missionary is not to "command" but, as guest, to be present in situations of mutual learning and conversion. If presence in a missionary context does not lead the missionary to be more critically aware of his own heritage, then it is not mission. The practical significance of Taylor's work for Mugambi is that missionaries and local church leaders will need to be trained differently. Inductive methodologies, personal encounter, and presence will become more important than "dogmatic instruction and institutional formation." Part of such training will involve the concept and practice of a missiological "reversal" where mission will need to be reconceived to include the re-evangelization of Europe and North America. That is to say, Taylor's approach overturns the dominant model of mission practiced before the Second World War in Africa where "heathens" needed "civilization" before conversion and where the measure of such civilization was the foreign missionary. There is then a continuity between the best of mission Christianity, seen especially in the work of Taylor, and the practice of African theology they propose.

Mission Christianity and colonial interests intertwined. It is within the context of the modern missionary movement and the colonial context of Kenya that the thoughts of Mbiti and Mugambi emerge.[11] The fact that Christianity came to East Africa primarily through the "invasion" of foreign missionaries is, however, neither something to "weep over nor rejoice about."[12] It did not need to happen that way, nor does the missionary movement account for the growth of Christianity in East Africa. African missionaries, the end of colonial rule, and ATRs are, at the very least, equally important in the expansion of Christianity in Africa.[13]

Mugambi identifies seven reasons for the emergence of the modern missionary movement, which cannot easily be separated from imperialist aspirations. First, Protestantism needed new converts to counter Roman

10. Mugambi, Introduction in Taylor, J., *Primal Vision*, xiii. Compare Dedji, *Reconstruction and Renewal*, 12–44.

11. Mbiti, "Future of Christianity (1970–2000)"; Mugambi, *CTSR*, 4–17.

12. Mbiti, *CMA*, 1. See Mbiti, "Christian Eschatology," 32–45; Mugambi, *FLTR*, 79–83.

13. Mbiti, "Future Of Christianity" (*CC*), 389–90; Mbiti, *BATAC*, 7–12; Mugambi, *BBE*, 7–11; Mugambi, "Missiological Research," 542–45.

Catholicism.[14] Second, revivalism created growing resources for overseas evangelism.[15] Third, campaigns against slavery and the need to "rehabilitate" freed slaves provided scope for foreign involvement.[16] Fourth, growing geographical knowledge expanded the vision of foreign expansionism.[17] Fifth, improvement in transport and communications made travel easier. Sixth, rising North Atlantic nationalisms increased the notion that Europeans and North Americans were "heralds of civilization."[18] Seventh, the threat of secularism motivated evangelicals especially to counter its spread elsewhere in the world.[19] Mugambi argues that such motivation affects understandings of mission in East Africa. Mission is the conversion of "heathens" and thus the salvation of as many "souls" from hell as possible.[20] Mission is civilizing Africans, improving the economic life of Africa, it is (especially from the late nineteenth century) teaching Africans about a God they had some vague notions about.[21] In more recent times, and especially in the wake of the Second World War, "development" has replaced older models of much mission activity in Africa. Yet, despite its redistributive claims, Africa becomes both more pauperized and more Christian than ever before. For Mugambi,

---

14. This is something acknowledged in, for example, *The Colonial Church Chronicle*. England's imperial expansion was providential. It provided the opportunity for Anglican expansion and would counter the Roman Catholic criticism that it was "insular." See N.a., "Rise and Progress"; N.a., "Extension of the Reformed."

15. Strong corrects the perception that British missionary culture begins with evangelicals. See Strong, *Anglicanism and British Empire*, 13–19.

16. The 1873 treaty signed between the British and the Sultan of Zanzibar abolishing in law the seaborne traffic of slaves meant the CMS took charge of a freed slave settlement near Mombasa. See *Church Missionary Gleaner* vol. 2, 85; *Church Missionary Gleaner* vol. 3, 10, 96.

17. Krapf's vision for interior expansion was warmly received by the *Church Missionary Intelligencer* as "England's answer to the Papal aggression."

18. A stress on "civilizing" African converts is not consistent throughout foreign mission history. From the 1860s, a shift toward an evangelism only approach was emerging. Mission was the proclamation of the "simple Gospel message to the greatest number possible." See Porter, "Overview, 1700–1914," 55. It should be noted that this was already the emphasis that Krapf and Rebmann had brought to Kenya twenty years earlier. They stressed the need for personal conversion and had no desire to introduce Africans to European "civilization." For Krapf, a "civilized" unbeliever is worse than a "savage" who is committed to traditional religion. See Ng'eny, *Rabai to Mumias*, 48.

19. Mugambi, *BBE*, 81–82. See Mugambi, *TAHCC*, 166–69; Strong, *Anglicanism and British Empire*, 10–40, 213–21.

20. He cites here Vidler, *The Church in an Age of Revolution*, 252. See also Mbiti, *NTEAB*, 51–61.

21. He cites here Evans-Pritchard, *Theories of Primitive Religion*.

such poverty is incongruous with the apparent growth of Christianity and unacceptable ethically.²²

Such criticism of the modern missionary movement is not only historical and theological for Mbiti and Mugambi. It is personal. For example, when Mbiti returned to Kenya to teach at an Africa Inland Mission (AIM) station, after completing a course of theological study in the USA, he was segregated from the white missionaries at the station. Despite working in Africa and having African American applicants since 1951 the AIM did not have Black missionaries.²³ When Mbiti questioned the AIM's racist policies, the missionaries reported him to the colonial authorities. Given that this happened during the Mau Mau movement (1952–60), the repercussions for Mbiti could have been very serious indeed.²⁴

In the experience of Mbiti and Mugambi and their writings, it is clear that mission Christianity, generally, taught converts to obey the colonial powers, and opposed nationalist movements.²⁵ Missionaries often presented the gospel in "other worldly" terms while importing their own cultural practices and complying with colonial rule.²⁶ For Mugambi, this means that missionaries were "extension officers in the process of Europeanization."²⁷ The greatest sin of mission Christianity, argues Mugambi, is that it failed to support the struggle for liberation in Kenya. Indeed, the lack of missionary support for national liberation is "the basis" for a critique of mission Christianity.²⁸ Mugambi argues that during the struggle for independence,

---

22. Mugambi, Introduction in Taylor, J., *Primal Vision*, xvi. Cites here Taylor, M., *Not Angels but Agencies*, 19. See also Ilo, *Church and Development*, 110–81.

23. See Mbiti, "When the Right Hand," 11. Mbiti is unaware that the AIM did have one "colored worker," Alice Wentworth. She had been with the mission since childhood. See Barnett, "Kenya Field Director." It appears that African American Christians sought to become AIM missionaries. However, Erik Barnett identified psychological, social, church, marital, and housing problems if African American missionaries were accepted. See Barnett, "Acceptance of Negro Missionaries from USA." See Davis, "General Secretary AIM."

24. Mbiti, Interview by Heaney, April 8. See Mbiti, "When the Right Hand," 11.

25. Mugambi, "Christian Mission in Context," 69–70; Mugambi, "History of the Church," 48. In an AIM handbook published in 1963, missionaries were advised not to take political sides and to entertain government officials—similar advice was given to CMS missionaries. See DePue, et al., "How Do 'You' Fit In," section 4.

26. Mugambi, *BBE*, 83; Mugambi, "Religion and Social Reconstruction," 21; Mbiti, *NTEAB*, 51–61.

27. Mugambi, *TAHCC*, 12–27. See Mbiti, *BATAC*, 26–33; Oliver, *Missionary Factor*, 163–292; King, K., *Pan-Africanism and Education*.

28. Mugambi, *CCAL*, 155–56. See Mugambi, "Christian Mission in Context," 67–70; Mugambi, *BBE*, 62.

the behavior of missionaries was "inconsistent with the Gospel." While they were happy to speak of "freedom in Christ," it was they who were citizens of the empire while Africans remained subjects of it. No concern for the loss of life, including those of devout Christians, seemed to provoke much empathy or sympathy. For Mugambi, such experience was formative and led to a strong distinction, as in Mbiti, between the gospel and missionary misappropriations of it in "Christianity."[29] In practice, therefore, mission Christianity communicated a sub-standard gospel in contrast to the biblical gospel proclamation of "total liberation" (Isa 61:1-2; Luke 4:16-22). Missionaries provided theological justification for colonialism.[30] Because of this association with imperialism and justification of imperialism, the foreign missionary movement is nothing less than "a scandal to the Gospel of Jesus Christ."[31]

Theological justification for colonialism exists. Given the role of the Church Missionary Society (CMS) in Kenya, it might be assumed that in referring to theological justifications for imperialism, Mbiti and Mugambi have in mind a work such as Max Warren's (1904-77) *Caesar, the Beloved Enemy.*[32] Even if they had not, it presents a particularly mature crystallization of a Christian missionary justification for imperialism. Warren's "theology of imperialism" justifies empire in reference to the theological categories of providence, vocation, order and, greater good.[33] Warren's theologizing, explicitly and implicitly, functions as a response to alleged cultural dysfunction. The rise of empire is providential because, unlike African traditions, it can act as a *praeparatio* for the Gospel. The universal vision of the empire, in contrast to the localism of traditional practices, inspires vocation. Colonization brings, in contrast to social structures that existed before, the permanent good of legislation, political betterment, and cohesion. The scope of the empire, again unlike traditional societies, can evoke in its subjects a commitment to a greater good and broader Commonwealth.[34] The mistake that Warren makes is that he emphasizes institutional expansion, which then finds its corollary in colonial expansion. The mission of both church

---

29. Stinton, *Jesus of Africa*, 26–27; Mugambi, *ACT*, 57; Mugambi, *TAHCC*, 17–18.

30. Mugambi, *BBE*, 56. See Mugambi, "Christological Paradigms," 147.

31. Mugambi, *CTSR*, 70; Mugambi, *BBE*, 62. See Mugambi, "Christian Mission after the Cold War," 65.

32. Warren, *Caesar, the Beloved Enemy*, 55–65.

33. Ibid., 30–41. See Kings, *Christianity Connected*, 34–35, 112–14.

34. Warren, *Caesar, the Beloved Enemy*, 26–40. This same notion of the inability of societies to relate to broadening horizons has also been employed to explain conversion. See Horton, R., "African Conversion," 85–108.

THE CRITIQUE OF MISSION CHRISTIANITY 37

and state is, therefore, to subdue the other. Indeed, Warren finds in the New Testament a "subordinationist ethic."[35] For Mugambi, the lack of support for nationalist movements and theological justifications for imperialism largely explains the rise of African Initiated Churches (AICs). This may oversimplify the historical issues in post-colonial African studies. For conversion is not always as clear cut an event as missionaries envisage.[36]

Elizabeth Isichei is no doubt correct when she argues that the choice for Africans was not simply one between "Christianity" and "tradition." Syncretism was always a live option.[37] It is unsurprising, therefore, that Simeon Kalume, the first African Anglican minister in Nairobi, wore charms and that not a few believers continued to consult traditional diviners or healers. In 1907, Yohana Nene, the first ordained African from Taveta, was suspended from the diaconate for apparently allowing his mother's skull to be removed from her grave.[38] Isichei correctly observes that religious meanings are changed, nuanced, and eroded "by journeys through time as well as by journeys through cultures."[39] Africans reading the Bible discovered lifestyles and theologizing which seemed to be accepted in the text but rejected by missionaries. Old Testament patriarchs had numerous wives and concubines, provision was made for levirate marriage, witches were executed, imperial powers were under God's condemnation, and the Apocalypse promised a calamitous end for "Babylon the Great."[40] Such contestatory readings is often associated with the emergence of AICs in Africa. However, Isichei rightly notes that the differences between such movements and the missionary churches are more apparent than real. For the conversion of Africans, by definition, creates a new community with a new "framework of discourse." Mission churches and AICs protest against the hegemony of colonialism and mission discourse.[41] Foreign missionaries were often keen to suppress any type of intermingling, whether that be liberation politics and theology or traditional wisdom and theology.[42] It is no surprise, therefore, that the biggest concentration of AICs is in South Africa, Zimbabwe, and

---

35. See Heaney, "Coloniality and Theological Method," 64–65.

36. See Strayer, *Making Mission*, 83. See Landau, "Language," 212, for examples of missionaries being "converted out of" their faith by those met in missionary contexts.

37. Isichei, *History of Christianity*, 132.

38. Strayer, *Making Mission*, 83–84.

39. Isichei, *History of Christianity*, 5.

40. Etherington, "Education and Medicine," 267. See Strayer, *Making Mission*, 80.

41. Isichei, *History of Christianity*, 10. See Sundkler, *Bantu*, 40, 55, 53–57, 238–301.

42. See Etherington, Introduction in *Missions and Empire*, 4. See Hastings, *African Christianity*, 24–25.

Kenya, where a small, conservative, and often violent community of white settlers sought to establish governance along racialist and racist lines.[43]

Mugambi insightfully takes a further step in his analysis. Where once missionaries and mission theologians justified colonialism either in published works or in mission practice, now some justify globalization. Once uninvited North Atlantic missionaries were enmeshed with the projects of imperialists. Now they are enmeshed in the projects of globalization. In terms reminiscent of Paulo Freire, whom he makes reference to, Mugambi argues that the arrival of missionaries is the inevitable consequence of North Atlantic exploitation. For the arrival of uninvited missionaries amounts to "false generosity" proposing to stand in for the absence of the brightest and best who have emigrated to Europe and Africa. Such "false generosity" props up an exploitative system under the guise of Christian ministry. In short, such mission baptizes globalization.[44] Freire writes:

> In order to have the continued opportunity to express their 'generosity,' the oppressors must perpetuate injustice as well. An unjust social order is the permanent fount of this 'generosity,' which is nourished by death, despair, and poverty.[45]

Jürgen Moltmann also concurs with such a prognosis, describing globalization as "the new magic word," which is simply a presently acceptable term describing what people in the nineteenth century called imperialism.[46] If this is indeed the case, and missionaries are involved in perpetuating an unjust system (globalization) or of unjustly practicing globalization, then radical action will need to be taken both by the church in Africa and beyond it.

Colonialists justified their presence and actions with reference to the emperor. Missionaries justified their presence and actions with reference to God. Colonial subjects were "convinced" by colonizers as a result of violence, the threat of violence, and the demonstration of the "universal" presence of the emperor. Missionaries could not demonstrate the universal presence of God in the same practical way, though not a few considered colonial conquest of Africa as evidence of the work of God.[47] From the perspective of many Africans, missionaries failed to justify their claim to have been sent

---

43. Mugambi, *BBE*, 56–63; Mugambi, *TAHCC*, 18–19.
44. Mugambi, "Religions in East Africa," 21–22. See Mugambi, "Challenges to African Scholars," 19; Freire, *Pedagogy of the Oppressed*, 25–27, 119–21.
45. Freire, *Pedagogy of the Oppressed*, 26.
46. Moltmann, "Liberation of the Future," 276.
47. Mugambi, "Problems of Meaning," 98.

Such subjugation is present also in Anglicanism. For Mugambi, Anglicanism in the African colonies was willing to suppress rival articulations of the Christian faith.[59] For it was the role of the "European masters" to interpret the Christian faith. Consequently, the whole modern missionary movement was based on "an erroneous theological presupposition" that identified the Christian faith with western civilization, and thus maintained, residually, a notion of Christendom.[60] To illustrate this, both Mbiti and Mugambi make reference to baptism as a re-naming ritual or ritual of civilization. The sacrament of baptism becomes colonial circumcision.[61] Mbiti asks, "Must we castrate our local spiritual creativity and become museums of the ancient treasures of Christendom? No!"[62]

Mugambi argues that missionaries did not follow the apostolic model of "synthesizing" the cultural context or heritage with the Christian gospel.[63] Rather, the "missionary curriculum" for converts "portrayed the imperial metropolis as the gateway to 'heaven.'"[64] For Mbiti this "cultural conditioning" is seen clearest in Church architecture, worship, music, art, theology, and structures. The suppression of "cultural values and tastes" has resulted in "a rebellion" against "cultural imperialism" (Mbiti) or "missionary imperialism" (Mugambi) by African Christians.[65]

For Mbiti and Mugambi, while an apostolic model for mission might not have been practiced by missionaries in Kenya, this does not equate to an absence of authoritarianism. On the contrary, foreign missionaries felt they were doing that for which Africans could not do for themselves. They were bringing them the very revelation of God.[66] Mbiti argues that such missionaries misunderstood the African context and had a deficient view of revelation.[67] Yet, it was the missionary movement that brought, sometimes unwittingly, a message of fulfillment to African traditions. The authoritarian nature of mission Christianity has not ended, however, with the coming of independence. Mbiti may be seen to suggest a type of neo-colonialism in

59. Mugabmi, *ACT*, 55.

60. Ibid.; Mugambi, *FLTR*, 19; Mugambi, "Some Perspectives," 53–54.

61. Mugambi, *BBE*, 95; Mugambi, *TAHCC*, 192–94; Mugambi and Guy, *CTAC*, 19–22; Mbiti, *NTEAB*, 116–17.

62. Mbiti, *BATAC*, 19.

63. Mugambi, "Problems of Meaning," 163; Mugambi, "Christian Mission after the Cold War," 66; Mbiti, "Christian Eschatology," 311.

64. Mugambi, "Responsible Leadership," 85.

65. Mbiti, "Gospel and Culture," 1–3; Mugambi, *CTSR*, 3.

66. See Mbiti, "Encounter of Christian Faith" (*CC*), 817–18.

67. Ibid.

mission Christianity where coloniality continues with foreign missionaries continuing to be empowered by larger forces at work. The church, observes Mbiti, "tolerates" foreign missionaries because the power and wealth that bring them to Africa resides outside Africa.[68]

Missionary acculturation cannot be denied. However, to expect Victorian era missionaries to have the same critical perspective as modern theologians may be unrealistic.[69] Furthermore, the very development of the thought of Mbiti and Mugambi itself might militate against such criticism of missionaries in colonial times. For the centers of learning, which they rightly accuse of inculcating Africans with European values and worldview, are centers they belong to as well. Mbiti, writing from the perspective of an African theologian in a different era, only later came to reject the idea of "indigenization." Likewise, while Mugambi did not give a wholehearted endorsement to *Nyayoism*, he did recommend Moi's *Kenya African Nationalism* as one source that shapes the "framework" within which theology in Kenya is done.[70] As history proved, neither *Nyayoism* nor the administration of Moi was benign, nor created a conducive context for Christian theologizing.[71] Yet, even within mission Christianity and within an emerging African Christianity, resistance to and rejection of acculturation was taking place.[72] Consequently, though tempered by historical awareness and due recognition for the mistakes African theology has also made, a critique of mission Christianity's practice of acculturation can still be sustained. Inevitably, such acculturation denigrates African forms of thought and practice.

Cultural subjugation includes rejection of African traditional practice by mission Christianity. Culture, for Mbiti, is human patterns of life responding to the human environment. Such response is expressed physically (in agriculture and arts), relationally (in institutions, laws and customs), and in human reflection on reality (in language, philosophy, religion, worldview).[73] Culture "is the context in which Christ is confessed, it is also the vehicle

---

68. Mbiti, *BATAC*, 205.

69. See Byaruhanga, *Bishop Alfred Tucker*, 23–42.

70. Mbiti, *BATAC*, 1–4. See Moi, *Kenya African Nationalism*.

71. Mbiti, *BATAC*, 1. See Githiga, *Church as the Bulwark*, 66–98. In his book explaining and justifying *Nyayoism*, Godia cites Mbiti as one thinker who "echoes the tone" of Moi in identifying the religious and ethical foundation of African life (p. 16–20). See also G. P. Benson, "Ideological Politics"; Cooper, *Africa since 1940*, 174–76; Nugent, *Africa since Independence*, 409–12.

72. See Mugambi, "Rites of Passage," 230; Mugambi, *TAHCC*, 1–11; Mbiti, *BATAC*, 15–16.

73. Mbiti, "Christianity and African Culture," 387.

of confessing him."⁷⁴ Mbiti understands culture as "that part of the total repertoire of human action" or the "total manifestation of a people's way of life and self-understanding." This includes what such action and self-understanding produces, "which is socially, as opposed to genetically, transmitted."⁷⁵ Such "total manifestation" of self-understanding and self-expression is witnessed in politics, economics, ethics, aesthetics, metaphysics, kinship, and religion whereas context is "the specific setting in which culture is lived by individuals, groups and communities at a particular time and place."⁷⁶ Their interpretation of culture, however, needs to be understood not just in relation to such definitions but in how they critique the practice of missionaries and the constructive proposals they make for an African theology.⁷⁷

For Mbiti, missionaries and their African converts, from the nineteenth century onwards, often exhibited a "bulldozer mentality" that assumed that African traditions were demonic and, therefore, needed to be "swept aside."⁷⁸ During colonial occupation people were "brain-washed" to consider African traditions to be inferior or useless.⁷⁹ For most foreign missionaries African practices were "repugnant."⁸⁰ Consequently, missionaries "scandalized, vandalized, and brutally tor[e] cultural life apart—without . . . clear theological justification."⁸¹ Traditional rites of passage were suppressed in colonial Kenya. Mugambi sees the colonial period in Kenya as a time when traditional "power relations" were disrupted leading to the break down of social cohesion.⁸² Rituals in regard to birth, adulthood, marriage, elderhood, and death were suppressed both by colonial officials and missionaries. Age and experience became replaced by academic and professional qualifications, church membership, and colonial patronage.⁸³

74. Mbiti, Introduction in *Confessing Christ in Different Cultures*, 24.

75. Mugambi, "Some Perspectives," 54–55; Mugambi, *FLTR*, 30. Cites Munro, "Culture," in Mitchell, *Dictionary of Sociology*.

76. Mugambi, *CTSR*, 119; Mugambi, *FLTR*, 30.

77. For broader discussions and developments on the nature of culture, see Geertz, *Interpretation of Culture*, 3–54; Geertz, *Available Light*.

78. Mbiti, "Confessing Christ in Multi-Faith," 138. See Mbiti, "Christianity and African Culture"; Mbiti, "Christianity and Traditional Religions," 432–33; Mbiti, *ARAP*, 8–18; Mugambi, *ACT*, 33; Mombo, "Theological Education," 131; Nwatu, "'Colonial' Christianity," 353–55.

79. Mbiti, "Literature and Oral," 93–94.

80. Mugambi, "Responsible Leadership," 85.

81. Mbiti, "When the Right Hand," 12. See Mugambi, *FLTR*, 77.

82. Mugambi, "Rites of Passage," 242.

83. Ibid. See also Mbiti, "Literature and Oral," 93–94.

The denigration of African cultures, for Mbiti and Mugambi, arises from an erroneous theology of mission. Such a theology assumed that the acceptance of Christianity meant the rejection of African culture. For such culture was alleged to be thoroughly superstitious and incompatible with the Christian gospel.[84]

Cultural subjugation is violence.[85] It is manifest not only in missionary policy but also in actual violence. Part of the reason, Mbiti argues, for the Akamba resisting the evangelism of western mission was its attendant violence. For example, missionaries beat some of the people, exploited their labor, assumed inherent superiority as missionaries, and racially discriminated against Africans. They separated themselves from the people and referred to Africans in derogatory terms.[86] Missionaries defined Africans as pagans. Mbiti quotes an AIM missionary's description of the Akamba in 1916: "the natives are unattractive, their hovels unsanitary, their customs revolting and their society depressing."[87] Hulda (sometimes Hilda) J. Stumpf of the AIM considered "the spiritual beliefs of the African" to be akin to

> . . . superstition rather than religion. They conceive of God not as an ethical deity or as a Father who knows and cares for His children, but rather as a power which must be propitiated. Likewise, the "ngoma," or spirits, are vindictive unless appeased. Fear, therefore, is the motive inspiring all their spiritual beliefs.[88]

She concludes, "We cannot understand the mind of the animist. He lives in continual terror. His whole world is peopled with millions of strange beings. Every path is haunted."[89] Lest it should be assumed that such attitudes belong to a missionary past, Mugambi references Stephen Neill who forty-five years later was still seeking to justify the term pagan for the "simple religions" who were not yet touched by civilization.[90] Mugambi rightly rejects the term because of the implication that Africans dwelling in rural societies are not civilized according to Western standards, and for equating conversion to Christianity with such civilization.[91] So too, Mbiti argues, that just as

84. Mugambi, "Fresh Look" (*IRM*), 343.
85. Fanon, *Wretched of the Earth*, 31–32.
86. Mbiti, "Christian Eschatology," 31.
87. Ibid., 5
88. Stumpf, "How Dark is Their Darkness?"
89. Ibid., 10–11.
90. Mugambi, *ACT*, 64. See Neill, et al., *Concise Dictionary*.
91. Mugambi, *ACT*, 64. Here he includes p'Bitek, *African Religions*; p'Bitek, *Song of Lawino*; Idowu, *African Traditional Religion*; Williams, C., *Destruction of Black Civilization*.

biblical criticism has emerged in the past two centuries it is now time for a critical approach to mission and evangelism.[92]

Conversion, if understood as the adoption of foreign missionary culture, results in "cultural inauthenticity."[93] This means that converts begin to see and respond to the world in foreign terms. If evidence was found of converts being involved in traditional "devilish" rites such as sacrifice, dances, and circumcision, they could be suspended from catechumenate classes preparing them for baptism.[94] Conversely, and writing specifically about 1940s Kenya and the circumcision controversies, Mugambi equates such denigration with the larger colonial context. For "African resisters" viewed such missionary policies as part of a larger project to deprive them of their identity. On one hand, white settlers alienated them from their land. On the other hand, foreign missionaries alienated them from their culture and religion.[95] "When you dismiss the cultural and religious heritage of a people, you have no right to convert that community."[96]

At times Mbiti and Mugambi portray the cultural denigration carried out by missionaries in too systematic of terms. Missionaries were often incapable of such systematic denigration. Furthermore, such overstatement can tend toward an analysis that undervalues the agency of African converts. Despite such a tendency toward overstatement, it seems that Mbiti's and Mugambi's general analysis of cultural denigration at the hands of missionaries is correct.

Missionaries in Kenya were involved in cultural denigration. However, given that Mbiti and Mugambi concede a degree of continuity between the theologizing of some missionaries and their work, the accusation of cultural inauthenticity can be leveled at them as well, as their work evidences a gradual move away from the particular. This will be further explored in subsequent chapters. Suffice it to say at this juncture, that the schooling and career of Mbiti and Mugambi in European and European styled institutions (AIM, Anglicanism, universities, and the WCC) inevitably affects and hybridizes the way in which they experience and analyze culture, context, and theology. However, in comparison to mission Christianity and approaches influenced by confessional theologies that influence resistance

---

92. Mbiti, "Christian Eschatology," 306.

93. Mugambi, "Problems of Meaning," 20–21. See Freire, *Pedagogy of the Oppressed*, 122–48.

94. Mbiti, "Christian Eschatology," 147, 297, 311–13.

95. Mugambi, "Some Perspectives," 207. See Mbiti, "Confessing Christ in Multi-Faith."

96. Mugambi, *FLTR*, 21.

to the emergence of African theology in dialogue with African traditional practice, Mbiti and Mugambi do strive for a more thoroughly contextual theologizing.[97] For they see the importation of denominationalism as a destructive foreign import.

Denominationalism mitigates against both the Christian Gospel and African sociality. Mbiti and Mugambi are critical of mission Christianity's introduction of competing forms of Christianity and its unwillingness to be involved in the ecumenical movement.[98] For Mugambi, who rejects the term "tribe" in reference to African sociality, accuses missionaries of introducing a denominational tribalism.[99] This can be understood quite literally. For if colonialism constructed "tribes" and hardened community boundaries (through, for example, imposition of the vernacular in primary schools, indirect governance through "chiefs," promotion of self-development along so-called ethnic lines, identity cards (*kipande*) stating ethnic origin, district administrative units relating to and/or strengthening ethnic boundaries, unequal allocations of resources, and banning nationwide political organizations) then missionary activity accentuated it. As has been seen, mission societies tended to work in particular "ethnic zones." Consequently, particular peoples began to be associated with particular denominations, for example, Anglicanism in Western Province, Roman Catholicism in Ukambani, and Presbyterianism in Central Province.[100] Indeed, denominationalism can divide families and can, according to Mugambi, cause more damage than ethnicity.[101] There is clear tension in the modern missionary movement. On the one hand, missionaries preached unity. On the other hand, they were involved in denominational rivalry while at the same time accusing the founders of AICs of "breaching the unity of Church."[102]

The Kikuyu conference of 1913 represented an early attempt at ecumenism in Kenya. Proposals were made for a single standard for church membership, a common code of discipline, an agreed approach to traditional customs, a common form of worship, and a degree of uniformity in ministerial training based on common recognition of the authority of the

97. For such a confessional approach, see Kato, *Theological Pitfalls*; Kato, "Eschatology in Africa." See also Mugambi, "Problems of Meaning," 165.

98. See Mugambi, Introduction in Taylor, J., *Primal Vision*, xxvii–xxxv; Mugambi, "Some Perspectives," 28–29; Mugambi, "Ecumenical Movement," 7–8.

99. Mugambi, *FLTR*, 203–4; Mugambi, "Religion and Social Reconstruction," 22.

100. Kundu, "Ethnicity and the Challenge," 160, 174. See in the same volume, Aseka, "Post-Colonial State"; Ogot, "Boundary Changes," 16–29.

101. Mugambi, "Christological Paradigms," 138–39.

102. Mugambi, *BBE*, 11. See Mbiti, "Dreams as a Point"; Mbiti, "Faith, Hope, and Love."

Scriptures and Creeds.[103] However, despite the early date of such ecumenical endeavor, it was ecumenism between mission societies not churches. African Christians were not involved, Roman Catholics were not involved, and there was no unanimity even amongst those who did attend. For example, Frank Weston, bishop of Zanzibar, baulked at unity with non-episcopal societies. Gradually others withdrew, including the AIM, not least because of the intransigence of Anglo-Catholics.[104]

Mugambi affirms Roland Oliver's prognosis (*The Missionary Factor in East Africa*), made first in 1952, that while the African church might be expanding at the circumference it is disintegrating at the center. Making reference also to Mbiti's work *The Crisis of Mission in Africa* (1970) Mugambi asserts that little has changed in the late twentieth century. He asks, what is the theological quality of African Christian expansion, how many theologians are the Churches producing, and can the African church sustain itself theologically?[105] It seems that he considers the likelihood of such self-sufficiency to be remote and, in part, this is as a result of internal fragmentation caused by imported denominationalism. When such denominationalism, which by definition resists ecumenism, is mixed with ethnicity "the political and economic poison resulting from it is impossible to neutralize."[106] Any practice of mission in the twenty-first century "must be for the promotion of an ecumenically open church, not for parochial, tribal, sectarian cultic communities."[107] This will only come about if the "logic of domination" is replaced by the "logic of solidarity."[108] Yet, as Mbiti recognizes, the impulse to denominationalism even if initially a foreign practice is now fervently practiced by many Africans.[109]

Any assessment of Mbiti's and Mugambi's contention that denominationalism is another form of cultural subjugation must begin with an acknowledgement that they are right to be frustrated by the historic unwillingness or ineptitude of the modern missionary movement's approach

103. Mugambi, "Ecumenical Movement," 10–11.

104. Ibid., 10–12. See Dedji, *Reconstruction and Renewal*, 64–65. An Alliance of Missions was eventually formed in 1918, to be replaced in 1943 by the Christian Council of Kenya, which became the National Council of Churches of Kenya (NCCK). See Anderson, W., *Church in East Africa*, 70–72, 106–8; Ng'eny, *Rabai to Mumias*, 58–64; Strayer, *Making Mission*, 9.

105. Mugambi, "Vision of the African Church," 237–38.

106. Ibid., 238–39. (Cites Jenkins, *The Contradiction of Christianity*.)

107. Ibid., 240. See Mbiti, "Eucharistie, Koinonia und Gemeinschaft."

108. Mugambi, "Vision of the African Church," 246–47. Cites Raiser, *Ecumenism in Transition*; Bonino, "Oikoumene"; on the logic of domination and solidarity.

109. See Mbiti, *CMA*, 4–5; Mugambi, *BBE*, 18–19.

to ecumenism. However, it has already been recognized that part of the very *raison d'être* of, at least, Anglican expansionism was to define itself over against Roman Catholicism. This is true also of the AIM. Because of such Protestant motivations they do not cooperate missionally with Roman Catholic societies. Expansionism serves ecclesiastical ends as well as missiological ends. It is unsurprising, therefore, that missionaries of the early 1900s were hesitant. Indeed, hesitancy still exists. In the 1970s, for example, the AIM use quotations from Mbiti's writing, without identifying him as the author, as illustrative of the "liberal ecumenism" that needs to be refuted in East Africa.[110] In contrast, for Mbiti and Mugambi, ecumenism is a vital part of mission.[111] For unity, they argue, unlike other foreign categories is traditionally esteemed by African communities.

Foreign categories were imported and assumed to be theologically and spiritually superior. Mbiti and Mugambi identify attempts to subjugate traditional thought and practice through the introduction of categories of thought and practice foreign to Africa. These categories include individualism, dualism, and futurism.

Before Mbiti's, now famous, encapsulation of African corporateness ("I am because we are")[112] Taylor describes the sociality of African human identity as "a centrifugal selfhood . . . interpermeating other selves in a relationship in which subject and object are no longer distinguishable. 'I think, therefore I am' is replaced by 'I participate, therefore I am.'"[113] In contrast, and as will be seen further in the next chapter, missionaries import a very individualist understanding of humanity. Mugambi sees this particularly clearly during the Cold War. Here individualism served to contrast the Christianity and capitalism of the West with the Soviet Union and its satellite and client states.[114] Such an emphasis was in danger of making Christianity "broadly irrelevant to the material needs of ordinary people."[115]

110. N.a., "Crisis of Church Leadership," 1. The quotations are from Mbiti, *NTEAB*.

111. Mbiti, "Mission Outreach," 177; Mugambi, *BBE*, 61.

112. Mbiti, *ARAP*, 141.

113. Taylor, J., *Primal Vision*, 27. See Mbiti, *ARAP*, 113. See also Yates, *Christian Mission*, 41.

114. For example, Robert Dayton, an AIM missionary, detected Russian influence in Africa in the era leading up to nationalism. Communists, he perceived, were promoting nationalism to later "reap the results" of the vacuum created. "Africa is calling, Russia is answering." Dayton, "Kenya Calls," film 4.

115. Mugambi, "Christian Mission after the Cold War," 69–72. The AIM saw Christianity as a bulwark against both Communism and materialism. The challenge it argued is clear, "Africa is calling, Russia is answering, what will our response be when Kenya calls?" Dayton, "Kenya Calls," film 4.

While individualism existed in missionary endeavor during this period it is doubtful if it deserves any special distinction.

Missionaries brought inherent dualisms in their theology. For both Mbiti and Mugambi the most serious dualism was that between spirit and flesh.[116] Mbiti observes that the practice of missionaries in Africa introduced a dualism in society not previously present. He notes that because of the attendant foreignness of the Christian message communicated in Africa by missionaries, converts are forced to exist in two worlds. Because of the foreignness of Christianity Mbiti observes that the Gospel has not permeated "into the total life of the people" so that a "pronounced dichotomy" between the "religious" and "secular" now exists.[117] He argues that mission Christianity seldom presented a God with recognizable power in African contexts. On the contrary, mission Christianity presented a remote God, removed from communities, uninterested in the daily struggle with evil, interested in individuals more than societies, concerned with their eternal welfare at the expense of their material welfare.[118] This understanding of God manifested itself in a very dualistic practice where, in contrast to traditional societies, the "spiritual" was valued above the "material."[119] Unsurprisingly, therefore, mission communities were organized hierarchically where those involved in the "spiritual" ministries had more authority in the church.

Mugambi sees a dangerous dualism at work in modern Africa between "religion" and "politics." He argues that such a dualism emerges in the Reformation in sixteenth and seventeenth century Europe. Politicians "schooled" in such a tradition often cause social disharmony by taking the concept of secularization "too literally." The "alleged emergence" of the secular-state is more ideological, he argues, than factual. It stands opposed to institutional religion, seeks to replace religion with nihilism, and is akin to fundamentalism.[120] Mugambi is correct to question the purported neutrality and elevated status of secularism. Indeed, in more recent times, the pervasiveness of secularism is being re-examined in Northern academies.[121]

---

116. Mugambi, "Religions in East Africa," 6–8. Mbiti comes close to similar thought. See Mbiti, *ARAP*, 212–16. See also Rowland, "Render to God." See also Rowland and Corner, *Liberating Exegesis*.

117. Mbiti, "Christian Eschatology," 289–90.

118. Mbiti, *BATAC*, 154–56, 165. For a recent example of the same diagnosis, see Matonya, *Real Power*.

119. Mbiti, *BATAC*, 159.

120. Mugambi, "Religion and Social Reconstruction," 13–14.

121. For an overview of the debate, see Clark, J., "Failure of a 'Grand Narrative'"; Morris, "Secularization and Religious Experience."

Futurism, Mbiti and Mugambi argue, is a concept imported to Kenya by missionaries. What precisely this means and a consideration of its impact on African experience and theologizing will be at the heart of the next chapter. Suffice it to say here, for Mbiti some of what was taught by the AIM was unbiblical despite their confidence to the contrary. For example, he is critical of them teaching the unbiblical notion that "in effect" the Messiah comes "visibly" three times.[122] Furthermore he argues, though Mugambi disagrees, that a future orientated temporality is not present in African communities.

Assessment of the identification of foreign categories again returns to the arguments and counter-arguments on the extent to which missionaries, at least in the early period in Kenya, might have been expected to be critical about such matters. Undoubtedly, individualism, dualisms of spirit and flesh and sacred and secular, as well as futurism are part of a European heritage that missionaries inevitably brought with them. At the very least, a more thoroughgoing engagement with the heritage of Kenyans would have made such dualisms much more obviously problematic. However, it should also be noted that Mbiti and Mugambi are not entirely free of dualist thinking. The most obvious example of this is in their distinction between Christianity and gospel. Tinyiko Sam Maluleke describes it as a "fantastic dualism—a neo-docetism . . ." and a way of thinking foreign to Africa.[123] Nonetheless, their depiction and criticism of missionary practice as they experience it in Kenya becomes important for defining their approach to African theology.

African Theology in the Writings of Mbiti and Mugambi

Mbiti and Mugambi observe that missionaries in Kenya at times transcended colonial interests. However, they argue that more often than not mission Christianity was intertwined with such interests and provided theological justification for imperialism and colonialism. Mission practices therefore emphasized acculturation, denigration of ATRs, denominationalism, and the imposition of foreign categories. In direct response to this fourfold cultural subjugation, African theologies can be characterized by four characteristics in the writings of Mbiti and Mugambi: African reflection, African sources, African universalism, and African agency.[124]

First, African theology is African theological reflection. African Theology begins with African experience and seeks to transform African

---

122. See Mbiti, "Christian Eschatology," 48–59, 241–44.

123. Maluleke, "Black and African Theologies," 10.

124. Muzorewa, *Origins and Development*, 3, identifies the first use of the term by P. D. Fueter. See Fueter, "Theological Education."

experience. For both theologians, missionaries largely understood mission to be acculturation. Consequently, the danger is that mission Churches, including the Anglican Church to which they both belong, has become "an instrument of cultural colonization or alienation."[125] The transformative affect of African theology must, therefore, prevent and redress this. By implication, it must have a decolonizing effect. This begins by disrupting missionary discourses with the theological reflection of Africans. African theology is, at its most basic, "theological reflection and expression by African Christians."[126] It is "systematic articulation of human response to revelation within a particular situation and context."[127] Mugambi prefers the ascription African Christian theology. For long before the arrival of Islam and Christianity, theological discourses were taking place in Africa.[128] For Mbiti "African" can embrace all races.[129] However, it appears that because of the "invasion" of mission Christianity from Europe and its attendant racism it is mainly a black theology and this is an emphasis seen particularly in Mugambi. Both Mbiti and Mugambi are critical of liberation theology. However, Mbiti might be seen to allude to a reflective cycle as often employed by liberationists.[130] Writing of the characteristics of theology done in "the South" he argues that it is "lived first and then written down later, starting out of practical ministry and moving into reflection."[131] The following chapter will demonstrate that this is a methodology he began with but later moved away from. Mugambi depicts contemporary African theology as being in "methodological crisis" as a result of the widespread adoption of deductive methodologies. This results in theologies more concerned with institutional Christianity than with the experiences of ordinary believers.[132] Undoubtedly Mugambi is correct to depict inductive theologizing as potentially more pertinent and accessible to more African believers. However,

---

125. Mbiti, *CMA*, 7.

126. Mbiti, "Biblical Basis in Present Trends," 72. See Mbiti, "Some African Concepts of Christology," 51–52. See Mugambi, *ACT*, 3, 1–12; Mugambi, *CTSR*, 1–35.

127. Mugambi, *FLTR*, 19–22.

128. Mugambi, *ACT*, 9.

129. Mbiti, *ARAP*, 130–35. See Mugambi, *ACT*, 11; Cone, *Black Theology and Black Power*, 3, 27–28.

130. Mbiti, *BATAC*, 230. See Mbiti, "Some Current Concerns," 12; Mugambi, *ACT*, 97; Mugambi, "Theology of Reconstruction," 144–45; Bediako, *Theology and Identity*, 334; O'Donovan, "Political Theology," 272–77; in the same volume, see Bennett, Z., "Action is the Life of All," 39–54.

131. Mbiti, "Christianity Tilts," 4. See Mbiti, "Theology of the New World."

132. Mugambi, *CTSR*, 1–9; Mugambi, *BBE*, 26–32.

as will be seen in subsequent chapters, he also tends toward a method of theologizing that undervalues marginalized experience.

If African theology begins with African experience its purpose is to transform such experience.[133] For Mbiti this means the construction of his theology accompanies a prior critique of missionary malpractice. Its transformative value is therefore measured by the extent it gives theological value to that which was demonized by missionaries—the traditional theologizing of African peoples. First and foremost Mbiti argues for and seeks to demonstrate the theological potency of African culture and practice.[134] The strength, and weakness, of Mugambi's understanding of the transformative potency of African theology is that it is broader than Mbiti's. For Mbiti the commonality of experience that forms the foundation upon which to build an African theology, at least initially, is particular and interfaces with foreign missionaries and the practice of ATRs. For Mugambi, along with this experience, he joins the political-economic exploitation of Africa.[135] "Africa" is, therefore, not intended to be an essentialized idea in their writings. Rather, it signifies a "collective consciousness" that opposes the hegemonic theology of the West and asserts that divine revelation and activity can be discerned in the histories and cultures of African peoples.[136] Not least in Africa's struggle for liberation.

For Mugambi transformation is "liberation-salvation." He argues, *contra* Mbiti, that African theology is part of the broad stream of liberative thought, which may include liberation theology but will not be bound by its characteristics or agenda, but must ultimately transcend it. African liberation, argues Mugambi, is not just one of the issues African theology must address. It is *the* task of African Christian theology. Mugambi, writing in the 1970s, recognizes that the dehumanizing of Africans takes on different forms especially in relation to racial discrimination and neo-colonialism. However, the "over arching goal" and "historical project" of liberation is to be both the place where African theology emerges and the task it must serve.[137] African liberation is to be enacted against cultural, economic, and

---

133. Mbiti, "Biblical Basis for Present Trends," 119. Contrast Pobee, "Contextuality and Universality," 5. See also Dickson, "African Theological Task," 46–47.

134. Mbiti, "Christianity and African Culture," 307–99. See Mugambi, *DDC*, 52–57. See also the statement published by the Ibadan Consultation (1966) in Dickson, *Biblical Revelation and African Beliefs*, 16.

135. Mugambi, *ACT*, 3–7, 22–23.

136. Mugambi, *TAHCC*, 140–50. See Mugambi, *FLTR*, 107–25; Kwok, *Postcolonial Imagination*, 40.

137. Mugambi, *ACT*, 13, 35–36, 28–31.

political imperialism.[138] African liberation is "aimed at liberating the African from all forces that hinder him from living fully as a human being."[139] Whether it be called inculturation, contextualization or liberation, argues Mugambi, the transformative function is the same: the freedom of the church from "the cultural garb of the missionary past." The church operates in a wider society and therefore theological inculturation is not possible without societal liberation (see chapter 6).[140] For this reason righteousness is crucial in African theology for Mugambi.[141] He argues that righteousness is important in biblical narratives and has immediate relevance in African contexts where "African life and culture have been submerged and distorted, either out of prejudice or ignorance."[142] God demands right relations and right actions between humans. For Mugambi, the means to such righteousness may include armed struggle in countries including Mozambique, Angola, Zimbabwe, and South Africa. That is to say, African theology is a practical project concerned with understanding the revelation of God for the economic, political, and social freedom of Africans.[143] It is not a dispassionate academic concern. On the contrary, it is the ongoing practical theologizing toward meeting human need in the building of "humane social order in the African setting."[144] The meeting of such human need in African contexts begins with an assumption that anthropology, unlike imported understandings of humanity, will be holistic. Neither thinker develops a systematic African anthropology. Rather, they build on the assumption of a holistic understandings of Christian transformation. For Mugambi, there cannot be liberation without salvation, nor can there be salvation without liberation.[145] For both, the significance of eschatology is not in its dialectical relationship with history but is significant because it can be understood historically.[146] While Mugambi does no major work on eschatology as will be seen in the following chapter, Mbiti does provide such a work.

138. Ibid., 59–60. See Mbiti, "Theological Impotence," 253.

139. Mugambi, *ACT*, 12.

140. Mugambi, *CTSR*, 24.

141. This identification of the importance of "righteousness" can be seen, more recently, to cause Mugambi to address issues of ethics. See Stückelberger and Mugambi, *Responsible Leadership*.

142. Mugambi, *ACT*, 13.

143. Ibid., 14. See Mugambi, "Christian Ideal," 70–96; Cone, *Black Theology and Black Power*, 22–23, 138–43.

144. Mugambi, *ACT*, 14.

145. Ibid.

146. Ibid., 14–15. Cites here Cone, *A Black Theology of Liberation*; Cone, *Black Theology and Black Power*.

Mugambi, however, in more recent times has proposed a new way of doing African theology in a post-Cold War setting, which neither seeks simply to "overthrow" foreignness or "domesticate" Christian theology in Africa. He seems to be suggesting that the danger of both approaches is that the West determines the nature of the African response. This can no longer continue. The need is now to move beyond the "exodus era." This movement from "Exodus" to a theology of reconstruction will be examined in chapter 6 as an apparent new source of African theology.[147]

Second, African theology depends upon African sources such as ATRs, examinations of practical theological syntheses, analysis of African biblical interpretations, and documented African Theology.

Missionaries often denigrated African traditions and practices. In contrast, Mbiti and Mugambi see ATRs as foundational to the development of African theology as it arises from written, oral, and symbolic traditions.[148] Within the context of the era of independence ATRs have added significance. For many emerging African nations the importance of their own sources of wisdom for public life was considered essential.[149] African Theology reflecting on ATRs begins with traditional experiences and conceptions of God.[150] This will be dealt with in chapter 4. Suffice it to say at this juncture, the outstanding contribution is Mbiti's *Concepts of God in Africa* (*COGA*). In *COGA* Mbiti has gathered together information on the beliefs of some two hundred and seventy peoples from written and other sources.[151] For Mbiti, African theology means, therefore, an emphasis on continuity between African traditions and Christian theology.[152] He argues that, since independence, the relationship between African cultures and religions is "probably the most outstanding issue to emerge."[153] Consequently, the delineation of

---

147. Mugambi, *ACT*, 6–17.

148. Mbiti, "Biblical Basis for Present Trends," 119; Mbiti, "Ways and Means," 333–37. See Mugambi, "Problems of Meaning," 15–17; Mugambi, "Some Perspectives," 104; Kinney, "Theology of John Mbiti," 65–66.

149. See Isichei, *History of Christianity*, 325–50; Hastings, *African Christianity*, 78; Stanley, *Bible and Flag*, 23–31; Taylor, J., *Primal Vision*, 18–25.

150. Mbiti, *NTEAB*, 186. See Idowu, *African Traditional Religion*, 140 65.

151. Mbiti, *COGA*, xiii–xv. See Mbiti, *NTEAB*, 25–32, 56–61; Mbiti, "Afrikanisches Verständnis"; Mbiti, *BATAC*, 42–44; Mugambi, *ACT*, 49–50.

152. Mbiti, "Encounter of Christian Faith" (*CC*), 817–18; Mbiti, "God, Sin, and Salvation" (*CCTWC*), 162–65; Kinney, "Theology of John Mbiti," 66. See Boesak, *Farewell to Innocence*, 35–37.

153. Mbiti, "Christianity in Independent Africa," 77.

traditional conceptions of God become important for African theology.[154] Indeed, such tradition becomes the very locus for African theology.

For Mbiti, African theology will emerge "out of the Church in Africa." It will be a "theology of triangular syncretism."[155] This is a term he only ever uses once. It points to the practice of bringing together the strands of traditional Christian theologies from beyond Africa, the Bible interpreted by Africans, and the theology of African religious concepts and practices. For Mugambi, Africans become Christians because they recognize in it a new way of life that is "qualitatively better than their traditional existence" (for example, protection from harm, hope for eternal life, new forms of worship, literacy). However, despite the proselytizing intent of missionaries often what emerged was a synthesis between mission Christianity, African readings of the Bible, and the continuing endurance of African traditions.[156] Converts were involved in processes of "reciprocation" between "Christianity and the cultural-religious milieu."[157] However, while synthesis is the inevitable result of African theological agency, syncretism is something to be avoided if that means a "process and way of thinking in which the essential message of the Gospel is so mixed up with other ideas that the teaching of Jesus Christ is no longer central."[158] Such christocentric concern (see chapter 5) results in Mbiti abandoning any continued attempt to argue for a theologically positive understanding of the term syncretism. Rather, a dialogic relationship between context and biblical context might be seen as a more preferable way of proceeding. When Africans read the Bible they experience a world where, while there are many dissimilarities, much is familiar. The translation of the Bible into African languages means access to the scriptures more directly and therefore more independently. This results in a practical and dialogical relationship between scripture and tradition, and a re-evaluation of oral tradition.[159] The Bible in African languages facilitates theological judgment.[160]

---

154. Mbiti, *NTEAB*, 186. See Idowu, *African Traditional Religion*, 140–65.

155. Mbiti, "Christian Eschatology," 311. In recent conversations with the present author, Mbiti confessed that he was surprised that he used "syncretism" in a positive fashion. Mbiti, Interview by Heaney, April 9. See Mbiti, "Some African Concepts of Christology," 51–52; Mbiti, "African Theology" (*IT*), 149–50.

156. Mugambi, "Some Perspectives," 127–28.

157. Mugambi, *TAHCC*, 2–3.

158. Mugambi, "Some Perspectives," 128; Shorter, *African Christian Theology*, 23.

159. Sanneh, *Whose Religion*, 10–11, 18, 24–26; Maluleke, "Black and African Theologies," 4–5. See West, *Academy of the Poor*, 93–98.

160. Mbiti, *BATAC*, 28–42; Mugambi, *BBE*, 6, 59–60.

> Missionaries introduced the Bible as a negation of African culture. There has been a hermeneutical clash, dictated by a chasm of ideological viewpoints between North Atlantic missionaries and their African converts. Are North Atlantic missionaries in Africa interested in Africans, or in themselves? Whose interests have the missionaries served? Is it out of self-sacrifice that they have come to Africa?[161]

Mbiti recognizes that a more independent hermeneutics had effects on nascent African nationalism. Referring to those involved in the struggle, he writes that they were:

> ... exposed to the biblical view of salvation. Most of these had embraced the Christian faith, and all had been educated in Christian schools ... The Exodus account in the Bible was certainly a great inspiration to many, and the cry was as God put it through the mouth of Moses and Aaron to Pharaoh: 'Let my people go!'[162]

Likewise, Mugambi argues something similar:

> Those who could read the Bible and the catechism could also read other books. Those who could write sermons could also write other things, and those who could count the number of converts they made, could also utilize their arithmetical knowledge in other spheres of life.[163]

As the Bible became available in African languages, Africans began to see that the scripture had some dependence upon oral transmission. The Bible itself and the cultures depicted within it value oral tradition. Mbiti submits, therefore, that the role of the oral tradition should not be forgotten when African theologians seeks to interpret the Christian message. African traditions are not located primarily in historical annals, but are alive in the community through the communication orally of history and myth.[164] It remains the case even in more recent times that the population of Christians is disproportionate to rates of literacy in Africa.[165] Mbiti argues that African interpretation will need to be careful that it does not simply continue the Western emphasis on the written word and formal schooling while ignoring

---

161. Mugambi, E-mail correspondence to Heaney, February 22, 2009.

162. Mbiti, *BATAC*, 163.

163. Mugambi, "Some Perspectives," 60.

164. See Shorter, *African Christian Theology*, 48–51; Idowu, *African Traditional Religion*, 83–86.

165. Mbiti, "Bible in African Culture," 29.

the rich tradition of African oral art.[166] Mugambi also affirms traditional forms of education. A society that does not depend on a book culture depends much more on "multidirectional communication" and values less the solitary scholar or the priestly monologue. Mbiti proposes that African interpretive practice should seek to maintain this multidirectional communication through sponsoring public reading of the Bible, scriptural story telling, Bible memorization, songs and hymns directly based on scriptural passages, biblical plays, and comparative studies on oral traditions in the Bible and in Africa.[167] However, written theologizing should not be discouraged or ignored.

Given the proliferation of published works by African theologians since the 1960s, these also become an inevitable source for African theology. Mugambi worries that African theologians of the 1960s and 70s have had "an overdose of European influence" but that their work might serve as a useful beginning. For Mugambi, the investigative dimension of African theology will focus on the systematizing and analyzing of the work done by African theologians concerned with "total liberation." Systematizing along with collecting documentation from conferences, sponsoring further conferences and consultations, holding consultations with AICs and Black American theologians, and the publishing of reflections of new generations of scholars all, for Mugambi, form part of what it means to practice African theology.[168] When such work is done the general contours of theological content as well as intent emerges.

Third, in contrast to imported denominationalism, African theology is part of a universal quest for divine truth. African theology is an exercise in theological particularism which is not sectarian but rather part of what they see as the universal or catholic project of Christian theology. African theology may have the effect of disrupting dominant theological discourses taking place ecumenically and globally. For this reason Mbiti and Mugambi allude to and depict its emergence as a new Reformation. Mbiti writes, in 1971, "The Church in Africa is suffering from a conservatism which makes it look like a relic of medieval European Christianity deposited here and left to rust and rot away."[169] Consequently, as the European Reformation of the sixteenth and seventeenth century, especially in light of vernacular

---

166. See Mbiti, "Biblical Basis for Present Trends," 119.

167. Mbiti, "Bible in African Culture," 30–33. See West, *Academy of the Poor*.

168. Mugambi, *ACT*, 15–16. In 1969, the AACC made an attempt to reach out to AICs along with conservative evangelical groups and Roman Catholics. See Utuk, *Visions of Authenticity*, 93.

169. Mbiti, *CMA*, 3.

translations of the Bible, challenged traditional orthodoxy, so too Africans, equipped with their own translations, are challenging the orthodoxy and authority of foreign missionaries.¹⁷⁰ This is seen clearest in the emergence of AICs, but is not limited to them.¹⁷¹ As Protestants in Europe did not believe they were jettisoning catholicity, so too Mbiti and Mugambi understand the particularity and contextualization of African theology not to be a denial of catholicity but a demonstration of it. This is a catholicity that appears, at first, to be "bottom up" and not "top down." They desire not to engage Christianity as a "tradition" for they hold to ancient and worthy African traditions, rather they desire to experience the "Gospel" and as a result join a worldwide (catholic) church that has experienced the same.

In contrast to Christianity (which is a located culture-bound response to the gospel), Mbiti defines the gospel as the existential meeting of God with a particular religious community. It is this distinction which eventually results in his rejection of indigenization and his re-evaluation of the spirituality of African traditional communities. Because God meets people in the specificity of their situation, the idea that Christianity is a "ready-made commodity" to be indigenized is rejected. For what is of primary theological concern to both African tradition and the biblical tradition is not the engagement with a culture-bound religion, but an existential encounter with God.¹⁷² Consequently, Mbiti sees the need for independent African theology not only arising from the nature of the African context, but also from the nature of the gospel itself. Part of the acceptance of the gospel is the realization that God is active in the world. Universality or catholicity is, therefore, not predicated upon a synchronization of orthodoxy with theological formulations from the West. Rather, it emerges from a conviction that God is at work in the world. As a result of this belief, Mbiti identifies ATRs as the place where God reveals God's self to Africans. Consequently, the gospel (encounter) is indigenous to Africa while at the same time transcends all cultures.¹⁷³

Mbiti and Mugambi identify the importance of universality in African theology as a means to demonstrating the integral part the reflection of African Christians play in any practice of catholicity. However, dangers also exist when universality is stressed. For the very integration of African

---

170. Mugambi, *BBE*, 6, 59–60. See Mugambi, *ACT*, 22–23; Mbiti, "Bibel und Bibelübersetzung," 7.

171. Mugambi, *CTSR*, 13–14. He cites Barrett, *Schism and Renewal in Africa*, as suggesting the idea of African Reformation.

172. See Bediako, "African Theology," 433; Boesak, *Farewell to Innocence*, 17–18.

173. See Mugambi, "Some Perspectives," 53; Mugambi, *TAHCC*, 91–95.

theology may result in its marginalization. There exists "unequal relationships" rooted in "the dominance of the former colonial and missionary past," which can suppress the contextual articulation of African Christians.[174] Such dangers, however, might be avoided if the theological agency of Africans is made clear, contended for, and practiced.

Fourth, in place of foreign categories of thought and practice, African theology contends for African theological agency. Such agency, as would be expected, is not construed individualistically. Mugambi writes, "God is the subject with which theology is concerned. A theologian explores the responses of his community of faith to God's revelation."[175] Mbiti is right to argue that the concept of community is central to both the Old and New Testaments and that the socio-political arrangements of ancient Israel have "many echoes in African life."[176] He simply observes, "African life is centered on community."[177]

It is Mugambi who is especially aware of the dangers of constructing "Africa." He writes, "Africa is not a cultural bloc that has always existed; it has been constructed."[178] While both Mbiti and Mugambi want to affirm major commonalities of tradition and experience on the continent of Africa, they appear at times to seek to counterbalance such generalizations with an affirmation on the centrality of community. Theology is, therefore, a "discourse about God," which can both be expressed theoretically and lived practically in community.[179] For Mugambi, as will be seen in chapter 6, such an emphasis on community has particular ecumenical significance.[180]

For Mbiti and Mugambi community in African life manifests itself with reference to, for example, blood and marital kinship, land, peoples, clan, and ritual. The network of community descends from people, to clan, to subclan, to extended family, to individual families, as well as to the community of the departed. One is related to the community present all around, but also relationships are to be maintained with the spiritual world.[181] Death

---

174. Mugambi, *CTSR*, 8.

175. Ibid., 20.

176. Mbiti, "Bible in African Culture," 35.

177. Ibid., 36. See Mbiti, "African Concept of Sin"; Bediako, *Theology and Identity*, 308–12.

178. Mugambi, "Churches and Reconstruction," 38. See Mugambi, "Religions in East Africa," 3–5.

179. Mugambi, *ACT*, 7.

180. See Dedji, *Reconstruction and Renewal*, 66–70.

181. Mbiti, "'Hearts Cannot be Lent,'" 6–7; Mbiti, *NTEAB*, 138–40, 153–56; Mbiti, "African Concepts of Human Relations"; Mugambi, *FLTR*, 198; Mugambi and Kirima, *African Religious Heritage*, 61–78, 94–117.

only begins a process of taking the departed "back" to a larger community which always surrounds, and even pervades, the mundane realities of everyday life.[182]

How Mbiti defines community is associated, by Mugambi, with rural understandings of community. In Kenya most continue to have a connection to such "homes." However, such roots are being repressed in modern day Africa by fellow Africans. For Mugambi identifies differences in understandings of "community" between those who continue to live in rural Africa and governmental policy makers. He argues a government can objectify community. That is to say, civil servants consider community to be the material for governance and the result of governance.[183] An African theological affirmation about the agency of community, therefore, not only stands in contrast to much mission Christianity but also stands in contrast to much modern African political attitude. Neither mission Christianity nor African governments have been able to "come to terms" with the traditional sense of community.[184] Consequently, for African theology to affirm the centrality of community is not just a rejection of individualism, it is also a desire for right action in and toward African peoples.

An emphasis on community has the potential to counteract a universalizing that ultimately silences the voices of specific Christians in specific contexts. However, it is doubtful that Mbiti and Mugambi have demonstrated, in comparison to liberation theology and later developments in African theology, the practical significance of such an emphasis on the resources to be found in local African communities. For because of the rather broad definitions of African context they assume and because of, despite the rhetoric, the undervaluation of experience, many Africans are excluded in their writings. Chief among those excluded are women.[185]

Conclusion

According to Mbiti and Mugambi, foreign missionaries tended to denigrate African traditions and practice. In seeking a more contextualized form of

---

182. Mbiti, *NTEAB*, 127–39. See Mugambi, "Rites of Passage," 240–41; Mugambi, "Some Perspectives," 120–26.

183. Mugambi, "Churches and Reconstruction," 36–37; Mugambi, "Responsible Leadership," 84–96.

184. Mugambi, "Churches and Reconstruction," 37. See Mugambi, "Rites of Passage," 228–45.

185. See Oduyoye, "Critique of John Mbiti's View"; West, *Reading Other-wise*; Somé and Bennett, "Christian Base Communities"; Ruether, "Feminist Theology"; Phiri and Nadar, *African Women*; Aniagolu, "First African Womanist Workshop."

theology Mbiti and Mugambi affirm African sources for their theology. Consequently, it appears that the experience of African traditionalists will have a role in the emergence of an African theology (see chapter 4). Missionaries introduced denominationalism to Africa. Mbiti and Mugambi are determined to make African theology ecumenical. In their writings universality, apparently arising from particularity, is seen in their stress on christocentrism as a means of unity in community and fellowship between communities (see chapter 5). Foreign missionaries understood and practiced mission as acculturation. In contrast, Mbiti and Mugambi argue against any synchronizing of the African church with imported theology. Rather, African theology begins with theological reflection on the particularities of African contexts (see chapter 3). Missionaries introduced foreign categories of thought and practice to Africa that included individualism, dualism, and futurism. In contrast, African theology affirms a communitarian theological agency, which moves beyond the power relations of reactionary and contestatory configurations of theology to a (re)constructive practice (see chapter 6).

The depiction of mission Christianity in the writings of Mbiti and Mugambi is not only important in appreciating the context or content of their writing. It has methodological and theological importance. As a result of an examination of how missionaries are depicted in their writing it becomes clear that this interface between Africans and missionaries becomes the initial site for the emergence of this African theology. Yet despite these criticisms of mission Christianity and the potentially constructive moves they identify, the contextual nature of their theologizing is gradually undermined. However, it is not undermined from outside African theology but undermined in the very development of African theology beginning with Mbiti's research on the temporality and eschatology of the Akamba people and their engagement with missionaries of the Africa Inland Mission.

3

Eschatological Issues and Context
Mbiti and the Akamba

MBITI'S WORK ON CHRISTIAN eschatology in relation to Africa is well known. However, what has not been recognized until now is that this work on eschatology occasions a methodological shift that may have widespread repercussions for later African theologies. For when a comparison is made between Mbiti's initial research on Akamba eschatology (1963) and his later publications a shift becomes apparent. When his initial research is compared to *African Religions and Philosophy* (1969), *Concepts of God in Africa* (1970), and then the publication of *New Testament Eschatology in an African Background* (1971), which is based on his 1963 research, a shift away from the particularism of context toward a more generalized concept of African theology is apparent.

This chapter has three main sections. First, Mbiti's criticism of mission eschatology as the most important disjuncture between foreign missionary thinking and traditional African thought and practice is identified. Second, Mbiti's specific interpretation of Akamba temporality in dialogue with his reading of Christian eschatology is outlined. Third, Mbiti's eschatology has been severely criticized. I will respond to these criticisms through the constructive move of reading his eschatology according to his own initial method. I argue that reading Mbiti's eschatology in such a manner provides at least three benefits. It recovers the innovation in his contextualism. It disarms much of the criticism of his eschatology. It highlights the subjugation present in this specific context thereby giving further credence to the hypothesis that his work bears comparison with a (post-colonial) theology that, at its best, takes as its point of departure such colonial subjugation.

A Theological Critique of Mission Eschatology

The original point of departure for Mbiti's work on eschatology is foreign missionary malpractice. However, the point of departure for his theological work changes and with it I argue the very nature of his project. Further, I will argue that a return to his initial methodology undercuts much of the criticism of his work.

Mbiti's work appears to be the only scholarly and critical examination of the theology of the AIM. His unpublished dissertation is concerned with missiological effectiveness.[1] The purpose of his research is therefore to make the work of Christian mission in "tribal Africa" more effective.[2] In *NTEAB* the emphasis shifts from missiological effectiveness to theological analysis and to conceptual relationships and coherence.[3] The depiction of mission eschatology in both remains crucial. However, in *NTEAB*, the material is reordered, giving the impression that it is African traditional practice which is the point of departure and not the experiences and reactions of Akamba converts to AIM mission teaching.[4] Despite the continued interest and

---

1. "The underlying theme is a question which relates to practical issues, viz.: 'How can African societies be effectively evangelized so that the Christian faith can penetrate deeply and firmly into the African soil?'" Mbiti, "Christian Eschatology," 1.

2. See Mbiti, "Christian Eschatology," 1, 46. Compare with Mbiti, *NTEAB*, 23. He reiterates this again, in a chapter omitted from the published book, when he writes, "The primary task in this study is to find out how tribal Africa can be evangelized intelligibly and effectively so that the people can hear and understand the Christian message, and in turn embrace the faith firmly." Mbiti, "Christian Eschatology," 286. See Mbiti, *NTEAB*, iv. Ironically, this emphasis is similar to that stressed in a missionary manual found in the AIM archives. "The religion of the peoples should be studied in order to find clues and relationships that might lead to contacts. This could open doors . . . to the things of Christ and His Word." DePue, et al., "How Do 'You' Fit In," section 4.

3. Mbiti, *NTEAB*, 3–4, 23. This is not to say that Mbiti abandons the idea of a theology of mission. See Mbiti, *BATAC*, 189–222.

4. An *emic* or internal approach is the original point of departure. An *etic* approach comes to dominate as traditional practice is now abstracted from the practice of a particular, in this case Akamba, community. Arguably, such a move betrays the fabric of Western ways of thinking that Mbiti criticizes. By the time *ARAP* is published the shift is very clear (see 19–36). See Pike, *Language in Relation*, 37–39. See Mugambi, "Problems of Meaning," 3; Mugambi, *TAHCC*, 183–91; Schreiter, *Constructing Local Theologies*, 57–61; Gyekye, *Essay on African*, 189–95; Muller, L., "Thematic Comparison," 116.

criticism that Mbiti's African temporality and eschatology provokes, until now, this shift in his approach to the topic has not been recognized.[5] There can be little doubt that in making the shift from the former (in his PhD thesis) to his later published work he seeks to give experiences from the broader African context the primacy in his eschatology and theology. In the final analysis, however, he is in danger of succeeding in doing the opposite. This, as yet unrecognized, criticism might well be the most severe criticism that could be made of Mbiti's presentation of African temporality and eschatology. For as will be seen, criticisms of Mbiti's eschatology (by Gillies, Musopole and Mugambi) have concentrated on, what will be termed here, philosophical and social objections that pay primary attention to how he understands African and mission temporality and how that affects emerging African theology. In sum, I propose that a reading of Mbiti's eschatology using his own initial method should be pursued. In doing this, a critique of his published work will emerge along with constructive moves beyond such critique. To begin where Mbiti began is to begin with experiences of mission malpractice in his home community.

The AIM, later to found the Africa Inland Church (AIC), was largely responsible for the evangelization of the area of eastern Kenya (Ukambani), which Mbiti identifies as the context for his initial study.[6] The AIM, founded in the USA in 1895, is a Protestant interdenominational society recruiting missionaries largely from evangelical and fundamentalist churches.[7] The founder of the AIM, Peter Cameron Scott, like Ludwig Krapf had a vision for a chain of mission stations across Africa.[8] When Cameron arrived in Kenya in 1895 he, again following Krapf, saw in the Akamba a people who

---

5. This is a shift that Mbiti had already made in two other publications produced after the completion of his Cambridge PhD, but before the publication of *NTEAB*. *ARAP* and *COGA* are predicated upon a concept of a generalized ATR that is "the strongest element" in the "traditional background." Mbiti, *ARAP*, 1. It should be noted that in the second edition of *ARAP* (1989), Mbiti notes that he now uses "African religion" over "African religions" to "emphasize . . . the commonalities and potential unity" of the tradition. Mbiti, *ARAP*, xiii.

6. The country of Ukambani and the people have historic importance as well. Krapf saw them as crucial to his missionary vision. Krapf, *Vocabulary of Six*, vii; Mbiti, *NTEAB*, 10–23. See Mbiti, *Akamba Stories*, 18–20.

7. Mbiti, *NTEAB*, 3–4; Mbiti, "When the Right Hand," 10; Waller, "They Do the Dictating," 83–126; Oliver, *Missionary Factor*, 171, 228; Torrey and Hulburt, *What we Stand For*. See Sandgren, "Kamba Christianity," 174–82; Anderson, D., *We Felt like Grasshoppers*; Richardson, *Garden of Miracles*; Gehman, "African Inland Mission," 118–44; Anderson, W., *Church in East Africa*, 62–64.

8. Stauffacher, "History of the AIM," 2. Scott's vision was inspired, in part, by his reading of Krapf. See Atieno-Odhiambo, "Mugo's Prophesy," 5–15.

would carry the gospel inland. The first AIM missionary station was, therefore, founded among them.[9] Mbiti does not present a detailed analysis of the AIM's teaching on eschatology. Rather, he makes reference to some of their publications as indicative of mission eschatology, which, like the theology of Krapf and much of Kenyan Anglicanism, he characterizes as individualistic and futuristic.[10] Mbiti observes that such an understanding of Christian eschatology is even affirmed by missionaries in the face of New Testament non-temporal symbolism.

First, AIM missionaries, like Protestant missionaries more generally, tended to teach eschatology in individualistic terms. Spear concurs with Mbiti. He describes the AIM as "perhaps, one of the most extreme examples of individualistic Protestant pietism."[11] The AIM teaches a premillennial return of Christ along with a literal resurrection of the body, eternal salvation for individuals who convert, and eternal perdition for all others. In place of a deep awareness of community and a traditional understanding of time, missionaries emphasized the importance of personal faith and individual future recompense.[12] There is real danger in such missionary teaching of reducing eschatology to little more than a concern for the future destiny and prosperity of converts. In Mbiti's Cambridge dissertation, it is plainly the case that his proposals for an African understanding of eschatology are defined in contrast to such teaching. It is when this is not recognized that Mbiti's work can be oversimplified and a sense of "the African sense of common life" can be seen as the sole departure for his theology.[13] Undoubtedly the African sense of commonality is important to an emerging African theology However, its importance cannot be assessed independent of how Mbiti sees missionary practice in a particular context ignoring and

---

9. See Anderson, D., *We Felt like Grasshoppers*, 20–23; Anderson, W., *Church in East Africa*, 62; Stauffacher, "History of the AIM," 5–6; Morad and Arensen, "Spreading Tree," 8–24; Hulburt, "Star-Points," 27–28.

10. Mbiti, "Christian Eschatology," 32–34, 40–59, 241–44; Mbiti, *NTEAB*, 3–4. See Taylor, C., "Conference on Evangelical Fellowship"; Spear, "Towards the History," 4–5.

11. Spear, "Towards the History," 14.

12. Mbiti, *NTEAB*, 49–51, 63–64, 82, 90, 159–61; Board of Directors of the AIM, "Minutes of the Meeting." See Mbiti, "Bible in African Culture," 36; Mbiti, *COGA*, 219–20, 231; Mbiti, "Christianity and African Culture," 26–40; Martey, *African Theology*, 14–17.

13. Musopole, *Being Human*, 5, 42–43. Musopole makes reference (p. 43 f.n. 6) to Mbiti's dissertation, but in citing its scope of enquiry, provides a quotation from the later published work of Mbiti, *NTEAB*. There is no evidence that Musopole has identified the importance of the shift in Mbiti's point of departure. See Mugambi, Introduction in Taylor, J., *Primal Vision*, xxiii–xxiv.

eroding it.[14] It is for this reason, as has been seen, that the original structure of Mbiti's argument will shape the approach of the current chapter.

Second, in Mbiti's experience missionaries in Ukambani emphasized the futuristic dimension of eschatology amongst a people who had very limited conception of the future. For Mbiti, the eschatology presented by these missionaries emphasizes a "here-after," which encourages a "psychological escape" from present trouble.[15] Such eschatology is linear, progressivist, and futuristic.[16] Mbiti is rightly critical of the AIM's eschatology where "few aspects of the futurist element of eschatology" are stressed. Consequently, African converts are required to change their conception of humanity's postmortem destination from recessing towards the ancestors to an unfolding future.[17] Such eschatology, which seems to have little or no present theological or existential significance can only result in escapism and quiescence.[18]

Akamba Christians were greatly discouraged that Christ had not returned as emphasized by the missionaries. Such disillusionment, due to a lack of rigorous contextualism on the part of the missionaries, results in the introduction of a dualism not previously present in Akamba society where Christian converts are forced to live in two worlds.[19] Equally, such discouragement could also result in an intensification of millenarian expectation. This is especially the case in AICs that broke away from mission churches. Mbiti goes as far as to argue that this disjunction between a foreign (missionary) understanding of time and an African understanding of time is a

---

14. See Musopole, *Being Human*, 5–12; Bediako, *Theology and Identity*, 334.

15. Okullu, *Church and Politics*, 2–18. See Mbiti, "Christian Eschatology," 130–35; Mbiti, *NTEAB*, 60; Mugambi, *ACT*, 96–99; Mugambi, *BBE*, 8–9; Mbiti, "New Testament and the Akamba," 21; Gitari, "Church and Politics"; Buthelezi, "Towards Indigenous Theology," 63–64; Musopole, *Being Human*, 39–44; Stanley, "Future in the Past," 107–9, 115–16.

16. ". . . a linear view of time [is] . . . time conceived in terms of a straight line, progressing from one point to the next towards an ultimate end." Parratt, "Time in Traditional," 118, see 122–23. See Mbiti, *NTEAB*, 57; Mbiti, "Christian Eschatology," 48–59.

17. Mbiti, *NTEAB*, 63, 86–87.

18. See Mugambi, "Some Perspectives," 99–100; Throup, "'Render, unto Caesar,'" 143–76; Sandgren, "Kamba Christianity," 174; Okullu, *Church and Politics*, 2–5; Sabar-Friedman, "Church and State"; Musopole, *Being Human*, 48; Welbourn and Ogot, *Place to Feel at Home*, 33–35, 63–64.

19. Mbiti, "Christian Eschatology," 289–90. Mugambi makes a similar point by referring to Taylor's concept of Christianity in Africa being a "classroom religion" and questioning the importance of the often vaunted growth of African Christianity. See Mugambi, "Fresh Look" (*IRM*), 343–44.

key reason for the proliferation of AICs.[20] This is difficult to substantiate. It may well be the case that this is a factor. However, as Mugambi recognizes and Mbiti later acknowledges, it appears that issues such as the suppression of African leadership, denial of African discernment, hesitancy in incorporating or adapting traditional customs into the church, translation of the Bible into African languages, and lack of support for nationalist movements seems as likely to provoke the desire for the formation of AICs.[21]

Third, not only do AIM missionaries interpret Christian eschatology in individualistic and futuristic terms, they also interpret eschatologically significant, non-temporal symbolism in such terms. *Gehenna*, fire, treasure, city, country, tears and pain, eating and drinking, and heaven become detached from christology resulting in a "materialization" of the symbols so that the promise of a "new world" takes precedence over the centrality of Christ in Christian eschatology.[22] For Akamba Christians such eschatological symbols become an end in themselves and are not realized in any sense now. Consequently, *gehenna* and *fire*, as reflected in the doctrinal basis of the AIM, refer exclusively to a future punishment for individuals who do

---

20. Mbiti, *NTEAB*, 18–21, 57–61; Mbiti, "Bible in African Culture," 34–35. See Mbiti, "Christian Eschatology," 40–41; Mbiti, "Future of Christianity" (*CC*), 392–93. Too often the AICs are presented as models of African theologizing, and the primary source for genuine African theology. As is the case with the African Brotherhood Church (ABC), which broke away from the AIC, they do not necessarily develop a theology distinct from the missionary founded church. Indeed, such AICs can accentuate the teaching of mission Christianity and reach logical but radical conclusions beyond missionary teaching. More recent research suggests that AICs are actually in decline, being overtaken by Pentecostal churches often associated with bodies in the United States of America. See Welbourn and Ogot, *Place to Feel at Home*, 55–61, 90–104, 137; Turner, *History of African Independent Church*, 5–8, 197–207; Turner, *African Independent Church*, xvi–xviii, 182–93, 202–20; Sundkler, *Bantu Prophets*, 17–18, 30, 32–64, 80–99, 170–79, 295–300; Gifford, "Some Recent Developments," 515–19, 525–28; Anderson, W., *Church in East Africa*, 122–23.

21. See Mugambi, *ACT*, 44–47; Mugambi, "Ecumenical Movement," 13; Mbiti, *BATAC*, 16–17. See Barnett, "Acceptance of Negro Missionaries"; Mugambi, *BBE*, 6–9, 18, 56; Mugambi, "Christological Paradigms," 159; Waller, "They Do the Dictating," 102–9; Spear, "Towards the History," 7–8, 14–15; Muzorewa, *Origins and Development*, 55. The founding of the ABC in 1945 by Simeon Mulandi seems to have much more to do with missionary authoritarianism and malpractice than any conflicting notions of temporality or other philosophical or theological concepts. Such authoritarian malpractice did not exclude violence. For on more than one occasion, colonial officers had to intervene to protect the Akamba from missionary violence or threat of violence. Sandgren, "Kamba Christianity," 169–95.

22. Mbiti, *NTEAB*, 89–90, 116.

not confess Christ as opposed to functioning as christological symbols of negation and judgment which can apply to the here and now.[23]

The eschatological significance of *treasure* relates to traditional Akamba beliefs where it is believed that wealth or poverty is translated into the next world.[24] AIM teaching reforms this notion to include the idea that the behavior of individuals in the present affects their reward ("treasure in heaven"), understood as "concrete material goods," in a heavenly *city* (see Heb 13:14; Phil 3:20-21; Gal 4:25-31). The New Testament christocentric emphasis, where the "riches of God" dwell in Christ and where symbols of fellowship with God through Christ are employed is replaced by a focus on reward beyond fellowship with the divine. Again it is seen that the imported eschatology brought to the Akamba is an "intensely anthropocentric and physicalized future."[25]

An eschatological *country* or fatherland makes up part of the New Testament's symbolism.[26] What appears to be promised in primarily temporal and geographic terms in the Old Testament, is now fulfilled in relational and eschatological terms in the person of Christ. However, as with the other concepts, what is emphasized in Akamba Christian thought is not the reality which the symbol might be pointing to, but to the symbol itself as eschatological (future) material reward. Consequently, the result is indifference to the present and escape to a "fictitious reality" where *tears and pain* will be dealt with having little expectation or activism to deal with suffering now.[27]

Eating and drinking has no spectacular significance in the Akamba conception of the next world. For, as has already been seen, such a world is very much continuous with the present. In the New Testament, the messianic banquet has both future and present significance. For eating and drinking symbolizes fellowship with God that is, at least in part, realized now in Christ (John 4:14, 6:27, 33-35, 48-58, 7:37; Rev 21:6, 22:17). Because missionaries emphasize the future aspect of these symbols, to the detriment of present significance, Mbiti argues that the Akamba are robbed of contextual significance for the sacraments. As will be seen therefore, an important part of an emerging African eschatology for Mbiti includes an emphasis on the sacramental.

Mbiti addresses the idea of *heaven* as it relates to the community of faith. While the New Testament symbolism is spatial, the emphasis falls on

23. Ibid., 67, 69-70. See Board of Directors of the AIM, "Minutes of the Meeting."
24. See, for example, Matt 6:20, 13:44-45, 19:21; Luke 12:33.
25. Mbiti, *NTEAB*, 74, see 70-75. See Mugambi, *TAHCC*, 79.
26. Heb 11:14-16, 12:18-29. See 1 Pet 2:11, 9:26; 2 Pet 3:11-13; Rev 21:1-2.
27. Mbiti, *NTEAB*, 78-81. See Waller, "They Do the Dictating," 84-85, 105.

theocentric worship and fellowship.[28] For the Akamba, because God exists in a distinct ontological category, there is no expectation that humans could somehow exist with God.[29] AIM teaching, however, encourages the idea that God who lives beyond the heavens (*matu*) offers a utopian dwelling place for believers to ascend to. While AIM teaching might have brought salvific hope to Akamba eschatology, it caused an unnecessary cosmological inversion. In Mugambi's terms, mission cosmology contrasted the monosectional view of reality that Africans affirmed.[30] Missionaries introduced the novel idea that post-mortem existence was located not on earth but in the sky.[31] Mbiti argues again that this undermines the christocentrism of many New Testament texts. For AIM teaching localizes heaven, either in terms of the temporal or spatial, thus tending to undermine any theological significance the symbol might have apart from it acting as a distraction from present suffering. In contrast, an African eschatology will be practical with the church participating in the life of God, in Christ, now. The church is an eschatological community where the presence of God is continually experienced and anticipated in her liturgical and sacramental life.[32]

In summary, Mbiti argues that the eschatology taught by the AIM is missiologically ineffective, biblically deficient, and christologically weak. Little of Mbiti's reading of Christian eschatology here can be seen as original.[33] This is not his initial aim. On the contrary, the first step is to begin to identify the eschatological issues as they are raised in the context where AIM missionaries and Akamba Christians theologized. The next step is to begin to resolve the issues already identified, such as an eschatology that does not take into account Akamba experience, an eschatology which is extremely individualistic, futuristic, and anthropocentric, and begin to outline an emerging African eschatology. For Mbiti this will mean arguing that there is theological significance to be found in, so-called, two-dimensional temporality such as that held by the Akamba.[34]

---

28. Mbiti, *NTEAB*, 85–89.

29. Mbiti, *COGA*, 12–16, 19–29, 161–243.

30. Mugambi, *ACT*, 79; Mbiti, *NTEAB*, 122–23. See Spear, "Towards the History," 6–7.

31. Mbiti, *NTEAB*, 63, 86–87.

32. Ibid., 88–89.

33. Indeed a comparison between Mbiti's proposals and the work of C. F. D. Moule highlights the latter's influence on, ironically, an African eschatology. See Moule, *Origin of Christology*, and further below.

34. Mbiti, *NTEAB*, 38–50. See Barr, *Biblical Words*, 147–52.

Akamba Time-Consciousness

Mbiti makes the argument well that the mission eschatology imported to Ukambani was deficient. AIM missionaries were often guilty both of seeking to universalize their particular theology and of being unprepared to consider the potential of Akamba traditional thought being compatible with Christian eschatology.[35] In contrast to mission eschatology, which emphasizes a progressive linear future, Mbiti argues for a realized dimension in an emerging eschatology with special reference to, what can be termed, Akamba temporality and the Christian sacraments. In contrast to AIM teaching, which is overly individualistic and anthropocentric, Mbiti identifies the importance of Akamba corporateness and its relation to an emerging eschatology with specific reference to resurrection.

First, Mbiti's understanding of Akamba temporality can be summed up into what one might refer to as *composition, future,* and *direction*. Time is a *composition* of events.[36] A day, month, and year are constituted by certain events taking place. Events "produce" time.[37] Yet there is an "ontological rhythm" ever at work at the individual and corporate level. For individuals this will include birth, puberty, initiation, marriage, procreation, old age, death, entry into the presence of the departed, and entry into the company of the spirits. For communities, this ontological rhythm is marked by the seasons and the agricultural activity which accompanies them. A given event does not belong to a particular moment but an event creates a moment.[38]

The *future* is virtually non-existent in the Akamba context.[39] Mbiti is unable to identify any myths about the future or any concept of the end of the world. Furthermore, he argues that often African languages cannot bear the weight of any future beyond the regular and rhythmic cycle

---

35. See Mbiti, "Christian Eschatology," 297, 311–13. African traditions were often considered "demonic" by missionaries. In contrast, Mugambi argues that it was the traditional background that was the key contributing factor for his acceptance of Christianity. Mugambi, *ACT*, x, see 132–33.

36. Mbiti, *NTEAB*, 29; Mbiti, *ARAP*, 24–29. See Musopole, *Being Human*, 45–47; Gillies, "Bantu Concept," 17–18; McTaggart, "Unreality of Time," 458; Bonganjalo, "Corporate Personality," 67.

37. Mbiti, *NTEAB*, 29; Mbiti, *ARAP*, 24–27. See Gillies, "Bantu Concept," 24–25; Parratt, "Time in Traditional," 119.

38. Mbiti, *ARAP*, 31; Mbiti, "African Concepts of Time" (*Afrika*); Mbiti, "African Concept of Time" (*ATJ*). See Gillies, "Bantu Concept," 24; Shoemaker, "Time Without Change," 68–79; Lowe, "Indexical Fallacy," 69.

39. Mbiti, *NTEAB*, 24; Mbiti, *ARAP*, 27–29. See Bediako, *Theology and Identity*, 323–28; Kato, *Theological Pitfalls*, 61–67. From a Northern context, see Lowe, "Indexical Fallacy," 69–70.

of daily life.⁴⁰ Because time is seen as inextricably linked to events, it is virtually impossible to speak of the future beyond the immediate. Time is two-dimensional, consisting of a long past (*tene*) and a dynamic present (*mituki*).⁴¹ A progressive linear concept of time is, therefore, foreign to Akamba thinking. Mbiti claims that the "now period" (*mituki*) in Akamba conception sublates what in Western conceptions would be considered to be future. This now-period consists of events that are about to occur, are in the process of occurring or have recently occurred. This period is "an experiential extension" of the present moment conceptualized as embracing a very limited future. *Tene* is not simply restricted to the concept of "the past" that Western missionaries working in Ukambani would recognize. *Tene* overlaps with the now-period. The now-period disappears into the *tene*. In short, the now-period refers to that which is experienced by the present community and the *tene* period is that dimension to which the experiences of all communities of every age belong. The *tene* period acts, therefore, as a mythical foundation for the identity of the present community, which is ever moving toward its ancestors.⁴² The present is based upon such pre-history. For because of this pre-history, societies gain historical depth, ontological foundation, social solidarity, and relationship to the land.⁴³

The *direction* of Akamba history is the opposite of the understanding of history by the AIM missionaries in that it recesses or moves backwards.⁴⁴ J. E. McTaggart notes:

> If . . . events are taken as moving by a fixed point of presentness, the movement is from future to past, since the future events are those which have not yet passed the point, and the past are those which have.⁴⁵

---

40. Mbiti, *NTEAB*, 30–32; Mbiti, *ARAP*, 21–23. See Booth, "Time and Change"; Byaruhanga-Akiiki, "Philosophy and Theology of Time"; Byaruhanga-Akiiki, "Luo Philosophy of Time."

41. The New Testament, argues Mbiti, has more than one understanding of temporality. Such a plurality of temporal concepts includes two-dimensional understandings. See Mbiti, "Christian Eschatology," 59–74; Mbiti, *NTEAB*, 24–50; Mbiti, *ARAP*, 27–29; Mbiti, "Afrikanisches Verständnis." For a contrary view, see Gyekye, *Essay on African*, 169–86.

42. Mbiti, *ARAP*, 28; Mbiti, *NTEAB*, 27–29.

43. Musopole, *Being Human*, 51–52.

44. Compare Mbiti, *NTEAB*, 24–25; with Mbiti, *ARAP*, 29–31. See Musopole, *Being Human*, 48–56; Gale, "Time, Temporality," 76.

45. McTaggart, "Unreality of Time," 470 f.n. 1. See Gale, "Time, Temporality," 68; Loux, "Time: A-Theory and B-Theory," 251.

While Akamba thought may be two-dimensional, McTaggart's comment is helpful in illustrating how one might understand the "backward flow" of history. Consequently, if there is a sense of temporal progressivism at work in missionary understandings of history, time, and eschatology, it is not generally present in Akamba society.[46] Their history, argues Mbiti, is not moving toward a *telos*, nor, in theological terms, is there any expectation of a messiah figure or final judgment.[47] Inevitably, Mbiti's understanding of traditional temporality comes in for much criticism (see below). Given the Akamba understanding of temporality, where the long past and the now-period take precedence over any sense of future, Christian eschatology in this context will have a strong realized dimension. Mbiti argues that in a ritually and symbolically rich context, a key means to communicate this will be through the sacraments.

Akamba Time-Consciousness and the Eschatology of the Sacraments

Mbiti submits that in an African setting the sacraments will be the primary means to convey "eschatological realities."[48] The Akamba do not have any concepts that correspond to the Christian sacraments. Libations, blessings, offerings, sacrifices, humanizing ceremonies, and circumcision are not theocentric events, nor do they have eschatological connotations. That is to say, they do not necessarily invoke the presence of God nor do they function in any redemptive sense.[49] Equally, under the tutelage of AIM missionaries, Akamba Christians understand baptism primarily as the means of initiation into a new life signified by the taking of a Western name and therefore assimilation into a culture now governed by "civilized" (missionary) norms. The significance of baptism is almost entirely social and cultural with the candidate attaining maturity by distancing him or herself from "heathendom."

---

46. That is not to say that the mission eschatology depicted by Mbiti conceives of such "progress" as an inevitable improvement in human conditions. On the contrary, the end of time will be consummated by the judgment of God on the very many who have not been converted to Christ. Mission is therefore part of what Moltmann characterizes as "the conservative syndrome." See Mbiti, *ARAP*, 30; Moltmann, "Liberation of the Future," 268–73.

47. Mbiti, *ARAP*, 29–31, 182–83; Mbiti, *Akamba Stories*, 17. See Parratt, "Time in Traditional," 123; Barr, *Biblical Words*, 140–42.

48. Mbiti, *NTEAB*, 91. See Mbiti, "Hope, Time."

49. Mbiti, *NTEAB*, 91–96. See Mbiti, *COGA*, 178, 194–217; Taylor, J., *Primal Vision*, 89–102.

In no sense is such baptismal practice "eschatologically orientated."[50] While such a cultural understanding of baptism might conform to some of the intent missionaries had, the understanding many of the Akamba have of the Eucharist is precisely what evangelical missionaries would be seeking to avoid. Biblical text and missionary authoritarianism result in the sense that something both dreadful and "magical" takes place in the Eucharist.[51] It appears, especially in the light of 2 Corinthians 11:27–32, which seems to invoke threats of magic and curse, that at the Eucharist much can be lost for the sake of very little gain.[52]

Against this background, Mbiti begins to identify components of a practical eschatology of the sacraments emerging from the context. It will include and emphasize paedobaptism, contextually appropriate liturgy, an undermining of magic, humanization, and a theological expansion of the concept of kinship.[53] Humanizing is a ritualistic process through which children are incorporated into the community of humans.[54] Mbiti is correct here when he identifies a strong relationship with baptism. For baptism is a "sacrament of birth" incorporating those who undertake it into the body of Christ. An understanding of community then is extended theologically to include a sense of christological kinship as foundational to identity.[55] Mbiti argues that the Eucharist will relate to and challenge traditional practice. On the one hand, Mbiti argues that the cross eliminates any need for sacrifice as practiced traditionally.[56] On the other hand, Mbiti argues that the Christian sacraments, and the Eucharist especially, provide an opportunity to trans-

50. Moltmann, *Spirit of Life*, 147; Mbiti, *NTEAB*, 108–13. Indeed, even today, baptism can be little more than a naming ceremony. See Mugambi, *BBE*, 16–24, 92–100; Mugambi, "Rites of Passage," 233.

51. AIM missionaries created a system of church discipline for those who offended apparently Christian norms. As well as barring offenders from Holy Communion for wide ranging "sins," which included circumcising children, polygamy, drinking beer, and allowing one's child to attend the Roman Catholic school. Short of excommunication, the most fearful means of discipline was the "seat of shame." Sandgren, "Kamba Christianity," 180–82. See Taylor, J., *Growth of Church in Buganda*, 244.

52. Mbiti, *NTEAB*, 113–16.

53. Ibid., 183–84. See Kirigia, "Liturgical Developments"; Chesworth, "Anglican Liturgical Reform."

54. Lindblom, *Akamba in British*, 33–34. For a more recent treatment of humanizing processes, see Mosha, *Heartbeat of Indigenous*.

55. Mbiti, *NTEAB*, 117–18, 145–51. See Mbiti, *Akamba Stories*, 6–8; Sawyerr, *Creative Evangelism*, 92–93; Moltmann, *Theology of Hope*, 155; Middleton, *Kikuyu and Kamba*, 79.

56. Mbiti, *NTEAB*, 116–26; Mbiti, *COGA*, 179. See Lindblom, *Akamba in British*, 218–24; Oborji, "In Dialogue," 21–22.

form an African understanding of the relationship between the physical and the spiritual.[57]

It may be the case that when read today there is little of Mbiti's proposals in regard to the eschatology of the sacraments that appear controversial. However, in the 1960s and 70s when Africans were still under-represented in Church structures and when African theology was emerging, much of what Mbiti proposed was contentious. For example, to associate baptism with traditional rites, including circumcision and clitoridectomy, is controversial. For it means the affirmation of a theology of continuity that directly contradicts the approach of the AIM. His proposals can be seen as controversial too when set in historical context. The AIM lost up to 95% of its membership amongst the Kikuyu as a result of propagating the view that circumcision is incompatible with Christianity. The controversy served to radicalize the Kikuyu prior to the Mau Mau movement. During the British suppression of Mau Mau, up to 11,000 Africans were killed and between 130,000 and 300,000 Kikuyu remain unaccounted for.[58] Nonetheless, Mbiti presses on with seeking theological bridges between traditional practice and wisdom and with Christian faith. He continues with a Christian contextualizing, for in both joy and sorrow corporate identity is given priority over individual identity by the Akamba. For Mbiti such corporateness is theologically significant.

Akamba Corporateness, the Spirit World, and Resurrection

The purpose of this section is twofold. First, in response to mission eschatology that is excessively individualistic, Mbiti's understanding of Akamba corporateness will be outlined. Second, the theological implications of such corporateness, especially for how the spirit-world and resurrection are to be understood by the emerging eschatology, will be identified.

First, central to what might be called Akamba ontology is the notion of community, which includes present and departed members (see chapter 2).[59]

57. Mbiti, *NTEAB*, 125.

58. Elkins, *Britain's Gulag*, 366. See Waller, "They Do the Dictating," 102–9; Spear, "Towards the History," 7–8, 14–15. In the wake of this controversy, the Kikuyu Independent Schools Association (1934) and the African Independent Pentecostal Church was founded. See also Edgerton, *Mau Mau*, vii, 107–13, 137–38, 150; Anderson, *Histories of the Hanged*. The practice of clitoridectomy was eventually outlawed by the Kenyan government in 1982. Kyle, *Politics of Independence*, 32.

59. Mbiti, "Bible in African Culture," 36, see 132. See Mbiti, "African Concept of Sin"; Mbiti, *BATAC*, 172; Bediako, *Theology and Identity*, 308–12; Musopole, *Being Human*, 5–10. Mugambi argues helpfully that "community" should take precedence,

It is the duty of all to maintain good relationships with the community both living and departing.[60] Mbiti contrasts imported concepts of individualized selfhood with traditional understandings of ontology where the corporate is primary. "I am because we are, and since we are, therefore I am" is now a widely disseminated summation of traditional ontology seemingly coined by Mbiti.[61] Central to any African religion is a concern for the relationship between those who have died and those who remain.[62] To this extent, Akamba tradition is also concerned with the eschatological. Mbiti observes that such concern brings one to the heart of the African worldview.[63] To begin with eschatology, argues Mbiti, is to begin where God is already at work prior to the arrival of missionaries.[64] To begin with eschatology is to address a set of questions important both to the Akamba and to the AIM missionaries in Ukambani.[65] For both the evangelized and the evangelists, death is not annihilation. Indeed, Mbiti argues that in Akamba ontology it is inconceivable that humanity could be destroyed. Mbiti does not make it clear as to why this should be so. Akamba ontology consists of five modes of existence: God, spirits, humanity, non-human life and inanimate objects. God is conceived chiefly as creator and, therefore, it may be that Mbiti is suggesting that if humanity was destroyed God would no longer be creator and therefore he would, in effect, cease to exist. Consequently, the whole fabric of Akamba ontology would unravel.[66]

Death plays its part in this ontology as a process of taking the departed to the spirit-world. It is assumed that humans are composite beings made up of, for example, body, breath, heart, life and mind. In the spirit-world

---

along with "people," over the use of "tribe" (nation) in post-colonial Africa. For not a few African "nations" (tribes) straddle Western drawn boundaries in Africa. Mugambi, *From Liberation*, 199–200. See p'Bitek, *African Religions*, 9–16; Ogot, "Boundary Changes," 29.

60. Mbiti, "'Hearts Cannot be Lent,'" 6–7; Mbiti, *NTEAB*, 6–7, 30–40, 138–40, 153–56. See Mbiti, "Christian Eschatology," 193–97; Mugambi, *TAHCC*, 135–39; Sawyerr, *Creative Evangelism*, 30. See Lindblom, *Akamba In British*, 209–16; O'Leary, *Kitui Akamba*, 57–64, 92–101.

61. Mbiti, *ARAP*, 141. See Musopole, *Being Human*, 10; Mugambi, *ACT*, 81; Mugambi, *TAHCC*, 136.

62. Mbiti, while using "religion," is aware of its limitations. See Mbiti, "Christian Eschatology," 289, 298–99; Mbiti, *Akamba Stories*, 14–17; Mbiti, *BATAC*, 165; Mbiti, *ARAP*, 19.

63. Mbiti, "Christian Eschatology," 5.

64. See Ibid., 305–12; Mbiti, "Encounter of Christian Faith" (*CC*), 818.

65. Mbiti, *COGA*, 264.

66. See Mbiti, *ARAP*, 20–21, 50–61; Mbiti, *NTEAB*, 132.

humans are given another body that is somehow identical to the body they had in the now-period.[67] In the spirit-world they first become members of the living-dead, then spirits (*Aimu*) before being incorporated into a state of collective immortality, thus losing any sense of individuality.[68] Mbiti's depiction of Akamba beliefs on death undermines the AIMs judgment that African beliefs concerning post-mortem existence are "dim, shadowy and undefined."[69] The Akamba can refer to dying in terms such as "following the company of one's grandfathers" and "going back."[70] At death the whole human being, apart from the body, moves "backwards" to join the departed members of his or her household.[71] Those recently dead are best described as the "living dead" for they are alive both in spirit and in the memories of their loved ones. The departed live in a world which is neither different nor removed from this world: "neither below nor above the ground, but everywhere and close to the physical."[72] It is only after about five generations when the departed can no longer be remembered by name that they are considered dead. At this time the departed survive as spirit in the state of collective immortality.[73] The world of the spirits is believed to be close to the human community but no one knows where. The spirits are believed to exist in a mode of being between humanity and divinity. They pervade the community, their ability to possess members of the community is well known (and not uncommon), possession can enable people to become mediums, women have spirit husbands (which form the foetus in the uterus), and spirits can act as guardians.[74]

The spirits in Akamba thought are distinct from the living-dead. For unlike the latter, they are not regarded as family members, they do not visit places that were familiar to them in life, and they have particular abilities such as flying and assuming different shapes. It is believed these spirits are

67. Mbiti, *NTEAB*, 130–31. See Mbiti, "Person Who Eats Alone."

68. See Mbiti, *NTEAB*, 127–46; Mbiti, *Akamba Stories*, 15–16; Mbiti, *ARAP*, 31–34.

69. Richardson, *Garden of Miracles*, 18. It should be noted that, in words omitted from *NTEAB*, Mbiti did initially describe the Akamba spirit-world as "'without form and void.'" Mbiti, "Christian Eschatology," 215.

70. Mbiti, *NTEAB*, 127–33, 139; Musopole, *Being Human*, 53. See Mbiti, *ARAP*, 20–34, 163.

71. Mbiti, *NTEAB*, 130–43. See Sawyerr, *Creative Evangelism*, 108–12.

72. Mbiti, *NTEAB*, 137, see 133. Sawyerr and Idowu argue that at least some traditional societies hold to a paradisiacal understanding of post-mortem existence. Sawyerr, *Creative Evangelism*, 109–10; Idowu, *African Traditional Religion*, 188–89.

73. Mbiti, *NTEAB*, 30, 63, 133–34; Idowu, *African Traditional Religion*, 184–86.

74. Mbiti, *NTEAB*, 134–37; Mbiti, *Akamba Stories*, 14–17; Middleton, *Kikuyu and Kamba*, 92; Lindblom, *Akamba in British*, 29–30.

present almost everywhere and influence the day to day life of the people. Because they inhabit an intermediary stage between humanity and God, the human community is responsible for regulating relationships with them through sacrifice. For example, sacrifices ensure that they are not allowed to get too close or too far away from the human world. For if either were to happen it is believed that the spirits would cause misfortune.[75]

Second, the idea of community, made up of those present and departed, is a feature of New Testament eschatology. It is understood in terms of the *body of Christ*, which shall experience *resurrection*. While such an image of corporateness and resurrection appears not to have been important to mission eschatology (favoring instead individual conversion and heavenly post-mortem existence), Mbiti argues it is potentially significant in an Akamba context and therefore in an emerging African theology.[76]

Mbiti demonstrates no desire to develop a detailed demonology or angelology. For both Akamba and New Testament eschatology are concerned primarily not with the nature of the departed nor the spirits but, he argues, how the nearness of the spirit-world affects human communities. In familiar theological terms this is seen most clearly in the New Testament's concept of the reign of God.[77] Christ is depicted in the New Testament as inaugurating this reign by bringing to bear the eschatological intent of God for the wholeness of his creatures and creation now. The pinnacle of the inauguration of this reign is his defeat of Satan at the cross. In sum, according to Mbiti's reading of the New Testament, incorporation into the eschatological community is dependent upon and determined by Christ. Such incorporation "in Christ" stands distinct from "the sheer fact of survival" in Akamba traditions. The passivity of survival gives way to an eschatological participating so that God, and not survival, becomes the object of hope.[78] The dimensions of this corporate fellowship are depicted by Mbiti in terms of communion with God, others, and the departed. Of particular significance, given the Akamba background of the spirit-world, is how Mbiti understands the relationship Christians have with the departed. While conceding that the New Testament is virtually silent (see Heb 12:22–29) on how the living relate to the departed, this does not hinder Mbiti in identifying

---

75. Mbiti, NTEAB, 134. See Mbiti, *Akamba Stories*, 110–15, 151–52, 186–91, 216–18; Lindblom, *Akamba in British*, 214–16; Middleton, *Kikuyu and Kamba*, 91–93; Hobley, *Ethnology of A-Kamba*, 10.

76. See Mbiti, NTEAB, 151–53. The influence of Mbiti's Cambridge supervisor can be seen here. See Moule, *Origin of Christology*, 47–96.

77. Mbiti, NTEAB, 140–43.

78. Ibid., 140–44. See Moltmann, *Theology of Hope*, 16; Metz, *Theology of the World*, 115.

a limited correspondence between the *Sanctorum Communio* and Akamba understandings of the departed. He is careful to ground any understanding of communion with the departed christocentrically. Human fellowship with God (in Christ) cannot be complete for those existing in the spirit-world if it does not include those who live in the present world as well. Furthermore, life in Christ, pre-mortem and post-mortem may justify practices such as praying for the dead. Beyond that, Mbiti begins to affirm a universalism where all will eventually be incorporated into Christ.[79] It is interesting to note that Mbiti does not seek to justify his universalism from the perspective of the African stress on corporateness. For no doubt he could argue that if the ancestors are not incorporated into the new humanity found in Christ then this humanity remains less than whole and as such would contradict the very essence of what "salvation" means. That he does not do so might, again, demonstrate his conviction that an African theology must be christocentric and not anthropocentric. While one may not find any of this particularly contentious, against the background of the Akamba and their evangelization by a conservative Protestant mission society, Mbiti's proposals are nothing less than revolutionary.[80]

As taught by the AIM, *resurrection* is seen chiefly in individualistic and futuristic terms. The Akamba have a concept of *resurrection* or resuscitation. Such resurrection only takes place in the *tene* period and is primarily corporate.[81] With the coming of missionary Christianity a traditional understanding in Akamba thought of post-mortem survival was simply re-affirmed while being replaced from the past to the now-period. In contrast, Mbiti is correct to argue that any understanding of resurrection will be determined by how one understands the resurrection of Christ. For Mbiti a christocentric and corporate understanding of resurrection is one that comes closer to the biblical traditions than what was met by the Akamba in the teaching of AIM missionaries. Mbiti argues that an understanding of resurrection that is christocentric will recognize the church is born and exists in an eschatological era. That is to say, "eternal life" is the realization

---

79. Mbiti, *NTEAB*, 179–80, see 186.

80. Ibid., 145–56. This is well illustrated by AIM judgment of Mbiti: "if all goes well, he will probably be our first African to enter into the higher ranks of our educational personnel." Ferrin, "To Ralph T. Davis," September 15. Ferrin adjudged that he "is above the average, and that he is a good one to take a 'risk' on—if we have to take a risk." Ferrin, "To Ralph T. Davis," September 22. However, in light of Mbiti's academic career, Raymond Wolfe cites Mbiti as an example of Africans educated overseas who display "relative overall ineffectiveness and power for God even in secular life, let alone as active in the Church." Wolfe, "Random Thoughts."

81. Mbiti, *COGA*, 265. See Mbiti, *NTEAB*, 157–59.

of resurrection, which has "broken in" to the now-period. This realization is found "in Christ" and therefore is inherently and ultimately corporate. Consequently, any notion of a future resurrection will not be material and that ultimately, individuality will be subsumed into a new mode of existence.[82] Mbiti is aware that these eschatological issues will not be resolved. However, his understanding of them is in marked distinction to the teaching the Akamba received from foreign missionaries. It is no coincidence that Mbiti's understanding of post-mortem existence, while christocentric, affirms his understanding of the Akamba concept, which ultimately results in an eschatological loss of individuality. Such contextual work on eschatology did not simply create controversy amongst the AIM. A wider audience of scholars engage and critique Mbiti's Akamba Christian eschatology.

Philosophical Objections: Western and African Temporality

Critics, such as Francis Gillies argue that Mbiti has neither a very sophisticated grasp of Western nor African concepts of time. However, while outlining Gillies critique, I argue that he misunderstands the scope of Mbiti's work and at key points fails to understand Mbiti's argument. Gillies has at least three objections to Mbiti's work, which will be dealt with in turn.

First, Gillies is critical of Mbiti for not setting his work in the historical context of developing theology. On the one hand, Gillies criticizes Mbiti for introducing notions of eschatology that owe much to modern theology. He argues that the proposals he makes for an African eschatology were not available to the missionaries he critiques.[83] At least two responses are possible to this objection. However, at the center of Mbiti's argument is the assumption, one which, no doubt, AIM missionaries would be happy to share, that the New Testament text itself is a sufficient source for the missionaries to enact very different approaches to engagement with the Akamba. As has been seen, Mbiti often undermines AIM eschatology, not by appeal to a strand of modern theology unknown to these missionaries, but by an intensification of the very theological presuppositions they themselves hold. Consequently, he argues for an eschatology that is more biblical and an eschatology that is more rigorously christocentric. In addition, there is evidence that even with the growth of work done on eschatology in modern theology AIM eschatology remains futuristic and individualistic. There is

---

82. Mbiti, *NTEAB*, 160–78.
83. Gillies, "Bantu Concept," 18–20.

little evidence that Mbiti's critique of mission eschatology would have to change even now.[84]

On the other hand, referring to Jürgen Moltmann, Johann Baptist Metz and Karl Rahner, Gillies criticizes Mbiti for not integrating the thought of modern theologians in his engagement with eschatological issues in Africa. He argues, if due attention had been paid to such developments, Mbiti would have constructed an eschatology that would have included a concept of the future which was neither linear nor ontological, but the reality which penetrates and influences all presents.[85] At best there is some tension in Gillies critique at this juncture. It is not clear how he can sustain criticism of Mbiti's work which, at one and the same time, is critical of him for introducing modern theology into the debate and critical of him for not introducing modern theology into the debate. Mbiti does engage with Moltmann making reference to his *Theology of Hope*. He does so as an illustration of the seeming inability of Western theologians to conceive of time in any other terms than a threefold linear dimension.[86] Whether Mbiti's protest against the dominance of such a concept of time in modern theology is ultimately convincing and whether he can provide a constructive alternative will be seen in the following section. Despite Mbiti's criticism of Moltmann, similarities exist.[87] Both Moltmann and Mbiti emphasize the primary position of eschatology in a theological system, both emphasize the realized implications of eschatology, and both argue that any understanding of resurrection is conditioned by the resurrection of Christ. However, as has been seen, Mbiti's argument for a christocentric understanding of eschatology that is not understood as the prolongation of the future dimension of time or "movement into the open time of the future," is framed largely in terms

---

84. See Stanley, "Future in the Past," 118.

85. Gillies, "Bantu Concept," 19–20.

86. Mbiti, *NTEAB*, 38. See Moltmann, "Liberation of the Future," 265. See Moltmann, "World in God," 39–41; Bauckham, *Moltmann: Messianic Theology*, 4–22. Mbiti refers to Barr, *Biblical Words for Time*, as an honorable exception. It would have to be noted that while Barr might approve of Mbiti's general approach using Akamba practice as foundational to his conceptions of time and history, he would rightly disapprove of any move to extract a theory of temporality based on "dubious lexical methods" (see Mbiti, *ARAP*, 21–23; Mbiti, *NTEAB*, 26–27). Indeed, Barr's primary concern in this work is not to construct a theological understanding of temporality, but to counter the rise of "lexical studies" and the methods upon which they are founded. Nonetheless, he is useful to Mbiti, for he rejects any readings of biblical texts that are predicated upon particular understandings of time, or any interpretation of biblical texts which purport to demonstrate "biblical" conceptions of time or eternity. Barr, *Biblical Words for Time*, 142, 153–62.

87. Mbiti, *NTEAB*, 32–50.

that arise from the context of Akamba converts engaging with foreign missionaries.[88] He is cognizant both of the limitations of missionary theologizing and Akamba temporality and seeks to, by taking account of both, move beyond them to a more contextual Christian eschatology that ultimately critiques African categories as well as mission malpractice.

Second, for Mbiti, Akamba time is a composition of events. Gillies understands Mbiti to be contrasting this idea with time as an ontological reality.[89] Again Gillies chooses to critique the eschatological proposals independent of the missionary setting that Mbiti begins with in his dissertation and does not even ignore in *NTEAB*. Gillies argues that Mbiti's concepts of Western and African temporality are far too simplistic. Therefore, Mbiti ends up comparing and contrasting views that neither represent Western theology nor philosophy, and views which are not representative of African thought. This, at first sight, seems to be a serious objection. However, Gillies appears to be guilty of the very same error. For Gillies does not ground his critique historically in terms of the development of Mbiti's thought, nor in relation to the context from which his thought emerges. As has been noted, there is a discernible shift in Mbiti's approach to the subject when his earlier research is compared to later published works. It is the latter upon which Gillies's objection is based. There is no evidence that he has read Mbiti's earlier dissertation. There is no evidence that he identifies any shift in the point of departure for Mbiti's eschatology. For had he done so, he would have been able to, with some justification, accuse Mbiti of abandoning a method that more successfully engages African experience theologically and thus substantiate his criticism that Mbiti's work is unrepresentative of African views.[90] Despite this, Gillies is on the whole correct to observe that Mbiti has a tendency to make general or universal claims for his work.[91] This is less the case in his original Cambridge dissertation. If the initial point of departure in Mbiti's work is kept in view, Gillies-like criticisms are less potent. For Mbiti is *not* comparing and contrasting the so-called Western view of time with the African view of time. On the contrary, he is critiquing the eschatology of a specific group of missionaries in a specific place at a specific time. This is done so that the presuppositions of AIM temporality might be

---

88. Ibid., 77; Moltmann, *Religion, Revolution*, xii.

89. Gillies, "Bantu Concept," 24. See Parratt, "Time in Traditional," 117; Gyekye, *Essay on African*.

90. For this kind of objection, see Diagne, "Prospective Development," 62.

91. Care must be taken not to overemphasize this universalizing. See Mbiti, *ARAP*, 5, 127–29; and the following chapter (on ATR) of this book. See also Gyekye, *Essay on African*, 172–77, 185, 190–91.

compared and contrasted with Akamba temporality in light of New Testament eschatology.

Gillies simply argues that Mbiti is incorrectly interpreting Akamba practice. Time does exist as an ontological reality amongst the Akamba. It already exists to be "stamped" by events. The primacy of event, from the existential perspective, does not stand in contradiction to the notion that time exists independently of practice.[92] Indeed, as will be seen presently, Mbiti concedes that traditional societies can conceive of a future of up to two years hence. It appears that time can, therefore, be distinguished from event. It is not obvious that Mbiti needs to deny the ontological reality of time. Furthermore, if these issues are historicized the comparison between mission temporality and Akamba temporality may shed light on what Mbiti is proposing. *Contra* Gillies it is not clear that Mbiti denies the ontological reality of time in Akamba thought. Rather, the point he seeks to make is that unlike the missionaries who came to Ukambani with, what might be termed, a notion of temporal linear progressivism, the Akamba very much lived in the "now-period."[93] It remains the case that time is not conceived of in abstract terms. Temporality is conceived of, as Parratt also recognizes, in relation to particular past events such as the agricultural cycle or ritual cycle. Consequently, with Mbiti, Parratt argues that such temporality is "grounded in the past" by seeking to bring about in the now-period what has happened before.[94] The assertion that Gillies will make about the future outlook of those who live subsistent lifestyles may be tempered if not challenged outright. For, *contra* Gillies, subsistence living can be understood as orientated towards the past as much as it can be understood as orientated towards the future. Simply stated, the desire is that the provision for life garnered by those in the past might also be experienced in the now-period.

Third, even if Mbiti's work is seen as primarily focused on the particular, with the admitted tendency to universalize, the specific claims he makes

---

92. Gillies, "Bantu Concept," 25–26; Musopole, *Being Human*, 147–49. In Gerhard Lindblom's research, which Mbiti uses, he observes that the Akamba take great care to measure time in relation to the position of the sun. Time is measured using markings on, for example, well placed trees. Such measurement, independent of event, seems to challenge Mbiti's assertion that event takes primacy over "time." Lindblom, *Akamba in British*, 338–40. See Gyekye, *Essay on African*, 169–77.

93. See Mugambi, *African Christian Theology*, 81.

94. Parratt cites, in support of this view, Beidelmann, "Kaguru Time Reckoning"; Bohannan, "Concepts of Time"; Evans-Pritchard, *The Nuer: A Description*, 108; Eliade, *Myth of the Eternal Return*; Eliade, *Patterns in Comparative Religion*. See O'Leary, *Kitui Akamba*, 67–74.

for Akamba understandings of the future may still be indefensible.[95] As has been seen, Mbiti argues that, unlike the futuristic eschatology of the missionaries, the Akamba have virtually no concept of the future. In response, Gillies submits that the Akamba understanding of chronological time is very similar to Western conceptions and therefore the contrast Mbiti makes is, at best, only one of degree. It must be conceded that Mbiti does modify his understanding of a limited future in African thought by referring to an ontological rhythm. There is, therefore, a certain tension in his conceiving of time that may leave room for the concept of an imagined future beyond what Mbiti proposes. He further modifies the notion of the now-period by making reference to the "invasion" of technology, education, and Christianity, which is influencing traditional understandings of time.[96] It is unclear as to what Mbiti might exactly mean here. It appears that he is contrasting an emphasis in modern and Western thought on the hope of "progress" with a traditional and African emphasis on the certainty of an eternal return to the community of the departed. Hope, in the former case, is invested in future advance and in the latter, hope is invested in relational proximity to one's community. If this is the case then Mbiti is arguing that a progressivist linear concept of history, where humanity continues to progress toward betterment, is being adopted by Africans as a result of colonization and evangelization.[97]

If chronological time-consciousness is grounded on the inevitability of the rhythm of nature then, as Mbiti identifies, it is unreal until experienced. In other words, a distinction is being made here between "future" and "time." Gillies argues that the sense of future that Mbiti concedes, that the Akamba affirm, is the very same concept of an "infinite future" affirmed in Western conceptions. This concept of the future is not based on an ontologically linear concept of time but is simply a "fundamental biological category."[98] Westerners and Africans conceive of the future with this sense of chronological inevitability upon which plans are made for providing for the future. Consequently, Gillies concludes that Mbiti is incorrect to identify a fundamental difference between Western and African concepts of the

---

95. The question of *direction* will be dealt with in the next section, as it applies best to the objections dealt with there.

96. Mbiti, *Akamba Stories*, 18; Mbiti, "Christian Eschatology," 103–4.

97. Mbiti, *Akamba Stories*, 17–18. See Mbiti, *ARAP*, 35–36, 282–98; Gyekye, *Essay on African*, 176–77.

98. Gillies, "Bantu Concept," 21. See Gyekye, *Essay on African*, 171–72.

future. Furthermore, given that the Akamba may live at a subsistence level they may be *more* concerned with this future than many Westerners.[99]

These criticisms of Gillies, which may well over-emphasize the tendency Mbiti has for universalizing in the absence of any engagement with his earlier work on the subject, fail to engage with the historical setting in which Mbiti examines "Western" and "African" temporality. It is one thing for Gillies to critique Mbiti's understandings of Akamba temporality at a conceptual level. However, while his critique raises crucial questions (which will be further dealt with below by revising Mbiti's insights), it remains less than convincing because he does not similarly address or recognize the conceptions of temporality that Mbiti was responding to in the context of Ukambani. Gillies remains silent on the issue of whether Mbiti or Akamba converts misunderstood the eschatology delivered to them by the AIM. What can explain the feeling of conceptual inversion or the despondency that Christ had not returned as promised in the "future"? For the criticism of Mbiti by Gillies to be compelling, he would have to identify constructive alternatives to these historical questions that, in large part, provoked Mbiti's research on Akamba temporality in the first place. Yet, the reason that Gillies can raise his objections with little reference to the particularism of context is largely the result of Mbiti abandoning his own initial method. There is, however, another type of objection, which takes very seriously the historical and social setting of such theologizing. Consequently, objections raised in relation to the social implications of Mbiti's reflections on eschatology will be addressed in the next section.

Social Objections: African Temporality and "Backwardness"

Arguably, objections that purport to explicitly demonstrate the negative social repercussions of Mbiti's work are more serious than any objection concerning its theoretical theological coherence. What might be termed a social objection is that which argues a "backward" looking understanding of time and history legitimizes the view that African (traditional) societies are under-developed as a result of African culture. This is a less common objection. The objection will be dealt with in two steps. First, some of the possible social implications of such a view will be identified. Second, reasons for the outright rejection of such a backward looking concept arising from a revised Mbitian temporality will be examined.

First, in presenting traditional concepts of temporality Mbiti is in danger of reaffirming the picture of Africans too often painted by foreign

---

99. Gillies, "Bantu Concept," 20–22.

anthropologists, explorers, missionaries and colonialists. Musopole understands Mbiti to be doing exactly that:

> Unless something is done to the concept of time, Mbiti warns, people in Africa will remain backward-looking rather than forward-looking. They will remain without hope, unprogressive and prisoners of ritual and a mythical past instead of being makers of history.[100]

Such views, as Mugambi is particularly aware, were used in the colonial era to legitimize brutal practices both by missionaries and colonialists. Indeed, Mbiti experiences missionary attempts to reject and suppress African agency and African traditional practice.[101] However, he does not seem to be aware that it is very possible that such cultural subjugation was predicated upon the very same image of Africans he is in danger of promoting. What might be termed representative domination is not unrelated to praxis in the social and political arena.[102]

Mugambi is critical of Mbiti's understanding of the direction of time, which he calls a "stereotype."[103]

> Conventional wisdom as articulated in Europe and North America seems to suggest that Africa is doomed to annihilation. Yet there is no good reason to suggest that the failures of the past will prevail in the future. Human beings, as creators of culture, are capable of working in the present to ensure that the future will not be like yesterday. Indeed, culture is the achievement of human beings in community, as they endeavour to ensure that the future need not be like yesterday.[104]

Mugambi's hopes for an African future, however, are harder to assert if Mbiti's understanding of Akamba temporality applies to Africa more generally.

---

100. Musopole, *Being Human*, 56. See Moltmann, *Religion, Revolution*, 3–6. See Diagne, "Prospective Development"; Beyaraza, *African Concept of Time*; Smith, D., "Time and Not the Other"; Kwanya, *Debate on African*; Òkè, "From an African Ontology."

101. Mbiti, "Role of Jewish Bible," 223. See Sebastian, "Mission without History."

102. Mugambi is alert to this and makes reference, for example, to the work of Edward Said. See Mugambi, *From Liberation to Reconstruction*, 78–79; Maddox, "African Theology," 26; Said, *Orientalism*, 95–97; Heaney, "Conversion to Coloniality."

103. Mugambi, *FLTR*, 88, see 110–11. See Mugambi, *GHN*, 13–41; Mugambi, *CCAL*, 71–76; Mugambi, *TAHCC*, 135.

104. Mugambi, *From Liberation to Reconstruction*, 88. It must be acknowledged that Mugambi has also, though for different reasons, complained about the lack of "technological and philosophical innovation" in Africa. See Mugambi, "Problems of Meaning," 76.

It appears that Mbiti is guilty of depicting African culture as inherently regressive. Indeed, Mbiti explicitly raises the question whether the slow rate of improvement and seeming lack of long term development planning in Africa has been partly the result of such a "past orientated" temporality.[105] Mugambi, rightly, rejects such implications.[106] He proposes that relationality and not temporality is the most important factor in African cultures. Mbiti's proposal that the African concept of time is the key to understanding African philosophies and religions is rejected by Mugambi. For such a proposal "oversimplifies African philosophical thought."[107] Indeed, in Kenya, the Mau Mau movement was predicated upon, or at least appealed to, an African traditionalism, yet this seeming conservatism became the impetus for radical change. Mugambi concurs with Mbiti that the now-period is the most intense period for many Africans.

> Africans are obsessed neither by the past nor by the future. What happens *at present* is of great concern in traditional African thought because it may completely alter future relations, and because what happens *now* is what later generations narrate as history.[108]

Any social failure (backwardness), Mugambi argues, is in large part the result of colonial structures being "superimposed" on traditional structures with no attempt at synthesis. So too the concept and practice of "development" is predicated upon imported assumptions.[109] Theologically, the image of backward looking traditions can continue to legitimize a missionary project in Africa that continues to espouse theologies of discontinuity and deny African agency.[110] Such issues will be further addressed in chapter 6 when Mugambi proposes a renewed approach to African theology.

> While it is true that Africans place much emphasis on what they consider and believe to be the important events in their past, it

---

105. Mugambi, *FLTR*, 81.

106. It must be noted that Mugambi did not always reject such arguments. For he has claimed that the inherently conservative nature of traditional societies prevents examination of the assumptions traditional knowledge is based upon. This, along with the colonial education system, "indoctrinated" Africans against innovation or inventiveness. Consequently, he can be seen to argue for a decolonized theologizing, which will bring such innovation and inventiveness back to Africa. See Mugambi, "Problems of Meaning," 15, 77–78.

107. Mugambi, *GHN*, 23.

108. Mugambi, *ACT*, 81.

109. See Escobar, *Encountering Development*.

110. Mugambi, *FLTR*, 88–106.

is also true that they feel bound by their experience to maintain the present and future social, religious and political beliefs and implications which those important past events cast on their understanding... The commitment to the past means to Africans that all the things they do in the present should ensure a future structure of the community which has a continued relationship with that past. Such a commitment cannot accurately be said to have its end only in the present.[111]

If Africans cannot conceive of a future then, traditionally, they have no "means or principles" for perpetuating their communities.[112] But this is not the case. For Mugambi marriage, initiation, and leadership succession are all future orientated practices and processes. Consequently, "just as the past is marked by events which have been experienced, so is the future anticipated in terms of events which are expected to happen, affecting the family and the community as a whole."[113] Relation or relationality, and not temporality, is "in deed, thought and expression, a fundamental concern of African peoples in their religions, philosophy and social organisation."[114]

Second, not only do the implications of such "backwardness" alert the theologian to the potential ill effect of Mbiti's proposals, but alternative interpretations from Kenya may deem them entirely unnecessary. If this is the case, then the constructive responses to Akamba temporality that Mbiti has "yet to see" may come into view.[115]

As the Mau Mau movement demonstrated in very stark terms "an alternative future" is conceivable within African temporality presenting itself as traditional. Gillies might be seen to recognize that this type of "future" should be distinguished from a chronological future. For it is, by definition, a break from the chronological. In a bid to illustrate this Gillies makes reference to the Exodus story, which arises from historical experiences, as a means to create an alternative future.[116] However, Mbiti argues that no such myths exist in Akamba religion.[117] Gillies proposes two possible responses

---

111. Mugambi, *GHN*, 23.
112. Ibid. See also Beyaraza, *African Concept of Time* vol. 2, 100–19.
113. Mugambi, *GHN*, 24.
114. Ibid., 25.
115. Mbiti, Interview by Heaney, April 7.
116. It should be noted that the Exodus story was utilized by nationalists in Kenya. The East African Association (1921) depicted Africans as in need of a new Moses to lead them in a new Exodus. See Anderson, D., *Histories of the Hanged*, 9–10, 287–90, for a brief sketch of the religious journey of a key Mau Mau leader.
117. Gillies, "Bantu Concept," 22–23.

to this backward temporality and the absence of future orientated myth. Mbiti's argument would be undermined if future orientated myths could be identified or if his assertion that Akamba life is governed by traditional religions could be weakened.

It appears that there is no agreement about such myths as they seem to emerge quite late in the traditions and may be admixtures of traditional and later Christian beliefs.[118] Gillies proposes that a more fruitful approach is to deny the common assumption that traditional African societies are consummately religious. Gillies is arguing that an imagined future could exist outside traditional religions and could be activated in response to particularly "alienating" circumstances.[119] It seems that a proposal like this, which to some extent revises the role or understanding of "traditional religion" could be incorporated into Mbiti's thesis, especially given the fact that he is prepared to modify his initial understanding of a lack of future in Akamba thought to include a period of up to two years.[120] For example, his depiction of Akamba temporality as a composition of events, as having a very limited notion of the future, and of being orientated towards the past could be revised to refer to this as the *normative* understanding of traditional temporality. If this were the case, then it could be argued that in, for example, very traumatic circumstances the future could be envisaged in contrast to this normative temporality. This seems especially the case if the chronology of time itself was threatened so that what might be expected to emerge from the now-period was under threat. It seems that some form of modification like this would allay the worst fears of Mugambi. It would affirm African agency against any notion of cultural determinism and it would add to the debate on conversion in traditional societies.[121] In sum, such a modification again justifies and illustrates the strength of Mbiti's initial methodology by bringing together belief (tradition) with practice (the experience of Africans).

If the context is given methodological primacy again then myths of the future, which Mbiti is unable to detect in traditional Akamba thought, could possibly be discovered in ongoing African practice (such as the Mau Mau movement). A static pristine past is not possible, nor is it a particularly useful foundation to build upon. If Mbiti had persevered with his initial approach, the recognition he makes that ongoing African experiences can be a source

118. See Williams, J., *Hebrewism of West Africa*, 340–56; Gray, R. F., *Sonjo of Tanganyika*, 97–98, 107–8; Parrinder, *African Mythology*, 8; Gyekye, *Essay on African*, 177.

119. Gillies, "Bantu Concept," 22–24. See Gyekye, *Essay on African*, 205–8.

120. Mbiti, *African Religions*, 23–28.

121. See Horton, R., "African Conversion."

of theology without either displacing traditional practice or seeing more contemporary practice as a threat to it, could have been clearly integrated into his early work on eschatology. As will be seen presently, there are other ways of conceiving of the now-period and imagined futures that, although not dealt with directly here, would also make sense of some Mau Mau leaders seeing their roles as prophetic. Consequently, while not being seen as religious in an Mbitian sense the imagined future is nonetheless thoroughly religious. This is especially the case if, as the next section deals with, biblical eschatology relates to Akamba temporality in ways Mbiti did not recognize.

Theological Objections: Biblical Temporality and Christology

The theological objections identified here focus on the possibility that Mbiti underestimates the possible relationship between New Testament temporality and Akamba temporality and over-christologizes eschatology.

First, it may be that both the AIM missionaries and Mbiti's reading of New Testament eschatology is shaped by a modernist understanding of time. For the AIM, such reading is largely uncritical. Mbiti seeks a more critical and contextual approach, but he may be guilty of reading New Testament eschatology through a modern lens and therefore be involved in theologizing from a perspective more similar to the missionaries than he is aware of. Bruce Malina, seemingly unaware of Mbiti's work on African and New Testament temporality, sets out a comparison between "traditional" temporality and "modern" temporality.[122] Unlike Mbiti, Malina does not see a "future" in the New Testament that is in tension with traditional temporalities. For Malina, the New Testament writers were "present orientated." Malina's depiction of biblical and traditional temporality has striking similarities to how Mbiti depicts Akamba temporality. By implication, it is therefore possible that a Malinian approach to temporality may provide a more thoroughgoing means of relating Akamba temporality to the New Testament than Mbiti's approach does.

For Malina, both in antiquity and in the contemporary world, future-orientation as a primary focus is an aberration.[123] Future-orientation functions only when present survival (food, clothing, shelter, security) is relatively certain. This was seldom the case in antiquity and, it might be added, is often not the case in Africa today.[124] In large part, future-orientation as a primary focus is a consequence of the Industrial Revolution. Time

---

122. Malina, *Social World of Jesus*, 179–214.
123. Ibid., 185.
124. Ibid., 184–85.

becomes non-social. It can be measured. People can be paid for time. It is "clock time." It is abstract.[125] In contrast, New Testament temporality is present-orientated where the present "covers a broad sweep marked off only by the horizons of the imaginary past on the one side and the imaginary future on the other."[126] Consequently, the perceived problems of a delayed *parousia*, the tensions between the "now" and the "not yet" and apparent three-dimensional temporality are not inherent in the New Testament text but are the product of liberal, post-industrial, post-Enlightenment eisegesis.[127] They are the product of anachronistic and ethnocentric readings of the biblical text.[128] The veracity of Malina's claims are not the focus of the present section. Rather, a Malinian approach to the New Testament provides the possibility of a further revision of Mbiti's stated approach. For it provides a way of understanding time and of reading the New Testament that relates more closely to the Akamba than either the AIM or Mbiti provide.

Malina's depiction of the traditional now-period parallels how Mbiti depicts Akamba temporality. Reality is the "experienced world and experienced time."[129] It is "based upon procedures rooted in the organic nature of things."[130] The present can, therefore, endure depending on the "process or event involved."[131] "The antecedent and the forthcoming blend in with the continuing."[132] The now-period embraces not only what is presently happening but what is also presently "forthcoming." Conceptions and practices of time, therefore, are not concerned with "present" and "future" but with the actually-present and the present-forthcoming. The now-period takes in what moderns would see as both present and future. What is distinct about Malina's approach, however, is how he takes into account time beyond the experienced world. This is "imaginary time." The imaginary world cannot be "directly or immediately" related to the "universe of experience."[133] It cannot be "validated" by experience. For it exists beyond the "horizon of the experienced world."[134] This identification of imaginary time and how present orientated societies relate to its possibilities, as opposed to the potentialities

---

125. Ibid., 182–208.
126. Ibid., 185.
127. Ibid.
128. Ibid., 210.
129. Ibid., 188.
130. Ibid., 191.
131. Ibid., 189.
132. Ibid., 190.
133. Ibid., 192.
134. Ibid., 195.

of the now-period, in the past and in the future may provide an Mbitian approach with a more thoroughgoing contextualism. For example, Malina argues that in biblical literature imaginary time is the exclusive domain of God.[135] It is not continuous with human experience and is unrelated to any present events. With this Malinian revision, an Mbitian approach need not look for future-orientated myths. Rather, an analysis of the prophetic, important in both traditional and Christian communities as access to God's imagined future could be the focus.[136] In sum, such Malinian revisions point to the possibility that Christian eschatology is problematic for the Akamba and Mbiti not because of New Testament eschatology but because of the assumptions that both AIM missionaries and Mbiti possess. Mbiti seeks to relate Akamba temporality to "New Testament" temporality by admitting the need to reform the former. However, it may be that Akamba temporality is more biblical than either Mbitian or AIM readings of eschatology.

Second, Mbiti seeks to understand New Testament temporality christologically. While Mbiti recognizes a limited relationship between biblical worlds and African traditional contexts his christocentric intent may ultimately prevent a thoroughgoing contextualization. That is to say, according to his work, eschatology must be made subordinate to christology. "Eschatological realities become meaningful only insofar as they are christologically grounded."[137] Consequently, he, like the missionaries he critiques, is critical of any theologizing that theologically decenters Christ. Again, however, it is possible that such an emphasis shares more in common with AIM missionaries and much less with the New Testament. It could be argued that Mbiti is more christocentric than the New Testament itself.

Not all would see such christocentrism as plainly evident in the New Testament.[138] As Mbiti accuses missionaries of not being biblical enough because of their ultimate lack of christocentrism, so such criticism can be inverted and applied to Mbiti. He is not biblical enough because his eschatology is too christocentric. The very type of theologizing that Mbiti and missionaries reject may be the very type of theology that is found in the New Testament. For example, Mbiti argues that the geographical and spatial promises of the Old Testament (country or fatherland) are christologically and relationally superseded in the New Testament. He is critical of missionaries for giving the impression that eschatology is spatial. But it can be argued that this may well be precisely the way in which the writers of the New Testament thought

135. Ibid., 192.
136. For prophecy in ATR see, for example, Mbiti, *ARAP*, 248–52.
137. Mbiti, *NTEAB*, 44.
138. See Bauckham, "Emerging Issues."

(for example, Rev 20). A "biblical" approach may be delayed by Mbiti's christologizing with a vengeance. While Mbiti may be more christocentric than the New Testament text itself, the New Testament text may be more African than Mbiti. For an argument can be made that the New Testament centers not on christology but on re-creation. Therefore, God's desire is to re-create and Christ is the means to that ultimate end. Christ is not, however, the ultimate end in himself. Rather, "When all things are subjected to him, then the Son himself will also be subjected to the one who put all things in subjection under him, so that God may be all in all" (1 Cor 15:28).

In the final analysis, while it is correct to identify the particular Akamba context as the place where Mbiti's initial work on eschatology emerges, it may be that his eschatology is more in continuity with the thought of foreign missionaries than what might be evident in an initial examination. Again, here is evidence that the Akamba context is not as prominent as it might have been. Furthermore, the criticism can be made that this is the reason why a more radical contextualism is not made between a Christian eschatology and Akamba traditions. In the end, Mbiti represents an approach to eschatology owing much to a perspective shared by the AIM missionaries he criticizes. It might be less than fair to judge him against more recent scholarship on the New Testament world (for example, Malina). Nonetheless, it remains a pity that a first generation African theologian did not at least identify a counter position (a more radical contextualization) to the one he chose (christocentrism), even if that counter position was not one he ultimately affirmed.

Conclusion

The point of departure for Mbiti's theology is identified as the particular context of Ukambani and the encounter the people had with AIM missionaries. However, Mbiti makes a critical mistake when he moves away from this context as the locus for his work on African temporality and eschatology as it opens him up to unnecessary criticism. In response, I argue that care must be taken in critiquing Mbiti's understanding of Akamba temporality when it is abstracted from the particular context. As will be seen in subsequent chapters this move away from the particularism of context is but the first step in a gradual, though unintended, move away from the particularism of experience (chapter 4), community (chapter 5), and coloniality (chapter 6) evidenced in the writings of Mbiti and Mugambi. Whatever else it may mean to do post-colonial theology, it will mean taking these issues more seriously (chapter 7).

Figure 1

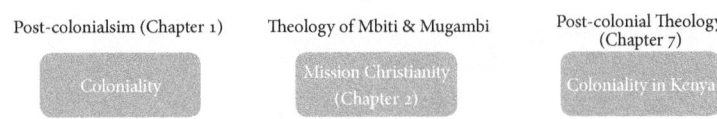

In this chapter, I argued that even when the immediate and initial Akamba context of Mbiti's research is kept in view, it appears that some revision of Mbiti's presentation of Akamba temporality is needed and this is seen particularly in reference to the social objections raised in response to his work on eschatology. The depiction of Akamba time as recessing into the past has the real potential of being construed as "African backwardness." This in turn has resonances with the legitimization of brutal colonial and missionary methods and of the assumption that Africa is inherently incapable of "progress." I argue that a revised Mbitian position will submit that an Akamba temporality (which is event centered, has a limited concept of the future, emphasizes the now-period and flows backwards) is *normative*. This does not exclude the possibility, especially in traumatic circumstances, that an historical, liberative future (as opposed to a chronological future) cannot be conceived of and brought about.

In the final analysis, Mbiti argues that Christian eschatology is a "christological phenomenon" that challenges all concepts of temporality. He does not deny that three dimensions of time has explanatory power in Christian eschatology.[139] Rather, he argues that such an understanding should be an *extension* of traditional temporality and not its replacement. To the extent that his thought can be read from the particularism of the initial context, his approach broadly succeeds in making Akamba temporality part of the source for an emerging African theology. Nevertheless, a more thoroughgoing contextualization is possible but not considered by Mbiti because of his insistence on making eschatology subordinate to christology. It can be argued that such christocentrism is a legacy of mission Christianity. However, independent assessment of how Christian understandings of God and Christ are integrated into this emerging African theology may make such an assessment premature. For that reason, the following chapters will address the subjects of how the African theology under present consideration understands God and Christ. The methodological shift initiated by Mbiti has influence on Mugambi, as he also views ATRs as the emergent locus for African theology. Consequently, the move away from the particular is further strengthened as attributes of so-called ATRs are abstracted from traditional religious experience as the means to, what I will call, theistic contextualism.

---

139. Mbiti, *NTEAB*, 182–83. See Mbiti, *ARAP*, 127–29.

4

The Theological Significance of African Traditional Religions

Engaging the Religio-Cultural Experience of Africa

AGAINST THE BACKDROP OF missionaries denigrating ATRs, Mbiti and Mugambi argue that God is known in the African traditional heritage independent of foreign missionary activity. This, therefore, grants the African religious heritage theological significance, which Mbiti sees in terms of *praeparatio evangelica*. Mugambi sees it in terms of re-mythologization and as part of a wider project for African "reconstruction."

African Traditional Religions as Theological Foundation

Mbiti estimates, in the absence of extensive research, that ATRs dominate two-thirds of Africa.[1] Despite this, foreign Christian missionaries, along with anthropologists, often depicted African traditions as devoid of any meaningful theologies.[2] During colonial occupation, Mbiti observes that many Africans were "brain-washed" with the assertion that "African heritage" was inferior and "altogether useless." This background was to be forsaken in favor of embracing "the cultures of the colonial rulers."[3] Yet, such

---

1. Mbiti, "Traditional Religions," 61–62. See Mbiti, "African Religion and World Order," 361–70; Mbiti, "Literature and Oral"; Mbiti, "Flowers in the Garden."

2. See Mbiti, *ARAP*, 10–11. See Stinton, *Jesus of Africa*, 9; Bediako, "Understanding African Theology," 2.

3. Mbiti, "Literature and Oral," 93–94. Mugambi explicitly states that religion is as

heritage was the locus from which Africans responded to the Christian gospel and it continues to inform the way in which they respond to modernity.[4] Despite the "bulldozer mentality" of foreign missionaries and many of their converts it is ATRs, argues Mbiti, that in large part account for the great numbers of converts to Christianity:

> Millions have put their faith in Jesus Christ. They confess Him as Lord and Saviour not in a vacuum, but in a religious and cultural context which has deep roots in the history and world view of African peoples. The success story of Christian presence in Africa, in which within one century, Christians have increased from 10 million or 9% of the total population in 1900 to about 320 million or 48% in 1994, and the numbers continue to soar, cannot be separated from African religiosity. The presence of African Religion within African Christianity is very strong and active. It is enriching and shaping Christian presence and people's experience, expression and understanding of the Gospel.[5]

Mugambi identifies the traditional religious background as the key contributing factor for his acceptance of Christianity above and beyond any evangelistic effort by missionaries or African Christians.[6]

The Christian message as understood by many Africans is largely world affirming. For God is seen to be involved in human history.[7] Belief in God, therefore, is centered on the perception of divine activity. God rescues individuals from danger, peoples from being destroyed, and saves the innocent.[8] Unlike a mission Christianity, where belief could be abstracted from practice, in African conception belief and consequence cannot be so easily separated. The coherence of faith is not measured by how one set of theological propositions relates to another. Rather, faith coheres when it is practical. One does not simply believe, for example, in the attribute of omnipotence, one stakes one's circumstances on the belief that God is all powerful. It is such a practical understanding that allows Mbiti to argue that a fundamental function of religion in African societies is to give protection to the adherent or community. The power of God is, therefore, not simply seen in the biblical text or subsumed into doctrines of providence and

"aspect" of "culture," see Mugambi, *FLTR*, 31; and see chapter 6 of the present study.

4. Opoku, "Introduction," 9. See Mbiti, "Hand to Mouth," 2–3.

5. Mbiti, "Confessing Christ in Multi-Faith," 138. See Mbiti, *BATAC*, 11–13; Mbiti, "Traditional Religions," 62.

6. Mugambi, *ACT*, x.

7. See Mbiti, *COGA*, 166–76; Mbiti, *BATAC*, 153–54.

8. Mbiti, *COGA*, 69–70.

sovereignty. God empowers believers to prophesy, to heal, to forgive, and to repent.[9] Consequently, the African theology that emerges from Mbiti's writing, is a living faith grounded in practice. However, this does not mean it is uncritical. On the contrary, conversions to the Christian faith are often only taken after significant reflection, dialogue, and argument. The decision to commit to the Christian faith is not solely taken on the basis of theoretical coherence, nor explanatory power, but also on the basis that existentially, the salvation unveiled in the Christian Gospel makes a positive difference in day to day life.[10]

For Mbiti ATRs include oral history of each people, myths, stories, narratives, biographies, religious names of people and places, religious concepts and practices, social institutions, ethics, and proverbs. ATRs can be seen to be dominated by six main themes: God, divinities, spirits, humanity, death and the afterlife, and magic.[11] At the time of Mbiti's initial research, in the 60s and 70s at Makerere, ATRs were primarily a rural phenomenon. However, even then, they were adapting to urban life. Such adaptation is seen in the many traditional medical consultants, in AICs, in its importance in nationalist discourses, and in the continued interest it generates for researchers.[12] Given that written sources that Mbiti uses for ATRs are largely from the nineteenth century, oral sources become particularly important. By 1970, in a bid to record such orality, Mbiti had collected 1,500 stories and over 2,000 proverbs and riddles, which he estimated represented 90 percent of the Akamba heritage.[13] Such research provides a powerful counter-discourse against foreign attempts to denigrate traditional wisdom. However, as Mugambi observes, the work must continue.

Mugambi argues that since Smith's *African Ideas of God* (1950)[14] most missionaries assumed that traditional societies have a defective understanding of God and an inadequate understanding of human destiny. In Smith's own words, "there was no need to persuade pagan Africans of the existence of God: they are sure of it, but not sure of Him as a living power in their

---

9. Mbiti, *BATAC*, 138–54. See Peel, *Religious Encounter*, 217–25; Mugambi, "African Experience," 49–58.

10. Mbiti, *BATAC*, 230.

11. Mbiti, "Traditional Religions," 62–65. See Smith, E., "Whole Subject," 2–14; Mugambi, *TAHCC*, 142–48.

12. Mbiti, "Traditional Religions," 67; Mugambi, "African Heritage," 169–78. See also Grillo, "Divination: Epistemology, Agency."

13. Mbiti, "Literature and Oral," 94. During his time at Makerere University, Mbiti was involved in field work on African religions with his students. It was largely from these sources that *COGA* emerged. Mbiti, Interview by Heaney, April 7.

14. Smith, E., *African Ideas of God*.

individual experience."[15] Despite, argues Mugambi, Mbiti's *African Religions and Philosophy* (1969), which may have more in common with *African Ideas of God* than Mugambi cares to admit, "African Religion" is a term and concept that has been resisted in the North Atlantic academy. In 1981, the *World Christian Encyclopaedia* had no place for it. It does not appear in the index of the *International Review of Mission*. Not until 2000 did the indexing of the Library of Congress list it. The North Atlantic "intelligentsia" preferred to name Africans. "The prejudice is overwhelming."[16] Only Geoffrey Parrinder's *Religion in Africa*, argues Mugambi, stands as an isolated attempt to establish African religion in the field of anthropology.[17] In theology things are not much better. Indeed, Mugambi argues that social evolutionism was as much an inspiration for attitudes and practices as was the Bible.

Paul maintained (Acts 17) that the Athenian "unknown god" was the same as the God who sent Jesus.[18] However, under the influence of social evolutionism many missionaries believed that African religions were primitive and yet to ascend from animism to polytheism or monotheism.[19] By the end of the first quarter of the twentieth century a shift in missionary thinking occurred.[20] For if assumptions such as those that portrayed Africans as animists were true, how was biblical translation to be done? If African cultures had no concept of "God" how was there to be any translation or conversion? Mission is predicated upon some form of continuity.[21] A shift was made, therefore, from depicting Africans as animists to depicting them as deists.[22] The need that missionaries were now meeting was the introduc-

15. Smith, E., "Whole Subject," 1, 16–35.

16. Mugambi, Introduction in Taylor, J., *Primal Vision*, xix–xxii. See Mugambi and Guy, *CTAC*, 33. In a recent web search on the University of Oxford's *SOLO* system, still no matches were found in the *International Review of Mission*, accessed May 18, 2013.

17. Mugambi, Introduction in Taylor, J., *Primal Vision*, xix–xx. Parrinder, *Religion in Africa*.

18. This is a text important to Tillich (see below) in explicating his apologetic or answering theology. See Tillich, "Theologian (Part 3)," 129–32.

19. Mugambi, "Problems of Meaning," 99–100.

20. Mugambi cites Smith, E., *African Ideas of God*; and Idowu, *African Traditional Religion*, 51–69, 140–72.

21. Mugambi, Introduction in Taylor, J., *Primal Vision*, xxv, and chapter 6; Mugambi, *FLTR*, 21–22.

22. Mugambi, "Problems of Meaning," 101. Smith identifies three stages: dynamism (belief in impersonal forces), spiritism (belief in non-human spirits or "discarnate" human spirits), and theism (belief in God as controller of natural forces and human destiny). See Smith, E., "Whole Subject," 16–30. See Tylor, *Primitive Culture*; Evans-Pritchard, *Theories of Primitive Religion*; Radin, *Primitive Religion*; McVeigh, *God in Africa*.

tion of an immanent God who "expected moral righteousness as defined by missionary external piety."[23] Such attitudes dominated through the colonial period, into the twentieth century and have been maintained, observes Mugambi, by "many western missionaries in post-colonial Africa."[24] For Mugambi, such conclusions were reached because "Euro-Christian" criteria were used in assessing the "theological adequacy" of African religious and cultural practices.[25] It is assumed, he argues, that Africans are "the most unsophisticated lot among humanity" for they possess no great centers of worship. In response Mugambi argues, "if you have a worldview in which God, humanity and nature are integrated, in which the whole world is your temple, what do you need a temple for?"[26]

In ATRs God is "spatially immanent, but ontologically transcendent."[27] This vision of a "profoundly immanent" God in ATRs "shook missionary anthropology from its foundations" with the publication of Taylor's *Primal Vision*. Mbiti's *Concepts of God in Africa* confirmed this from the perspective of an African scholar.[28] Consequently, "the brief interruption of . . . the European imperial period has not succeeded in distancing Africa's post-colonial present with its pre-colonial past." A "pre-colonial substratum which forms the ontology and ethos of contemporary African individuals and communities" exists, which "the invading religions" with their ideas of "development" and "modernity" were unable to uproot.[29] This "pre-colonial substratum," however, can result in "whitewashed" conversions. For underlying "the veneer" of Christian commitment there exists a "strong African cultural identity." That is to say, as Mbiti recognizes also, Christianity is something that many Africans associate themselves with, but it has not penetrated into their worldview or psyche. If Christianity can be proven to be "supplementary and complimentary" to the traditional substratum, then "African religiosity will be enhanced creatively and re-constructively."[30]

---

23. Mugambi, "Problems of Meaning," 101.

24. Ibid.

25. Ibid., 169.

26. Mugambi, "Churches and Reconstruction," 41.

27. Mugambi, "African Heritage," 170.

28. Mugambi, Introduction in Taylor, J., *Primal Vision*, xxvi. At the same time, E. Bolaji Idowu was rejecting deistic projections onto ATRs from a West African perspective. See Idowu, *Olodumare: God in Yorùbá Belief*.

29. Mugambi, "Religions in East Africa," 20–21. See Mbiti, "African Theology" (*IT*), 141–57.

30. Mugambi, "Religions in East Africa," 26, 21; Mbiti, *ARAP*, 19–21.

As the interaction between colonialism and African agency became a key locus for the emergence of nationalisms and independence, so the interaction between mission Christianity and African theologizing becomes a key locus for African theology. It is unsurprising, therefore, that African theology strives for a position that emphasizes a continuity between tradition and Christianity.[31] For Mbiti, Christianity in its "Western form" has sought to "exterminate" ATRs. In contrast, ATRs have "accommodated" Christianity.[32] For "to be an African (in a traditional society) is *ipso facto* to be religious."[33] In sum, Christianity is indigenous to Africa.[34] In a bid to substantiate these claims Mbiti published *African Religions and Philosophy* (*ARAP*). Alamin M. Mazrui adjudges that it is a seminal contribution to Pan-African thought. It became a "classic" African interpretation of indigenous cosmology, ethics, and traditional theology.[35] Mbiti and, following him, Mugambi argue for a commonality of belief across a wide range of African traditions and practices, which together form ATRs. For before foreign missionaries came Africans had experience and knowledge of God.

God and African Traditional Religions

In their writings, Mbiti and Mugambi lay out a rich vision of God arising from ATRs. That vision begins in the revelation of God as creator. For in traditional societies, God is originator and sustainer of the universe and the topic of creation is most widespread in the myths of ATRs.[36] To talk of God is to conceive of God as creator and to speculate about the origin of life is to talk about God. Consequently, argues Mbiti, "God is beyond the nature of himself being created."[37] God belongs to a distinct ontological category. Consequently, African peoples describe God as the source, first creator, everlasting, the beginner. He is associated with the heavens where he dwells. However, many myths suggest that the heavens had originally been linked to the earth. This linkage had somehow been broken either by humans, ani-

---

31. Mbiti, "Encounter of Christian Faith" (*CC*), 817–18; Mbiti, "God, Sin, and Salvation" (*CCTWC*); Kinney, "Theology of John Mbiti," 66.
32. Mbiti, "Traditional Religions," 62.
33. Mbiti, "Literature and Oral," 91.
34. Mugambi, *CCAL*, 155.
35. Mazrui, "Cultural (Re)Construction," 128.
36. Mbiti, "Creation in African Religion" (*Worlds*), 57–68; Mbiti, "African Names"; Mbiti, "Wandlungen des Afrikanischen Menschenbildes."
37. Mbiti, "Creation in African Religion" (*Worlds*), 58–59. See Mugambi, "Traditional Religion," 14–15; Mugambi, "African Heritage," 170–72.

mals or as the result of some disaster. Despite this, God continues to be the "Sustainer" and "Upholder."[38] This idea is now well accepted:

> A critical examination of the scholarly literature on traditional African religions shows that most African peoples do have a concept of God as the Supreme Being who created the whole universe out of nothing and who is the absolute ground of all being.[39]

If the creation of the universe features in a myth it always precedes the creation of humans. Traditional creation narratives include stories that relate to God creating an original husband and wife, God the potter making humans from clay, and God bringing humans out of a termite hole. Stories of humans being created elsewhere and lowered onto earth are not uncommon.[40] Human creation begins with a husband and wife or with two pairs of humans. God is sometimes given assistance, especially in West African myths, in creating. God is assisted by spirit beings or by other creatures such as the chameleon, lizard, snake, and praying mantis. The moon, sun, and stars also can assist God in creation.[41]

While the original state of humanity might be considered "paradisal," it did not last. This is represented, for example, by the coming of death, the separation of heaven and earth, the loss of food supplies, the coming of disease, conflict, and the loss of knowledge or abilities. The "primal gifts" of immortality, rejuvenation, and resurrection were the most significant losses. Traditionally humans are considered to be "ultimately good." Consequently, the source of evil is nonhuman.[42]

While Mbiti identifies a strong traditional knowledge of God, he identifies a very weak traditional concept of sin. Mbiti concurs with Christian Baëta, "'sin' is really relevant only in so far as it is a potent cause of bodily, mental, and social disorder."[43] Sin, it is argued, relates to the breaking of traditional community codes. If "sin" is committed, the proper relational balance within the community is restored by the offender offering libation or sacrifice. Mbiti sees the biblical witness challenge this traditional understanding by asserting that sin is internal as well as external, is fundamentally

38. Mbiti, "Creation in African Religion" (*Worlds*), 59–64.

39. Gyekye, *Essay on African*, 195–96. Note the Tillichian terminology here.

40. Mbiti, *Concepts of God in Africa*, 161–66; Mbiti, "Encounter of Christian Faith" (*CC*), 818; Mbiti, "Creation in African Religion" (*CJR*), 31–38; Sawyerr, *Creative Evangelism*, 44–65.

41. Mbiti, "Creation in African Religion" (*Worlds*), 58–62.

42. Mugambi, *BBE*, 27. See Smith, E., "Whole Subject," 6–9.

43. Baëta, "Conflict in Mission," 290–99, 293.

against God not community, and the relational balance is set right not by the action of offenders but by the salvific action of God.[44] Mbiti may be correct in what he affirms, however, his denial of a serious concept of sin in traditional society may need to be challenged. For while the "essence of . . . sin lies in the violation of the solidarity of the community" the community's very existence depends on God and therefore sin can be identified, at least indirectly, as against God. It is also the case that in certain communities the sin of an individual is conceived of as an offence against a particular spirit. Harry Sawyerr rightly argues, "if all the spirits are believed to derive their power from God, then sin . . . must inevitably be against God."[45]

From these ontological suppositions Mbiti identifies intrinsic, eternal, and active attributes of God. Intrinsic attributes include omniscience, omnipresence, omnipotence, transcendence, immutability, and immanence. According to Mbiti's research, while there exists a theological tension between the transcendence and immanence of God, in traditional theology there is no evidence that the immanence of God goes to the extreme of pantheism. According to the Lugbara, God can temporarily live in rivers, trees, and mountains. There seems to be no belief however that rivers, trees and mountains are God.[46]

The eternal attributes of God include the belief that he is spirit, self-existent, pre-eminent, cause of all things, invisible, incomprehensible, immutable, and one. The Bacongo assert, "'He is made by no other, no one beyond him is.'" The Karanga, in terms strongly reminiscent of Exodus 3:14, declare, "'It is he that is God'. . . 'He is who he is.'"[47] As has already been seen, in much traditional theology it seems that God is ontologically distinct.[48]

The active attributes of God include conceiving of God as creator, sustainer, sovereign, healer, and savior.[49] God is the Grand Ancestor, the Great Weaver, Carpenter, Originator, Moulder, Architect, Builder, Father/Mother, Grandfather/Grandmother, Parent, Designer.[50] This activity is not unrelated to the conviction that God is moral. God's moral attributes in-

---

44. Mbiti, "'Hearts Cannot be Lent,'" 7–11; Mbiti, "African Concept of Sin," 182–84; Mbiti, "God, Sin, and Salvation" (*CCTWC*), 165–67; Mbiti, "ὁ σωτηρ ἡμῶν," 408–12; Mbiti, *People of God*, 3–7; Mbiti, *Voice of Nine*, 4–6; Mbiti, *Death and the Hereafter*, 8–10.

45. Sawyerr, *Creative Evangelism*, 32, see 43.

46. Mbiti, *COGA*, 3–26; Idowu, *African Traditional Religion*, 152–53.

47. Mbiti, *COGA*, 19–21.

48. See Mbiti, *NTEAB*, 86–87, 138.

49. Mbiti, *COGA*, 19–87, 161–76; Mbiti, "Creation in African Religion" (*Worlds*), 58–60. See Idowu, *African Traditional Religion*, 149–51.

50. Mbiti, "Creation in African Religion" (*Worlds*), 58, 64–67.

clude pity, mercy, and kindness, though love is seldom included. While love is not often directly attributed to God as an abstracted concept, his nature is known through his active involvement with peoples as one who brings comfort and goodness and is constantly faithful. The moral nature of God is seen by some to imply that the universe he created is inherently moral.[51]

God does not abandon humanity. Rather, in ritual and in symbol God's presence is assured. The symbolic becomes, therefore, crucial. Mount Kenya symbolizes the "magnificence of God," an animal without blemish symbolizes the perfection of God, rain symbolizes God's blessing, birth symbolizes both the child's arrival to join the generation of those who are born and the parents' transition into a new stage of elderhood. God's presence is affirmed in the community through such symbols in ritual and ordinary life.[52] Indeed, for Mugambi, the conviction of God's presence with the community largely explains instances of traditional resistance to missionary incursion. Resistance was predicated upon devastatingly clear logic. If God is for us then anyone purporting to speak and act in God's name will champion our interests against the invading powers.[53] Similarly, Mbiti associates the revival of ATRs with political independence and nationalism.[54] God stands on the side of the community. God continues to send rain, give children, and sustain life. Humans can reach God in prayers, sacrifices, offerings, invocations, songs, and rituals. Procreation serves to "keep death at bay."[55] Thus, procreation is the most important aspect of marriage and marriage may often be considered void without children. Having children is to be godlike. For it continues the creativity of God in the world. Children ensure immortality.[56]

Mbiti simply defines worship in the context of traditional religions as acts of "turning to God."[57] Prayer is mostly associated with significant occasions such as rites of passage, harvest, planting, hunting, war, and drought.[58] Intermediaries are common in traditional contexts and chief among them

51. Mbiti, *COGA*, 31–52.

52. See Mugambi, *TAHCC*, 203–7; Mbiti, "Kosmologie und Menschenbild."

53. Mugambi, "Problems of Meaning," 99–100.

54. Mbiti, "Growing Respectability," 56–57. See Muzorew, *Origins and Development*, 55–56.

55. Mbiti, "Creation in African Religion" (*Worlds*), 58–63.

56. Mbiti, *LAMA*, 42–49; Mbiti, *ARAP*, 133. Such theologizing has been rightly criticized in African women's theology. See Oduyoye, "Critique of John Mbiti's View," 341–65.

57. Mbiti, *COGA*, 178. See Taylor, *Primal Vision*, 76–84.

58. Mbiti, *COGA*, 194–217; Mbiti, *NTEAB*, 91–96. See Mugambi and Guy, *CTAC*, 242–44; Mugambi, *TAHCC*, 122–24; Alagoa, "Ijaw as Moral Community," 4–5.

are what is referred to as the living-dead (see chapter 3). In "the ontological structure" of African religions they occupy the position between living humans and the spiritual world. The conviction that such intermediaries are needed, according to Mbiti, arises from the structure of many traditional societies. Socially it is the predominant custom that those considered to hold lower positions need intermediaries to communicate with those in higher positions.[59] In traditional religions, as well as the ancestors, elders, priests, prophets, oracles, diviners, "medicine-men," "witches," and rainmakers are employed to intercede with God on behalf of the people.[60] Such practice is very much understood as bringing benefit to the life of the community now as opposed to the prospect of any eschatological reward.[61]

Mbiti sees potentially fruitful exchange between traditional worship and the practice of the Christian sacraments.[62] The Eucharist relates to and challenges traditional practice. On the one hand, Mbiti argues that the cross eliminates any need for sacrifice as practiced traditionally.[63] On the other hand, Mbiti argues that the Christian sacraments, and the Eucharist especially, provide an opportunity to transform an African understanding of the relationship between the physical and the spiritual:

> The Sacraments form the nexus between the physical and the spiritual worlds, and through the concrete and material realities, eschatological realities become evident and available in the temporal and physical realm . . .[64]

Baptism could potentially enrich the custom of "humanizing." Humanizing is a ceremony where it is believed that infants are incorporated into the community of humans. However, it is Sawyerr who seems to better understand the potential for a contextualizing understanding of baptism when he compares it to the blood initiation rituals:

> . . . Christians . . . belong to a corporate existence built upon the blood-covenant of Jesus Christ. By baptism we become buried into Christ's death . . . The African initiate is told that he must

---

59. See Mbiti, *NTEAB*, 132–33; Sawyerr, *Creative Evangelism*, 96; West, *Academy of the Poor*, 114–18.

60. Mbiti, *COGA*, 220–30.

61. Mbiti, *NTEAB*, 68, 72, 138; Mbiti, *COGA*, 259–60. See Shorter, *African Christian Theology*, 121–22; Idowu, *African Traditional Religion*, 187.

62. See Mbiti, *NTEAB*, 116–26; Sawyerr, *Creative Evangelism*, 92–107.

63. See Mbiti, *COGA*, 179; Oborji, " In Dialogue," 21–22.

64. Mbiti, *NTEAB*, 125.

die to his or her early life, but he must yield to the genius of the cult to live to the tribe . . .[65]

Baptism as initiation affirms the inherent worth of infants as full members of the community (body) as a consequence not of human effort or racial identity but based on the divine activity and grace of God. Indeed, it can be argued that a particular African stress on community can enrich not only the sacraments, but the practice of theology itself.

Despite the seeming dominance of Christian categories in how Mbiti and Mugambi present God in ATR practice they contend for, as has been seen in chapter 2, a theological hybridizing in African Christianity. Indeed, unlike Mugambi, Mbiti is critical of Taylor's *Primal Vision* for being too sympathetic and not critical enough of the African traditional world. For Mbiti, Taylor draws too sharp a distinction between "African" and "European" practices where the latter pollutes the former.[66] Conversion, as has been seen, is not as clear cut an event as missionaries would have hoped for. Syntheses are always being made. For Mugambi "the Christian teaching about God was superimposed on the traditional African concepts."[67] The concept of "God" introduced by missionaries in East Africa was "merged with traditional African concepts of deity." While African names for God amongst African peoples may have differed, there was a general belief that God's power and presence transcended one group. He was God also of the world. Consequently, there was a widespread acknowledgment that different societies with different names for God were worshipping the same deity. Referring both to Mbiti and S. G. Kibicho, Mugambi observes that while people may have been converted to Christianity, not least because of the continued use of the name of their deity, most believed they were worshipping the same God before and after conversion.[68] Christian teachings, brought by missionaries, were "superimposed" upon the African traditional beliefs. Consequently, "fellowships of faith" were established that "were distinct from both the traditional African community and the missionary society, but related to both."[69]

In contrast to Western missionary and anthropological denigration of African religiosity, Mbiti and Mugambi argue that God is present in ATRs. For Mbiti, the God of the Bible whom missionaries assumed they were introducing to Africa "is none other than the God who is already known in

65. Sawyerr, *Creative Evangelism*, 92–93.
66. Mbiti, *ARAP*, 15–16.
67. Mugambi, *ACT*, 44. He cites here Song, *Compassionate God*, 1–20.
68. Mugambi, "Some Perspectives," 105–10. See Kibicho, "Kikuyu Concept."
69. Mugambi, "Some Perspectives," 113.

the framework of our traditional African religiosity."[70] Indeed, "the Western missionary is merely heeding a call whose echo has long reverberated throughout the edifice of African religiosity."[71] As will be seen presently, this theistic contextualism grants ATRs or the ARH theological significance.

The Theological Significance of ATRs: Mbiti and *Praeparatio Evangelica*

Africans believe that God exists and that God is one. Mbiti cites evidence that amongst the Shona and Ndebele there is even a form of trinity.[72] Both Mbiti and Mugambi make comparisons between the Jewish heritage that formed the context for the emergence of Christianity and the African traditional heritage. For Mugambi, the Old Testament patterns of devotion are not dissimilar to African traditions, yet missionaries were keen to quash any such connections being made. Indeed, he asks to what extent Judaism might be considered an African religion, given the scriptural testimony that Moses received his revelation in Africa.[73] He refers to African traditional religion as one of four Abrahamic faiths, as it—like Judaism, Christianity, and Islam—draws its teachings and practices from traditional sources in Upper Egypt.[74] Mbiti writes:

> ... Christianity finds in traditional religion, a common vocabulary by means of which to communicate its own message . . . In a sense, Christianity finds in Africa its OT, its early church situation, and its life in the modern world. Nowhere else in the history and geography of Christianity are these three worlds found simultaneously and coexistentially.[75]

Already, therefore, the purpose of their work is evident. In chapter 2, it has already been seen that because tradition becomes the locus for their theology substantiating the continuity between ATRs and Christianity becomes a crucial task. How this continuity might be understood is the subject at hand presently. For Mbiti such continuity is understood primarily in terms

---

70. Mbiti, "Encounter of Christian Faith" (*CC*), 818. See Sanneh, *Whose Religion*, 18–20; Parrinder, *African Mythology*, 19.

71. Mbiti, "When the Right Hand," 19.

72. Mbiti, *COGA*, 23, 29–30, 91–93. See Posnansky, "Archaeology, Ritual," 31–34; Parrinder, *Religion in Africa*, 39–43.

73. Mugambi, "Religions in East Africa," 4.

74. Mugambi, "Responsible Leadership," 93.

75. Mbiti, "Growing Respectability," 57.

of *praeparatio evangelica* and for Mugambi it is understood in terms of re-mythologization. Both concepts have weaknesses. I will argue that Mbiti's and Mugambi's thought on the continuity between ATRs and Christianity is better understood as correlation or contextualization.

At the 1910 Edinburgh World Missionary Conference it was declared that "primal religions" had almost no significance in terms of acting as a theological *praeparatio* for conversion.[76] In contrast, Mbiti adopts the term to demonstrate the theological significance of ATRs. ATRs "prepared the ground" and were the "basis" for the expansion of Christianity. He applies Hebrews 1:1–2 to the Christian faith in African contexts. Once God communicated through the ancestors. Now he has communicated through Christ.[77] This seems a very straightforward understanding of *praeparatio evangelica* where ATRs are adjudged to have providentially prepared Africans to receive the Gospel of Christ. However, though Mbiti is easily understood to say this and is widely understood to say this, it is not in fact what he understands himself to be arguing.

The term *praeparatio evangelica*, at least in retrospect, is used by Mbiti empirically and not theologically. That is to say, he uses it to simply describe what happened. For Mbiti, the primary emphasis is not on the theological role of tradition-as-preparation as much as it is on the empirical fact that Christianity is predicated upon ATRs in Africa.[78] He does not want to build any theological or providential claim upon this fact. Mbiti is not arguing that this should be how traditional religions are understood theologically or missiologically, nor does he provide any definitive explanation for the conversion of African people to Christianity. Consequently, that ATRs are a source for African theology arises not because of a particular judgment *in abstracto* of their inherent theological nature or worth. It is a source of theology because this forms a large part of the history and context of the African church. In short, Mbiti wants to avoid a supercessionism where ATRs are replaced by Christianity and thus reduced in theological significance. Given this, he would have served his readers better by choosing a different term. Adopting the term *praeparatio evangelica* can create some confusion when readers make it bear more than Mbiti intended.

---

76. Stinton, *Jesus of Africa*, 9; Bediako, "Understanding African Theology," 2.

77. See Mbiti, "Bible and God's Revelation," 7; Mbiti, "Traditional Religions," 62; Mbiti, "Future of Christianity" (*CC*), 390; Mbiti, "African Theology" (*IT*), 150; Mugambi, "Principles and Methods."

78. See Eusebius, *Praeparatio Evangelica*.

Latterly, Mbiti has intimated that "correlation" may have been a better category to adopt over the category and concept of *praeparatio evangelica*.[79] For such a term may be more suited to carry the intercultural communication possible between ATRs and the Christian Gospel that Mbiti wishes to sustain. That such a move away from *praeparatio evangelica* is necessary is seen not least because of how it is associated with Eusebius who uses the term to give an account of the Jewish-Roman-Greco histories that would lead pagans to Christianity. The purpose of the early Christian apologists was to define and defend a Christian identity against pagan or Jewish identities. The purpose of Eusebius's work, in seeking to undermine Greek hegemony and the supposed supremacy of Greek culture, was to argue for "the total rejection of one's ancestral ethnic customs for a new [Christian] way of life."[80] The negative repercussions of adopting the term by Mbiti is further apparent when it is recognized that fundamental to Eusebius's argument in the *Praeparatio* was an ethnic (*ethnē*) construction of Christianity over against inferior ethnicities.[81] While this historical antecedence does not serve Mbiti's adoption of *praeparatio evangelica* well it is even more directly problematic for African theology because of its association with Max Warren's imperialist theology (see chapter 2).[82]

In contrast to the theological, ethnic, and imperialist associations attached to the term *praeparatio evangelica*, Mbiti and Mugambi argue for continuity between ATRs and the Christian gospel. They both reject a Barthian dialectical type of theology, apparently owned by many missionaries, in favor of an analogical approach to theology.[83] In practice, argue these theologians, missionaries who came to Africa maintained that special revelation was found in Christ and that general revelation was found either in pre-Christian Judaism or in Western cultures and philosophies. Non-Western religions, and arguably especially such religions found in Africa, were at odds with Christian revelation. The emerging theology in Africa seeks to rebut this estimation of African religions and the distinction between general and special revelation.[84] Any theology that distinguishes between "general"

---

79. Mbiti, Interview by Heaney, April 8. See Mbiti, "Convergence and Divergence," 1–12.

80. Johnson, *Ethnicity and Argument*, viii, 1–14.

81. Ibid., 11–54.

82. Warren, *Caesar, the Beloved Enemy*, 28.

83. It is not an emphasis owned by missionaries alone. See Kato, "Critique of Incipient Universalism." "Dialectical theology" was not a term Barth approved of, see McCormack, *Karl Barth's Dialectical Theology*. See also Tracy, *Analogical Imagination*.

84. See Musopole, *Being Human*, 11; Mugambi, "Bible and Ecumenism," 74–77.

and "special" revelation is rejected by Mugambi. Mbiti also feels uncomfortable with such a distinction.[85] Again, the apparent stress on christocentrism (see chapter 3) is weakened by other theological commitments.

If God is creator of the universe and sustainer of history then he has created Africa and sustains African history: "many theologians even today maintain the doctrine of the universal providence of God and also, with self-contradiction, subscribe to the theory of 'General' and 'Special' revelation." Election, therefore, understood as the claim that a particular strand of monotheism is God's unique choice for revelation, is particularly troublesome for Mugambi.[86] He writes:

> It is philosophically and theologically inconsistent to maintain that God is the creator and the director of all human history and also, that some peoples are outside that history which God directs.[87]

Given this critique, the theological significance of ATRs for Mugambi will be outlined presently.

The Theological Significance of the African Heritage: Mugambi and Re-Mythologization

As has been seen, Mugambi prefers the term "African Religious Heritage" (ARH). For he is, rightly, concerned that the impression might be given that ATRs can somehow be abstracted from the African way of life. In traditional African thought and practice religion and culture are inseparable. The term "religion" may mislead. For one may be converted to a religion or may choose a religion. In contrast, one does not opt in or out of one's heritage.[88] The ARH should be understood as a "social phenomenon with many dimensions."[89] If Christianity can be proven to be "supplementary and complimentary" to the traditional substratum, then "African religiosity will be

---

85. Mbiti, Interview by Heaney, April 8. See Smith, "Whole Subject," 32–35.

86. Mugambi, "Problems of Meaning," 102, 110 n. 18. See Mwase, "Kuona, An African Perspective."

87. Mugambi, "Problems of Meaning," 102.

88. Mugambi, *TAHCC*, 141–42. Mbiti also, in more recent times, has referred to the term "indigenous religious heritage" as a more general term while still affirming the use of ATR. Mbiti, "'African Religion,' Article for *Encyclopedia of Bioethics*."

89. Mugambi, Introduction in Taylor, J., *Primal Vision*, xix; Mugambi, *TAHCC*, 128. He is here indebted to Smart, *Dimensions of the Sacred*.

enhanced creatively and re-constructively."[90] As will be seen, the theological significance of ARH, for Mugambi, is part of his wider project for African "reconstruction." The focus of this section, however, will be to examine his proposals for "re-mythologization." However, Mugambi's proposal for "re-mythologization" must be seen not only against the backdrop of mission Christianity but also against the backdrop of criticisms of African Christianity within Kenya. For this reason the critique of Christianity by so-called cultural conservatives will be addressed first.

First, Mugambi is not nearly as pessimistic about the future of the African heritage as are Kenyan opponents of Christianity. Mugambi depicts opposition to African Christianity as either cultural-historical or intellectual-philosophical.[91] Ngũgĩ wa Thiong'o argues that the experience of Christianity in Kenya is an aspect of Western culture used to disrupt African heritage in order to facilitate colonialism.[92] Okot p'Bitek, at one time a colleague of Mbiti at Makerere University, doubts whether Christianity is "intellectually satisfying" to the extent that Africans should opt for this faith at the expense of their religious heritage, which, prior to the coming of missionaries, gave meaning for centuries. He argues that Christianity is theologically incoherent (he is particularly disparaging of the doctrine of the Trinity) ethically incoherent (it is socially divisive because it divides communities into "believers" and non-believers), and distorts ATRs for its own use.[93] Consequently, many missionaries and African cultural conservatives agree that African traditional heritage and Christianity are incompatible. However, Mbiti and Mugambi recognize the danger in conceiving of the debate in such binary terms.

For Mugambi, ARH "adjusted," "adapted," and "blended" various influences during the dominance of Mission Christianity and colonialism.[94] What results, for both Christians and non-Christians, is a "new way of life" that is neither completely "traditional" nor completely "European."[95] Culture is, therefore, dynamic. It tends to change, or develop, or dissipate.[96]

---

90. Mugambi, "Religions in East Africa," 21; Mbiti, *ARAP*, 19–21.

91. Mugambi, "Some Perspectives," 210–38.

92. Ibid., 212–22. See wa Thiong'o, *Decolonising the Mind*, 5–25.

93. p'Bitek, *African Religions*, 52–69, 80–120. See Mugambi, "Some Perspectives," 213–14, 226–28, 231–38.

94. As has already been noted, Mbiti also recognizes this hybridity in his early work and refers positively to "syncretism" (see chapter 2).

95. Mugambi, *TAHCC*, 128.

96. Mugambi, *CTSR*, 20.

Consequently, while ARH remains foundational to Mugambi's practice of African theology this does not make him a cultural conservative.[97]

In Kenya, there are both socially "conservative" and socially "transformative" practices.[98] However, it is not possible to return to the past. Equally, because of the resilience of the African heritage, it is not possible to ignore or suppress the foundational dynamics of traditional societies. Rather than moving forward on the basis of conservative or transformative social policies, what is needed is re-mythologization (see below).[99] African Christians belong to wider communities which have, argues Mugambi, their foundations in traditional practices.

> If their Christian experience is going to be meaningful and effective, they cannot afford to cut themselves off from the rest of the community or from their own cultural and religious past. The Gospel should help them to live more fully, more abundantly, *as Africans*.[100]

> ... religion has a prominent place as the norm-setter in the long term project of social reconstruction. Africa, particularly, needs the services of the churches and other religious groups, because they are among the social institutions having the facilities and resources for leadership development. At a time when state apparatus in many African countries seems desolate, the churches and other religious agencies can, and should, provide a stabilizing and catapulting influence, on African societies.[101]

---

97. See Mugambi, *TAHCC*, 189–91. Teaching the African heritage is not, he argues, destructive of the African Christian faith. Rather, the teaching of the African heritage is the "foundation" for Christian faith. "A person whose house is founded on a rock will not fall: An African's rock is his own background. This is the attitude which I recommend as a basis for African Christian theology" (p. 191).

98. Mugambi is clear that "conservative forces" are not always of "negative value" any more than "transformative forces" are always positive. A society cannot be "totally dynamic." See Mugambi, *RSCR*, 37; Mugambi, *CTSR*, 54–55.

99. Mugambi, "African Heritage," 167–68; Mugambi, "Bible and Ecumenism," 75; Mugambi, *FLTR*, 77–78. See Mugambi, *RSCR*, 30–31, here Mugambi also identifies cultural reformers, iconoclasts, cynics, and prophets. However one understands Mugambi's notion of re-mythologization, it is inevitable that it will be closely related to his proposals for a theology of reconstruction. Consequently, while aware of the close relationship of the two practices, this section, within the overall theme of the present chapter, will seek to establish what Mugabmi means by re-mythologization independent of reconstruction.

100. Mugambi, *ACT*, 10.

101. Mugambi, *RSCR*, 46.

Theological reconstruction is a project of re-mythologization, in which the theologian thus engaged, discerns new symbols and new metaphors in which to re-cast the central Message of the Gospel.[102]

Second, Mugambi defines "re-mythologization" in contrast to his understanding of Rudolf Bultmann's demythologization and the problem of biblical literalism in Africa.

> . . . the Demythologizers would like the Bible to be stripped of all myths, so that the *Kerygma*—the essential Message—could be laid bare . . . this approach leads nowhere, because most of the essential Message is coded in myths, metaphors, parables and analogies . . . Myth is indispensable in cultural constructions of reality. At one cultural period one set of myths may be discarded, but another set immediately takes over. Thus, the so-called myth-free interpretation of *Kerygma* in Bultmann's method only re-casts the Gospel in a new mythological garb. The anti-metaphysical positivism of the late 19th and early 20th centuries to which both Bultmann and Barth succumbed, produced a new metaphysics, which was just as mystifying as the previous world-views . . .
>
> It is reasonable . . . to suggest that *re-mythologization* would be a more effective response when metaphors and idioms become obsolescent, irrelevant or out of context. Theological reconstruction is a project of re-mythologization, in which the theologian thus engaged, discerns new symbols and new metaphors in which to re-cast the central Message of the Gospel.[103]

Mugambi fails to identify that while he and Bultmann have distinct judgments on the nature of myth (a term that Bultmann did not use consistently), both are concerned with the practice of making Christianity heard in more recent contexts.[104] Despite this, the focus here is to be clear on what it is that Mugambi is proposing for a practice of re-mythologization. Unfortunately, as is too common in Mugambi's writing, he identifies a seemingly new departure or development yet provides less than full elucidation of it. Re-mythologization is one such underdeveloped idea. As will be seen, in chapter 6, re-mythologization is sublated into his proposals for a theology of reconstruction. Indeed, in a recent explication of reconstructionism he

---

102. Mugambi, "Bible and Ecumenism," 75.

103. Ibid., 74–75. See Mugambi, *FLTR*, 36–37.

104. See Jaspers, "Myth and Religion," 144; Rowland and Corner, *Liberating Exegesis*, 69–74.

entirely omits any mention of re-mythologization.[105] It is, nonetheless, a term pregnant with significance especially against the backdrop of the ARH. It shall be proposed presently that, like Mbiti, he is involved in a contextualizing process but, unlike Mbiti, he is concerned with the identification or development of new myths for communicating the hope of the Christian gospel.[106] In other words, Mugambi's concept of re-mythologization, in contrast to Mbiti's contextualizing, identifies the ARH as an ongoing and dynamic reality and dialogue partner for African theology.

Mugambi's proposals for *myth-making* begin with Bultmann. For Bultmann, the gospel is not myth nor does it need mythical expression in the modern world. In a context where people no longer believe in a "spirit world" or demonic powers the gospel can still have significance.[107] De-mythologization "implies the removal or elimination of myth in the act of interpreting, i.e., understanding and communicating, the essential meaning of the Bible."[108] Myth is not of the essence of the gospel. For Mugambi, myth is of the essence of the gospel. Consequently, while Bultmann seeks re-interpretation that excludes the mythic, Mugambi seeks re-mythologization which integrates new (African) myths. In Bultmann the essential *kerygma* must be detached from biblical mythologizing. For expressing the *kerygma* in mythical language may lead to an obscuration of the essential Christian message.[109] For Mugambi, expressing the Christian message always necessitates myth. For the Christian message is always experienced in particular contexts through particular myths.

Mugambi argues that myth "bears truth in a special way which cannot be duplicated by science and logic."[110] In reference to Karl Jaspers, Mugambi defines myth as having historical, sacred, and symbolic elements. Myth tells a story expressing intuitive insights as opposed to universal concepts. It does not "cloak" any "general" ideas which could be better conceived and comprehended abstractly. Myth does not give voice to empirical concerns but rather relates sacred stories and vision concerning divinity. Myth is symbolic in that it carries meaning that is inextricably linked to the very language of myth. It cannot be "interrupted" or reduced to something less but must be grasped within the worlds of myth and re-interpreted in other

---

105. See Mugambi, "Theology of Reconstruction," 139–49.

106. See Dedji, *Reconstruction and Renewal*, 57–59.

107. Rowland and Corner, *Liberating Exegesis*, 73.

108. Morgan, "Rudolf Bultmann," 78. See in the same volume, Thiselton, "Biblical Theology," 520–37.

109. Morgan, "Rudolf Bultmann," 78; Thiselton, "Biblical Theology," 525.

110. Mugambi, *FLTR*, 37.

myths.¹¹¹ Given the continuity and discontinuity between Mugambi and Bultmann, it becomes clear how the African heritage would play a part in Mugambi's re-mythologization. For the African heritage could be seen to provide the mythic materials for gospel hope in Africa.¹¹²

> ... Africa must begin to make new myths, and re-interpret old ones, for the survival of its own peoples. The myth of a vanishing people, must be replaced by the myth of a resurgent, or resilient people. The myth of a desperate people must be replaced by the myth of a people full of hope. The myth of a hungry people must be replaced by the myth of a people capable of feeding itself, and so on.¹¹³

It is not clear how these so-called myths and counter-myths relate to Jaspers's and Bultmann's understanding of myth. It appears that Mugambi is not using the terms symmetrically. It also seems that these "myths" could easily be understood in non-mythic and "rational" terms. While drawing on myth as understood by Bultmann and Jaspers he will not be limited to using it in their terms. Consequently, he simply seeks to emphasize that theologians must provide "myths" to engender hope in Africa. If this is the case, then it becomes clearer how he can sublate re-mythologization into a theology of reconstruction concerned not only with personal and ecclesial reconstruction, but with cultural reconstruction also (see chapter 6). For such myths of hope are part of a cultural reconstruction needed after colonialist and imperialist subjugation. Nonetheless, Dedji's poignant observation makes clear the danger of such a generalized appeal to myth-making:

> ... one may wonder the extent to which theologians can go on forging new myths without giving support to despotic leaders ... Considering that African people from West to East have gone through disillusioning experiences with 'great' political myth-makers, can African theologians start afresh that business of myth-making regardless of people's experiences?¹¹⁴

---

111. Ibid.; Jaspers, "Myth and Religion," 144.

112. Mugambi writes of "re-cycling" traditional values. Such a practice has positive (ecological) connotations though the outcome would be unpredictable. Mugambi, *FLTR*, 78. See Kalu, "*Sankofa*: Pentecostalism." He argues, somewhat convincingly, that it is the traditional heritage and not urbanization or globalization that explains the growth of Pentecostalism.

113. Mugambi, *FLTR*, 37–38.

114. Dedji, *Reconstruction and Renewal*, 58.

As will be seen in chapter 6, this danger is particularly real for Mugambi who, at one time, appealed to Daniel arap Moi's political philosophy of *Nyayoism*.

If Bultmann provokes Mugambi's proposal of re-mythologization then, *prima facie*, it is Tillich's project of re-casting or re-modelling that provides him with the means to re-mythologization.[115] Indeed, it is in the context of rejecting Bultmann's de-mythologizing that Mugambi introduces Tillich. Arguing for his project of re-mythologization he writes:

> Paul Tillich, perhaps more than any other 20th century theologian, succeeded in this task of theological re-casting and re-modelling . . . These new metaphors were inspired by Tillich's endeavour to come to terms with North American appropriations of Christianity . . .[116]

According to Mugambi—making reference to ground of being, ultimate concern, and denial of courage to be—Tillich is a successful re-mythologizer.[117] While Tillich's success has since been questioned his purpose is clearly understood by Mugambi as seeking to make Christianity "understandable and persuasive" to modern skeptics. Mugambi seeks to do the same for Africans who have become victims of the brutality of that same modernity.[118]

---

115. Dedji states the obvious when he observes that, "Mugambi is among those theologians who are still influenced by Tillich." However, beyond referencing Mugambi's own admission that he admires Tillich and a correlative method, he provides little in the way of substantiating this claim. More than this is needed. For a theologian can claim to admire another theologian and even claim to adopt another's method while actually misunderstanding the other, failing to adopt his or her methods, or reinterpreting the method for a different context and use. Mugambi does not adopt Tillich straightforwardly or systematically. It is unsurprising, therefore, that Dedji does not explore the relationship in any detail. However, there are more Tillichian influences present in Mugambi and Tillichian prospects in Mugambi's idea of re-mythologization than is apparent to Dedji. He focuses, rightly, on the dominant proposals for "reconstruction" (which will be dealt with in chapter 6 of this study), but in doing so may too quickly pass over the significance of "re-mythologization." See Dedji, *Reconstruction and Renewal*, 57.

116. Mugambi, "Bible and Ecumenism," 75. What he might mean by obsolescence and irrelevance in a post-Cold-War and post-colonial context will be dealt with in chapter 6.

117. Martin Buber is also cited as an example of successful re-mythologization. Mugambi, "Bible and Ecumenism," 75–76.

118. Mugambi, "Theology of Reconstruction," 139–40. See Tillich, *Systematic Theology*, 34–68. That is not to deny that the brutality of modernity played a foundational role in Tillich's work. See Bayer, "Tillich as Systematic," 19. For responses and critiques see, for example, Kelsey, "Paul Tillich," 87; Tracy, *Blessed Rage*, 45–46.

Mugambi argues that in debates on resilience and change too often the focus is on the "transitory"[119] elements of culture (which include individual and family interests, social amenities, communal customs, societal infrastructure).[120] The aspects of culture that are particularly resilient, and one can assume can therefore be bearers of re-mythologization, are basic worldviews, basic values, and social structures.[121] Myth-making is, then, part of the reconstruction of culture, which becomes one of Mugambi's three levels for a theology of reconstruction.

Worldview is a disputed term with a particular history in European philosophy and theology.[122] Nonetheless, Mugambi employs it to define an African heritage that is "an integrated phenomenon, from which humankind is inseparable, whether physically or intellectually."[123] A worldview is the "epistemological foundation of every culture." Colonialism may have "seriously damaged" all other "layers of culture" but the foundation remains in-

---

119. Tillich argues that theologians should not be concerned with "preliminary concerns." Such concerns include judgment on the aesthetic value of art, the scientific value of a physical theory or medical methodologies, the best methods of social reconstruction, or about politics. Tillich, *Systematic Theology*, 12–13, see 61–62.

120. Tillich makes a distinction between "preliminary concerns" and ultimate concern. Indeed, he defines as the first criterion of theology the distinguishing between preliminary concerns and ultimate concern. Ultimate concern is that which "determines our being or not-being." Ultimate concern is that which has the power to threaten or save human beings. According to Tillich, the transitory or preliminary concerns can become "bearers" and "vehicles of the ultimate concern" (Tillich, *Systematic Theology*, 13). Tillich writes: "In and through every preliminary concern, the ultimate concern can actualize itself. Whenever this happens, the preliminary concern becomes a possible object of theology. But theology deals with it only in so far as it is a medium, a vehicle, pointing beyond itself" (Tillich, *Systematic Theology*, 12–14). Following Tillich's apologetic or answering theology (Tillich, *Systematic Theology*, 6–8), it appears that Mugambi will seek to get at "ultimate concern" in African contexts through the creation of new myths (Tillich, *Systematic Theology*, 6, 12). However, it is not clear that this is Mugambi's theological rationale. Nor is it clear that he is interested in meeting Tillich's first criterion of theology despite his identification of the "transitory" (Tillich, *Systematic Theology*, 12). Nonetheless, he does specifically identify aspects of African culture, which can become vehicles for re-mythologization and thus, in broad terms, he begins from a Tillichian position.

121. Mugambi, "African Heritage," 169, 174; Mugambi, *TAHCC*, 114–39. See Tillich, *Systematic Theology*, 38–47, 59–66.

122. I have explored the contextual, philosophical, and post-colonial problems with the concept elsewhere. Heaney, "Moral Scepticism." See also Naugle, *Worldview: History of a Concept*, 58–64, 332–33.

123. Mugambi, "African Heritage," 169. In delineating the non-transitory aspects of culture, Mugambi's cited sources include Koestler, *Sleepwalkers*; Birch, "Nature, Humanity and God."

tact. In this context, Mugambi makes an appeal to a Pan-African worldview as the means to decolonization and as the hope for African "renaissance."

Basic value-systems are build upon the foundational "layer." It is not clear how this layer is "derived" practically and logically from an African worldview but this is what Mugambi claims. For Mugambi, an emerging African value-system will be superior to the now defunct value-system of "Euro-Hellenism." Such a value system, argues Mugambi, seeks dominance over nature, operates on the basis of a mechanistic cosmology that is dehumanizing and un-ecological, unjustly vaunts the "triumphs" of science, and conceives of God either as object or concept. In contrast, an Africa value system is more ecological because it emphasizes the integration and unity of human and non-human creation, because it places God and community above the individual, because of economic practices that place more emphasis on service and human relations, because time, space, and matter are not first and foremost saleable commodities transferred by contract but are transacted ritually and symbolically.[124] There is a fair amount of unnecessary dichotomizing involved here but despite this, and maybe because of it, Mugambi's proposals for re-mythologization may become clearer.

Social structures make up the "third layer" in the "form and content" (Tillichian terms)[125] of every culture. By this, Mugambi is referring to politics, economics, ethics, aesthetics, and metaphysics as "components" of culture. Religion (which includes ritual symbolism, liturgies, doctrine, and communal organization) belongs to this layer of culture. It serves as the "custodian" of the society's worldview and value-system. Imperialism sought to replace African social structures with structures imported from the metropolitan center. However, while transitory practices in Kenya

124. Mugambi, "African Heritage," 171–72. See Mugambi, *TAHCC*, 111–50.

125. Tillich distinguishes between import (*Gehalt*), form (*Form*), and content (*Inhalt*). Form is the media for expressing content and import (e.g., a painting, social movement, organization, or a whole culture). Content is the objective meaning expressed in a given form (e.g., the subject of a painting or the principles of a social movement). Import is "meaning-giving power." It is that which is brought to expression in form. It is ". . . the sense . . . the spiritual substantiality, which gives form its meaning . . ." (Schweiker, "Theology of Culture," 143. See Tillich, *Systematic Theology*, 178–79). Import can shatter form because form can become inadequate to import. "The form is broken open to the power that endows it and its content with meaning." (Schweiker, "Theology of Culture," 143). Therefore, the mission of a theology of culture, according to Tillich, is to "trace this process in every sphere and creation of culture and to bring it to expression." The project is theological because the locus for reflection is import in contrast to the cultural sciences that reflect from the perspective of form (Schweiker, "Theology of Culture," 143). For Tillich every "domain can express the religious import, and in so doing can become theonomous, can manifest the depth of meaning-giving power in culture" (Schweiker, "Theology of Culture," 144).

were changed or disrupted the more foundational components of culture remain largely unchanged.[126] The transitory can, therefore, become re-mythologized to take account of new circumstances while at the same time remaining firmly rooted in the African heritage. In order to illustrate this, Mugambi makes reference to rites of passage:

> . . . the way ahead is for us to find ways and means in which to make the 'rites of passage' one of the foci for the promotion of cultural consciousness on a national scale, as a contribution towards a strong foundation for self-propelled national development and integration.[127]

An African Christianity and theology will need to draw on re-emergent values in order to provide re-mythologization which will meet the needs of a modern African nation.[128]

> Cultural renaissance is neither a blind return to the past, nor a blind leap into the future. The past is re-incarnated into the present, and owing to that re-incarnation, visions of the future are facilitated.[129]

It is only a common appreciation of the African heritage that will unify African nations. The African heritage will prevent the ongoing alienation between "the African elite" and the needs, beliefs, and practices of the majority in Africa. The acceptance of development or globalization arises, he argues, when Africans are distanced, through education, from the values of traditional African societies.[130] Consequently, while Mbiti and Mugambi are committed to making African traditional theologizing part of their work it is Mugambi who has a more expansive rationale. Arguably, it is Mugambi's bringing together such traditional thought and contemporary socio-economic conditions that best demonstrates a holistic theology reflecting traditional understandings of the integrated nature of life, thus marking it distinct from the North Atlantic paradigm of theologizing. Indeed, Mugambi envisages traditional wisdom as critiquing foreign paradigms of education, theology, and economics.[131]

---

126. Mugambi, "African Heritage," 172.

127. Ibid., 178.

128. Mugambi, "Bible and Ecumenism," 75. See also Mbiti, *LAMA*, 9–17.

129. Mugambi, "African Heritage," 165.

130. Mugambi, "Religions in East Africa," 16–17; Mbiti, *ARAP*, 282–98. See Tillich, *Systematic Theology*, 12.

131. Mugambi, "Religions in East Africa," 14–17.

Mugambi does not only associate the subjugation of African traditional heritage with cultural and theological issues but also with wider societal issues. For as a result of schooling, which continues to be shaped by colonial and neo-colonial assumptions, African elites are becoming alienated from their cultures and are therefore failing to analyze problems correctly and are failing to construct solutions that will have long term viability for all. Mugambi suggests that the "technological stagnation" in tropical Africa is primarily ethical not financial.[132]

> It is not the lack of a resource base that causes technological stagnation or retrogression. Africa is rich in a wide diversity of resources. The colonial legacy has ensured that these resources are extracted for the benefit of the industries mainly, though not exclusively, in the North Atlantic.[133]

For Mugambi, the contextualization of theology is a very practical matter indeed. For it is part of reconnecting with the vast majority of people in Africa who continue to "live according to traditional values and norms."[134] Indeed, he can say that in "the context of Christianity" the aim of reflecting on the African heritage is "to establish the base on which the Gospel will be proclaimed."[135] This proclamation and "propagation" does not exclude socio-economic renewal. For he argues that subjugation in one (cultural) area has repercussions for the way a society interacts in other areas. Consequently, Mugambi's contextualism does not succumb to the criticism that might be leveled at Mbiti's. For it would be possible to argue that these traditional religious understandings are now on the wane in an increasingly urbanized Africa. Mugambi will not allow this. For, he argues, not only that the vast majority of Africans dwell in rural settings but that even after conversion to Christianity the traditional worldview continues to dominate.

It appears that the promise of Mugambi's re-mythologization, especially in relation to ATRs, remains largely unfulfilled. To what extent his theology of reconstruction, which sublates his proposed practice of re-mythologization into proposals for cultural reconstruction, is successful will be seen in chapter 6. Before that, however, a constructive move to counter what constitutes a move away from African traditional religious experience will be proposed.

---

132. Mugambi, "Responsible Leadership," 84–96.
133. Ibid., 86.
134. Ibid., 85–86.
135. Mugambi, *TAHCC*, 186.

Criticisms of Myth-Making and Correlation: Religion, Unity, and Power

Three critical points on the way in which the theological methods of Mbiti and Mugambi move their theologies away from the particularism of traditional religious experience can be identified. These criticisms relate to the priority given to "religion," to the hypothesis of unity, and to power relations.

First, the priority Mbiti and Mugambi give to "religion" can be questioned.[136] The category itself is problematic (as they both recognize).[137] However, it is the assumption that it is in religion (even if seen as "holistic") that God is present that is particularly problematic. There seems no theological necessity for concluding that religion is the locus for God's revelation. Indeed, there are biblical and theological evidence for just the opposite (Isa 1:10–17, 58:6–11; Hos 6:4–6; Matt 25:31–45).[138]

> It is in the temple that we find God, but in a temple of living stones, of closely related persons, who together make history and fashion themselves. God is revealed in history, and it is likewise in history that persons encounter the Word made flesh . . . God's temple is human history; the 'sacred' transcends the narrow limits of the places of worship.[139]

Mbiti especially has chosen to build an African theology on "the places of worship." He is keen to distinguish the theological from the political where he is concerned with the former. However, this seems only possible if a prior assumption about the secular and religious is affirmed (even if only implicitly).[140] Worse still, discounting the political may make a focus on ATRs, worldview, or philosophy into a "diversion" from the exploitation of Africa.[141] Mugambi's re-mythologization, apparently drawing from ATRs, is meant to have social impact. However, if re-mythologization is defined in Jasperian terms it will take his further away from the particularism of African traditional religious experience. For Jaspers at least, re-mythologization includes a rejection of any philosophical naivety which assumes

---

136. See Rieger, *Remember the Poor*, 218–20.
137. See also Cobb, "Beyond Pluralism," 84; Ray, *African Religions*, xii–xiv.
138. See also Gutiérrez, *Theology of Liberation*, 106–20.
139. Ibid., 115.
140. Rowland, *Revelation*, 135. See Rieger, *Christ and Empire*, 313. Mbiti is not alone as an East African theologian explicitly eschewing the political. See Nyamiti, *Studies in African Theology*, 3–7. A notable exception is Mbiti, "Church and State."
141. Houtondji, *African Philosophy*, 37.

that ancestors, spirits, and demons exist in realist terms.¹⁴² Mugambi does not explicitly state that he recognizes such reification and its attendant antirealism. One might be forgiven for detecting it, however, in the rather facile examples of "myth" which he does provide. If this is the case, then the importance he, like Mbiti, places on ATRs does not include treating them in their own terms. There is a danger, therefore, that the move away from African traditional religious experience in an emphasis on ATRs and a generalized contextualization is itself a form of de-mythologization.

Second, the hypothesis of unity for ATR is widely criticized.¹⁴³ That is to say, a "basic cultural unity" in Africa that can act as a source and foundation for African theology to draw upon and build upon is rejected by critics. For the purported unity is formulated for the theological purpose of theistic contextualization. Okot p'Bitek plainly (over)states the move away from experience such theologizing exhibits, "The African deities of the books, clothed with the attributes of the Christian God, are, in the main, creations of the students of African religions. They are all beyond recognition to the ordinary Africans in the countryside."¹⁴⁴ Kwame Gyekye, reviewing *ARAP*, accuses Mbiti of "generalizations, over-simplifications, premature judgments and sparse analysis."¹⁴⁵ Paulin Hountondji rejects the very idea of an underlying "African" worldview as pseudo-philosophy. He argues it emerges not from African wisdom but from "Western ethnocentrism," which is in danger simply of expressing the dominant views of a particular context or particular philosopher or, in this case, theologian.¹⁴⁶ In contrast, Benjamin Ray argues that the depiction of a "unified traditional religion" can be understood as part of wider nationalist and pan-African discourses in the aftermath of independence.¹⁴⁷ Takatso Mofokeng is critical of Mbiti's attempt at "rehabilitating" African religions. His criticism comes close to the present author's criticism in light of the methodological shift from his early work. The validity of ATRs, argues Mofokeng, is directly proportionate to its application to contemporary contexts and the goal of liberation.¹⁴⁸

142. Jaspers, "Myth and Religion," 147.

143. Shorter, *African Christian Theology*, 46–48; Hountondji, *African Philosophy*, 60. See Shaw, "Invention of 'African Traditional Religion'"; Ray, *African Religions*, xii; Cox, *Rational Ancestors*, 15.

144. p'Bitek, *African Religions*, 88.

145. Gyekye, *Essay on African*, 190–91.

146. See Hountondji, *African Philosophy*, 58, 75–76; Shaw, "Invention of 'African Traditional Religion.'"

147. Ray, *African Religions*, xi–xii. See Platvoet, "From Object to Subject"; Cox, *Rational Ancestors*, 15.

148. Mofokeng, "Black Theology," 49.

Third, Mercy Oduyoye concurs with Mbiti and Mugambi. African "God-talk" begins in and with ATRs.[149] However, a stress on ATRs or African heritage may reinforce the *status quo* especially as it relates to the power of men in African societies.[150] For culture, tradition, or heritage is "frequently a euphemism to protect actions that require analysis" and delay liberative praxis which would ensure the full humanity of women.[151] For example, in relation to marriage, and its apparent stress on procreation, she rightly notes that there is the real possibility that African theology provides further sanction for oppression:

> The extremely harsh language used about women who cannot bear children explains the lengths to which parents will go to seek aid for daughters caught in this vicious assessment of the purpose of woman-being. Mbiti reports, '. . . whatever other qualities she might possess, her failure to bear children is worse than genocide . . . When she dies she will be forgotten.' 'The childless wife,' he continues, 'bears a scar which nothing can erase. It is an irreparable humiliation for which there is no source of comfort in traditional life.'[152]

Oduyoye's identification of a "vicious assessment" of the purpose of womanhood is well made. She simply asks, does immortality in African theology have anything to do with God? If, as is seen above, Mbiti emphasizes "immortality through procreation," is this not a dangerous truncated version of Christian hope (one which is at least as dangerous as the eschatology of mission Christianity examined in chapter 3 of the present work)? As long as (traditional) beliefs associating procreation with immortality and remembering one's ancestors remain "I do not see a way out."[153] Women are left asking, "whose voice is the voice of the ancestor?"[154]

---

149. Oduyoye, *Introducing African Women's Theology*, 39.
150. See Oduyoye, *Hearing and Knowing*, 56–76.
151. Oduyoye, *Introducing African Women's Theology*, 13, 22–38.
152. Oduyoye, "Critique of John Mbiti's View," 349. See Mbiti, *LAMA*; Mbiti, *ARAP*, 174–94.
153. Oduyoye, "Critique of John Mbiti's View," 355.
154. Oduyoye, *Introducing African Women's Theology*, 25.

Prospects for Myth-Making and Contextualization: Experiential Dialogue

The criticism of moving away from the particular in emphasizing the category of religion and of then defining an abstracted and generalized ATR that marginalizes those who suffer because of traditional taboos is well made. Nevertheless, critics do not often recognize that Mbiti and Mugambi are themselves aware of some of these problems. Both Mbiti and Mugambi are aware of the difficulties of applying the term "religion" to Africa. Indeed, in *ARAP* Mbiti simply refuses to define it other than to say, "for Africans it is an ontological phenomenon; it pertains to the question of existence or being."[155] That is to say, religion is not something that Africans chose. Rather, he argues, all of life is understood within the framework and with reference to the religious dimension of existence including God, spirits, and humans whether as part of the ancestors, the living-dead, or the living.[156]

Mbiti is aware of the danger of the hypothesis of unity. He states in his introduction to *ARAP*, "Traditional religions are not universal: they are tribal or national."[157] Because such traditions have historically been undervalued and are complex and dynamic the knowledge of them is incomplete. It should be noted that both the singular (ATR) and plural (ATRs) are used by Mbiti. More accurately, however, even when the singular is used there is the recognition of plurality. Thus, when the singular is used it is best understood as a "collective singular." ATR refers to the "religious systems" of Africans that have "evolved" over centuries with neither founding figures nor written scriptures.[158] Mbiti plainly states: "no formal unity" exists for ATR. Rather, there are "common elements" that, at this stage of the research, justify a broad definition of ATR.[159] Mugambi appeals to Mbiti's defence and adds his own.[160] Despite the diversity between European and American cultures, languages, and histories it is still common place to speak of the West and Western thought. For him, the introduction of apparent diversity in African traditional practice as a foil against ATR, especially if identified by those from outside Africa, he associates with the "divide and rule" ideology of colonialism.[161] Despite this appeal, by Mugambi, to power relations at work it

---

155. Mbiti, *ARAP*, 19.
156. Ibid., 1–7, 17–21. See Mugambi, "Religions in East Africa," 3–8.
157. Mbiti, *ARAP*, 5.
158. Mbiti, "Spirituality in African Religion," 1.
159. Mbiti, "When the Right Hand," 3.
160. Mugambi, *ACT*, 3–7.
161. Mugambi, *TAHCC*, 136.

is here that they are weakest when it comes to the implications for abstracting ATR from experience.

A constructive move will be proposed presently to counter the move away from the particularism of experience identified in this chapter. In brief, a reading or dialogue between experience and experience and not tradition and tradition will be proposed. Such dialogue will provide a fresh approach largely bypassing foreign categories while at the same time identifying a place for the theological agency of African traditional religionists as well as theological agency for Christians.

Mbiti and Mugambi often affirm the common Christian assertion that at the center of faith and experience is the person of Jesus Christ. Yet, despite such christocentric language they pursue a theistic as opposed to christological contextualization with ATRs. An experiential dialogue begins with the person and experience of Christ as represented in the Gospels and the practice and experience of African traditional religionists. In a bid to illustrate this and begin to define further the practice of experiential dialogue the recent work of Pieter Craffert is used. For Craffert seems to provide direction for what an experiential dialogue might be and do in an African context.

Craffert argues that "placing" Jesus in first century Galilee means more than "situating" him in a religious system (Judaism). Place, as Mbiti and Mugambi recognize, is also geographical and cultural. Craffert's particular contribution is to place Jesus within a traditional (in a sense close to how Mbiti and Mugambi understand African *Traditional* Religion) framework. This "shamanic complex" (which it can be argued relates well to African traditional religious experience),[162] argues Craffert, has distinct explanatory power. For it offers a framework for understanding Jesus as a "social personage," it coheres well with the practices of Jesus (recorded in the Gospels), it adds depth to understandings of his relationships to a particular community, culture, and historical context, and it allows cross-cultural and inter-religious comparison.

A shamanic complex describes the practice of a "religious specialist who experiences ASCs [Altered States of Consciousness] and who acts as inspired diviner and healer, and who can also control the spirits."[163] The

---

162. Indeed the shamanic is already a category utilized in the study of the experiences of African traditional religionists. See, for example, van Beek, "Innocent Sorcerer."

163. Craffert, *Life of a Galilean Shaman*, 163, see 135–68. He defines ASCs in terms of biological states (it is normal to the extent that with the right stimuli an ASC is possible for any human being), psychosocial phenomenon (ASCs are cultural events), and in terms of how such states are induced (induction methods vary widely but might be seen to come about as a result of either physiological (sensory) deprivation or

characteristics of such religious practice includes controlled ASC experiences, visions, possession, journeys, and "social functions" including healing, mediating, prophecy, divination, exorcism, and control of spirits. Such practices take place within a distinct milieu and make the shamanic figure discernible from prophets, priests, healers, sages, or rabbis. Unlike other religious social types, shamanic practices combine ASCs with other roles not usually combined in other actors in a traditional community (healing, control of spirits, divination, and didactic functions). Craffert takes care to define shamanic practice and then to put that into dialogic relationship with the ministry of Jesus. He concludes that Jesus was a Galilean shamanic figure and that an anthropological historical approach treats seriously his reported ministry.[164] In short, relating such a reading of the Gospels with the experience in traditional religion means that the ministry of Jesus is more directly contextualized with experience in ATRs than either Mbiti's or Mugambi's approach provides. If this type of approach was adopted it would also come closer to treating ATRs on their own terms and of viewing, in this case, the ministry of Jesus through such a lens.[165]

Of course Craffert's approach has similar weaknesses, and is therefore open to similar criticisms, to the approach Mbiti and Mugambi take to ATRs. For as Mbiti and Mugambi approach ATRs in etic terms, so too does Craffert define the ministry of Jesus in etic (shamanic) terms and depends upon a hypothesis of unity (shamanic practices, which vary widely, have a unity that allows comparison and the adoption of a general term).[166] Nonetheless, had a Craffert-type approach been adopted, a contextualizing that brings the Christ of the Gospels closer to the practice of African traditional religious communities might have been achieved. It would appear from the writings of Mbiti and Mugambi that such is their intent even though, as has been seen in this chapter, the very opposite (in a move away from the particularism of experience) is what happens. Suffice it to say, at this juncture, the practice of such experiential dialogue will be further explored especially in relation to a symbolic approach to christology in the following chapter.

---

physiological (sensory) overstimulation, see 147–55, 165–66. For the African context see Mbiti, "African Traditional Medicine," 313–16; Mbiti, "God, Dreams and African Militancy."

164. Distinct from either a positivist or postmodernist approach. See Craffert, *Life of a Galilean Shaman*, 156–96, 420–22.

165. See Kim, K., *Holy Spirit*, viii–xii, for a controversial practice of shamanic theologizing. It should be noted that a key difference between the theologizing at the World Council of Churches Cranberra Assembly and the application of Craffert here is that any constructive move on the basis of the thought of Mbiti and Mugambi, because of their appeal to christocentrism, will be christologically conceived.

166. See Craffert, *Life of a Galilean Shaman*, 167–68.

Conclusion

Mbiti's approach to African temporality and eschatology signifies a move away from the particularism of context. The subject of the present chapter signifies a move away from the particularism of African traditional religious experience. For in an exercise of theistic contextualization the category of religion is prioritized, the unity of ATR is assumed, and those who suffer within traditional (patriarchal) societies are marginalized.

Theologically, for both Mbiti and Mugambi, ATRs become the locus for the further emergence of African theology. For Mbiti, the importance of ATRs is that they (historically or empirically) provide continuity between traditional thought and the Christian message. It is part of the African Christian story, it remains part of the story and, therefore, continues to be important theologically. Mugambi concurs but also has a broader vision for the theological importance of the African heritage. He sees a social function with a re-mythologization of the African heritage serving national unity. Both demand that a properly African Christian theology take account of ATRs. For it is the continuity, in contrast with the discontinuity found in much mission Christianity teaching, between ATRs and the Christian gospel that makes theology African.

Their desire for theistic contextualization through an appeal to ATRs, which entails a move away from experience, seems a very Northern way of doing theology. However, the purpose of such an approach is not to acquiesce to foreign conventions but to counter the dominance of voices from beyond Africa. While they do move away from experience in their presentation of ATRs and the ARH some acknowledgement would have to be given to the fact that their addressing the issue of theistic contextualization itself arises from their own experience. Nevertheless, a move away from the particularism of experience does prevent experience from having an explicitly methodological and theological role to play. In response to such criticisms, a constructive move is proposed that would bring the experience of traditional practices into dialogue with the practice of Jesus as depicted in the Gospels (experiential dialogue). Given that Mbiti and Mugambi choose a theistic contextualization to dominate their approach to ATRs and the ARH and not a christological contextualization, their christocentrism may not be as important or as thorough as the rhetoric they employ would suggest. It will be the task of the next chapter to test this very assumption as the nature of their christology is examined.

5

Christ and Symbol in African Community

> Later on, He came, this Son of Man:
> Like a child delayed He came to us.
> The White Man brought Him.
> He was pale, and not the Sunburnt Son of the Desert.
> As a child He came.
> A wee little babe wrapped in swaddling clothes.
> Ah, if only He had been like little Moses, lying
> Sun scorched on the banks of the River of God
> We would have recognized Him.
> He eludes us still this Jesus, Son of Man.[1]

THIS CHAPTER WILL HAVE three tasks. First, the major christological themes in the writings of Mbiti and Mugambi will be briefly identified as Christ and culture, Christ and catholicity, Christ and cross, and Christ and salvation. Second, the themes will be analyzed to reveal tendencies toward a Christ transcending culture, a top-down catholicity, reductionist emphases on the cross, and narrow emphases in understanding salvation. It will be argued that these tendencies constitute a movement away from the particularism of faith communities in Kenya. Third, given this move away from the particular, a constructive move relating to a symbolic approach to christology and christopraxis is proposed. A symbolic approach will be proposed to further the thought of Mbiti and Mugambi towards connecting their christologizing with the importance of symbol in African traditional religious practice.

---

1. Setiloane, "I am an African," 128–31.

Christopraxis is as an ontologically significant contextualization between the humanity of Christ and the suffering humanity of Africa.

For Diane Stinton, two factors above all else inspire African christology. These are colonialism and missionary malpractice. The association of Christianity with colonialism and missionary malpractice, especially seen in the denigration of African cultures have clear christological consequences.[2] According to Stinton, despite these experiences of colonial Christianity and missionary malpractice, first generation African theologians (1950s–80s) did not develop African christologies in their writings. Stinton adjudges that christology is "latent" in first generation African theology.[3] She argues that this is the case because of a preoccupation with ATRs and the desire to establish a theological continuity between this African heritage and their received Christian faith. It is the case that Mbiti and Mugambi do not develop and write fully fledged systematic christologies. This apparent lacuna in their work is then seen as part of a wider "christological crisis" in Africa.[4] While the present writer would not characterize Mbiti's and Mugambi's work on theistic contextualization as a "preoccupation," it does have significance for their christologizing. The significance, however, is not that it creates a christology that is "latent." Rather, instead of dealing with christology according to the methods and themes dictated by a more dogmatic or systemic approach they take a more practical approach. Arising from a study of their writings, christological themes emerge that focus primarily on how Christ benefits people rather than on questions about, for example, the divinity and humanity of Christ.

Christ and Culture

Culture is made by humans and makes humans.[5] For Mbiti, the gospel is God given and distinct from culture. However, it is given in a particular cultural milieu. The universalizing of the particular begins on the day of Pentecost, "from the day of Pentecost onwards, the gospel traverses one culture after another. No culture can monopolize the gospel since it is public property. But the gospel needs culture because it cannot be proclaimed in a

---

2. Stinton, *Jesus of Africa*, 29. See Bahemuka, "Hidden Christ," 7.

3. Stinton, *Jesus of Africa*, 4–9, 16–18. Stinton sees the 1980s as the decade when African christologies emerge in earnest. See Stinton, "African Christianity," 4–5. For recent work in the area, see also Nyamiti, *Studies in African Theology*, 65–146; Nyamiti, "African Christologies"; Akper, "Person of Jesus Christ"; Schreiter, *Faces of Jesus*.

4. See Stinton, *Jesus of Africa*, 6; Mbiti, "Some African Concepts," 51.

5. Mbiti, "Gospel and Culture," 1–2.

vacuum." Christianity, which is distinct from the gospel, is the result both of the message of Christ and the culture of a particular place and time. There is, then, a kind of theological reciprocity between gospel and culture. On the one hand, the gospel judges and saves culture "exorcis[ing] cultural demons and sanctify[ing] cultural values."[6] On the other hand, the intelligibility of the gospel is dependant on culture. "Culture is the context in which Christ is confessed, it is also the vehicle of confessing Him."[7]

> Culture knows no eschatology to which it may take humanity. Only the Gospel has an eschatology for both man and the whole creation (cf. Rom 8:19–21). In this case, the Christian is a cultural pilgrim and not a settler, moving with his cultural baggage towards the eschatological goal of the Gospel. At best, culture can only equip us to hear the Gospel and answer the voice of Christ when He calls us corporately to Himself, out of and within our different cultures.[8]

Despite this, an assumption has existed that the "older Churches" can think, speak and build churches on behalf of African believers. In contrast, the local church should "swallow up" missionaries.[9] Such attitudes and practices create "spiritual pygmies." For Mbiti such practice has christological consequences. For such relationships of dependence displace the role of the Spirit of Jesus Christ. Without the work of the Holy Spirit, christologically conceived, christocentrism is supplanted.[10]

Echoing Stinton's analysis above, Mugambi quotes a sermon from J. G. Donders that points to Christ contextualized into colonialist and imperialist practice and culture:

> Jesus is a stranger in Africa
> He is an expatriate,
> He comes from another world.
> He is a product of the west
> He is an imperialist
> He is a colonialist
> He is pretentious.[11]

---

6. Ibid., 2–3.
7. Mbiti, Introduction in *Confessing Christ in Different Cultures*, 24.
8. Mbiti, "Gospel and Culture," 4.
9. Mbiti, "Christian Eschatology," 308–9.
10. Ibid., 308.
11. Mugambi, *CCAL*, 157.

The Gospels depict a Jesus who acknowledged "the dignity and cultural integrity of other people" in a new community. This community, according to Mugambi, was to be distinguished by an "evolv[ing] fuller sense of self and an awareness of the universality of humankind." The uniqueness of Christianity is, therefore, not inherent. Rather, it is "derived from its universal appeal, which, ideally goes so far as to ensure that no culture has ascendancy over any other, but rather that the equal validity of all is affirmed."[12] Jesus did not come to subvert or abolish particular cultures. Jesus is fulfillment of tradition. Consequently, Mugambi sees the ministry of Jesus as a competing vision for the future of tradition against a conservative religious institution that sought to let the past of tradition condition thought and practice.[13] The mission of God "takes human form" and inaugurates a new era in the "totality of human experience."[14] Indeed, in one place Mugambi defines the incarnation as "the core of the Christian faith." However, he does not dwell on ontological questions. Rather, he immediately moves to its practical meaning. Incarnation means inculturation. Thus, the gospel is "culturally coded."[15]

Inculturation cannot be separated from liberation in Mugambi's thinking.[16] It seems that Mugambi's understanding of "gospel" as a message often imported in foreign cultural terms means that there is a need for an ongoing process of contestation toward a more thoroughly inculturated gospel. This stands in distinction to Mbiti's more existential understanding of gospel where people have an immediate and personal encounter with God (see chapter 2). Consequently, it is possible for Mbiti to identify the possibility of a christological relationship between Christ and ATRs. At the heart of Mbiti's argument is the proposal that God reveals God's self in traditional religious experiences.[17] It is revelation that theologically ennobles the African heritage. Christ, even if unnamed, provides access to the God known as the creator in traditional belief. Christ, therefore, will be known as "the one who strengthens kinship"[18] both at the human level (for corporateness is now founded not only in race or custom but in redemption and church)

---

12. Mugambi, *FLTR*, 90.

13. Mugambi, *BBE*, 8.

14. Ibid., 9.

15. Mugambi, *CTSR*, 71–72.

16. Ibid., 71–73.

17. More recently, Mugambi has clarified this reference to Macquarrie, calling it an "allusion." Mugambi, E-mail correspondence to Heaney, February 22, 2009.

18. Mbiti, "Christian Eschatology," 304; Mbiti, "Some African Concepts," 61–62.

and at the level of God and humanity.[19] Mbiti sees a christocentric African practice move people from a tribal solidarity to a christological solidarity.[20]

There are christological titles that cohere, to some degree, with traditional beliefs (Son of God, Lord, Servant). Consequently, Mbiti can say, Christ "was not 100% absent from traditional African religious insights and practices."[21] Some christological titles (Messiah, Christ, Son of David, Son of Man) have no coherence.[22] Yet, other titles could be newly conceived given an African cultural context (for example, Jesus the Circumcised). For material in the Gospels (such as genealogy[23] and circumcision[24]), which are generally undervalued outside Africa, may become key in opening new understandings and dimensions in Christology.[25] It is this more practical dimension in christology, and by implication soteriology, that is to be stressed in an African christology. Such emphases in African Christology might be seen, observes Mbiti, in five functions that are important in an African context. Christ, as has been seen, is not necessarily absent in ATRs. Christ is fulfiller of tradition or reconstructionist. Christ is the master of initiation. He is savior and victor (*Christus Victor*)[26] not only through the cross but in transformative ministry mastering the spirit-world and sickness. He brings realization of the eschaton in such practices. Function, therefore, is emphasized over ontology.

In the Christology of both Mbiti and Mugambi, there is a complex web of issues relating to the issue of Christ and culture, which neither thinker fully resolves. On the one hand, it is recognized that the revelation of God is incarnated and inculturated in the person of Jesus of Nazareth. For Mugambi especially, this christological inculturation is but the beginning of an ongoing process of inculturation which, in practice, means that Christ is never fully comprehended in one culture. On the other hand, both writers

---

19. Mbiti, "Christian Eschatology," 304. This idea is developed further by Nyamiti, *Christ as Our Ancestor*. See Mbiti, "Is God a Hindrance."

20. Mbiti, "Some African Concepts," 61–62.

21. Mbiti, "African Theology" (*IT*), 150. See Mbiti, "Is Jesus Christ in African Religion."

22. Mbiti, "Some African Concepts," 57–62.

23. Mbiti, "Bible and God's Revelation," 5.

24. Mbiti, "African Theology" (*IT*), 143–44; Mbiti, "Christusbekenntnis," 5; Mbiti, "Confessing Christ in Multi-Faith," 140–45.

25. Mbiti, "African Theology" (*IT*), 143.

26. Mbiti, "Some African Concepts," 54–57. See Stinton, "Africa, East and West," 124. It is not that Mbiti is proposing a theory of atonement here as in Aulén, *Christus Victor*. Rather, he is emphasizing that, from an African perspective, the victory of Jesus over the spirit-world is significant.

provide a severe criticism of foreign missionaries who came to Kenya with their inculturated Christian gospel. Yet, it seems such criticism is predicated upon an acontextual "Archimedean point" from which such a judgment can be made. Therefore, some means of holding this tension between the inculturated realities of christology and a more objective or, as it is in Mbiti's thought, existential christology is needed. An appeal to catholicity may be seen as a strategy towards achieving such balance.

Christ and Catholicity

Africans possess a theological agency independent of any acceptance of the Christian gospel brought by missionaries. For example, although it was not presented in clear terms in the missionary journalism of the time, it was under the leadership of the so-called Bombay Africans that the church grew in the freed slave communities Rabai, Godoma, and Fulladoyo.[27] These centers, often coming into conflict with foreign missionaries, formed the "first genuine African church in East Africa."[28] Abe Sidi (d. 1885) led the Giriama Church at Jilore, which was founded by Africans and pastored in its early years by Africans alone, but later taken over by foreign leadership.[29] For Mugambi such processes of christological contestation are part of a broader struggle for liberation.[30] It is important to note that even Mugambi with his emphasis on inculturation and human finitude can, at times, distinguish gospel from culture. Neither thinkers interrogate such a notion as thoroughly as they might. Nor do they provide any means of analyzing power relations even though they criticize missionary domination and recognize that christologizing has social implications. They are, however, conscious of the function of christology on what might be termed ecclesiological sociality. That is to say, an emphasis on African culture and christological inculturation does not for either thinker lead to isolationism. On the contrary, it is because of christology within African theology that the African church is catholic.

Mbiti identifies a christological center for the church. The church "cannot have its centre in New York or London, in Geneva or Nairobi, or Jerusalem or Madras, but only in Jesus Christ."[31] The Bible and Christ are what

27. Reed, *Pastors, Partners*, 112–13, 129–30.
28. Ibid., 80.
29. Ibid., 153–55.
30. See Mugambi, "Some Perspectives," 105–10; Mbiti, "Confessing Christ in Multi-Faith," 138; Mbiti, *BATAC*, 11–13; Mbiti, "Traditional Religions," 62.
31. Mbiti, "Christian Eschatology," 309.

join the Christian community worldwide. "Our faith is built around Jesus Christ. Therefore, Christian theology falls and stands with christology."[32] While ATRs are not explicitly christological, Mbiti argues that African theology should be christocentric. This emphasis, over against missionary denominationalism, might be explained as an attempt to establish the practice of African theology within the catholicity of Christian faith.[33] Consequently, Mbiti writes:

> The Christian message is one and remains unchangeable around the person of Jesus Christ. But the people employ their cultures, their world-views, their hopes and fears, their experiences and disappointments, their songs and cries, their celebrations and tears and the totality of their being in order to understand that message, to interpret it, to institutionalize it, to celebrate it and weave it into their daily life. This then, results in a Christianity which bears both the local imprint and also a universal imprint.[34]

For Mbiti, Christianity is a "universal and cosmic faith," which was "universalized on Calvary, and cosmicized on the first Easter Day." The task of African theologians is now to "localize this universality and cosmicity."[35] This localization is essential. For only with localization is Christianity's universality and cosmicity meaningful.[36]

For Mugambi, "The Church is the community which derives its identity from its commitment to Jesus Christ." It is a "trans-historical" community "anchored in the commitment of its members to Jesus Christ" with a "corporate obligation" to practice the demands of Christian discipleship. For Christ has inaugurated a new type of community. A community based not "on cultural identity" but on "faith in God through Jesus Christ." Consequently, because everything except faith is peripheral, Christianity becomes a "universally open religious movement." It incorporates peoples from any culture without, in principle, prejudice or discrimination.[37] In proclaiming the fulfillment of prophetic hope in Luke 4 Jesus pledges to make such hope a "living reality." Mugambi understands Jesus to be making a commitment to work against dehumanization seen in poverty, captivity, oppression,

---

32. Mbiti, "Dialogue between EATWOT and Western Theologians," 102. See Mbiti, "Theologische Zusammenarbeit," for his reflections on the development of EATWOT.

33. See Mbiti, "African Theology" (*IT*), 146, 156.

34. Mbiti, *BATAC*, 20.

35. Mbiti, "Christianity and Traditional Religions," 145.

36. Ibid., 145–46.

37. Mugambi, *BBE*, 12–16.

prejudice, illness, and estrangement from God. The symbol that captures this consistent and practical opposition to dehumanization is the Kingdom of God. For Mugambi, the definition of it as, for example, the reign of God is of little consequence. Rather, his focus is seeing the kingdom in practical action against dehumanization.[38]

The problem with the Christian declaration that Christ represents all humanity because he is "above" or "beyond" history, gender, race, and/or culture is that this beyondness is never, in practice, beyond the particular. Mbiti and Mugambi, of course, do recognize the European and imperial Christ in Africa. However, they fail to see clearly that the former may create the latter. That is to say, they fail to see that the universalizing or abstracting of Christ from culture may be the very move that creates the European Christ. Indeed, it is particular theological and philosophical presuppositions that accommodate such a move. Tsenay Serequeberhan, critiquing post-Enlightenment European thought, rightly recognizes that the elevation of the universal "Man" and universal enlightenment is predicated upon exclusionary assumptions disabling the very idea at its moment of acclaim.[39] The same criticism of a universal Christ is closely related to a tendency in the way they view catholicity as a top-down practice. For catholicity may also be challenged as an imperialist construct and practiced through domineering power relations that demand consent and make declarations on the "orthodoxy" of one theology over another.[40] It is the contextualizing dynamic of catholicity that does not serve the wider project. For a move from the "universal" to context is again a move away from the particular and the experiential. Given the experiences of oppression and suppression that Mbiti and Mugambi testify to, one might have expected a resistance to a practice of Christian catholicity practiced from the universal to the local. It might have been expected that any practice or theory of catholicity from the perspective of contextual theologians might have began with the local community of faith. That is to say, the practice of catholicity espoused by Mbiti and Mugambi might have been expected to be "bottom up" and not "top down." Such a dynamic of catholicity might have been further informed by christology itself in that the crucified lord of the church experiences alienation on the margins of society and on the margins of empire. However,

---

38. Ibid., 39–51.

39. Serequeberham, "Critique of Eurocentrism," 144. Kant, for example did not see reason and rationality to be indigenous to Africa (p. 149). See also McCarthy, *Race, Empire, and the Idea*.

40. See Rieger, "Christian Theology."

while Mbiti and Mugambi affirm christocentrism it is not necessarily the case that they affirm crucicentrism.

Christ and the Cross

> For Jesus the saving of people . . . [was not left] . . . to the cross. When I read the gospels and follow Jesus . . . this is not a Jesus on the cross . . . this is a Jesus who saved people. He healed them, he comforted, he embraced those who were on the peripheries, he gave them assurance and that is the saving work of Jesus which for me is far more meaningful than just hanging [on a cross] . . .[41]

In Mbiti's research, he draws attention to missionary teaching in Ukambani that focused on the death of Christ. The impression was given, especially through the hymns brought by the missionaries, that Christ remained on the cross.[42] An overemphasis on the cross, for Mbiti, distorts the salvific potency of the Christian message. For example, a church crucifix is "a distortion of the Jesus I see in the Gospels . . . that dead Jesus does not appeal to me. I want the living Jesus." For Mbiti, the sins Jesus was concerned with were those conditions which marginalized people from community. Unfortunately, this understanding of sin, which he argues owes much to Jewish understandings, has been "hijacked" by Christian theologians and clergy.[43] Christ is savior and the salvation he offers, from an African perspective, is not solely grounded on his passion and cross. Rather, his whole ministry, including his engagement with spirits and sickness, affects the way in which salvation is understood. Salvation must be practical and contextual or it is not experienced as salvation.[44] Indeed, Mbiti doubts that Jesus invested much theological significance in the literalness of the cross. For the idea of taking up the cross (Matt 16:24; Luke 9:23) emerges in a first century Jewish context and must, therefore, have Jewish significance. In Jewish scripture a sign or mark could be taken up or worn as an indication of lamentation. Those who lamented for the sin of the people marked themselves out as God's true people (see Ezek 9:4). If this is what Mbiti is referring to then he understands Jesus as calling the Jews of his day to a similar spirituality and

---

41. Mbiti, Interview by Heaney, April 7. See Mbiti, *BATAC*, 166.
42. Mbiti, "Christian Eschatology," 244. See Jenson, *Systematic Theology*, 179.
43. Mbiti, Interview by Heaney, April 7.
44. Mbiti, *BATAC*, 166.

distinction. To take up one's cross, metaphorically, is to greatly lament over Israel.[45]

For Mugambi, "The crucifixion was . . . a dramatic theological critique of human political systems."[46] For, in his death, Jesus demonstrated that "there was an absolute qualitative distinction" between his kingdom and human kingdoms (John 18:33–36). The relationship, argues Mugambi, between God's kingdom and human kingdoms is that the former should inform the governance of the latter. Consequently, spiritual poverty, concern for the suffering, righteousness, mercy, purity of heart, peacemaking, love, justice, reconciliation, sincerity, and humility are given priority (see Matt 5:1–12).[47] For Mugambi, the christological crisis in Africa is not that theologians have failed to develop textual and systematic christologies. Rather, the "scandal" is that "for five hundred years, the West has chosen the Christ without the cross, while the people of Africa live the cross without the Christ."[48] Stinton quotes Mugambi as saying:

> I am wrestling with a contradiction: The gospel proclaims good news in specific cultural and historical terms (Luke 4:16–22). Yet missionary Christianity has reached Africa as terribly *bad news*, in which people have been taught in church to despise their culture, their ancestry, their history and their knowledge. How can Jesus the Son of God, who created Africans in His own Image, condone such dehumanization? Either this negative teaching is theologically erroneous (heretical); or it is imperialist ideology rather than theology; or the God this teaching proclaims is an idol created in the image of its proclaimers. The implications of this concern are far reaching and it is too early to predict the outcome.[49]

Africa has trod the way of the cross while missionary Christianity has proclaimed and practiced an imperialist lordship. Post-colonialist theologians are, more recently, also taking up such criticism.[50]

An African proclamation of Christ and the cross will need to be different. Part of the christological contextualizing needed, according to Mugambi, will be a rejection of mission Christianity's exclusivist soteriology.

---

45. Mbiti, Interview by Heaney, April 7. See Wevers, *New Century Bible Commentary: Ezekiel*, 71.

46. Mugambi, *ACT*, 87.

47. Ibid., 87–88.

48. Ela, "Memory of the African People," 18–19, cited by Stinton, *Jesus of Africa*, 37.

49. Mugambi in Stinton, *Jesus of Africa*, 26.

50. Rieger, *Christ and Empire*, viii.

That all must submit, through conversion, to an (imperial) Christ alienates Christians from other traditions in Africa including, Mugambi argues, the African traditional heritage. Such exclusivist soteriology he depicts as "prejudiced missionary teaching."[51] Indeed, he sees the genesis of such thinking as the "formalization of Christianity as the religion of the elite in the 'Christianized' Roman Empire."[52] In contrast, he makes reference to John Hick's proposals in *God and the Universe of Faiths* and *God Has Many Names*.[53] In Africa, argues Mugambi, a Hickian-type approach will reduce religious antagonism in religiously diverse settings while "enhancing national unity." It will also mean a redefinition of "mission" to exclude "the divinely instituted obligation to convert everyone to their own religious convictions."[54]

The writing of Mbiti and Mugambi in relating the cross to the African situation of suffering is, undoubtedly, apposite. However, it might well be that both Mbiti and Mugambi further distance their work from the Christian faith community in Kenya by reducing the message of Matthew 16:24 and Luke 9:23 to Jewish (albeit messianic) lamentation and of citing John Hick's work in such a positive manner. It is very far from clear that such thinking on the significance on the cross of Christ relates well with the beliefs and practices of Christians in Kenya.[55] Not least because, as Mbiti and Mugambi recognize, the cross and the salvation it brings in Kenyan Anglicanism is not an academic concern.

Christ and Salvation

In Africa, argues Mbiti, the most important function of religion is that it protects adherents. Salvation is predicated upon the belief that the object of one's worship has the power to sustain one's life against enemies. As Christ demonstrated in the Gospels, the function of the Holy Spirit today is to cure, heal, and provide good health and victory over evil. A key factor in people moving church or denomination in an African context is that the new church can provide healing. Healing, notes Mbiti, is equated with

---

51. Mugambi, "Problems of Meaning," 154.

52. Mugambi, E-mail correspondence to Heaney, February 22, 2009.

53. Hick, *God and the Universe*; Hick, *God Has Many Names*. For a recent engagement see Muck, "Theology of Religions."

54. Mugambi, "Problems of Meaning," 156–57.

55. See Mugambi, "Evangelistic and Charismatic Initiatives," 111–44. See also Kings, "Proverbial, Intrinsic"; Kings and Morgan, *Offerings from Kenya*, 46–50; Tovey, *Inculturation of Christian Worship*, 130–49; Stinton, "African Christianity," 3–14.

salvation.[56] African Christian practice results in a broader understanding of salvation than what was imported by mission Christianity (often preaching a salvation for "souls" in "heaven"). Salvation is for here and now. Such an understanding, argues Mbiti, is influenced by ATRs and African readings of the Bible. ATRs are often dominated by themes of struggles to survive physical and spiritual threats. "As long as one is alive in this body, physical threats have spiritual consequences and spiritual threats have physical consequences."[57] The same life struggles are found also in the biblical text. The salvation of Christ is experienced, therefore, in the present world in a daily victory of life over death. But salvation is even broader than this. It has a cosmic dimension:

> ... people stretch their salvation experience into the world of the divinities, the spirits of nature and of the departed, the mystical realities of magic and witchcraft, and so on, so that salvation through Jesus Christ can be seen and experienced to reach out beyond physical realities[58]

Commitment to Christ mediates the salvation of God, which is protection against harm from whatever quarter harm could come from. In short, salvation is life (John 10:10) and it is Christ who converts human life into sacramental life.

> To exist, in Africa, is to be involved in a sacred transaction: and Christianity in our continent has no greater service to render than to transpose the existence of this religious man of Africa into the existence brought about by the Gospel light, by Jesus Christ, so that the entire life of Africa can proclaim Christ as Lord and King.

> The act of Redemption, though it took place under 'Pontius Pilate,' was lifted out of Time so that every portion of Space and every moment of Time could be affected by and saturated with that redemptive act of God through Jesus Christ.[59]

---

56. Mbiti, *BATAC*, 138-51. Indeed, it is not uncommon for priests and pastors to testify to losing members of their congregation to AICs or Pentecostal churches when claims are made of spectacular healing or some other manifestation of apparent divine power.

57. Ibid., 156.

58. Ibid., 165.

59. Mbiti, "Christianity and East African Culture," 4.

The above quotation is from an address Mbiti gave to Makerere University Christian Union in 1967. It is arguably the most explicit, pellucid, and evangelical comment Mbiti makes on the nature and scope of Christian salvation. A younger Mbiti has not yet defined *praeparatio evangelica* in a primarily empirical manner. Rather, "God has not left Himself without witness in Africa, and this intensely religious life of the African, is a God-given 'praeparatio evangelica' (preparation for the Gospel)."[60] Mbiti's critics may not see this standing in tension with the rest of his work. They may see it as a glimpse of the real (missionary) motivation of his work as a consistent invitation to a fuller, christologically conceived, life.[61]

For Mugambi, Jesus was killed "for the sake of righteousness." This he sees as a very different option to that recommended by the oppressors who exhort the oppressed to "turn the other cheek" (Matt 5:38–42). Such "warped" theologizing is, for Mugambi, an exercise of theological power that, along with economic, military, and technological power, is used to usurp the agency of the oppressed to determine their own morality and destiny. This amounts to blasphemy. For such a demand, made by oppressors, is one that only God can make. In contrast to human oppressors, who seek subservience, God in Christ brings liberty. Mugambi stresses an understanding of liberation in the here and now, thus laying much less stress on theological definitions of atonement.[62]

Mugambi recognizes that despite his reading of Christian salvation as something that must include liberation in a context where people suffered much in contexts of coloniality, the Gospel depiction of Jesus does not seem to initially provide this. In the context of Roman domination, however, Mugambi does not see Jesus' refusal to join the Zealots as signaling a quiescent approach to Israel's predicament. Rather, for Christ, and Christian theology, the issue of violence and non-violence is "subsidiary." Survival, freedom, justice, and humanization are "logically and theologically prior" to questions of violence and non-violence.[63]

The restoration of African human dignity includes a positive appraisal of African heritage and practice (inculturation), which is part of a

60. Ibid., 4.

61. It should be noted that the early Mugambi also possesses much more missiological intent. Thus, in the article that began his academic career, he writes, "If the Gospel could be taught through a traditional approach," his own people (the Embu) would "consider it their own and original . . . This would remove from most of them the present feeling that they are only participating as 'invited guests' in foreign religion that is not their own." Mugambi, "Traditional Religion," 56.

62. Mugambi, *ACT*, 100–103.

63. Mugambi, *BBE*, 44.

transformative continuum moving towards wider transformation in the society as a whole (see chapter 6). Jesus came into conflict with the ruling elite. He encouraged "the peasants and the marginalized urban dwellers to affirm their dignity."[64] Jesus, like the majority of Africans, was a rural dweller and most of his ministry, argues Mugambi, was directed towards rural society. This, he observes, would have been unexpected for a teacher of his stature who might have been expected to base himself in the cosmopolitan capital of Jerusalem. He chose peasant followers. He gave his first sermon, not at temple or synagogue, but on a hill (Matt 5–7). Mugambi chooses to contrast this model of ministry with what missionaries do in Africa and submit that Christian ministry in Africa needs to be improved in rural societies.[65] While Jesus did not join the Zealots against Roman imperialism he did empower his followers to resist being treated as objects by either political or religious leaders. Jesus stands within the prophetic tradition, especially in the Sermon on the Mount, and obliterates all ethical and theological justification for exploitation and oppression. Mugambi concludes, "In the socio-political domain, this ethical stance results in the disruption of the *status quo*, even when there is no programme of revolutionary action."[66]

Mugambi rejects any false dichotomizing between a contextualist and liberationist christology. An African theology will both draw on African traditional heritage and seek to address the suffering in a post-colonial Africa.[67] Hope comes from Christ, and to illustrate what this means Mugambi identifies, but does not elaborate on, twenty-seven possible "paradigms" that might further the development of African christologies.[68] However, because

---

64. Mugambi, *CTSR*, 64–65.

65. Mugambi, *ACT*, 91–95.

66. Mugambi, *CTSR*, 65–67.

67. Mugambi, *FLTR*, 8–10. See Bujo, *African Christian Morality*, 125; Bujo, *African Theology*, 71.

68. Mugambi, "Christological Paradigms," 136–61. Mugambi labels the paradigms occupational (Jesus is fisherman, carpenter, and teacher, see Matt 4:18–22; John 21:1–13; Matt 13:55; Mark 6:3; Mark 1:22); cultural (Jesus is circumcised, see Luke 2:41–51); familial (Jesus as family member, obedient to his parents, but ultimately transcending family to reach across boundaries, see John 4:39; Mark 7:26; John 19:20, 7:35; Matt 8:5; Mark 15:39; Luke 7:2); genealogical (Jesus is son of David, son of Abraham, thus Jesus can be, in Africa, ancestor, see Matt 8:5–13); theocentric (Jesus is son of God, see Mark 1:1); cosmocentric (Jesus is the self-disclosure of God, see Rom 1:20, 8:22; 2 Cor 5:17); eschatological (Jesus is herald of hope); biocentric (Jesus declares human achievement is dependent on God and sacred, see Matt 4:1–10; Mark 10:17–22); ideological (Jesus is the ideal liberator, see Luke 4:16–22); liturgical (Jesus is teacher of liturgy, see Matt 6:7–15); ritualistic (Jesus fulfills and reforms ritual, see Mark 2:27); ontological (Jesus is identified with God the creator, see John 8:58); charismatic (Jesus as possessor of

he sees the role of a theology of reconstruction (chapter 6) as crucial for African theology, it is through this lens that his own christological reflections might be seen most clearly. A theology of reconstruction, for Mugambi, needs to be developed now that Kenya has won its liberation and lives in a post-colonial context. Jesus, therefore, is understood as a reconstructionist.

> It is quite clear that Jesus, in his public ministry, was actively and simultaneously involved in both personal and social reconstruction. He mobilized his followers to become involved in social change, having convinced them of the necessity and urgency to change their attitudes towards themselves and the world.[69]

According to Mugambi, Jesus is more of a "reconstructionist" than he ever was a "liberationist." It is not clear what Mugambi is denying here but what he is affirming is a particular reading of Luke 4:18–19 and the Sermon on the Mount where Jesus was calling for "a new social consciousness" so that his followers might "regain [their] dignity under the Roman Empire."[70] Mugambi argues that Jesus "did not condemn campaigns against colonization and imperialism," but rather, affirmed the possibility of love, justice, and peace if "human political systems adhered faithfully to the ideals of the kingdom of God."[71] What is noteworthy about the above argument, which makes up a chapter in Mugambi's *African Christian Theology* entitled "The Cross as a Christian Symbol," is not what he affirms about the work of Christ, but what he does not. Reading this chapter along with the other chapters on "The Kingdom of God and the Kingdom of Men," "Jesus and Rural Society," "Poverty and the Kingdom of God," "The Church in Education and Liberation," "Political Power and the Power of the Cross," and "Christology and Ecclesiology," one is struck by the absence of any developed discussion on atonement.

---

spiritual gifts for teaching and healing, see Mark 1:21–22, 27); mystical (Jesus is a mystic, see Matt 3–4, 14:22–27; Mark 1:35–39; Luke 9:28–36, 22:39–46); aristocratic (Jesus is King); anthropocentric (Jesus is son of man and son of woman); juridical (Jesus is judge, advocate, counsel, mediator); homiletic (Jesus is preacher, see Matt 5); epistemological (Jesus is source of all knowledge and wisdom); therapeutic (Jesus is healer); counseling (Jesus is counselor, see John 3, 11); normative (Jesus is author of principles, seen primarily in the command to love God and neighbor); ecclesiological (Jesus is founder of the church and church is a fellowship of those following Jesus, see John 14–17); pneumatological (Jesus as Spirit and sender of the Spirit); dialectical (Jesus is controversialist); festive (Jesus as celebrant of ritual); and historic (Jesus as the one who alters history).

69. Quoted by Stinton, *Jesus of Africa*, 221.
70. Mugambi, "Theology of Reconstruction," 147–48.
71. Mugambi, *ACT*, 89.

Neither Mbiti nor Mugambi develop a theory of atonement. Rather, when choosing to identify the significance of the message of Christian salvation, they focus on what they adjudge to be important in an African context. For Mbiti, drawing on ATRs, protection becomes key to how salvation is understood. For Mugambi, reflecting on the subjugation experienced at the hands of missionaries and colonialists, agency or freedom becomes key. In part, these emphases stand in continuity with their assessment of psychical need in traditional and post-colonial communities in Africa and in contrast to the Christ and gospel brought by foreign missionaries. However, it is not clear to what extent this understanding of salvation does in fact relate to the beliefs and practices of believers in the church in Kenya. Even a cursory consideration of the history and liturgy of, for example, the Anglican Church of Kenya demonstrates a broader understanding of salvation is at work.[72]

Beyond Latency: Symbolic Christology and Christopraxis

The christology in the writings of Mbiti and Mugambi is only "latent" if a systematic approach is the only way to christologize. It is only underdeveloped if systematizing is the only way to establish (or practice) christology. Because they deal with christological issues in a more practical manner, and because of a prior commitment to a non-christological conception of God (chapter 4), they do not necessarily follow the methods, agenda, or themes that might be expected by scholars from beyond the context or from scholars who operate from within a dogmatic or systematic frame. Nevertheless, their approach to christological issues may not be as thoroughly contextual as expected. Indeed, their approach evidences a further move away from the particular. In this instance, it is a move away from the particularism of faith communities.

First, there is a move away from the African traditional religious experience. For especially Mbiti's christologizing persists with a Christ transcending culture and with an emphasis on salvation that is too narrow. This narrowness is particularly highlighted against the background of the rise of Pentecostalism with some groups maintaining emphases not at all dissimilar to mission Christianity. Despite this, Kalu argues that Pentecostalism grows because of the "power theme" arising from African traditional religious

---

72. See again Kings and Morgan, *Offerings from Kenya*; Tovey, *Inculturation of Christian Worship*, 130–49. See also Reed, *Pastors, Partners*; Ward and Wild-Wood, *East African Revival*; Spear and Kimambo, *East African Expressions*; Kalu, *African Pentecostalism*.

understandings and expectations.[73] To redress this move away from the African traditional religious experience a symbolic approach to christology will be proposed. Second, there is a move away from Christian communities of faith. For top-down power relations may marginalize local theological agency and a tendency toward a reductionist reading of the cross of Christ may undermine the contextualizing potency between the marginalization of the cross and the suffering of communities of faith in Africa. In response, christopraxis will be introduced to counter this.

Approaching Symbolic Christology

Both Mbiti and Mugambi attempt a contextualization of African traditionalist experience and practice with theistic experience and practice. However, this same contextualizing with experience in ATRs is not extended to the subject of christology. Mugambi does call for such a constructive move when he writes, "The traditional African view of God ought to be related to African Christology."[74] He does not, however, develop such a relationship.

Mugambi cites Tillich as one inspiration for contextualization and Mbiti concedes that correlation or contextualization would have been a better category than *praeparatio evangelica* (chapter 4). However, it is not being proposed that the writings of Mbiti and Mugambi be considered Tillichian or that their thought should be converted to Tillichianism. Indeed, the present writer has serious reservations about Tillich's approach to christology.[75] Nevertheless, Tillich's identification of the role of symbol may create potential for how a constructive move between African traditional practice and christology could be envisaged as an extension of the thought of Mbiti and Mugambi.

For Tillich, Jesus mediates the ultimate ground of being but cannot be confused with it. Jesus is finite. Jesus is the Christian symbol, *logos*. He is not what is to be known. Rather, he is its medium.[76] In short, Tillich locates the theological significance of the *logos*'s function by distinguishing

---

73. See Kalu, *African Pentecostalism*, 249–70. See also 4, 68, 216.

74. Mugambi, "Christological Paradigms," 142.

75. Such reservations might be seen to particularly relate to Tillich's "audacious declaration of freedom regarding historical fact" (Reijnen, "Tillich's Christology," 68, see 68–71). For reviews and responses to Tillich's christology, see, for example, Reijnen, "Tillich's Christology," 56–73; Cameron, "Historical Problem"; Ogden, "In the Spirit." See also Forsyth, "Implications for Christology."

76. Kelsey, "Paul Tillich," 90–93. For Tillich's christology see, for example, Kelsey, *Fabric of Tillich's Theology*; Clayton, "Is Jesus Necessary," 147–63; Reijnen, "Tillich's Christology," 56–73.

it ontologically from divinity. A symbolic christology, therefore, seeks to hold in tension both the integrity of the symbol and what is symbolized without collapsing one into the other. Had Mbiti and Mugambi developed a similar type of symbolic christology, they too would have been able to more readily affirm the integrity of African traditional symbolic practice, thereby preventing a move away from African traditional religious experience. Conversation, dialogue, and relationship would mean, then, an attentiveness to symbols in both ATR practice and Christian practice that could point to the divine.[77] Such a Tillichian-type approach begins with traditional symbolic practice. For example, the symbolism associated with initiation, saving, and healing, according to Mbiti and Mugambi, is important in traditional religious experience (see chapter 4).[78] The practice of such symbols as well as their relation to the act of, for example, healing could be christologically significant. For this local symbol could be brought into, for example, Christian liturgy as a means not only of connection with the traditional community but as a symbol towards the divine. This would be a practical and symbolic christologizing that would exist independent of, at least initially, the metaphysical categories and definitions at work in Northern theologies, which Mbiti and Mugambi succumb to in chapter 4. Indeed, both referents for the symbol (healing and divinity) may well co-exist even in liturgical practice.

For Tillich, "who Jesus is follows from an explanation of what he did to 'save' us. Furthermore, 'salvation' and 'revelation' name two aspects of the same reality. 'Salvation' means 'healing.'" The parallel between Tillich's thought here and with the practical christology in Mbiti and Mugambi is stark. Mbiti and Mugambi begin with an emphasis on the assumed function of Jesus (for example, saving, initiating, and healing) in an African context. That is to say, significance is found in what Christ does. For Tillich, the significance of "Jesus the Christ as the power of New Being" finds its significance against an existentialist backdrop. While the Tillichian resonance will not be present here, in the same way there is an experience of estrangement in African contexts as well. Not least, an estrangement from African traditional communities and experience and estrangement from an imperial or foreign Christ.[79]

77. For a recent, useful study of symbol in African traditional religious experience, see Ray, *African Religions*.

78. See Ray, *African Religions*, where symbol is explained usefully as "visible token of the god, of man, of the sacred community of the numinous or his intermediary." Ritual then constitutes a "concentration of references or messages about values or norms dealing with a two-way traffic between the known and the unknown" (p. 34). See also Agorsah, *Religion, Ritual*; MacGaffey, "Kimbanguism."

79. Kelsey, "Paul Tillich," 94.

A symbolic christology does not "destroy or deny other symbols of God's love and salvation."[80] Rather, Christ is the *symbolon* of God revealing God. Jesus is the "symbolic self-expression" of the Father to the world. As symbol, Jesus makes the symbolized reality present. Jesus is the concrete symbol of God. Such a symbolic understanding affirms revelation but denies any ontological "objectification" of Jesus' divinity. Consequently, other symbols formed in different philosophical, religious, and cultural milieus that might point to divine reality are affirmed and not replaced.[81] Sebastian Karotemprel, summing up the significance of symbolic Christology, writes what appears to be words that cohere well with the theological autonomy and legitimacy that Mbiti and Mugambi seek to give to ATRs:

> Symbolic Christology does not undermine the autonomy and legitimacy of other religious mediations of God and his salvation. The symbol of *Logos* implies God's immanence and presence to all beings. The Christian can expect the same immanence and presence of God in other religious mediation and traditions . . . 'Other religions are judged valid in principle by Christians on the basis of their religious experience of God as *Logos* or God's Word in Jesus.'[82]

It is not necessary that such a symbolic approach, redressing the tendency of moving away from practices of traditional communities through symbolic practice, be reductionist. For, as has been seen, both Mbiti and Mugambi refer and allude to Chalcedon-type language and incarnational language. Rather, a symbolic approach might be seen as one means to practice a more open dialogue with the particularism of an African context where ATRs continues to be significant.[83] It is suggestive of, in theologically post-colonial terms, porous boundaries (see chapter 8) for ecclesiological practice. Such an approach may further build on the outward looking desire of their writing (towards ATRs), thus re-connecting their thought with traditional community experience. It will be proposed presently that christopraxis could

---

80. Karotemprel, "Introduction: Christology and Mission," 23.

81. Karotemprel, "Introduction: Christology and Mission," 22–23. See Haight, *Jesus, Symbol of God*.

82. Karotemprel, "Introduction: Christology and Mission," 23.

83. See also Tracy, *Analogical Imagination*. What is being suggested here seems to relate to Tracy's approach. For while Tracy promotes the analogical (in terms of the present study, this is seen in the implications for the "symbolic"), he does not deny that the dialectic (in the terms of the present study, this is seen in "christopraxis") is also needed. The Christian analogue is always Christ.

have similar implications for relating their christologizing more consistently with the christological commitment of Kenyan Christian communities.

Approaching Christopraxis

As has been seen, the need for christopraxis emerges as a response to the depiction of top-down power relations (catholicity) and a reading of the cross that may weaken the relationship between the marginalization and suffering of Christ with other marginalized and suffering people. How christopraxis is to be understood as a constructive move in light of that is the task of the present section. Christopraxis simply refers to what Christ did and what Christ's followers should do. It emerges from a reading of Christ influenced by those who have experienced coloniality and disempowerment. It is an understanding of divine power shaped by the ministry and cross of Christ. Christopraxis is divine power exercised in the ministry and passion of Christ not from the top-down or from the center-out but from the margins. The practical vision of christopraxis will be further integrated into the current argument in chapters 7 and 8. There it will be considered as part of a comparison between Mbiti and Mugambi and post-colonial theology as a means to power analysis. Presently, the focus is christological and christopraxis will begin to be defined. Christopraxis can be seen to include criticism of imperial logic, rejection of the *status quo*, and an emphasis on ontological equivalence.

First, Mbiti and Mugambi recognize that often foreign missionary activity distorted christology for an African context. What they do not consider is that the christology the missionaries subscribe to may not just be the consequence of domineering practices of power (coloniality) but may be the cause of domineering exercises of power.[84] Rieger, surveying the christology of Paul, Nicaea, Chalcedon, and Anselm, rightly argues, "if the relations to empire of each of these ancient approaches go unnoticed, it is more likely than not that the spirit of empire will be perpetuated in our own time."[85] Rieger calls for, after Frederick Herzog, an "historico-self-critical" analysis of christology.[86] This critical approach is needed both by those who theologize within traditional colonizing centers and by those who theologize in (chronologically) post-colonial contexts. A practical christologizing will need to include, or be aware of, a critical re-reading of the "lordship" of

---

84. For a useful historical study of an Anglican religio-imperial discourse, see Strong, *Anglicanism and British Empire*. See also Heaney, "Views of Colonization."

85. Rieger, *Christ and Empire*, 313.

86. Ibid., 315.

Christ in imperial contexts.[87] Rieger demonstrates where such a re-reading might take a practical christology:

> ... Christ the Lord differs dramatically from the Roman [or British] emperor as lord. We find here the old theological principal of *via negativa* rather than the *via eminentiae*. The lordship of Christ is not to be understood as a higher form of (but similar to) the lordship of the Emperor (*via eminentiae*). The lordship of Christ is the contradiction of the lordship of the Emperor (*via negativa*).[88]

Such a christological approach to, in the present context, coloniality does not simply critique the presenting issues of colonial and missionary subjugation. It seeks to identify and reject imperial logic. Such a logic proposes to bring benefit to all from the top down. It is a logic which, therefore, is built upon the suffering of the weakest.[89] While Mbiti and Mugambi rightly critique imperialist or foreign christology the further step of critiquing imperial logic is needed. For without this critique contextual and liberation christologies can be captive to the empire through a top down christologizing. Such issues will be further explored in chapters 7 and 8.

Second, a generalized view of ATRs can become the abstracted locus for a Christ who affirms patriarchy and marginalization. In a more constructive move, christopraxis rejects the *status quo* highlighted, not least, by the reaction of womanist and feminist theologians to African theology.[90] For a contextual approach to christology, especially one that generalizes context and experience, may not transform situations of marginalization. In response, christopraxis, *contra* Mbiti, is unavoidably political. Rieger's words are apposite, "Empire theology does not have to be a conscious enterprise; many of its oppressive tendencies are produced by default."[91] In Mbiti and Mugambi, writing in the light of colonialism and mission Christianity, there is a tendency to top-down contextualizing seen, not least, in an appeal to catholicity. In contrast, to proclaim the lordship of Christ, as the Messiah from the margins, is to proclaim and practice a resistance against top-down globalizations. For, as Rieger sees, "empire theology" is not just theology that explicitly justifies empire (see chapter 2). It is theology that considers the imperial situation and economy normal. This is why theologizing that

---

87. Ibid., 24–54.
88. Ibid., 53.
89. Ibid., 53–54.
90. See Oduyoye, *Hearing and Knowing*, 120–37.
91. Rieger, *Christ and Empire*, 34, see 34–40.

putatively stands independent of politics is perilous. It is in danger of accepting an imperial (or globalized) "normalcy" and "logic."[92] Such issues will be further explored in the following chapters.

Third, christopraxis is ontological solidarity. In giving ATRs a foundational place in their theology both Mbiti and Mugambi demonstrate, to some extent, the possibility of solidarity between ATRs and the Christian church. However, their christologizing, as has been seen in this chapter, moves away from the particularisms of both traditional African religious communities and Christian communities. Christopraxis is not simply the identification of the presence of Christ in the theologizing of Kenyans beyond mission Christianity or in opposition to mission Christianity. For solidarity can be practiced predicated on a notion of bringing those on the margins into the center or practiced as a condescension to bring those below up to some imagined superior level. Such solidarity is based upon hierarchy and manifests itself in hierarchy.[93] As has been seen in this chapter, Mbiti's *praeparatio evangelica*, even if it is understood in more empirical terms, may result in just this kind of hierarchy and condescension. In contrast, christopraxis is ontological solidarity. That means that the humanity of Christ is co-equal with the Akamba and with Kenyans. Christopraxis is defined by a solidarity that affirms not only the co-equality of divinity and humanity in Christ but the co-equality of Christ's humanness and, in this case, African humanness.

Christ is a human "under pressure, suffering, [and] struggling against the powers of empire."[94] The co-equality of this humanness means that Jesus is in solidarity with a particular experience of humanness thereby incarnating a vision of the divine no longer removed from sites of struggle.[95] This kind of solidarity, christologically conceived, results in a practical doctrine of God. God is present in the marginality of African theological voices, in the marginality of African women, in the marginality of adherents to ATRs, and in the marginality of poor people. To know this God is to act. The espoused christocentrism of Mbiti and Mugambi, therefore, can become more contextual and practical with the constructive move of christopraxis.

Conclusion

Four christological themes emerge in the writings of Mbiti and Mugambi and undermine the complaint that in first generation African theology

92. Ibid., 32–33.
93. See Ibid., 82–100.
94. Ibid., 98. See also Song, *Jesus, the Crucified People*, 210–11.
95. Rieger, *Christ and Empire*, 98–99, 255.

christology is "latent." Rather, the christologizing of Mbiti and Mugambi tends toward a more practical approach. Despite this, there is again the tendency to move away from the particular. In this case, it is a move away from the particularism of Kenyan Christian faith communities. However, it is Mugambi who calls for a return to context through a reappraisal of context. Given political developments in a post-colonial context at the end of the Cold-War, Mugambi proposes a reappraisal of both the African context and African theology. Instead of avoiding the political he seems to make it the very point of departure for a new and reconstructionist approach to theology. It appears, *prima facie*, that Mugambi's return to the context in reappraisal at last provides redress for the shift away from the particular inaugurated by Mbiti's work on temporality and eschatology. For that reason, his theology of reconstruction will be outlined and assessed in the following chapter. As will be discovered, however, instead of contextual redress his theology of reconstruction may well embed the move away from the particular. In the final constructive move of the book, it will be argued that in order to address this shift away from the particularism of coloniality some means of power analysis is needed. It will be argued, in chapter 7, that such analysis will emerge now that a fuller comparison of the writings of Mugambi and Mbiti with the emergence of critical post-colonial theology is possible.

6

Coloniality and Mugambi's Theology of Reconstruction

MUGAMBI, LIKE MBITI, is an innovative thinker. This is seen particularly clearly in his theology of reconstruction. It should be noted at the outset, however, that while Mugambi identifies a new approach to African theology, on the whole his theology of reconstruction is captured in a series of intimations. He concedes this when he writes that he will only "paint the mural of reconstruction in broad outline, hoping that others can supply the details with finer brushes and in more varied colors."[1] In short, at the very outset Mugambi concedes that his reconstructionist theology will not in fact be contextual. It is only an approach which arises from thirty years of contextual theology that has gradually moved away from the particular that can, at one and the same time, propose a renewed approach for contextual theology while at the same time conceding from the outset that it will be a generalized and abstracted approach.

This chapter consists of five main sections. First, a brief section analyzing Mugambi's rationale for a theology of reconstruction will be submitted. The following three sections will outline Mugambi's intimations toward a theology of reconstruction which are personal, cultural, and ecclesial. The final section will identify criticisms his proposals attract especially in relation to the exercise of power in social analysis. Consequently, I will submit a further constructive move towards the practice of power.

---

1. Mugambi, *FLTR*, 17.

Mugambi's Rationale for a Theology of Reconstruction

First, the African context is moving into a new era that Mugambi defines as post-liberationist. In the 1970s, Mugambi urged that African theology should be done out of a desire for liberation and towards the goal of liberation.[2] Liberation "must be the overarching goal—the historical project—out of which and for which an African Christian theology must emerge."[3] During this "Exodus era" Moses is the "paradigmatic role model" for leaders of movements seeking freedom from "the imperial system of oppression."[4] He argues that, in the light both of African readings of scripture and the African heritage, colonial subjects had a "divine mandate" to fight for independence.[5] Righteousness, important in biblical narratives, has immediate relevance in African contexts where "African life and culture have been submerged and distorted."[6] God demands right relations and right actions between humans. For Mugambi, the means to such righteousness is practical and can translate into armed struggle in Africa. African theology, for its part, is a practical project concerned with understanding the revelation of God for the economic, political, and social liberation of Africans.[7] For theologians, the "primary" question is "how [can] African Christians . . . be liberated from domination by the missionary legacy on which they have been nurtured, to enable them [to] participate as full members of the international Christian community"?[8] In other words, liberation fighters seek to defeat the political and military imperialist regime and African theologians seek to defeat mission Christianity for it is part of the "imperial entourage."[9]

For Mugambi, inculturation and adaptation are but variations of the dominant liberative impulse in African theologizing.[10] His understanding of liberation, therefore, does not correspond straightforwardly with liberation theology.[11] This is well illustrated from an incident at the inaugural

2. Mugambi, *ACT*, 13.

3. Ibid.

4. Mugambi, Foreword to *Theology of Reconstruction*, ii. See Mugambi, *FLTR*, x–xv; Mugambi, "Social Reconstruction"; Mugambi, *CTSR*, 53. See also Nugent, *Africa Since Independence*, 10–19; Chatterjee, *Nation and its Fragments*, chapter 2.

5. Mugambi, *ACT*, 56. See Mugambi, "Problems and Promises," 55; Muzorewa, 55–56.

6. Mugambi, *ACT*, 13.

7. Ibid., 14.

8. Mugambi, *FLTR*, 23.

9. Mugambi, "Christian Mission and Social," 65; Mugambi, *CTSR*, 21.

10. Mugambi, *FLTR*, 24, 38–42.

11. See Petrella, *Future of Liberation Theology*, for a criticism of any theology that

conference, in Dar es Salaam in 1976, of the Ecumenical Association of Third World Theologians (EATWOT). Mugambi, along with other African theologians, rejected the way in which Latin American theologians were "bulldozing" their agenda of class struggle as the framework for theology. Despite the dominance of Latin American understandings of liberation, African, as well as Asian, practices of liberation are distinct and no one can have a monopoly on the term.[12] The politics and history of each context will be different and how that is understood will, in part, shape a theology for that context. Mugambi seeks a reappraisal of the context and theology in a post-colonial setting.

Second, since the era of independence the broad context for African theology is post-colonialist. Yet, Africa often stands "mainstream political theory on its head." Mugambi argues that nationalism did not lead to the creation of nation-states in Africa. Rather, nations were created by the seeming arbitrary cartography of colonialists. It is only in the light of this colonial fact that nationalisms arose. Consequently, "African states have labored for thirty years to create African nationalist consciousness in their citizens."[13] This has largely failed, argues Mugambi, because the state is often seen as neo-colonial or an extension of the colonial state.[14] Indeed, Bethwell A. Ogot argues that the Kenyan state is not so much a given but a "site of political contestation, a source of conflict and debate."[15]

---

claims "liberation" without prioritizing the material, see for example 122–43.

12. Mugambi, *FLTR*, 2–5, 10–12; Mugambi, *CTSR*, 169; Mugambi, Foreword to *Theology of Reconstruction*, ii–iii. Mugambi refers to Liberation theologians as "'Latin American' only in citizenship. In thought, they are an extension of Euro-American thought . . . Liberation theology in South America did not include the thought of Native and Afro-Latin Americans!" Mugambi and Guy, *CTAC*, 31–32. For early considerations and definitions of African liberationist practice, see Appiah-Kubi and Torres, *African Theology en Route*, 67. It should also be noted that the Kenyan context may be more complex. For example, class conflict can be subsumed within ethnic conflict. For ethnic (a problematic term in itself) conflict is very often focused on access to economic benefits, patronage, and the "resources of modernity and capitalist economic accumulation." See Clark, "Against Invisibility"; Berman, et al., "Patrons, Clients," 466–77; Adar, "Assessing Democratisation."

13. Mugambi, "Churches and Reconstruction," 37; Mugambi, *TAHCC*, 136–39; Mugambi, *FLTR*, 81–83. See Mugambi, "Religions in East Africa," 4–5; Gibellini, "African Theologians," 4; Held, "Development of the Modern State," 74–106, 115–17; Zack-Williams, "Five Decades On."

14. Mugambi, "Churches and Reconstruction," 38; Mugambi, "History of the Church," 49–50. See Aseka, "Post-Colonial State," 92.

15. Ogot, "Introduction," 1. See Mugambi, *TAHCC*, 166; Mugambi, *FLTR*, 220–21; Berman, et al., "Patrons, Clients," 500–501; Davidson, B., *Black Man's Burden*.

At independence the new nations were bound into loans with exorbitant interest rates. Repayment had to come in the form of "hard currency" over against the constant devaluing of "soft currencies." The prices of exports, mainly of raw materials, could not be fixed by the exporters. Consequently, "the pauperisation of the nations of Africa, the Caribbean and Pacific (ACP) was by design, not by accident."[16] In African post-colonial states "the former colonial masters have continued to maintain economic dominance that was assured at the negotiated settlements."[17] As control of the country was once sought in direct political rule it is now, argues Mugambi, sought indirectly by means of economics, technology, and culture.[18] Against this backdrop, mission Christianity "rejoices" over Africa's religiosity while Africa becomes more and more indebted to the nations that missionaries come from.[19] Given such a situation, some kind of reconstruction beyond liberation is needed.

Third, in more recent years Africa is moving into an era of reconstructionism. Reconstruction is needed after liberation and this, argues Mugambi, begins with a conscious movement out of the "Exodus" era and mentality. The end of the "Exodus era," for Mugambi, is marked by three events.[20] In 1990, the founding of the Republic of Namibia, the release of Nelson Mandela, and the collapse of the Soviet Union take place.[21] The Exodus motif no longer makes sense because now African unity would not be predicated upon resistance to "external 'pharaohs.'" Now, the focus would be on reconstruction. African politics, culture and theology have emerged from a colonial bondage and now the search for new metaphors and idioms begins. For Mugambi, under the influence of Paul Tillich, Martin Buber, and Karl Jaspers, a theology of reconstruction is, therefore, an

---

16. Mugambi, "Responsible Leadership," 82. Interestingly, Mugambi cites Arturo Escobar's 1995 work, *Encountering Development*, which has direct links with post-colonial criticism. Indeed, Escobar cites, among others, Said and Bhabha as aiding newer (decolonizing) ways of "thinking about representations of the Third World." See Escobar, *Encountering Development*, 5, 26–54. Undoubtedly, the situation in sub-Saharan Africa is more complex than Mugambi admits. Not least is the factor that African states play in economics. See Woodward, "The Cost of Credit," 6–55; Edelman and Haugerud, *Anthropology of Development*; Schydlowsky, *Structural Adjustment*; Woods, *The Globalizers*.

17. Mugambi, *BBE*, 62.

18. See Rieger, *Christ and Empire*, 241–42, 271–79, 314.

19. Mugambi, "Religions in East Africa," 17. See Mbiti, "Is God a Hindrance."

20. Mugambi, *CTSR*, 71–77.

21. Ibid., 29. Mugambi calls Mandela "the most prominent symbol of the Exodus Metaphor in Christian theology." See Mugambi, "Future of the Church," 35.

attempt at "re-mythologization."[22] This desire for such re-mythologization and, therefore, the very desire for a theology of reconstruction, illustrates not so much a move beyond Mbiti's approach away from the particular but a further embedding of his approach. For it is traditional cultural values, myths, and symbols that are to be revitalized. A theology of reconstruction "presupposes that the social foundations of the old culture are essential for the sustenance of the new society." The "reconstruction motif" is now "much more relevant and potent" as alienated peoples "return to rebuild their destroyed cities, towns and villages."[23] They are to be reconstructed "in symbiosis with the biblical message." This, in turn, will lead to them being re-cast to meet the needs of African churches and societies.[24] Such reconstruction, Mugambi argues, must be practiced at personal, cultural, and ecclesial levels.

Personal Reconstruction

A Christian is "a person who has accepted the Christian faith and made his own decision to become a follower of Jesus Christ."[25] African theology will be determined by those who experience "the power of the gospel."[26] "Inner transformation" is needed. It is such transformation that leads Moses to become a liberation leader, thus bringing together both "spiritual" and social emancipation. The reconstruction of Israel from a "slave community to a liberation one" is predicated upon such personal reconstruction.[27] Personal reconstruction is, therefore, an encounter with God that leads to practice towards social activism. Such reconstruction, argues Mugambi, is not simply part of the narrative of Moses.

> Although Moses is brought up in the king's palace as one of the king's princes, his encounter with God emancipates him and gives him the courage to confront Pharaoh. Nehemiah becomes spiritually emancipated when he encounters God through the cries of his people. As a result of that encounter, he . . . leads a movement of reconstruction in the city of his ancestors. The movement of reconstruction, though guided by technical experts, is essentially a spiritual project, inspired by the inner

22. Mugambi, "Bible and Ecumenism," 75.
23. Mugambi, "Social Reconstruction." See Mugambi, *FLTR*, 23–32.
24. Dedji, *Reconstruction and Renewal*, 45.
25. Mugambi, *TAHCC*, 87.
26. Mugambi, *ACT*, 11; Mugambi, *TAHCC*, 18–21.
27. Mugambi, *FLTR*, 39. See Mugambi, *CTSR*, 68.

commitment to do the will of God. Likewise, Paul becomes spiritually emancipated when he encounters God on the road to Damascus, and converts from a leading persecutor of Christians to a leading defender of Christianity.[28]

From these personal "conversion experiences" a variety of reconstructive projects emerge. Moses reconstructs the "collective consciousness of his people" enabling them to resist Pharaoh and be liberated. Nehemiah reconstructs the "collective consciousness of the disenfranchised people" giving them hope to rebuild their community. Paul builds Christian communities throughout the Mediterranean region on the basis of the freedom of Christ. From these conversions and constructive practices Mugambi concludes, "there is an intimate connection between spiritual emancipation and the processes of Liberation and Reconstruction." Without "inner spiritual motivation" it is unlikely, argues Mugambi, that any liberative or reconstructive project would be possible.[29] Consequently, Mugambi can summarize a theology of reconstruction as having as its goal "the re-definition of our social consciousness, so that it is consistent with our affirmation of the Christian faith."[30] People must "continually reconstruct" themselves in "readiness for the tasks and challenges ahead."[31] Such personal reconstruction is empowered by the Christian gospel, which Mugambi illustrates by citing Jesus' parable of the Pharisee and tax collector (Luke 18:9–14), his words to the crowds in Matthew 23 critiquing pharisaical hypocrisy (Matt 23:1–13), and hymns by Benjamin M. Ramsey (Teach me thy way O Lord), Frances R. Havegral (Take my life and let it be), and Charlotte Elliott (Just as I am, without one plea). Empowered by this gospel of divine acceptance and freedom through humility and dedication Africans can "forge their own self-image and self-understanding."[32]

It is because of this holistic understanding of liberation-salvation that Mugambi rejects "dialectical thought," "dialectical discourse," and critiques theologies of liberation.[33] Unlike African thought, the "European intellectual tradition especially since the Enlightenment, has been dominated by the Hegelian Dialectic." This, Mugambi understands, to be a cycle or spiral of ideas moving from thesis to antithesis to synthesis and new thesis. In a critique reminiscent of post-colonial theology (see chapter 7), Mugambi

28. Mugambi, *CTSR*, 68.
29. Ibid.
30. Mugambi and Guy, *CTAC*, 21.
31. Mugambi, *FLTR*, 15.
32. Ibid., 88.
33. Mugambi, *CTSR*, 165–66; Mugambi, "Missiological Research," 545–47.

sees theologies of liberation as framed within such a dialectical framework. The goal then becomes the "dislodgement of the oppressor *from power*, and the accession of the oppressed *to power* after their liberation." Unfortunately, Mugambi's thought is less than pellucid when it comes to his criticisms of liberation theology. A primary reason for this is that he persists in using terms and thought from liberation theology while, at the same time, seeking to distance himself from liberation theology. He is more indebted to liberation theology than he admits and, as will be seen, his innovation is less marked than his rhetoric would suggest. Nevertheless, his criticism of liberation theology caught in so-called Western dialectical thought is sound and his desire to engage theologically with issues relating to ongoing struggles in Africa is a contextual move in fitting with his purpose as an African theologian.

In Africa, people have suffered for liberation and have suffered at the hands of the "elite" who jostle to power only to fail in practicing consensus politics. Unlike such theologies of liberation a theology of reconstruction, he argues, is a genuinely new way of doing theology. A theology not led by the elite for the sake of the oppressed masses against their oppressors but a theology where "all sectors of the population are invited to participate in the inauguration of a new social order."[34] For without salvation there can be no liberation and without liberation there can be no salvation.[35]

> Theological discourse in Africa should come to terms with this integral approach to the Gospel. It is not necessary to opt for either the liberational or the salvational approaches. Rather, African theologians ought to discern an approach which integrates liberation with salvation, and *vice versa*.[36]

In short, theological agency is predicated upon human agency, more generally, which is itself predicated upon self-determination in cultural, political, social, and economic terms.[37]

Dedji observes that Mugambi has consistently resisted the polarization in theology and practice in Africa between "salvation" and "liberation" or any configuration of theology that is predicated upon an "us-them" or

---

34. Mugambi, *CTSR*, 165–66. See Mugambi, "Religion and Social Reconstruction," 22–23. Mugambi bluntly states: "Neo-colonialism was the actual result of decolonisation" (p. 22).

35. Mugambi, *ACT*, 14.

36. Mugambi, *FLTR*, 7.

37. Ibid., 9–10. See Shorter, *Toward a Theology*, 247.

"winner-loser" dichotomy.[38] Salvation must be total.[39] Salvation can no more be reduced to class struggle than it can be reduced to spiritual disembodiment. Salvation-Liberation is both theological and socio-political.[40] Therefore, like Mbiti, Mugambi claims to have serious reservations about liberation theology. For Mbiti these reservations center on importing political ideology into theology. Mbiti rejects liberation theology because, he argues, theology can have transformative effects in a plurality of socio-political contexts and with a plurality of political commitments. Mbiti wants to make a distinction between contextual and political theology. Mugambi does not want to do this. "As an aspect of liberation, inculturation is indispensable. This is because the process of liberation is incomplete without cultural liberation."[41] The danger in Africa, argues Mugambi, is that theologians have sought inculturation without liberation. However, inculturation is a dimension of liberation. Therefore, *contra* Mbiti, he rejects any attempt to see contextual theologies as alternatives to liberative (but not liberation) theologies. Contextual theology deals with the emancipation of culture that, if it is to have effect, must be integrated with political and economic liberation.[42] He does not want so much to make a distinction between contextual and political theology as much as he wants to reject the importation, implicit or explicit, of any ideology that confirms the marginalization of people in Africa. In no way should African theology endorse the marginalization of Africa as the "Third World." On the contrary, its liberative function is to resist such marginalization and empower Africans to theologize in their own terms.[43] Consequently, liberation for Mugambi is the "penultimate process" eliminating dependency and affirming integrity and independence in the socio-political sphere. Salvation is the "ultimate hope" that transcends "the finitude of natural and historical processes" towards "total self-realization" and "self-fulfilment."[44]

Despite such calls and hopes for personal reconstruction, it remains unclear how particular and individual conversions lead to particular reconstructionist impulses or practices. It is not necessary that conversion leads to (reconstructionist) activism. Indeed, conversionism can lead believers away from social activism. The causal relation between conversion and

---

38. Mugambi, *FLTR*, viii–ix. See Dedji, *Reconstruction and Renewal*, 51.
39. Mugambi, *ACT*, 12, 14. See Boff and Boff, *Salvation and Liberation*.
40. Mugambi, *ACT*, 12, 14; Dedji, *Reconstruction and Renewal*, 49–50.
41. Mugambi, *CTSR*, 72.
42. Ibid., 72–73.
43. Mugambi, *FLTR*, 11; Mugambi, *BBE*, 68 f.n. 5.
44. Mugambi, *ACT*, x, 12–16.

reconstruction remains unproven in Mugambi's intimations toward personal reconstruction. However, there does seem to be a clearer relationship between the history of Kenya and the need for cultural reconstruction.

Cultural Reconstruction

African theology is forged within the context of brutal and vicious racism and colonialism. In circumstances where such racism and colonialism have been overcome now reconstructed people, argues Mugambi, need to begin to reconstruct their culture and society. There is always the danger, Mugambi observes, that a society can become "enveloped into the cocoon of traditionalism."[45] However, African culture is "not some archival, fossilized set of practices."[46] Modifications occur. "Culture is alive when the people who have evolved it are determined to preserve the most basic elements while modifying the superficial aspects and incorporating new ones to maximize the chances of survival."[47] Mugambi's "modifications" (reconstruction) relate to what he sees as key components of culture—ethics, politics, economics, and aesthetics.[48]

First, cultural reconstruction is ethical. Mugambi's proposals for political, economic, and aesthetic reconstruction can be seen as an initial attempt to ethically and practically ground reconstruction. This relationship between ethics and cultural reconstruction is seen most clearly when Mugambi's assessment of ecumenism is noted. Writing about ecumenism, Mugambi sees ecumenical practice as a grounding of the center of "the Christian ethic"—love.[49] If love is at the center of Christian ethics then Christian commitment must strengthen, not diminish, "cultural identity."[50] It can be assumed if love strengthens cultural identity then colonialism and missionary practice associated with colonialism are very far from an

---

45. Mugambi, *FLTR*, 77.

46. Mugambi and Guy, *CTAC*, 83. See Mugambi, *TAHCC*, 90.

47. Mugambi, "Future of the Church," 50.

48. Mugambi, *FLTR*, 16. See Mugambi, *TAHCC*, 129–31. He also includes "religion," but that will be dealt with in the following section when ecclesial reconstruction is considered. For it is to Christianity that Mugambi appeals when writing about religion and reconstruction.

49. Mugambi, "Future of the Church," 45. He quotes but does not cite William Barclay at this point: Barclay, *Christian Ethics for Today*. See also Mugambi, "Towards Ecumenical Consensus."

50. Mugambi, "Religions in East Africa," 21; Mugambi and Guy, *CTAC*, 21–22. See Mbiti, *ARAP*, 19–21.

outworking of a Christian ethic.[51] Indeed, the "cultural integrity" of Kenya has been suppressed under foreign rule and foreign mission (see chapter 2). However, Kenyan "national identity" cannot be developed without a "national consciousness" or a reconstruction of "cultural integrity." His proposals for a theology of reconstruction are, therefore, "articulated" within the context not only of "global capitalist hegemony" but also of "internal civil strife in Africa."[52] Such strife has particularly affected rural communities.

Mugambi observes that it is largely rural and traditional communities that guard and promote an "African ethic."[53] If these communities are in danger of disintegration then African ethics are in danger. Urbanization, he argues, brings just such a danger resulting in a "severe" threat against "traditional social structures."[54] Urban centers in Africa bring "dehumanizing" tendencies associated with individualism, anonymity, mobility, opportunity, flexibility, and plurality.[55] Writing in 2001, Mugambi adjudges the past twenty years in Kenya to be a period of cultural "anarchy" under the influence of globalization, privatization, and liberalization. The best that can be said is that "national norms" are pluralistic.[56] In response, ethics within a theology of reconstruction are concerned with reconstructing "value systems."[57] He quotes Clifford Geertz who "succinctly articulates" the role of religion in social ethics. Geertz proposes that religion gives to values a "metaphysical grounding."[58] Morals "evolve as ways and means of regulating behavior within specific cultural contexts."[59] Mugambi explains that when "priorities change, the value system also has to be adjusted, either to remind the people of forgotten priorities, or to re-organize the hierarchy of values."[60] It is not clear if Mugambi affirms Greetz's assessment that such grounding is a construction of the human imagination.[61] However, Mugambi's interest is not ostensibly in philosophies or theories of ethics. Rather, his focus seems more practical. For that reason he moves to reconstructionist proposals for

---

51. Mugambi, *TAHCC*, 127–28; Mugambi, *FLTR*, 31, 78.
52. Mugambi, "Theology of Reconstruction," 143.
53. Mugambi, *FLTR*, 73.
54. Ibid., 75. See Mugambi, "Christian Mission in Context."
55. Mugambi, *FLTR*, 75.
56. Mugambi and Guy, *CTAC*, 71–73.
57. Mugambi, *FLTR*, 17.
58. Ibid., 82. See Geertz, *Interpretation of Culture*, 126–31.
59. Mugambi, *CTSR*, 50–51.
60. Mugambi, *FLTR*, 17.
61. Geertz, *Interpretation of Culture*, 131.

what appear to be concrete problems in the Kenyan and African context: politics, economics, and aesthetics.

Second, cultural reconstruction is political. In place of the disintegration of African ethics, a theology of reconstruction will seek African union in place of division and togetherness in place of disharmony. To that end, Mugambi has proposals for African democracy and proposals for the means to wider African solidarity.[62] In Africa, there have been proposals made for philosophical foundations for the state based on the conviction that "Africans needed social systems founded on the African cultural and religious heritage."[63] African theologians must, therefore, "reckon with" nationalism or become irrelevant.[64] The earlier Mugambi made an appeal to *Nyayoism* as a Kenyan foundation for African theology. However, because of colonial history, he now recognizes that the post-colonial state has "been in crisis from the beginning." Repressive laws on the statute books were not removed and power was transferred to "an African elite without any public debate."[65] Such leaders "almost without exception" govern in ways not dissimilar to colonialists. They "demand to be obeyed, not emulated!"[66] Despite this, Mugambi identifies African countries, including South Africa, Mozambique, and Uganda, as providing a glimpse of how African "ideology" can shape political practice. For example, South Africa's Truth and Reconciliation Commission is "an innovation unprecedented in history" and founded on the "African belief that confession is therapeutic, even when the damage done by the offender is irreparable."[67] Mozambique's power-sharing government reflects the African conviction that "the loser is just as important as the winner, because without losers there can be no winners." The Uganda Movement system stands as an African alternative to multi-party systems. A "Westminster model" promoting "adversarial politics through political parties" does not "resonate" with the African heritage. In the African heritage the primacy and unicameral nature of community means there are no political parties. There is, therefore, an "inclination" towards "one-party democracy." For consensus is more important than majority opinion.

62. Mugambi, "Religion and Social Reconstruction."
63. Mugambi, *CTSR*, 39–40.
64. See Mugambi, *TAHCC*, 19; Mugambi, "Theology of Reconstruction," 148.
65. Mugambi, "Religion and Social Reconstruction," 22. See Magaga, "African Dream," 89; Godia, *Understanding Nyayo*. It must be noted, however, that Mugambi is well aware that theology cannot be done in an "ideologically neutral" manner. Indeed, he would much prefer a theologian declares his or her "ideological orientation." In this way, he has been consistent with his own advice. See Mugambi and Guy, *CTAC*, 62.
66. Mugambi, "Religion and Social Reconstruction," 26.
67. Mugambi, *CTSR*, 40.

Eldership is the key qualification of a leader and that leadership will not distinguish the "religious" from the "political."[68] According to Mugambi the Ugandan system is "internationally acclaimed as 'democratic' without political parties."[69] These impulses and glimpses of African heritage in African politics leads Mugambi to submit practical political proposals.[70]

In the period of reconstruction, Mugambi proposes that African nations return to earlier proposals for a continent wide federal republic and a common continental language.[71] A federal Union of African States is "long overdue."[72] Mugambi references the significant contribution that Kwame Nkrumah (first president of a newly liberated Ghana from 1957) makes to pan-Africanism. The Cold War thwarted his vision of a continent-wide federal republic through the "balkanization of the continent." However, the end of the Cold War and the rise of the European Union leads Mugambi to again call for practical African unity.[73] To promote and consolidate such continent-wide "integration" Nkrumah also proposed that Africa have a uniting language (Kiswahili). It appears that Mugambi wishes to reconstruct such proposals at the end of the Exodus era.[74] For Mugambi quotes as affirmation the conclusion of V. B. Thompson that without Pan-Africanism there is "No Africa."[75] This reinvigorated Pan-Africanism is not only political

---

68. Mugambi, "Religion and Social Reconstruction," 13–14, 21–23. These are not original points. See Nkrumah, *Consciencism: Philosophy*, 100–106.

69. Mugambi, "Religion and Social Reconstruction," 13.

70. Mugambi, *TAHCC*, 129–39; Mugambi, *CTSR*, 42, see 57–58.

71. See Thompson, *Africa and Unity*.

72. Mugambi, *FLTR*, 212. The African Union was founded in 2002. For recent work on the African Union, see Gebe, "Quest for a Union Government"; Landsberg, "Reflections on the African Union." Other articles in the same edition include Mbeki, "African Union at Ten"; Zondi, "African Union and the State."

73. Mugambi, *CTSR*, 41, 57–58; Mugambi, "Foundations for an African Approach," 9–10. See Mugambi, *FLTR*, 152; Nkrumah, *Consciencism: Philosophy*, 117–18. For more critical appraisals of Nkrumah, see Rooney, *Kwame Nkrumah: Vision*, 350–64; White, "Kwame Nkrumah: Cold War Modernity."

74. See Mugambi, *CTSR*, 39–43, 50; Mugambi, *FLTR*, 210–25.

75. Mugambi, *FLTR*, 210; Thompson, *Africa and Unity*, 313. While Mbiti is keen to shun "political theology," he also shares similar sentiments when he writes, "Rather than try to do the impossible and extremely explosive job of reversing and revising the colonial boundaries, modern African states have agreed to retain and respect these colonial boundaries, however painful they may continue to be. It would be a more positive step forward if the states would unite and thus swallow up or forever abolish these colonial divisions." Mbiti, *ARAP*, 133.

and cultural, it is anticipated also to "evolve internal markets for goods and services."[76]

Third, cultural reconstruction involves economics.[77] Africans, Mugambi asserts, are "double losers" because they can neither set the prices for what they export (mostly raw materials), nor set the prices for what they import (mostly manufactured goods). This is seen particularly clearly in agriculture. For too much land is set aside for growing cash crops when many suffer food shortages each year.[78]

> Suppose peasants in a particular locality decide that coffee prices are low, and choose to plant flowers instead. They earn more money, only as long as the flowers are fetching good prices in the export market. Since the earnings are still determined externally, the incomes of these peasants will remain fragile and dependent.[79]

For Mugambi, Kenya suffers under the arrangements of "economic apartheid," which will only be exacerbated by the Millennium Development Goals.[80] For they, along with structural adjustments, continue the dependency and indebtedness of Africa to the "developed" nations. While poverty alleviation is the "ostensible" objective "systematic pauperisation has become the actual result."[81] Only a complete restructuring of economic relationships will address these injustices.[82] Undoubtedly, Mugambi would agree with Rieger who writes, "A mere insistence on equality that does not also seek to overturn the basic presuppositions that undergird the unequal distribution of power is not enough."[83]

Mugambi proposes a multifaceted approach calling for action at both grassroots and national levels. It is the church in Africa that is often the social institution that has closest contact with "the peasants." At a grassroots

---

76. Mugambi, *CTSR*, 41, 57–58; Mugambi, "Foundations for an African Approach," 9–10. See Mugambi, *FLTR*, 152.

77. Mugambi, *CTSR*, 43.

78. Ibid., 44–45; Mugambi, *FLTR*, 212–14.

79. Mugambi, *CTSR*, 44.

80. See www.mdgafrica.org. See also Kim, K., *Concepts of Development*.

81. Mugambi, "Religion and Social Reconstruction," 24–25. See Mugambi, *FLTR*, 64–67. See also Mkandawire and Soludo, *African Voices*; Young, R., *Postcolonialism: Historical Intro*, 27.

82. Mugambi, "Responsible Leadership," 82–83, argues for Fair Trade, citing Stückelberger, *Global Trade Ethic*; Ghai, *Renewing Social and Economic Progress*; Devarajan, et al., *Aid and Reform*.

83. Rieger, *Christ and Empire*, 224. See Mugambi, *FLTR*, 214.

level Mugambi proposes that "extension officers" be based in local communities to help them "improve their farming, processing and marketing practices."[84] For self-sufficiency in "staple foods is the first step towards restoration of dignity in Africa."[85] Improvement might be made through crop diversification, food processing, and the introduction of low management crops (Mugambi identifies sugar cane as an example).[86] Whatever technical course is followed the most important aspect of such work is the strengthening of social structures. For, Mugambi claims, it is not "natural disaster" that is the primary cause of hunger but "social instability."[87]

Internal markets in Africa are "fragile or non-existent." An African Union would "open up markets within the continent and remove travel and immigration restrictions." It would mean that each state would be focused on attracting capital and trade from every part of the continent. Such a federation would also present a "trading bloc," a "united Africa would certainly be strong enough to compete in the world market" and it would become an important "lobby within the United Nations." Such a lobby may be strong enough to demand an end to European protectionism.[88] Such lobbying power would counter the imposition of a Northern agenda and Northern cultures.

Fourth, cultural reconstruction is aesthetical. It is not only ethical and political practice that has been imposed on Africa. Aesthetically, foreign values have been "superimposed" upon traditional practice. Despite this, Mugambi sees traditional aesthetic resilience in preferences for large families where community defines human identity, architectural preference for the circle over the right-angle, the dominance of black, red, and green as Colors integrated into the flags of independent nations and the blurring of performer and audience.[89] However, something more robust is required. Aesthetic reconstruction is needed and it is to the publication of proceedings of a conference at University College, Nairobi that he points to as "perhaps" the most convincing approach to this. Of the essays in *Black Aesthetics* Mugambi identifies those authored by B. A. Ogot and Ali Mazrui as the most important.[90] Though Mugambi does not identify in any detail what it

---

84. Mugambi, *CTSR*, 45, see 58–60; Mugambi, *FLTR*, 213–15. Mugambi mentions water harvesting and low cost irrigation, 215.

85. Mugambi, *FLTR*, 214, see 220–22.

86. Ibid., 222.

87. Ibid., 86. For this insight, Mugambi cites Byron, *Causes of World Hunger*, 5–15.

88. Mugambi, *FLTR*, 212, 223, see 83–89.

89. Mugambi, *TAHCC*, 129–39.

90. Gurr and Zirimu, *Black Aesthetics*. See Mugambi, *CTSR*, 46–47.

is about these two essays that serves his reconstructionist approach they can be summarized presently as proposals for self-knowledge, extension, and indigenization.

From Ogot arises the need for self-knowledge. This means coming to terms with a more realistic understanding of Africans in history and in art. A reconstructionist "theme" will not simply apportion blame externally but will "as a priority, focus on self-criticism, self-evaluation and re-dedication."[91] Ogot writes, "the African is a normal human being who is capable . . . of exhibiting a whole galaxy of human virtues . . . In the same way, we have to accept that he is very capable of committing all kinds of crimes and sins."[92] Grounding such realism can be achieved through extension programs as art taken to the people. Mazrui identifies several theatrical groups in East Africa that have successfully done this. However, extension is not one-way. Rather, "old arts" must too be brought to the "new educational system."[93] For example, oral literature and traditional oral historians must be given opportunity to engage with the universities of East Africa.[94] As well as such grassroots practice, educational curricula must continue to be extended. In Anglophone educational institutions the literature that is being studied must be continually "internationalized." The result will be that the "foreignness" of English will become "no longer . . . identifiable with what is British."[95] Consequently, a reconstructionist approach to aesthetics will continue to enact two "paradoxical processes" in more African literature and orature (localization) and a greater diversity of sources (internationalization).[96]

Colonial languages, including English, need not continue to reverberate according to the cadences, grammar, or vocabulary of the metropolitan centers. Rather, the metropolitan language must be continually "domesticated" and "indigenized."[97] Mazrui notes that such indigenization in "the profound and the superficial, the imaginative and the mediocre, the polished style and the halting expressions of semi-literacy" is the means to the construction of a new culture.[98] In a similar way, African languages, including Kiswahili, must continue to be modernized to take into account

91. Mugambi, *CTSR*, 48.
92. Ogot, "A Man More Sinned Against," 23.
93. Mazrui, "Aesthetic Dualism," 40–41.
94. Ibid.
95. Ibid., 43.
96. Ibid., 45.
97. Ibid., 49.
98. Ibid., 50.

cultures and situations which they had not before had to articulate (for example, modern law, technology, international literature and culture).[99] All such construction and reconstruction seems to serve Mugambi's definition of aesthetic reconstruction as entailing an "appreciation of the values upon which a society is founded, and a commitment to build on this foundation mode of life which is constructively responsive to the challenges of the present and the future."[100]

As will be seen in the following section, it is religion, and the Christian church in particular, that Mugambi identifies as the key social institution to embody and promote such ethical, political, economic, and aesthetical reconstruction. For that reason his understanding of ecclesial reconstruction becomes crucial to the practicability of his proposals. However, before proceeding to the next section, it should be noted that in his proposals for cultural reconstruction his appeal to the particular and experiential is substantially weakened by a rather uncritical view of African political systems and arrangements. The same uncritical approach is also evident in generalized or even romanticized views on the pacific nature and role of rural communities.

Ecclesial Reconstruction

For Mugambi "religion" is a "sub-set" of culture and not a "super-structure over culture."[101] The starting point for his reconstructionism is not therefore, in the end, experience or even personal conversion. Rather, it is the more abstracted understanding of the "African cultural and religious heritage" that relates to "religion" as the most "basic stratum" for a reconstructionist project.[102] Christian religious reconstruction, relating to the African heritage, is for Mugambi obviously the task of the African church. The task of such reconstruction is missional, theological, and ecumenical.

First, ecclesial reconstruction is missiological. Just as Mbiti's initial articulation of African Christian eschatology is designed to equip the Kenyan church in mission, so also Mugambi initially prioritizes Christian mission in his first articulation of a theology of reconstruction.[103] Indeed, no "movement can merit the title 'church' unless it is a missionary community."[104] The

99. Ibid., 41–43.
100. Mugambi, *CTSR*, 49.
101. Mugambi and Guy, *CTAC*, 169.
102. Mugambi, *CTSR*, 37–38.
103. Mugambi, "Future of the Church," 36. See Mugambi, *FLTR*, 21–22.
104. Mugambi, "Future of the Church," 36; Mugambi, *FLTR*, 240, see 167–73. See

mission that Mugambi has in mind is the reconstruction of theology, knowledge, technology, pastoral care, ecumenism, healing, and management. These he calls the "new frontiers" of evangelization.[105]

In Africa, there is a "crisis of knowledge," which can be understood as a "great gap" between the schooled and the unschooled and between the church and science and technology.[106] The African church has tended to be "defensive" in the face of science and technology. However, in a rapidly changing context the church must work on launching programs and guidance on science and technology as part of its mission. The danger of not doing so is the loss of "schooled Africans" to the church.[107] For example, there is sometimes "open antagonism" between "scientific medicine and traditional African medicine." A reconstructive approach to mission will seek a holistic approach where "the doctor, teacher, pastor and social worker may all co-operate to heal a patient within a family context." Such integrated mission cannot be allowed, however, simply to function on the basis of "evangelical unity." There must also be commitment to "ecumenical unity." Integrated mission is common witness but it is also a working together for "visible expressions of united Christian witness, fellowship and service." Towards this end church "management procedures" need to be modernized in order that personnel, finances, assets, time, donations, and grants are more efficiently and effectively used.[108] There is little detail in Mugambi's proposals here. More would help his readers garner a greater sense of what he envisages practically.

Second, ecclesial reconstruction is theological.

> Theology is indispensable in the process of reconstruction, because it provides the epistemological axioms on the basis of which social institutions are legitimized. If African Christian theology continues to justify epistemological dependence on ecclesiological packages from the North Atlantic, African churches will find it increasingly difficult to afford and sustain church structures which are culturally irrelevant and alien. Conversely, African Christian theologians can constructively discern the needs of African communities, and help in the shaping of ecclesial structures which inductively respond to these

---

Mbiti, "Mission Outreach."

105. Mugambi, "Future of the Church," 40–43.
106. Ibid., 41.
107. Ibid., 42.
108. Ibid., 40–43. See Mugambi, "Vision of the African Church," 246–47.

needs with efficacy. This introspective method in theology has great creative potential in the future of African Christianity.¹⁰⁹

For Mugambi, "Theology is the means by which the Church rationalizes its process of ecclesial reconstruction."¹¹⁰ A theologian must, therefore, be a "servant of the community of faith to which he or she belongs."¹¹¹

As has been seen, Mugambi's reconstructionist emphasis finds its biblical foundation not in the imagery of the Exodus but in the post-exilic.¹¹² In Africa, he argues, liberative practice concentrates on conflict, reconstructionist practice concentrates on peace. Liberation focuses on the oppressor, reconstruction focuses on the liberated agent. Liberation conceives of the oppressors as objects, reconstruction sees the liberated as subject. Liberation locates the center of power with the oppressor, reconstruction locates the center of power with the liberated. Liberation aims to destroy, reconstruction aims to rebuild. Liberationists employ weapons, reconstructionists employ tools. Liberationist movements are regimented, reconstructionist movements are decentralized. Liberationist movements have a central command, reconstructionist movements emphasize personal initiative. Liberationist movements have hierarchical leadership, reconstructionist movements have horizontal leadership. Liberation stresses competition, reconstruction stresses cooperation.¹¹³ In these ten antitheses, where Mugambi contrasts the practices of liberation in Africa with the practices of reconstruction, he makes little attempt to justify why he has isolated these specific antitheses. He simply compares the examples of Moses and Nehemiah. Moses, he argues, operates like a war commander whereas Nehemiah operates like a manager at a construction site.¹¹⁴ More is needed from Mugambi at this juncture. At best, his antithetical list crystallizes his interpretation of dominant practices of liberation in Africa, in their political, cultural and theological forms, which in turn allows him to introduce how a theology of reconstruction might succeed and subsume such struggles for a new era. At worst, he abstracts and misjudges liberative practice and nationalist movements, which he then uses as a foil against which to introduce his own innovations. Nonetheless, the antitheses do serve to illustrate why Mugambi thinks fresh developments are needed.

109. Mugambi, *CTSR*, 31.
110. Mugambi, *FLTR*, 17.
111. Mugambi, "Future of the Church," 40.
112. Ibid., 35. See Mugambi, "Theology of Reconstruction," 140.
113. Mugambi, *CTSR*, 74–75.
114. Ibid., 75.

Deuteronomy (1:19–40) provides him with a new "metaphor" or "motif." Moses and his generation were barred from the promised land because they "relied on Egypt as their point of reference" and, therefore, "remained in ideological bondage." In contrast, argues Mugambi, the book of Deuteronomy is a call to the people to "establish their own identity while maintaining friendly relations with all the neighbors."[115] For there is no "classic" culture. There is no possibility for the "permanent achievement" of a single and universal culture. Culture is dynamic. A theologian with this understanding of culture, notes Mugambi, views theology as an ongoing process and focuses on method as a way of engaging with ongoing cultural changes.[116] What is needed, seeing the contributions of the past as foundational but reformable, is to practice theology in response to changing circumstances while seeking to change such circumstances. Despite Mugambi's apparent equalitarianism, it is the "responsibility of the African elite, including theologians" to be the agents of such change. It is the elite who will lead "the process of reconstruction, so that the continent can take its respectable place among other regions of the world."[117]

The method, according to Mugambi, for engaging theologically with ongoing change in African culture is reconstructionist and it is to Tillich that he turns to for an example of what that might entail. Mugambi's confidence in Tillich is clear when he writes, "perhaps more than any other 20th century theologian [Tillich], succeeded in the task of discerning new symbols and metaphors in which to re-cast the central message of the gospel."[118] Mugambi is less concerned with the success of Tillich's correlating theology in a Northern context and more concerned with attempting to develop the method for theological reconstruction in Africa.[119] Such development results in his proposals that African theologians and churches must ground such remythologization.[120]

Third, ecclesial reconstruction is socially engaged. In African societies, churches, through the power of the pulpit, apparently remain "the most powerful and the most accessible instrument of communication in

115. Mugambi, "Future of the Church," 35.

116. This emphasis on method is something that Mugambi takes from his reading of Bernard Lonergan. See Mugambi, *CTSR*, 20; Lonergan, *Method in Theology*. See also Mugambi, "Theological Method," 5–40.

117. Mugambi, *ACT*, 27–28.

118. Mugambi, "Bible and Ecumenism," 75.

119. Dedji, *Reconstruction and Renewal*, 57. See Tracy, *Blessed Rage*.

120. Mugambi, "Bible and Ecumenism," 75. See Dedji, *Reconstruction and Renewal*, 57.

Africa."¹²¹ For this reason they have great potential to be the "social institutions" to resist and replace "colonial images" of Africa. It is in the replacement of such images that Mugambi actually identifies an example of what it might mean to create new myths (re-mythologize) for Africa. Instead of the colonial image of Africa as the "sleeping question mark" and "the dark continent" churches must provide new myths. In place of the myth of a "vanishing people" new myths of a "resurgent people," a "resilient people," and a hopeful people must be proclaimed. In replacing the myth of a "hungry people" the myth of "a people capable of feeding [themselves]" must now be promoted.¹²² Churches, then, have the potential to "transfigure" Africa's identity as the means to such re-mythologization.¹²³

> 'You see the trouble we are in, how Jerusalem lies in ruins with its gates burnt. Come, let us rebuild the wall of Jerusalem, so that we may no longer suffer disgrace.' I told them that the hand of my God had been gracious upon me, and also the words that the king had spoken to me. Then they said, 'Let us start building!' So they committed themselves to the common good. (Neh 2:17–18)

According to Mugambi, in the biblical text it is Nehemiah who through "participatory management" leads social reconstruction for his people. Post-colonial Africa is in a position not dissimilar to Nehemiah's Judah.

> There are many Sanballats, Geshems and Tobiahs in the media, in politics, in diplomatic circles and in business. They are also in the World Bank and in the IMF; in embassies and universities; in churches and mission agencies; and in media houses and corporations . . . It seems to me that at this time in history, the figure of Nehemiah is most encouraging and most inspiring for Africa today. We can find and emulate prophets of hope, who encourage the poor and weak to keep struggling, even in the midst of great disaster. God is in charge of history, even when principalities and powers mess it up. Hope will eventually triumph over despair. This is the essence of the theology of reconstruction.¹²⁴

Societal reconstruction begins with the church in a context where Kenyan political leaders have distanced themselves from the realities that ordinary Kenyans live with and have continued to gather wealth and power

---

121. Mugambi, *FLTR*, 49–50, see 47–51, 225.
122. Ibid., 37–38.
123. Ibid., 49–50.
124. Mugambi, "Theology of Reconstruction," 147.

onto themselves. There is a gap in understandings of community. That is to say, there is a gap between the governing elite's understanding of community and the African heritage. Mugambi suggests that community within the African heritage, seen today especially in rural societies, is understood in relation to kinship, family, and networks of relationships. From the perspective of government, community is objectified as a series of relations to be served or manipulated.[125] Consequently, Mugambi sees the role of the church as a possible mediator between the assumptions and worldview of the ruling classes and that of the ordinary people. For "there is a great difference between social reality as experienced and understood by the opulent, and social reality as experienced and understood by the destitute."[126] The churches, he argues, will "come of age" when they become the "'social conscience' of African peoples and nations."[127] However, such maturation is predicated upon unity. Mugambi's reflections on post-colonial ecclesial reconstruction are centered on the agency of the churches and their capacity for unity. Mugambi sees the ecumenical movement, beginning in the twentieth century, as contributing greatly "towards the correction" of the errors of the cultural imperialism of much missionary activity in Africa.[128]

Fourth, ecclesial reconstruction is ecumenical. Mugambi is an experienced and committed ecumenist and his proposals for ecclesial reconstruction include an expansion and advancement of ecumenism in Africa.[129] "The plague of Christianity in Africa is its internal division and rivalry, not external threat."[130] For Mugambi, the diversity of agencies, the denominationalism, the competition and the rivalry imported by missionaries and inherited by African believers in the nineteenth century is scandalous. It amounts to a "denominational partition" of Africa mirroring imperialist arrangements at the Berlin Conference (1884–85). The "great hope" found in the ecumenical movement is that it may enable "people of all cultures to proclaim their identity without shame or fear."[131] Ecumenism is particularly prized by Mugambi because he sees it mirror an "inclusive perspective"

---

125. Mugambi, "Churches and Reconstruction," 34–37.

126. Mugambi and Guy, *CTAC*, 105.

127. Mugambi, "Religion and Social Reconstruction," 32.

128. Mugambi, *TAHCC*, 89; Mugambi, *FLTR*, 205–9. For an overview of the situation up until the 1980s, and especially in light of Vatican II, see Mugambi, et al., *Ecumenical Initiatives*, 5–26; Mugambi, "Ecumenical Movement," 5–28.

129. Mugambi, "Ecumenical Movement," 6.

130. Mugambi, *FLTR*, viii, see 196–98.

131. Ibid., 106. See Mugambi, et al., *Ecumenical Initiatives*.

already present in the African heritage.[132] In general terms, "[t]he African value of social solidarity is held so dear that no family would try to isolate itself from other families because of its religious beliefs."[133] Furthermore, as with the African heritage, there seems to be a permanency or stability with the churches not evident in other social institutions:

> In Africa, the Church remains the most influential and the most sustainable social institution, especially in the rural areas. Political parties, trade unions and co-operatives are transient . . . Churches, in contrast, have a permanence which transcends particular national boundaries and generations of leaders.[134]

While there are positive developments in ecumenical relationships in East Africa, sectarianism is all too prevalent in the churches.[135] This is especially the case when theological education is considered. Theological education is often delivered along denominational lines and, because of that, often replicates curricula from outside Africa. Mugambi concludes that the "adverse implications of such exclusiveness for the construction of a nation in post-colonial Africa are staggering."[136] That is to say, "[t]here can be no unity in a country if churches remain divided."[137] Ecumenical programs and institutions need to be established and promoted. However, this remains a great challenge in the face of confessionally based donors.[138] Nonetheless, especially with the introduction of the Bible in local languages, itself a product of ecumenical work, ongoing renewal, reformation and even schism becomes likely as African hermeneutics emerge.[139]

Fifth, ecclesial reconstruction is hermeneutical. Like Mbiti, Mugambi accords the Bible, always read from specific contexts, a central place in Christian identity and practice.[140] It is the "scriptural foundation," the "basic source," the "final authority," and the "unifying focus" of the Christian faith.[141] For Mugambi, the Jewish and Christian scriptures are "an anthology

---

132. Mugambi, *FLTR*, 206.

133. Mugambi, et al., *Ecumenical Initiatives*, 43.

134. Mugambi, *FLTR*, 225.

135. Mugambi, "Ecumenical Movement," 12; Mugambi, "Challenges to African Scholars," 12–14.

136. Mugambi, *FLTR*, 102–3, see 43.

137. Ibid., 105.

138. See Mugambi, "Challenges to African Scholars," 7–8.

139. Mugambi, et al., *Ecumenical Initiatives*, 8–10, 163–65.

140. See Mugambi and Guy, *CTAC*, 283; Mugambi, *FLTR*, 142.

141. Mugambi, "Bible and Ecumenism," 68, 73.

of stories, told from a variety of perspectives, put together to convey the dynamics of a community of faith... It is their contextual specificity that gives them universal appeal."[142] Consequently, the Bible is a "cultural document" and not a "super-cultural manual."[143] Because "language is a cultural product, its meaning is intertwined with the culture that produces it." The Bible is not to be venerated as a religious object "independent of cultural influences." It is not some kind of "talisman" or "magical wand." Rather, the Bible is to be "liberated" from "cultural imprisonment" in order that it can be understood in each language and cultural setting.[144] To that end, Mugambi affirms what he sees as a Tillichian approach, which he defines over against Bultmann and Barth. Mugambi oversimplifies a Tillichian approach as:

> ... discernment of the meaning behind the words in the Bible — towards the *Word* hidden in the *words* of the Bible. Such an approach requires some training in philosophy, and it is rewarding because it leaves the controversial biblical texts intact, and yet goes *beyond* them to discern the divine message they carry.[145]

In interpreting the biblical texts in Africa, neither a literalist (which he sees as continuing to dominate in the African church) or a demythologizing approach will contribute to social reconstruction. For both approaches devalue the part symbol, myth, and culture play in the text and the interpretation of the text.[146] Africa needs, argues Mugambi, an "ecumenically inclusive, critically consistent and contextually tuned approach to the Bible, utilizing the latest tools of biblical analysis."[147] This will result in a hermeneutic of discernment:

> ... we shall have to discern the principles behind religious precepts in the Bible, rather than obey the letter of religious 'law.' We shall have to discern the 'spirit' rather than the 'letter' of biblical instruction. In my view, this is what Jesus meant by instructing that Sabbath was made for humankind, not the other way round. (Mark 2:27-28)[148]

---

142. Mugambi and Guy, *CTAC*, 113.

143. Mugambi, "Challenges to African Scholars," 15-17. Mugambi and Guy, *CTAC*, 169.

144. Mugambi and Guy, *CTAC*, 177-78.

145. Mugambi, "Bible and Ecumenism," 74.

146. See Mugambi, "Challenges to African Scholars," 80-82.

147. Ibid., 84.

148. Mugambi and Guy, *CTAC*, 170.

Hermeneutically, neither the text nor the context are constant. Rather, the reader is involved in a movement between the given texts, cultural readings of the texts, and the reader's context.[149] Undoubtedly, this will lead to a pluralism of interpretation. However, according to the African heritage, deviations from the majority (reading) can be tolerated if both minority and majority maintain respect for each other.[150]

As with Mbiti's appraisal of the context in chapter 3, Mugambi's reappraisal of a post-liberationist context promises innovation and particular practice. However, as with Mbiti, there is a tendency even in his commitment to a practical theology of reconstruction to move away from the experiential and the particular. At this juncture, this is seen when religion is defined primarily in cultural as opposed to experiential terms, when reconstruction is to be led by the elite creating the potential for the suppression of the voices of the majority, and when biblical reading towards reconstruction is professionalized by the necessity of the latest tools of biblical analysis.

Assessing Mugambi's Theology of Reconstruction

As he himself confesses, the characteristics he associates with a theology of reconstruction are, at best, intimations toward future practice. Consequently, as has been seen, his proposals at times lack clarity and remain abstracted from the particular. Indeed, it may be that it is this vagueness that is the chief problem with Mugambi's theology of reconstruction. For as has already be seen, Mugambi does not make the case for conversion leading to social activism, he exhibits a rather generalized and uncritical view of African politics and rurality, he defines religion primarily in cultural terms, and he professionalizes the practice of reconstruction with appeals to the agency of the elite and the specialism of biblical criticism. Despite his reappraisal of the context and intimations toward reconstructionist practice, each of these weaknesses seems to evidence a tendency toward a more generalized and abstract understanding of reconstruction. The focus of the criticisms in this section are threefold. Firstly, his claims to innovation can be tested. Secondly, his assessment of the context can be questioned. Thirdly, his identification of reconstruction from the biblical text is problematic. It will be argued that such assessment further underlines the tendency toward a more generalized understanding of African theology evident in Mugambi as well as Mbiti.

---

149. See Ibid., 155. Mugambi cites the work of Manus, *Intercultural Hermeneutics in Africa*.

150. Mugambi, *TAHCC*, 129–39.

First, Mugambi's emphasis on innovation can be tested. For if Mbiti is too quick to universalize his particular findings on the Akamba, then Mugambi may be too quick to claim innovation for his theology. This innovation might be questioned both from the context of earlier African theologizing and the context of earlier ecumenical theologizing.

It appears to be the case that Mugambi underestimates the contribution of earlier African theologies and theologians. Indeed, it is surprising, not least given the work of Mbiti, that in the 1990s when Mugambi was introducing the concept of "reconstruction" he was able to say that no "distinctly African contributions" in theology have emerged.[151] Stinton is, therefore, correct:

> The question remains . . . as to the extent of innovativeness represented by the proposal for reconstructive theology . . . One problem stems from the zeal to find new theological paradigms without adequate appreciation of the gains made in previous theologies.[152]

In 1981, in a personal report on a visit to Zimbabwe, Mbiti speaks of a "land reborn" and the need for the church to be involved in rebuilding beyond colonialism, European "civilisation," and foreign culture.[153] In 1971, over twenty years before Mugambi's *FLTR*, Mbiti was calling for a similar engagement with social development or reconstruction:

> National development should be for the betterment of society and if so then Christians ought to be at the very front lines, with the understanding that this is God's world and that God is transforming it through Jesus Christ.[154]

Mbiti, not unlike Mugambi, does little to give detail to what this might entail. He simply calls for involvement in culture, economics, industry, agriculture, ecology, politics, and reconciliation as part of the mission of the church.[155] While the concept of "development" might rightly be questioned by Mugambi, what cannot be doubted is Mbiti's desire for Africans to make (reconstruct) their own history and theology beyond missionary and colonial dominance.

---

151. Mugambi, "Future of the Church," 41.

152. Stinton, *Jesus of Africa*, 224. Of course, there are other theologies addressing social reconstruction beyond Africa. See, for example, Villa-Vicencio, *Theology of Reconstruction*, 1–17, 19–48, 117–53.

153. Mbiti, "Simbabwe: Ein Persönlicher Bericht," 4–5.

154. Mbiti, *CMA*, 8–9.

155. Ibid., 8–10.

Mugambi's claim to innovation is predicated upon a negation of liberationist theologizing. While there is much to commend in Mugambi's revised understanding of the liberative function of theology, especially seen in his critique of the Exodus motif, he may underestimate the ongoing relevance of liberation theology. Liberation theologians continue to be involved in social justice.[156] For it continues to be the socio-economically poor who suffer the most. While rejecting liberation theology, it may be that Mbiti, in rejecting its political and Marxist underpinnings, is the one who truly recognizes its significance. Mugambi associates national independence with an Exodus era for Kenya and the end of the Cold War as the beginning of a new era. However, the significance of the Exodus motif for national independence and the end of the Cold War for the poorest in Kenyan society may be exaggerated. In short, liberation theology may well continue to have significance in African contexts.

Mugambi omits from his writing on reconstruction the work of the South African scholar Charles Villa-Vicencio and the book, *A Theology of Reconstruction: Nation-building and Human Rights* (1992). This omission is particularly glaring when it does not even appear in the bibliography of *CTSR* (2003), which was written as a development of his initial intimations toward a theology of reconstruction. Villa-Vicencio's work on the subject emerges from an African context at roughly the same time as Mugambi is introducing his reconstructionist approach. It possesses significant similarities to Mugambi's writing.[157] For example, both see the gospel as inseparable from culture,[158] both adjudge the liberationist paradigm to be limited and in need of being transcended,[159] both see a new paradigm for theology emerging in the wake of events in the 1990s,[160] both see the church entering a "post-exilic" era,[161] both see reading or discerning "the signs of the time" as crucial to theological practice,[162] and both demand reconstruction of economic systems.[163]

---

156. See Petrella, *Beyond Liberation Theology*, 3, 45–147. See Mugambi, *ACT*, x.

157. See Villa-Vicencio, *Theology of Reconstruction*, xiii. It is surprising that even in the most recent publication of Mugambi's approach to a theology of reconstruction, a reference to Villa-Vicencio is omitted, and equally surprising is the omission of Mugambi's work in recent editions of Villa-Vicencio, *Theology of Reconstruction*.

158. Villa-Vicencio, *Theology of Reconstruction*, 46.

159. Ibid., 7, 274.

160. Ibid., 14.

161. Ibid., 23–37.

162. Ibid., 40–41.

163. See Ibid., 37, 197–253.

Not only does it appear that Mugambi underestimates the contribution of other African theologians and theologies but it appears he also underestimates the contribution of earlier ecumenical scholars. As has been seen, Mugambi proposes that a theology of reconstruction be an ecumenical and multi-disciplinary project. However, it is when he is taken at his word and his proposals are examined within a broader ecumenical perspective that the innovation of his approach might again be questioned. For Mugambi's theology of reconstruction might be seen less as a departure from earlier theological work and more a return to an older ecumenical social ethics now revised in light of a post-colonial Africa. Such a perspective is warranted not only because of comparisons with earlier ecumenical social ethics but also because Mugambi himself worked for the WCC. Dedji sees this, but not fully. He observes that Mugambi's stress on the interconnectedness of unity and mission is well attested to in international ecumenical movements, at least since the General Assembly of the AACC in 1969, and in bodies such as the World Council of Churches and the YWCA. He adjudges Mugambi's stress on ecumenical mission, though seeking to ground it in Africa, as "a duplicate" of existing hopes.[164]

Seen within the historical ecumenical movement, Mugambi's proposals for a theology of reconstruction become part of a stream of thought stretching back to the post-World War II era. In what became known as "ecumenical social ethics," questions of post-war reconstruction, decolonization, and nation-building became prominent. Such ecumenical social ethics, based on the so-called "middle-axoim" approach and calling for collaboration between theologians and decision makers in society, dominated ecumenical social thinking until the 1960s. This approach is seen in the work of, for example, J. H. Oldham and Ronald Preston.[165] One of the dangers of such an approach, however, is that it tends toward an elitism that overvalues the well educated and undervalues or silences other voices.[166] Forrester is correct, "It is dangerous to believe that people from the

---

164. See Dedji, *Reconstruction and Renewal*, 73–74.

165. Visser't Hooft and Oldham, *Church and Its Function*; Graham and Reed, *Future of Christian*; Forrester, *Beliefs, Values*. This practice of the middle axiom might further shed light on Mugambi's understanding of the church as "mediating" between government and people. For the role of the church would then, through its theologians, provide general ethical guidance for specific circumstances. See Koopman, "Churches and Public Policy," 11–12. It should be noted that Villa-Vicencio makes direct reference to middle axioms. See Villa-Vicencio, *Theology of Reconstruction*, 280.

166. Forrester, "Scope of Public Theology," 10–14. Forrester cites Eliot, *The Idea of a Christian Society*; Baillie, *What is Christian Civilisation*, as examples of such restorationist or reconstructionist impulses. See Koopman, "Churches and Public Policy."

academy, from the civil service and from the educated elite are able to read the Christian tradition with objectivity, and decide what is good for other people."[167] While Mugambi makes no special claim to objectivity, indeed he doubts its very possibility, there appears to be an echo of such elitism in his work. He bemoans the lack of "theologians" in the African church and, as already noted, he sees the reconstructionist task as the responsibility of an African elite which includes theologians.[168]

While Mugambi's theology of reconstruction might belong to this tradition of ecumenical social ethics it is also influenced by what replaced it. The new approach was affected by liberation theology and seen most clearly in the WCC's Programme to Combat Racism (PCR).[169] Mugambi, though critical of liberation theology, makes affirming reference to the PCR: "that programme has demonstrated in action, more than words, what it means to be the Church in situations gripped by crises of racial brutality."[170] Mugambi's theology of reconstruction might, therefore, be seen to be a return to an older ecumenical social ethics revised in light of liberation theology and post-Cold War circumstances in Africa. At the very least, there is evidence that his theology of reconstruction is in continuity with earlier work. A social ethics that, once again, is less confident about the direct application of theology to society in favor of a more complex and interdisciplinary approach.[171]

In sum, just as Mbiti too quickly universalizes his particular findings on the Akamba, Mugambi too quickly claims innovation for his theology. Despite his reappraisal of the context, it is because he does not attend to the particularity of his own context and his own experience as an African and ecumenical scholar that he can so confidently claim innovation. More contextual awareness would relate his theology of reconstruction to his experiences within, for example, the WCC and the precursors of African theology, not least Mbiti. Rather than too readily claiming innovation, a more constructive move would identify some means of connecting his work to a broader context and common experiences in situations of post-liberation

167. Forrester, "Scope of Public Theology," 12. Such an approach to social ethics was largely displaced by liberationist thought and practice, which once again brought to bear more radical and utopian theologies, see 14–16. Forrester cites Alves: "Where utopias are not imagined, ethics is reduced to solving problems within the established system." Alves, *Theology of Human Hope*.

168. Mugambi, *ACT*, 27–28. See Mugambi, *BBE*, 63–67. He does also refer to "ordinary" Christians (p. 92).

169. Forrester, "Scope of Public Theology," 14–16.

170. Mugambi, *BBE*, 56, 69–76.

171. Forrester, "Scope of Public Theology," 5–19.

and post-colonialism. It will be the purpose of chapter 7 that in relating the work of Mbiti and Mugambi to post-colonial theology a more judicious reading of innovation and a more transformative practice will emerge.

Second, Mugambi's contextualism, both in terms of his evaluation of the end of the Cold War era and his intimations toward reconstruction, can be criticized. Mugambi, as a reader of the "signs of the times," identifies the end of the Cold War as the occasion for a new paradigm in African theology. Dedji, however, argues that Mugambi overestimates the significance of the post-Cold War era for "ordinary Africans." Indeed, Mugambi himself admits to no real change when it comes to poverty, war, dictatorships, foreign demands for structural adjustment, invasive foreign cultures, and globalization.[172] Such subjugation and suffering is encompassed in what has already been referred to as coloniality and the admission of its ongoing reality along with Dedji's criticism evidences a further move away from the particular. A move away from the particular of coloniality towards more macro-level theorizing and analysis weakens Mugambi's contribution. This is underlined by the seeming incompleteness and nascency of his reconstructionist proposals. The danger is that Mugambi's myth of a "resurgent" or "resilient" people remains an "ideal dream" and a "pure slogan."[173]

Dedji deems the project of re-mythologization, as the apparent means to cultural reconstruction, to be like *Négritude,* which "can only succeed in making Africans dance magnificently in the clouds without being able to descend into the caves of their daily life. In this regard, Paul Tillich and Karl Jaspers have not been a good influence on Mugambi."[174] However, like Mugambi, Dedji underestimates the role of earlier African theologizing. For before Mugambi introduces Tillich and Jaspers, a methodological shift in African theology has already occurred. In this study, that shift is seen when comparing Mbiti's PhD with his later published works. It is not simply the case that Mugambi overlooks African involvement in the slave trade, civil war, and genocide.[175] Instead, a rather abstracted notion of "tradition" or "heritage" becomes both the point of departure and the court of appeal (the "clouds" in Dedji's analogy) for a theology of reconstruction. It is for this reason that Dedji's "ordinary Africans" are in danger of not being served

---

172. See Dedji, *Reconstruction and Renewal,* 75; Maluleke, "Half a Century," 84–114.

173. Dedji, *Reconstruction and Renewal,* 80.

174. Ibid., 87.

175. Dedji, *Reconstruction and Renewal,* 80; Villa-Vicencio, *Theology of Reconstruction,* 36.

by such proposals.¹⁷⁶ More concrete practice addressing issues such as reparation, including foreign governments and other foreign bodies such as mission agencies, may need to take place.¹⁷⁷ For genuine forgiveness and reconciliation might well relate more convincingly with Mugambi's own "salvation-liberation" rhetoric and get closer to the experience and needs of the grassroots.¹⁷⁸ Maybe a time will come when representatives of the modern missionary movement will be called to a missional Truth and Reconciliation Commission. Certainly, Mugambi's nascent attempts at analyzing power relations suggest more constructive and thorough theological power analysis is needed. This will be further explored in the following chapter as post-colonial theology is brought into dialogue with both Mugambi's and Mbiti's theologizing.

Third, concern can be raised about how Mugambi adopts Ezra-Nehemiah for his reconstructionist purposes. Elelwani Farisani sees Mugambi's focus on Ezra-Nehemiah as superficial.¹⁷⁹ For while Mugambi calls for a "critical" reading of the text of Nehemiah he does not achieve this himself. He is blind to the ideology of the text and "the conflict between the returned exiles and the *am haaretz*." In not even recognizing the conflict between these two groups, Mugambi suppresses the voice of the *am haaretz*.¹⁸⁰ Farisani succinctly states the problem:

> Mugambi, by using the reconstruction theme in Ezra-Nehemiah without isolating the ideological agenda of the text and identifying the group which is dominant in the text, has inadvertently identified reconstruction as that which is driven by the returned exiles at the exclusion of the *am haaretz*.¹⁸¹

Not only does Mugambi's placement of theologians among Africa's elite stand in tension with his proposals for reconstruction as a practice of the

---

176. Dedji, *Reconstruction and Renewal*, 80. See Villa-Vicencio, *Theology of Reconstruction*, 274, where he warns that the reconstructionist theologians cannot afford "... the luxury of taking refuge in generalities and principles with which few take issue and most will not dispute—primarily because such generalities are devoid of specific content."

177. For the ongoing case of Mau Mau veterans, see, for example, Cobain, "Mau Mau Veterans"; the online Editorial, "Kenya: Evil and the Empire"; Cobain and Hatcher, "Kenyan Mau Mau Victims," accessed May 6, 2013. See Heaney, "Views of Colonization."

178. See Dedji, *Reconstruction and Renewal*, 78–87.

179. Farisani, "Use of Ezra-Nehemiah," 32.

180. Ibid., 33–34.

181. Ibid., 34.

masses, his reading of Ezra-Nehemiah reveals that he is imperceptive to the marginalized in the biblical text.[182] A text which exclusively identifies the returned exiles as "Israel" is co-opted into a theology that is meant to aid African reconciliation and rebuilding.[183] Mugambi, and Villa-Vicencio, read the text from the perspective of the dominant and not the marginalized group. Indeed, given Farisani's unveiling of the ideological bias in the Nehemiah text it may apply more to post-independent Kenya (1960s) than post-colonial Kenya (1990s). For, according to Mugambi's own analysis, an elite and unrepresentative group took over governance after the colonial authorities left. Indeed, in the era of independence not a few of the governing elite were returned exiles and, like the returnees of Ezra-Nehemiah, they too can be accused of oppressing and suppressing the voice and wishes of the people of the land who had struggled through occupation.

The closer the text is read, the more problematic it becomes as a basis for a theology of reconstruction. For example, on the one hand Mugambi rightly castigates missionaries and mission policies for demanding that Christian polygamists abandon all their wives apart from their first. On the other hand, an African reconstructionist theology appeals to the example of Ezra and Nehemiah, the former of whom (Ezra 7–10) redefined the returned exiles in ethnic terms, and enjoined them to divorce their *am haaretz* wives.[184] A more critical reading, submits Farisani, would have provided more thoroughgoing transformative practices (around the themes of ethnicity, foreign debt, and the oppression of women) and would have prevented a naïve reading of the text.[185] It matters how the text is read. Mugambi recognizes this, calls for a critical reading, and then fails to read critically. Even Mugambi's most cautious critics note that the significance of the *am haaretz* must be addressed in the future if a reconstructive practice is not to be "delayed or disrupted indefinitely."[186] A critical reading matters, not least, because it reveals from which subject-position one is reading from and, therefore, what person or group of people one sees as the agents of reconstruction. Mugambi's uncritical reading of Ezra-Nehemiah may provide some analogous connection between the text and his intimations toward reconstructionism. However, it does so at the expense of failing to recognize the wider context of the returned exiles and failing to take into account the

---

182. Ibid.
183. Ibid., 36, see 38–44.
184. Ibid., 44.
185. See Ibid., 44–49.
186. Gathogo, *Liberation and Reconstruction*, 231.

experience of the marginalized within the text. The failure to analyze such power relations does not bode well for a theology of reconstruction.

Conclusion

The unifying factor of this study is the recognition that the African theology examined here moves from the particular of context (chapter 3) to a more generalized understanding of African theology (chapter 4). Such a move begins with Mbiti's work on African temporality and eschatology. Because he is one of the most significant figures in African theology his theological influence continues to be felt. Mugambi is one theologian who is indebted to him. That the move Mbiti makes in his work on temporality and eschatology away from a particular context has only now been identified, means that his methodological influence has also only now been recognized. Mbiti's methodological influence is apparent in the way Mugambi also gives ATRs a foundational place (chapter 4) and in the way he affirms Christian identity through christocentrism while being unable to christologize the experience of African suffering (chapter 5).

In this chapter, Mugambi's reappraisal of the context and his apparent innovative contribution of a reconstructionist theology is examined. However, even in this post-colonial reappraisal and innovation, the shift from the particular is not redressed but further embedded. For the causal link between social activism and personal reconstruction (conversion) remains unproven and abstract. Cultural reconstruction is weakened by a generalized and uncritical view of African political systems and rural societies. Ecclesial reconstruction is predicated upon an elitist approach to leadership and a specialist approach to reading the Bible resulting in the marginalization of voices in both text and context. Mugambi's innovation seems to be, therefore, overstated in that he fails to thoroughly connect his proposals with a wider context of former theological work both within Africa and within the ecumenical movement. His theology of reconstruction also, because of macro-level theorizing, may distance his analysis and proposals from the experience of the vast majority of people in his context. In short, the unintended consequence of his reconstructionist intimations is that he moves away from experiences of coloniality thereby failing to provide strategies for the unveiling and transformation of subjugation. His proposals may be a reappraisal of the "post-Exodus" context but they do not provide a means for him to overcome the methodological shift from the particular and experiential initiated by Mbiti thirty years previously. Indeed, his intimations toward a so-called theology of reconstruction can be seen as the culmination of a gradual shift away from the particular of context (chapter 3), experience (chapter 4), and community (chapter 5). This is evident when these shifts from the particular are compared with his three levels of reconstruction.

First, it is only with the shift away from the particularism of context (chapter 3) that proposals for personal reconstruction can assume that personal conversion will lead to social activism. In analyzing the context of Kenya, Mugambi is critical of missionaries (see chapter 2), many of whom it can be assumed will have experienced "personal reconstruction" or conversion, for precisely failing to exhibit the activism he now assumes arises from such conversion. Indeed, such failure of social activism, which Mugambi especially associates with efforts toward liberation, seems predicated upon an spiritualized individualism not dissimilar to his own understanding of personal reconstruction.[187] Second, it is only with the shift away from the experience of African traditional religionists (chapter 4) that proposals for cultural reconstruction can be predicated upon generalized and uncritical views of rural societies and traditional values in African politics. Those who experience, or who have experienced, traditionalist societies and traditional politics do not speak with unanimity about their contribution to African thought and practice.[188] Third, it is only because of the shift away from the particularism of faith communities (chapter 5) that proposals for ecclesial reconstruction can emphasize elitism and specialism. For, by definition, most people will neither belong to the elite nor possess theological or biblical specialism. Assuming that so-called specialists are the ones to lead ecclesial reconstruction begs the question and potentially veils domineering power relations. In sum, the power at work in individualism, tradition, and specialism remains concealed. Some means of analyzing such exercises of power is needed. The following chapter will propose that such means to analysis will begin to emerge now that a more thoroughgoing comparison of the writings of Mbiti and Mugambi with post-colonial theology is possible.

---

187. Oduyoye observes that individualism is not only a trait found in foreign practice, but also amongst African men. See Oduyoye, *Introducing African Women's Theology*, 26.

188. Certainly, Kato is one such dissenting voice. See, for example, Kato, "Christianity as an African Religion," 1–8, who in typical strident language refers to ATR as "depraved" (p. 2). Hountondji, already cited in chapter 4, speaks of the danger of a generalized ATR as simply expressing dominant views (Hountondji, *African Philosophy*, 33–70). See also Oduyoye, "Coming Home to Myself," 105–22; Oduyoye, *Hearing and Knowing*, 56–76; Oduyoye, *Introducing African Women's Theology*, 13, 22–38.

7

Comparing the Writings of Mbiti and Mugambi with Post-Colonial Theology

THROUGHOUT THIS BOOK I have proposed a series of constructive moves in response to the abstracting tendencies in both Mbiti's and Mugambi's work. In the previous chapter, a further constructive move was identified but not developed. That is because Mugambi's move away from the particularism of coloniality is the culmination of the moves away from the particular dealt with in chapters 3, 4, and 5 of the present study. Any constructive move responding to Mugambi's reconstructionism will have consequences for Mugambi's other writings and Mbiti's work also. Consequently, in seeking a means toward power analysis, in light of coloniality, this chapter will deal with both Mugambi's and Mbiti's work.

Post-colonial theology is, or includes, power analysis. It is unveiling coloniality. It is theologizing in light of coloniality. In chapter 1, post-colonial theology was defined and an initial proposal made that the writings of Mbiti and Mugambi compare favorably to it. This chapter will first deepen that comparison and then identify problems and further prospects for their work in relationship to post-colonial theology.

Post-Colonialism and the Writings of Mbiti and Mugambi

The present section will utilize the previous outline of post-colonialism and post-colonial theology to assess to what extent the writings of Mbiti and Mugambi might be considered to be critically post-colonial. It will be argued that such a comparison will eventually provide a practical means to power analysis, which is absent in the writings of Mugambi and Mbiti (see below). The categories of coloniality, agency, hybridity, resistance, and decolonization will constitute a framework for such assessment and construction. Each will be illustrated in reference to a major theme (mission Christianity, eschatology, African traditions, christology, and reconstruction) found in the writings of Mbiti and Mugambi and outlined in the previous chapters of this study. It is important to note at the outset that there will be an inevitable overlap between categories and major themes. However, for the purpose of illustrating the potential for a comparison between post-colonial theology and the writings of Mbiti and Mugambi, individual themes will be compared to individual post-colonial categories.

First, coloniality relates to mission Christianity and mission Christianity relates to coloniality. Post-colonial theology emerges from experiences of coloniality. Mission Christianity is characterized as distinct from colonialism but it is also characterized by acculturation, the denigration of traditions and traditional practice, denominationalism, and by the introduction of foreign categories of thought and practice (chapter 2). It is not so much that the writings of Mbiti and Mugambi are simply a response to such thought and practice and therefore potentially derivative of mission Christianity. Rather, the assumptions, theologizing, and practices of mission Christianity and the assumptions, theologizing, and practices of African converts become the interface for an emerging African Christian theology. In post-colonial terms, coloniality is experienced particularly intensely on this interface for Mbiti and Mugambi. As has been seen, Mbiti and Mugambi argue that missionaries in Africa often sought to "condemn, ridicule, belittle, attack and overlook" Africans and African customs in favor of a European interpreted Christianity.[1] Consequently, colonialism stunted the growth of the church.[2] Mugambi, from the work of Cees J. Hamelink, affirms the idea of "cultural synchronization." In contrast, what is needed is resistance and internal equality in the face of imperialism.[3] Young is correct to acknowledge that the best of post-colonial analysis focuses on "the question of representation, mediated with analyses of counter-histories or the effects of colonialism on colonial subjects and the forms of their subjectivity."[4] Both

---

1. Mbiti, "Role of the Jewish Bible," 223. See Mbiti, *ARAP*, 10; Sebastian, "Mission without History," 75–96.

2. Mbiti, "Future of Christianity" (*CC*), 389. See Pobee, "African Theology Revisited," 135–38.

3. Mugambi, *FLTR*, 7. See Hamelink, *Cultural Autonomy*, 33.

4. Young refers to Said, Bhabha, and Spivak as ". . . the Holy Trinity of colonial discourse analysis . . . acknowledged as central to the field" (Young, R., *Colonial Desire*, 163). For a powerful depiction of neocolonialism in Kenya, including the role of

Mbiti and Mugambi are involved in such counter-discursive writing and this fundamental concern in post-colonial literature of a desire to respond to the experience of colonial subjugation is present in their writings. At the heart of post-colonial studies is a desire to see, and transform, disciplines as they are disrupted by knowledge and experiences of subjugated people.

> ... at its simplest level, the postcolonial is simply the product of human experience, but more particularly the result of the different experiences of cultural and national origins, the ways in which the colour of your skin or your place and circumstance of birth defines the kind of life, privileged and pleasurable, or oppressed and exploited, that you will have in this world. Postcolonialism is about nothing more than that. It's a language of and for those who have no place, who seem not to belong, of those whose knowledge and histories are not allowed to count.[5]

In this very basic sense, the writing of Mbiti and Mugambi is post-colonial. As has already been seen throughout this study there is, however, a tendency to move away from the context in favor of making "tradition" the locus for their theology. It has been argued that this is, methodologically, a mistake. For it undervalues experiential knowledge and, therefore, the agency of those experiencing marginalization.[6] In short, the way the Akamba criticize AIM missionaries is evidence of contextual power analysis but this is undermined with a shift away from the particularism of context.

Second, as in post-colonial theology, Mbiti and Mugambi contend for the agency of marginalized peoples. Those beyond the North Atlantic academies, churches, and missions are not missiological objects but theological subjects.[7] Much post-colonial literature is concerned with examining litera-

---

Christian religion, see wa Thiong'o, *Barrel of a Pen*, 8–26; wa Thiong'o, *Moving the Centre*, 89–95; Parry, "Problems in Current Theories," 27–58; Ahmad, *In Theory*. (Young counters that while the colonial discourse analysis of Said, Bhabha, and Spivak may not include such thoroughgoing historical analysis, they do not deny that this is important—p. 163.) Bhabha counters Said's overconfidence in the successful instrumentality of orientalism by identifying ambivalence as central to the colonialist's interaction with "the Orient." That is to say, not only does colonial discourse operate as a construction of knowledge, but it also operates "... according to the ambivalent protocols of fantasy and desire" (p. 161). Spivak, also reacting against Said's totalizing argument, explores the possibility of "counter-knowledges," which rewrite the received accounts authored by the colonizing academics or the indigenous elite (p. 161–62). Young, R., *Colonial Desire*, 161, see 160–65.

5. Young, R., "What is the Postcolonial," 2.

6. See Young, R., *Postcolonialism: Historical Intro*, 62, 65.

7. Introduction in Douglas and Kwok, *Beyond Colonial Anglicanism*, 11.

ture produced in colonial times and in situations of coloniality in a bid to analyze how the colonizers represent the colonized and how, in response, the colonized seek to represent themselves.[8] Post-colonialism is, therefore, a quest for representative agency. It is a project aimed at disrupting dominant theological and missiological discourses from the margins. Indeed, for Young, it is the post-colonial "preoccupation" with those who come from "elsewhere" that he sees as constituting a "shared area of sympathy" between post-colonialism and Christianity.[9] A similar desire, it appears, is present in the writings of Mbiti and Mugambi as they contend for and seek to demonstrate African theological agency:

> Theologians from the South know the North fairly well because many of them have studied in the North and have drawn from its scholarly treasures, ecclesiastical ties, and church traditions. But the North does not seem to know the South to the same extent. Indeed, it seems to be ignorant of southern Christianity. Perhaps through dialogue, this inadequacy could be ameliorated. Theological education in the North has yet to integrate the South in its courses. There are a few attempts, especially in missiology courses. But the South deserves more than token or peripheral courses. Theology is more than theology of the North. The Church today had become truly global. So also theology must become truly universal: unless such a development is seen as a threat to both North and South.[10]

Mbiti goes on to call for a "fundamental re-examination and adjustment of academic content to reflect Christianity as a universal reality."[11] The study of theology must be intentionally cross-cultural. "Otherwise it remains impoverished, provincial and inadequate for global Christianity. Theology is where the church is . . ."[12] By implication both Mbiti and Mugambi have rejected the idea of the universal subject.[13] For the universal subject of modernity is revealed as the male European scholar.[14] If so-called Western theology is to be critical it must engage, in terms of dialogue, publishing, curricula, and hiring, with theology from beyond the powerful nations of the North.

---

8. Sugirtharajah, *Postcolonial Criticism*, 11.
9. Young, R., "What is the Postcolonial," 2–3.
10. Mbiti, "Dialogue between EATWOT and Western Theologians," 103.
11. Ibid.
12. Ibid.
13. See Kwok, *Postcolonial Imagination*, 132.
14. See Young, R., "What is the Postcolonial."

A concrete demonstration of this African theological agency is Mbiti's work on Akamba eschatology (chapter 3). Especially in his initial work on the Akamba and their interaction with foreign missionaries and Christianity, Mbiti develops what can be called a particularist approach towards African theological agency. For he addresses theological issues at a particular place and in a particular time.[15] In effect, he challenges the way theology is practiced by these missionaries and, by implication, challenges the way theology is practiced in North Atlantic academies. For he unsettles the identity of theologian, tradition, and context. For both Mbiti and Mugambi, theologians become those who reflect on their encounter with God with or without explicit reference to the Christ of Scripture. Tradition is expanded to include the pre-missionary wisdom of indigenous theologizing. Context, therefore, is not only the physical and cultural space that missionaries move into. It is also the public, political, and/or ecclesiastical space where some discourses are permitted, some are legitimized, some are suppressed and where others resist, subvert, and hybridize. Such African theology, even from what Josiah Young calls "the old guard," loses its significance when either the theologians themselves or readers of their theology separate it from experiences of coloniality.[16] To the extent that the innovations of Mbiti (chapter 3) and Mugambi (chapter 6) retain a particularist approach, they appear to relate positively to post-colonial criticism and thus seek some form of theological decolonization. In this context, a particularist approach will mean the recognition and search for theological significance arising from distinct groups asserting their identity and practice as resistance in the face of Western expansion.

Third, the work Mbiti and Mugambi do in relation to ATRs (chapter 4) bears favorable comparison with the post-colonial concept and practice of hybridization. The mission Christianity that Mbiti and Mugambi depict (chapter 2) is well represented in post-colonial literature. It is often portrayed as an imperialist project that promotes modern antonyms or binary opposites such as civilized/uncivilized, saved/damned, and Christian/pagan.[17] In contrast, Mbiti and Mugambi seek to relate African traditional beliefs and practices with the Christian gospel. Post-colonial texts are neither pure

---

15. Mbiti, "Christian Eschatology"; Mbiti, *NTEAB*.

16. Young, J., *African Theology*, 13–24.

17. The work of the Comaroffs offer a particularly strong example of a post-colonial and negative reading of missionary activity. Comaroff and Comaroff, *Of Revelation and Revolution*. For a response, see Stanley, "Conversion to Christianity," 315–31. See p'Bitek, *African Religions*; Boahen, *African Perspectives*, 36. See also the poetry of Mugambi, especially, "You Degrade Me, My Son," and "Rome," in Mugambi, *Carry it Home*, 5, 49–50.

retrievals of pre-colonial tradition or pure adoptions of colonialist convention. They are marked by hybridity. In their appeal to tradition (see chapter 4) both Mbiti and Mugambi seek to relate Christian gospel with African beliefs and practices. The foreign missionaries experienced and depicted by Mbiti often proceeded with the conviction that, in Africa, they had a theological *tabla rasa*. Missionaries were convinced and secure in their vocation that they were bringing the truth of God to Africans for the first time. However, as is seen in chapter 2, Mbiti and Mugambi argue that mission Christianity seldom presented a God with recognizable power in African contexts. The God of mission Christianity, in an ironic inversion of deistic assumptions, was remote and removed from daily realities and struggles.[18] Thus, a dualism between material and spiritual welfare was created.[19]

Mbiti and Mugambi argue that traditional African thought and practice is theologically significant, independent of the modern missionary movement. That is to say, they recognize that divine revelation exists pre- and post- the missionary movement. Theological knowledge does not primarily expand by missionary agency from Christians centers but emerges by divine agency from African experience and thought. Consequently, the fundamental theological category of revelation, along with the categories of theologian, tradition, and context, is hybridized. For the binary representations of "tradition" versus "revelation" are erased. As is seen in chapter 2, this encapsulates Mbiti's and Mugambi's analysis of the theological function of foreign mission in Africa. On the one hand, foreign missionaries often misinterpret the African context and have a deficient view of revelation.[20] On the other hand, it is the missionary movement which brings, often unwittingly, a message of fulfillment to African traditions. African Christianity is more than African tradition and it is more than the imported Christianity of foreign missionaries.

Mbiti notes the parallel between the oral propaganda of Mau Mau with a similar dynamic at work in oral theologizing in the church. There was a "merging" between British and African traditions. In the immediate aftermath of independence Mbiti portrays the situation as a "joint world."[21] Mugambi also moves away from "dialectical thought" and discourse, which he associates with liberation theology, and comes very close to contending for a practice of hybridity.[22] He appeals to the suggestion made by the Chi-

---

18. Mbiti, *BATAC*, 154–56, 165.
19. Ibid., 154–65.
20. See Mbiti, "Encounter of Christian Faith" (*CC*), 817–18.
21. Mbiti, Interview by Heaney, April 7.
22. Mugambi, *CTSR*, 165. See Maluleke, "Black and African Theologies," 8.

nese scholar C. S. Song that the past must be "'transposed' into the new key of the present, and the present transported into the new key of the future, in order for effective and meaningful social transformation."[23] Mugambi cites sources also from India, Europe, and Latin America concluding that the culture in each is critically blended.[24] From such critical "transposition" Mugambi draws five conclusions. Firstly, rediscovery of the past becomes the "basis" for analysis of the present and planning for the future. Secondly, the reconstructed past cannot be identical with the "real" past. Thirdly, rediscovering the past is always "ideological" whether that is acknowledged or not. Fourthly, rediscovery of the past is essential for any nation seeking to "make an impact on the world." Fifthly, technological and scientific successes are "directly related to cultural rediscovery."[25] Despite his positive appraisal of such cultural rediscovery and reconstruction Mugambi is clear that the question should not be what in the African heritage should be "presented and promoted." Rather, the resilience of African heritage should be "taken for granted" and a method towards critical transposition should begin by asking, what in "foreign cultures" should be "blended" with the African heritage?[26]

> After a short and violent conquest of Africa south of the Sahara by European empires, it appeared as if the foundations of African culture had been totally destroyed. But as the twentieth century draws to a close and the twenty-first century sets in, the African renaissance enters the scene of world history. Pan-Africanism paved the way for decolonisation, and the same movement will give momentum to this renaissance, irrespective of any ideological, religious or technological opposition from those who view it as a threat.[27]

---

23. Mugambi, *TAHCC*, 112. See Song, *Compassionate God*, 11–12.

24. The sources he cites in Mugambi, *TAHCC*, 112–14, are in the *Gandhi* film (1982); Erikson, *Gandhi's Truth*; Gandhi, *Bhagavad Gita*; Radhakrishnan, *Recovery of Faith*; Sharma, *Critical Survey*; Muller, H., *Uses of the Past*; Russell, *History of Western Philosophy*; Collingwood, *Idea of History*; Gibellini, *Frontiers of Theology*.

25. Mugambi, *TAHCC*, 113–14.

26. Ibid., 114–25. It should be noted that Mugambi avoids Song's preferred term for such "transposition." Song refers to transposition as "incarnation," whereas Mugambi adopts "reincarnation" to speak of "cultural renaissance," see Mugambi, *TAHCC*, 111–12. Song argues transposition is neither a matter of imitation or uncritical fusion, but ". . . a matter of an alien culture 'become flesh' in a native culture. A metamorphosis must take place in the cultures concerned." Song, *Compassionate God*, 11, see 10–12.

27. Mugambi, *TAHCC*, 116.

Hybridization decenters theology and prevents a continuation of oppositional theologizing.[28] In situations of coloniality it may provide a means of resistance against disempowering hegemonic forces and of providing enunciative space for those experiencing suppression. It is precisely this kind of resistance that the innovations of Mbiti and Mugambi are intended to provide.

Fourth, Mbiti and Mugambi seek to resist exercises of power harmful to thoroughgoing African theological contextualism. For Mbiti and Mugambi to speak of culture in Kenya is to speak of it in a context where colonial policy and missionary strategy often suppressed African initiation rites, African literature, African dance, African politics, and African religion. Mbiti may seek to prioritize culture and tradition in his theologizing, remaining hesitant about political and liberation theology, and does so by moving away from his initial particularist methodology. However, he is clear on the consequences of power relations for the church in Africa. As has been seen, Mbiti observes that the church "tolerates" foreign missionaries because the "decisions, the power and the wealth" reside there.[29] Mbiti strongly argues that the authoritarianism and wealth of mission agencies has created a "missionized" sense in the African church. That is to say, the agency of Africans has been supplanted by a power dynamic where the African church is "directed, controlled and even enslaved by external structures, theological education, traditions and spirituality. Its umbilical cord has not yet been severed."[30] Such arguments resonate strongly with other counter-discourses in post-colonialism.

Mugambi remains clear on the practical implications of broader power relations on the lives of Africans. He observes that "the power to name the world is vested in those who are able to exert themselves over the rest. Thus, the poor and the weak cannot name themselves. They have to be named by others!"[31] Consequently, the United Nations Development Programme *Human Development Report* clusters some countries together on the basis of race or religion and others are "developed." "Sub-Sahara" is particularly troublesome for Mugambi. He asks, "No other region is labeled on the basis of a desert, or forest, or a prairie! What is the significance of the Sahara Desert in international economics and politics?"[32] For Mugambi this enun-

28. Maluleke, "Black and African Theologies," 8.

29. Mbiti, *BATAC*, 205.

30. Ibid., 209. For a similar and contemporary view, see Byaruhanga-Akiiki, "Africa and Christianity," 179–95.

31. Mugambi, "Responsible Leadership," 80.

32. Ibid. See also website, http://hdr.undp.org/en/, where UNDP continues to use

ciative powerlessness underlines Africa's marginality. A marginality where Africans continue to suffer under globalizing capitalism to such an extent that they are "in essence, enslaved at home."[33] Both Mbiti and Mugambi recognize that the Christian gospel brings a message of freedom. However, this message did not translate into missionary support for independence movements. Indeed, the Jesus that was brought to Africa seemed to support colonialism and coloniality.[34] As has been seen, Mugambi is especially critical of any African christology that is contextual without also being liberative. That is to say, he rejects any false dichotomizing between a contextual and liberative christology.[35]

Because of the marginalization and suffering of Africa, Mugambi recognizes that there are problems now in referring to God as "king" or "lord." As a theologian who experienced the brutality of a British concentration camp ("protected village")[36] in 1950s Kenya, he writes, "A human king tends to oppress his subjects, and a human lord tends to exploit his servants . . . The superiors tend to assume absolute power over those who are inferior."[37] Mugambi resolves this theological tension to some degree by identifying that categories such as "king" and "lord" must be "qualitatively different" from historical experiences of kings and lords. He makes a further attempt to decolonize such terms by stressing that the concept and practice of freedom is a much more central theological concern and that any notion of divine kingship is subject to it. The analogy of God as king therefore stands as a critique of dictatorial regimes and the abuse of power in human relations.[38] The theological "concept" of the kingdom of God announced by Christ, therefore,

> . . . brings low the lofty assumptions of human kings (rulers), and elevates the low spirits of the human subjects, children and servants when they realize that in the judgement of God all human beings are placed on an equal status. In this insight lies the

---

the "Sub-Saharan Africa" categorization (2013).

33. Mugambi, "Theology of Reconstruction," 142.

34. See chapter 2 of the present study and Warren, *Caesar, the Beloved Enemy*; Strong, *Anglicanism and British Empire*.

35. Mugambi, *Liberation to Reconstruction*, 9–10; Bujo, *African Christian Morality*, 71.

36. In 1952, during the Mau Mau movement, he was removed from his home and held in a concentration camp ("protected village"). Reflecting on this experience, he says it "completely changed my life and that of people in my generation," see Mwase, "Critical Evaluation," 252.

37. Mugambi, *ACT*, 76–77.

38. Ibid., 77–79.

liberating power of the Christian gospel. This is the 'good news' which Jesus proclaims (Luke 4:16–22) and for which Mary the mother of Jesus thanks God (Luke 1:46–55). Human 'kings' are liberated from their lofty attitudes and conduct which dehumanize them as they dehumanize their inferiors, and those who are barred from exercising their freedom are elevated to realize their full dignity as human beings and as children of God.[39]

When Jesus announced the inbreaking of the kingdom of God he was referring to "an entirely new order." Such a new order means that, in the present, Christians will reject all of the "trappings and temptations of power, which dehumanize both the rulers and the ruled."[40] This expectation that the world should be "turned upside down" along with redefinitions of key biblical and theological terms (for example, king, sovereign, master) are, it can be argued, critically post-colonial moves. Indeed, the resistance of both Mbiti and Mugambi to a systematized christology can be similarly seen as a post-colonial move against the dominant way of christologizing. Both Mbiti and Mugambi have experience of so-called Western theologizing. They could well have opted for a systematic approach to African christology. They chose not to. Rather, there is evidence of practical christological reflection found throughout their writings. Read from a post-colonial perspective this option for the practical, though not as thorough as it could have been, is not simply a contextualist move. It is a resistant move against the homogenization of empire.[41] It is a move towards theological decolonization.

Fifth, both Mbiti and Mugambi seek theological decolonization. For Mbiti, African theology, at its simplest, is "theological reflection and expression by African Christians."[42] For too long, he argues, Africa has lived on "borrowed" or "inherited" Christianity.[43] "There is no permanent home for foreign Christianity in Africa."[44] As has been seen, the diversity of foreign mission agencies, imported denominationalism, competition, and rivalry imported by missionaries to Africa since the nineteenth century amounts, in Mugambi's view, to a "scandal."[45] In post-colonial terms, there appears

---

39. Ibid., 78.
40. Ibid., 79.
41. See Rieger, *Christ and Empire*, 77–80.
42. Mbiti, "Biblical Basis for Present Trends," 119.
43. Mbiti, *BATAC*, 7. This concern is still raised by African scholars twenty years since Mbiti voiced it. See Mombo, "Theological Education," 127–33.
44. Mbiti, *BATAC*, 19.
45. Mugambi, "Ecumenical Movement," 6.

to be a need for theological decolonization. This is well illustrated by Mugambi's call for a theological practice beyond the "Exodus-era" (chapter 6).

For Mugambi, globalization is an "intensification of the imperial legacy." This legacy begins, he argues, with the modern missionary movement preaching "civilization" and is continued in the proliferation of agencies dispensing "donations, relief supplies and consumer goods subsidized from the member-countries of the OECD." Under international pressure African markets have been liberalized while northern markets have been closed to Africans through tariff barriers. "Hypocrisy," Mugambi concludes, "has become more the norm than the exception in the dealings between the affluent and the destitute."[46] Against this background, and making reference to the apparent nationalism of the thirty-seventh Anglican Article of Religion ("The Bishop of Rome hath no jurisdiction over this Realm of England") Mugambi sees the theologies of Africa, Asia, and Latin America as part of a new Reformation within a broader movement for decolonization.[47] In biblical terms, as has been seen, it is Nehemiah who through "participatory management" leads social reconstruction for his people. If the Exodus text is foundational to liberation theologies, it is Nehemiah 2:17–18 that is foundational to a theology of reconstruction. Post-colonial Africa, argues Mugambi, is in a position not dissimilar to Nehemiah's Judah. International media, politics, diplomats, business leaders, academics, church leaders, World Bank, and IMF are akin to the Sanballats, Geshems, and Tobiahs of Israel's past. In contrast, "prophets of hope" encouraging the people to continue in reconstruction are what Africa now needs.[48]

As has been seen, from the emerging post-colonial theological literature and the centrality of coloniality already identified in this chapter, theological decolonization is both the consummation and summation of a post-colonial theology. It might be seen to include the practices of disrupting dominant theological discourses, erasing binary opposites, and creating enunciative space for theologizing in coloniality. There can be little doubt that both Mugambi and Mbiti are involved in such decolonizing moves not least in Mugambi's more recent intimations toward reconstruction. However, the comparison between their work and post-colonial theology is not without problems.

---

46. Mugambi, "Religions in East Africa," 16–17.

47. Mugambi, "Problems of Teaching," 13. See Mugambi, "Rites of Passage," 237; Cone, *For My People*, 41.

48. Mugambi, "Theology of Reconstruction," 147.

Problems and Prospects for Power Analysis

As well as the writing of Mbiti and Mugambi being compared to post-colonial theology, it can also be contrasted with post-colonial theology. Post-colonial theology has been identified as emerging from coloniality, proposing practices of marginalized agency, theologically hybridizing, resisting hegemony, and having decolonizing intent, so too criticisms of the writings of Mbiti and Mugambi are briefly identified from these same perspectives. In addition, problems and responses to comparing the writings of Mbiti and Mugambi with post-colonial theology will be discussed further in the conclusion. There it will be submitted that despite such problems the work of Mbiti and Mugambi should now be seen as part of a broad body of critically post-colonial theology. However, before such issues are explored it is important to now illustrate how a comparison of their work with post-colonialism could provide a means to power analysis as this is the constructive move that was deemed necessary as a result of the ill-defined intimations of Mugambi's re-constructionist theology.

First, several post-colonial criticisms can be made of the work of Mbiti and Mugambi. Both Mbiti and Mugambi have experienced the reality of suppression and oppression in Kenya. They have experienced this both from within and without the church and Mugambi has spoken of his experiences during the State of Emergency in 1951. It is for this reason that while the present study does identify a methodological shift away from the particular, it does not deny that their experiences of coloniality have a profound effect on their writing. Nonetheless, such a methodological move does mean that experience (coloniality) plays less of a part in their writing than it might have done otherwise. Indeed, Mbiti's initial positive appraisal of "syncretism," when theologizing on the theological interface between African theologizing and imported Christianity, is a practical example of how the methodological (and theological) significance of coloniality is weakened.[49] When "tradition" becomes the point of departure it is inevitable that "syncretism" becomes not the practice of ordinary believers on such an interface, but becomes the pole that a contextualizing theology must always avoid. This has repercussions for both practices of agency and hybridity.

In the present chapter, Mbiti's work on African temporality and eschatology is used as an illustration of an exercise of marginalized theological agency. As is seen in chapter 3, such Mbitian temporality has been the subject of much criticism. A post-colonial reading of Mbiti will seek to unveil the potential that his work reinforces colonial assumptions about

---

49. For the broader theological significance of coloniality, see, for example, Heaney, "Coloniality and Theological Method," 55–65.

"primitive" and "backward" Africa.[50] At this juncture, further criticism can be submitted. Because of Mbiti's insistence on the (unnecessary) dichotomy between a contextual and a political theology he fails to interrogate the relationship between so-called Western notions of "future" and empire. This failure seems to undermine claims to the post-colonial nature of this work, which set the tone for his other writing. In the face of the brutality of colonialism and the potential dystopias to be faced by humanity, James Perkinson submits that the very concept of a Western notion of the "future" should be considered as an imperial construct and McClintock argues that post-colonialism is a challenge to a Western notion of linear time.[51] This "future" has resulted in an ever increasing consumption of goods, of lands, and of the environment. To submit "alternative time orientations" must entail, therefore, an invitation for "'developed' social orders to come clean about the imperial enslavements, genocides, and extinctions that have everywhere been their condition of possibility (ever since the first turn to settled agriculture and progressive urbanization more than five millennia ago)."[52] In sum, Mbiti's purported exercise in marginalized agency via a representation of African temporality may forestall African theological agency not only by playing into the hands of colonialist stereotypes but also because of his failure to critique so-called Western "futures."

It can be argued that the apparent hybridizing in the writings of Mbiti and Mugambi, especially associated with their appraisal of ATRs and its relationship to Christian theology, falls short of a hybridizing equipped to contribute to theological decolonization. Rather, ATRs are co-opted to demonstrate a continuity between African Christianity and African traditions that is in danger of simultaneously justifying imperialist practices of Christian mission.[53] While the language of *praeparatio evangelica* has particular resonances with imperial Anglicanism (see chapter 2), it could be argued that fulfillment is itself a form of hybridizing. This may be so, but it is the inability of both Mbiti and Mugambi to see the hybridizing effects of ATRs on Christian practice and readings, compared to AICs for example, which weakens such a rebuttal.[54] It can be argued that because AICs remain closer to the particularism of context and experience they hybridize to a

50. See Perkinson, "John S. Mbiti," 465–66.

51. See McClintock, "Angel of Progress," 84–98.

52. Perkinson, "John S. Mbiti," 455–69. See Malina, *Social World of Jesus*, 184–85.

53. Muller, L., "Thematic Comparison," 119. See p'Bitek, *African Religions*, 7, 58–80.

54. See Welbourn and Ogot, *Place to Feel at Home*, 129; Turner, *African Independent Church*, 182–93, 202–20.

much greater extent. An emphasis on tradition as preparation leads both Mbiti and Mugambi to fear syncretism and prevents them from recognizing and promoting greater degrees of hybridization in the biblical text, Christian theology, and African Christian practice, which in turn weakens resistance to hegemony.

The Christ of Mbiti and Mugambi is not nearly as hybridized a figure as that seen in more recent post-colonial theology. For that very reason, Christ is less a challenge to the powers that be than he might have been. That is to say, the christological reflections in their writings, while pointing to a Christ beyond imperialism, presents a Christ of Africa arguably more recognizable to mainline (imperial) Christianity than to "traditional" Africa. Mugambi's writing attempts to transcend the limitations of a Mbitian contextualist approach by directly addressing imperialism and post-colonial issues (see chapter 6). The announcement of the kingdom of God is the inauguration of a new order for freedom and against dehumanizing powers. However, such christologically conceived freedom, while relating to nationalist struggles against colonialism and neo-colonialism, seems to leave other oppressions untouched. This gives the impression, as has already been seen, that the co-equality of this Christ's humanity does not relate to those most dehumanized including women who suffer under African patriarchy.

Africa has suffered much. In Mugambi's writing one gets a sense of this along with the anger and frustration that Africa continues to be marginalized by globalizing powers. Consequently, he proposes a shift from theology and practice that is liberative to theology and practice, which is reconstructive. However, the decolonizing effects of such a proposal are enfeebled because of the ongoing tendency to move away from the particular and the experiential. This is seen in a failure to connect with a wider context of prior theological work and in prioritizing historical shifts (for example, the end of the Cold War) that have little impact on the experience of most Africans. Like Mbiti's innovation his reconstructionism has further, unintended, marginalizing consequences. As has been seen in chapter 6, his reading of the Ezra-Nehemiah text is not critically post-colonial. Indeed, there are times when the understanding of the Bible that Mugambi and Mbiti have as a whole is less than critical. For Mbiti, the Bible "links Christians of all ages and places and provides us with an essentially neutral and ecumenical authority for the profession of our faith."[55] This stands in contrast to other

---

55. Mbiti, *BATAC*, 13, see 156–57. It should be noted, however, that there is, at certain junctures in their writing, the sense that this primacy is not straightforwardly based on some prior commitment to revelation. Rather, it may be predicated upon more contextual and existential concerns. The Bible is primary because it bears testimony to the revelation of God *and* because it addresses issues pertinent in African

post-colonial theologians who not only see missionaries and colonialists distorting the Bible, but who also detect in the biblical text itself colonialist thought and practice. This lack of critical awareness in approaching the biblical text is seen very clearly in how Mugambi appropriates Nehemiah. For his reading of the text suppresses the voices of the *am hareetz*, which is the very voice that a post-colonial reading of the text should be recovering. This inauspicious exegetical foundation is only compounded by a lack of material detailing what, in practice, reconstruction might look like in Kenya today. It might even be argued that had Mugambi demonstrated an awareness for the need to reconstruct the voice of those suppressed in Ezra-Nehemiah, he would have been in a better position to give more detail for his own reconstructionist impulse for Africa.

The criticisms identified here largely center on the inability of Mbiti and Mugambi to take account of power in their work of theology. Consequently, there are key dissimilarities as well similarities between their work and the work of post-colonial theologians. The next section will seek to demonstrate how a more constructive and practical move towards power analysis, taking into account the work of Mbiti and Mugambi, might be achieved.

Second, a comparison with post-colonial theology while opening up the possibility for a means to power analysis does not actually provide such analysis. It will be the purpose of the present section to briefly extrapolate from the comparison with post-colonial theology to a practice of power analysis. The practice of power analysis, emerging from a comparison between the writings of Mbiti and Mugambi with post-colonialism, can be summed up in terms of defining scope, prioritizing marginalized voices, discerning multiple causes, networking from below, and clarifying transformative goals.

Chapter 2 defines the context from within which both Mbiti and Mugambi develop their contextual theology. It is a context dominated by foreign Christianity and foreign colonialism. They experience coloniality. That is to say, missionary agents and colonial agents, both intentionally and unintentionally, are involved in a process that subjugates African cultural and theological agency. This focus on coloniality in context can be seen as the first means toward power analysis. That is to say, an analysis begins with the identification of scope—a particular context and a particular time is first identified.

As has been seen, however, in chapter 3 the focus on context is not always easy to maintain. Initially, Mbiti gives priority to Akamba theological

---

societies and by African churches.

reflection in light of the practice of the AIM. When that specific contextual focus is maintained the theological agency of the Akamba is kept in view and given voice. The second practice of power analysis is, therefore, the prioritizing of marginalized agency and marginalized voices. Power analysis, addressing a particular context or situation at a particular time, will give voice first to the most marginalized persons in that context. In an African context, it is likely that such people will be the poorest and will include women and other groups not normally given voice within society. For it is such people who are most likely to suffer the consequences of top-down power in a particular context and will provide perspective and criticism from beyond the *status quo*.

Chapter 4 puts ATRs into dialogue with theism. From a post-colonial perspective this can be seen as a process of hybridization where the African characteristics of divinity might have influence on theistic attributes of God and *vice versa*. It is a rejection of binaries of opposition. The God of theism is not to be defined in distinction from the God of ATRs. Rather, God is further defined in relationship to ATRs. This rejection of dualisms and oppositional binaries creates opportunity to define the third characteristic of power analysis. That is to say, an analysis of power relations in a particular context will always seek multiple causes. Because binaries of opposition are already rejected the cause of subjugation or suffering will not be reduced to one root. Multiple causes are sought after. The suffering of a local community is not simply the cause of the arrival of colonialists two hundred years ago. While such a binary opposition might fuel nationalism it will fail to uncover more immediate causes and therefore fail to develop more immediate ameliorations.

In chapter 5 it was argued that the christologizing of Mbiti and Mugambi distances their work from faith communities in Kenya. A symbolic approach and christopraxis was identified as a way to respond to this problem. The Christ that emerges in such an approach is close to traditional communities because his practice relates well to traditional practices. The Christ that emerges is close also to Christian communities because their proclamation of him includes the message that his humanity and their humanity are ontologically equivalent.[56] The suffering and subjugation experienced by humans in a particular community is equivalent to the suffering experience by the marginalized Messiah of the Gospels. Consequently, the ministry of Christ and the ministry of Christians in such communities is to resist top-down powers. A christologically conceived community (church)

---

56. For a further exploration of the practical potency of ontological equivalence in a very different context, see Heaney, "Towards the Possibility," 171–86.

in a particular context will, therefore, practice power analysis through networking with other christologically conceived communities. Power analysis involves, then, a networking and sharing of resources from other contexts of subjugation. For such "bottom-up globalizing" resources communities by the sharing of experiences and testimonies from other practices of resistance.[57]

The purpose of post-colonial criticism is, or should be, decolonization. Unfortunately, in some of the publications and discourses referenced in this chapter it is not always clear that post-colonial theologians are keeping this goal clearly in view. Mugambi seeks to provide a reappraisal of the Kenyan context in chapter 6 leading to apparent personal, cultural, and ecclesial reconstruction. However, as has been seen, his proposals are no less than the culmination of gradual moves away from the particular initiated by Mbiti's work on Akamba/African temporality and eschatology. His work is distanced from coloniality. In contrast, while post-colonialism may demonstrate discursive unveiling of power relations and discursively re-empower marginalized voices, a more grounded practice of power analysis is also needed. In the current context, processes of decolonization will be achieved when stated and measurable goals are in place. Already practices have been identified that can be measured. Scope must be defined, marginalized voices must be heard, multiple causes need to be identified, and networks (through, for example, internet or mobile phone connectivity) must be established. To the extent that these practices are taking place a decolonizing process is in operation. Thus, clarifying transformative goals initially and through ongoing assessment, especially as networks develop, needs to be set in place. For decolonization is not a state to be achieved but a critical stance and an ongoing process whether named "decolonizing" or not.

Conclusion

This chapter provides a further constructive move designed to counter the unintended marginalization present in the work of both Mugambi and Mbiti. For the emergence of post-colonial theology has created a body of literature much more aware of the experiences and voices of the marginalized. Chapter 1 outlined what post-colonialism and post-colonial theology might be. It is suggested that there are grounds for considering the significance of Mbiti's and Mugambi's writing as critically post-colonial. For it seems to emerge from coloniality, promotes African theological agency, theologically

---

57. For the idea of "bottom-up" globalization, see Rieger, "Between Accommodation and Resistance."

hybridizes, resists hegemony (especially as found with the coming and continued dominance of the modern missionary movement), and culminates in a bid to decolonize both the African church and African theology. However, at each of these points criticism can be identified, which weakens claims to their writing being considered critically post-colonial. For despite experiences of coloniality, abstracted notions of "tradition" or heritage seem to be prioritized, the agency contended for is in danger of strengthening colonialist assumptions, the apparent hybridizing is not nearly as radical as other post-colonial theologizing, their resistance to hegemony fails to thoroughly present a Christ in solidarity with the most powerless, and their intent towards decolonization is weakened by a further move away from the particular and the experiential in, for example, macro-level theorizing that embeds marginalization in the biblical text and in the contemporary context. In response to such criticisms a constructive response seeking to define and ground power analysis as defining scope, prioritizing marginalized voices, discerning multiple causes, networking from below, and clarifying transformative goals has been submitted.

In conclusion, at the very least, the writings of Mbiti and Mugambi can be considered part of the antecedents of the continuing emergence of post-colonial theology. For the anticipated criticisms raised about their writing have parallels in broader discourse in other literature considered post-colonial. While, like any theological writing, it does not always deliver on its (post-colonial) promise, it does demonstrate decolonizing intent, methodology, and themes. As has been seen, such intent is at the very heart of literature that is critically post-colonial. While unintended marginalization exists in their writings, a comparison with post-colonial theology provides opportunity to identify ways in which such marginalization can be redressed by a more intentional approach to power relations. This is demonstrated in a constructive move which grounds power analysis, demonstrating further potential for transformative practice. However, it remains to be seen how Mbiti and Mugambi might react to such a comparison, and part of the purpose of the final chapter will be to anticipate just that.

Conclusion

THE PURPOSE OF THIS brief conclusion will be threefold. First, an overview and summary of the argument will be provided. Second, in light of the conspectus an attempt will be made to anticipate how Mbiti and Mugambi might react to the argument that their writing should now be considered part of post-colonial theology. Third, the final brief section of the book will submit some further reflections on how the implications of the present study might be envisaged.

The question this book has sought to answer emerged from conversations, conferences, research, seminars, theology classes, and friendships in East Africa. From such experience a question crystallized: what is the ongoing significance of the theology developed by first generation African theologians? In response to that question, this study comparatively analyzes the work of John Mbiti and Jesse Mugambi in reference to their post-colonial context and through identifying major themes in their writing. As is seen in the preceding chapters, this analysis is not on the basis of the fact of contextualization. It is on the basis of the character of their contextualization.

The theology developed by Mbiti and Mugambi emerges from the particular but gradually moves away from it toward a more generalized understanding of African theology. Despite their criticism of mission Christianity (chapter 2) and its relationship to empire (chapter 1), there is movement away from the particularism of context (chapter 3), experience (chapter 4), community (chapter 5), and coloniality (chapter 6). However, ongoing significance for their work is sought in a series of constructive moves: prioritizing Mbiti's initial methodology, proposing experiential dialogue, affirming christopraxis, and integrating power analysis. This leads to a reappraisal of their work in light of the recent emergence of post-colonial theology. Their work, therefore, remains significant for African theology because of such constructive moves. Their work emerges, for the first time, as significant for post-colonial theology as, at the very least, precursory to critically post-colonial theology.

Conclusion

Conspectus

It is the discovery of a methodological shift, identified in this study for the first time, which becomes the unifying factor for the argument. An outline of how Mbiti and Mugambi represent and experience mission Christianity seems to suggest that such a context and such experiences are the point of departure for their theology (chapter 2). However, the particular is ultimately eschewed in favor of a generalized concept of tradition becoming the locus for their emerging theology. Consequently, the chapters on eschatology, tradition, christology and reconstruction can be seen as an examination of a series of gradual moves away from the particularisms of context, experience, community, and coloniality.

It is a comparison of Mbiti's Cambridge PhD with his later published works also dealing with temporality and eschatology that occasions the discovery of a methodological shift in the African theology under discussion (chapter 3). There is a movement away from the context (in Mbiti's thesis) as the point of departure for African theology to an appeal to tradition as the locus for African theology (in *ARAP*, *COGA*, and *NTEAB*). Because Mbiti has such a pervasive influence on African theology it is inevitable that such a shift has widespread repercussions. Certainly, for the present study, the primacy of tradition or heritage as the locus for African theology is apparent in Mugambi's work also. For both writers, a generalized concept of ATRs becomes the means to theistic contextualization (chapter 4) often at the level of metaphysical comparison. This abstracts their theologizing from the experience of African traditionalists and thus undervalues a more grounded contextualization between, for example, the practice of Jesus in the gospels and the practice of traditional priests or healers. That such a move is not made is symptomatic of wider tensions within their writing on the topic of christology. For, while they espouse christocentrism and tend to treat christological issues in a practical manner, a more thoroughly contextualist approach may be forestalled. Relating African traditional religious experience and Christian faith and practice (chapter 4) is not extended to include a contextualizing exercise between traditionalist belief and practice and Christian belief and practice. In addition, their hesitancy towards ontological reflection on the nature of Christ is not, it appears, evident in the faith communities they themselves come from. A disjuncture between their christologizing and both traditionalist and Christian faith communities in Kenya emerges. There is danger, then, that already marginalized communities in a post-independent Africa may further be marginalized by those theologizing on their behalf (chapter 5). Nevertheless, it appears that Mugambi's promise of a theology of reconstruction will redress this gradual shift away from the particular as he turns to a reappraisal of the post-Cold War context (chapter 6). However, when he submits his reappraisal of the post-colonial context he further embeds the trend away from the particular and experiential initiated by Mbiti four decades earlier. Because the methodological shift away from the particular and contextual is dominant, his reconstructionism largely fails to enable people to theologically critique power relations and redress the injustices of coloniality. Instead, his theology of reconstruction exhibits abstractions, generalizations, uncritical reflection on the biblical text and context, elitism, and specialism.

Despite such criticisms, Mbiti and Mugambi do provide or anticipate innovations in African theology and, especially through a series of constructive moves in this book, it is possible to begin to anticipate how their work might be developed in response to criticisms and, therefore, how their contribution may continue to remain significant for theology within and without Africa. As has been seen, at least four main constructive moves, evoked by the writings of Mbiti and Mugambi, are proposed. The constructive moves respond to identified weaknesses in the way they address eschatology (chapter 3), tradition (chapter 4), christology (chapter 5), and coloniality (chapter 6). In a study of the Akamba there is a move away from context. In response, the constructive move of reading Mbiti's eschatology according to his own initial method is proposed. In prioritizing ATRs as the locus for the ongoing emergence of African theology, there is a move away from experience. In response, the constructive move of experiential dialogue is proposed. In dealing with christological issues, there is a move away from faith communities. In response, the constructive move of a symbolic christology and of recognizing the importance of christopraxis is proposed. In a reappraisal of the context, a reconstructionist theology moves away from coloniality. In response, the constructive move of integrating power analysis via a comparison with post-colonial theology is proposed.

Constructive Moves

The first constructive move of this study is to read Mbiti according to his own initial method. Identifying the shift away from the particular for the first time is also to recognize that, prior to that shift, a different approach was taken. Reading Mbiti's eschatology according to his own initial method in his Cambridge thesis counters a move toward a more generalized understanding of African theology. It brings to the fore the subjugation at work in the Akamba context, thus opening up analytic space for an eventual comparison with post-colonial theology. It reveals the innovation of his research while, at the same time, weakening major criticisms of his eschatology. Reading Mbiti's eschatology with the context of the Akamba and foreign AIM missionaries as the point of departure diminishes the significance of the philosophical, social, and theological objections identified in chapter 2. For the temporality he defines, as it emerges from the experience of the Akamba, might be seen as *normative*. That is to say, his analysis of the Akamba is put into contextual perspective while allowing for the possibility of the reformulation of such temporality in particular (and possibly traumatic) circumstances. Indeed, an example of such circumstances in a situation of coloniality (Mau Mau) was identified as an example of how, in practice, a reformulation of normative temporality could take place. Recognizing the significance of coloniality as providing the possibility for temporality beyond the normative evokes a further (post-colonial) constructive move in chapter 7. For an extended Mbitian approach to temporality, arising from an Akamba context, could go on to interrogate the so-called Western notion of the future. For, as has been seen, the type of future imported to Kenya in missionary eschatology can be seen as an imperial construct where the future becomes associated with consumption.

The second constructive move proposes experiential dialogue as a response to a further move away from the particular evident in the writings of both Mbiti and Mugambi as they prioritize tradition over experience. Theistic contextualization between ATRs and Christianity becomes the priority over the experience and theologizing of believers in a particular context. In response, a dialogic practice that also provides criticism of African theology is submitted (chapter 4). For even in their attempts to contextualize (Mbiti) and re-mythologize (Mugambi) African tradition and heritage with Christian belief and practice, they further abstract their theologizing from African experience. This is highlighted through criticisms relating to the hypothesis of unity, the power dynamics at work in tradition, and the prioritizing of the category of religion. In response, a practice of experiential dialogue is introduced as a means to bring the experience of Christ closer to the experience of people in traditionalist communities.

For the practice of Jesus may provide a much closer relationship to African experience than the generalized and metaphysically conceived attributes of ATRs and theism. If such a reading of the Jesus in the gospels is possible, it highlights how the work of Mbiti and Mugambi might be developed back towards the particularism of traditional religious experience. It also highlights the ongoing danger that in the very act of seeking to overcome Northern ways of theologizing they, in fact, may embed such ways of theologizing in African theology.

The third constructive move is to envisage a christology that integrates the importance of symbol and christopraxis. While the priority Mbiti and Mugambi give traditional religion or heritage is designed to signify their work as *African* scholars, it is the language of christocentrism that is used to signify that they write as *Christian* scholars (chapter 5). However, because they have already moved away from context in conceiving of African theology in generalized terms (chapter 3) and in prioritizing theistic contextualization (chapter 4) there is danger that such an appeal to christocentrism will also become abstracted from the particular. Consequently, while they develop what might be referred to as a more practical and thematic approach (as opposed to a systematic approach) to christology the connection between faith communities and their christologizing is not as apparent as it might have been. In order to redress that distancing from traditionalist and Christian communities, a christology that integrates symbol and christopraxis is envisaged as a way of grounding further the intent of Mbiti and Mugambi. For symbol continues to be important to traditional religious practice and a symbolic christology may well be able to draw from this in its understanding of Christ. That is to say, a symbolic approach does not connect with a generalized traditional community in terms of metaphysical congruence. It connects through recognizing the importance of symbolic practice. From this recognition Christ can be seen as the symbol that makes the presence of God present, thus a christocentrism emerges that provides space for the revelatory potency of African traditional religious practice and community. Such theologizing may counter the deliberate marginalization that such communities experience, sometimes at the hands of Christians. Marginalization is further addressed in an appeal to christopraxis. For an emphasis on christopraxis takes as its point of departure the co-equality of Christ's humanness with African humanness. Christ as the marginalized and colonized Messiah, unable to exercise a top-down type of power, connects both with marginalized practices and experiences in a way that is not apparent in Mbiti's and Mugambi's christologizing.

The fourth constructive move is to recognize the necessity of power analysis in theology. It responds to the final stage in the move away from the particular understood as a move away from coloniality. As has already been seen, Mbiti's and Mugambi's writing moves toward a generalized understanding of theology. Such an abstracting tendency results in unintended marginalization. For when Mbiti moves from his initial method in African eschatology, the voice of theistic contextualization marginalizes the voice and agency of the Akamba. So too Mbiti's and Mugambi's christologizing, while exhibiting to some extent a practical approach, fails to connect with traditional symbolic practice and fails to emphasize the co-equality who, in part, shape post-colonialism. These include Kwame Nkrumah and Kenya's first president, Jomo Kenyatta.[5]

For Sugirtharajah, the genesis of post-colonial theory and practice is not crucial. Rather, what is important is if such practice has "diagnostic capabilities to promote the cause of the marginalized."[6] Indeed, post-colonial criticism itself should exhibit the hybridization it celebrates. It emerges from an interaction between colonizing countries and those who are colonized. Its origin is neither in the First nor the Third World. Rather, it is "a product of the contentious reciprocation between the two."[7] There is potential, therefore, that a practice of hybridity may go some way to counter the objection that post-colonialism is something imposed from without and a means of analysis predicated upon a protagonist-antagonist dualism. However, as will be seen below, this appeal to hybridity in post-colonial theology is not nearly as convincing given the apparent marginalization of African voices including those who actually experienced, in this case, coloniality at the hands of Europeans.

Second, the aforementioned elevation of hybridization may be questioned by Mbiti and Mugambi. As has been seen, while Mbiti used "syncretism" once in his writings in a positive manner he has not used it in such a manner since. Mugambi also has identified syncretism as a danger to be avoided by African theology. They may remain skeptical of any theology that has an inability to distinguish hybridity from syncretism. Both Mbiti and Mugambi are cognizant of the blending of sources in Christianity's history and seek to see that continue as Africans negotiate with Christian texts, thoughts, and practices. However, they see syncretism as a move beyond contextualization. This may relate to their commitment to a Christian gospel that is good news for Africa. That is to say, a fear of syncretism is a fear that the liberative and transformative effect of the gospel will be hindered by admixtures of teachings or practices that veil the freedom they have found in the person and message of Jesus Christ. This is the opposite concern of post-colonialism being a foreign imposition. Here, syncretism is the fear that theologizing no longer functions as a challenge to culture and society but simply legitimizes dominant practices. This is a concern the present writer shares. Indeed, such polarized legitimation could equally be directed at the field of post-colonialism more generally if it becomes associated with one particular perspective on Christian theology.

5. Young, R., *Postcolonialism: Historical Intro*, 217–52.
6. Sugirtharajah, *Postcolonial Criticism*, 14.
7. Ibid., 23.

If post-colonial theology, whether by design or default, becomes dominated by views aligned to radical or liberal causes understood in either theological and/or social terms it will have failed.[8] If it simply is another expression of, for example, antirealism, panentheism, postmodernism, or queer theologizing while at the same time giving less attention to other forms of marginalization it will not be nearly as hybridized as it claims. Unfortunately, the early indications signal just such failures. For example, in a recent edition of the *Journal of Anglican Studies* dedicated to post-colonial theology, only one of the main articles engaged with theology from beyond the traditional colonial centers and only one author was from beyond the Northern church.[9] The danger remains that post-colonialism, without reference to theologies emerging in former colonial contexts, can also be colonized for the benefit of academic elites in well resourced academic centers—even if such academics seek to challenge so-called Western hegemony. Nonetheless, there remains time for such an emerging field to rectify such trends. For example, a recent publication addresses the relationship between evangelicalism and post-colonialism.[10] It is hoped that such publications will provoke other research from other (hybridizing) perspectives not yet well represented, including African theology. In addition, it appears that if post-colonialism, especially as practiced in the North, is to respond practically to such anticipated concerns reparative partnerships with marginalized people and marginalized institutions will be needed.

Third, it is possible that Mbiti and Mugambi would further question their role in post-colonial theology in relation to the function of alterity. That is to say, they may have the sense that their function within post-colonial theology is reduced to providing "otherness" for a movement against Western hegemony. Sara Suleri captures such danger vividly when she objects to being treated like an "otherness machine." As scholars from beyond the West, the risk is that one's primary responsibility is for the "manufacture of alterity."[11] Anne McClintock's criticism of post-colonialism is apposite. She accuses scholars of post-colonialism of once more orientating the globe "around a single, binary opposition: colonial/post-colonial" so that non-European wisdom is only valued in relation to European wisdom.[12] Given

---

8. See Heaney, "Prospects and Problems," 29–42.

9. Even then, his focus was the Church of England. See Kasibante, "The Ugandan Diaspora," 79–86.

10. Smith, K., et al., *Evangelical Postcolonial Conversations*.

11. Appiah, "Is the *Post-* in Postmodernism," 356.

12. McClintock, "Angel of Progress," 85–86. See Hall, "When was 'the Postcolonial,'" 249.

such criticisms, Mbiti and Mugambi would likely further object to being integrated into the field of post-colonial theology.

Mark Taylor refers to a "discourse of otherness" which "dulls the liberationist edge."[13] Taylor sees the concept and practice of hybridity as standing in the way of resistance and transformation.[14] For this reason he, despite the post-colonial affirmations and practices of marginalized agency, hybridity, and resistance, wants to maintain a "necessary binary" of colonizer and colonized.[15] This is well meaning.[16] However, it is a mistake. For the dualisms and binary opposites problematized by post-colonial thinkers are not simply a rhetorical or theoretical option to be adopted or rejected. Rather, they get to the very heart of the matter. For hybridity, understood in the context of differentials of power, is the means to resistance. Taylor is correct, writing from an American context, to be wary of the influence of a "(playful) postmodernism" on post-colonial practice.[17] However, this need not be the nature or purpose of post-colonial hybridity. Alterity need not be the function of African theology in post-colonial theology. For alterity can be conceived of, in a post-colonial theology, as both immanent and transcendent. That is to say, otherness in a post-colonial theology will not just define something that exists beyond the theological context in question. Alterity is hybridized to be something that is found both, in the present case, within Northern theologies (see, for example, Rieger's identification of theological "surplus") and in African theologies.[18] Furthermore, the alterity of African theologizing in a post-colonial context is not designed to be the foil to which so-called Western theology might be defined and practiced. On the contrary, it largely functions to bring critique and judgment to Northern thought and practice thereby necessitating change toward some kind of practice of decolonization. How such change might begin to be envisaged is the focus of the following section.

It is beyond the scope of the present study to set out in detail what the implications of this might be for the Northern academy and church. However, given that the author is part of that academy and church some brief and initial reflections on the implications for the present work will be submitted. The implications of the present analysis will include the theological, missiological, and pedagogical.

13. Taylor, M., "Spirit and Liberation," 46.
14. Ibid., 45.
15. Ibid., 47.
16. Stinton, "Africa, East and West," 132–33.
17. Taylor, M., "Spirit and Liberation," 46.
18. Rieger, *Christ and Empire*, 9–11, 93–100.

Theological Implications

Paul Avis acknowledges that Anglicanism has spread largely because of empire.[19] The theological significance he draws from such history is the cultural competition between assimilation and contextualization. Questions of how imperial practices affect visions of God are ignored. Such failure remains a challenge to the purported rationalist and critical nature of so-called Western theology. The challenge is compounded when it is recognized that theologies emerging in colonial and post-colonial contexts explicitly critique such rationalism and theologizing. The post-colonial point here is not that Eurocentric rationalism fails simply because the idea of rational "Man" arises from particular traditions, cultures, and experiences. The point is that such rationalism explicitly excludes others and uses them to define modernist rationality over against the "irrationality" of the other. Colonized peoples, argues Kant, have displayed a passivity more akin to animals than to rational European men. They will be raised from their irrational indolence only through a civilizing mission. Theology and missionary activism built upon such understandings of rationality are exclusionary not as a by-product of history. They are exclusionary philosophically.[20] A theology influenced by voices beyond the Northern context and within the broad field of post-colonialism will not, therefore, be fixated with the aims of coherency nor with answering the rational skeptic. Rather, what might be termed the moral skeptic and the transformative function of theology will be in view. For attention is drawn to the experiences of colonialists (and missionaries) and colonized (and converts) that problematize, hybridize, and undermine such polar distinctions as self/other, pure/impure, sacred/profane, rational/chaotic. Post-colonial scholars seek to identify the underlying agenda that sustains such differences.[21] More constructively, post-colonial theologies identify and affirm the apparent hybridities present in Christian theology that will serve a multilingual, multiracial, multicultural world better. Christianity itself emerges as a hybrid intermixing metaphysics, philosophies, and identities within the larger context of the Roman empire.[22] In illustrating what that might mean theologically, post-colonial reflections on God will include issues of power, marginalization, hybridity, and decolonization already identified as key post-colonial themes (see chapters 1 and 7).

---

19. Avis, *Identity of Anglicanism*, 52. See Heaney, "Views of Colonization," 726–38.

20. See Serequeberhan, "Critique of Eurocentrism," 141–61; McCarthy, *Race, Empire, and the Idea*.

21. Bhabha, *Location of Culture*, 2–12.

22. Keller, et al., Introduction to *Postcolonial Theologies*, 13–14.

God and power: the genealogy of imperialism, especially as it relates to Mbiti and Mugambi, is Eurocentric. However, its present potency is not limited to region. Its "logics of rule" function also in chronologically post-colonial contexts.[23] Imperialist practice is still a desire for the extension of geographical, political, economical as well as intellectual, emotional, psychological, spiritual, cultural, and religious governance.[24] It is top down power disallowing or disarming alternative realities or alternative purposes.[25]

Rowan Williams, reflecting on the significance of the Nicene settlement, reminds Christians that God is not an individual. God's will is, therefore, not about "self-assertion" or "contest" for control.[26] The Trinity is non-individualistic, non-hierarchical, and differentiated. Consequently, such inherent ontological pluralism becomes a threat to the hegemonic processes of imperialism.[27] Most evocatively Williams writes, "God does not compete with us for space."[28] Humans colonize. God does not. The implications of such a vision of God "for ethics and for prayer and spirituality are enormous; and we are still discovering them."[29]

The divine does not compete for space. God's grace creates space for creation and fellowship with and between creation. A kingdom of eternal expansive grace stands in contrast to the expansionist over-reach of every human imperialism. Because of the communitarian (Trinitarian) revelation of God, particularisms of faith-responses, faith-communities, faith-traditions, and faith-stories emerge. Indeed, such pluralist particularisms are too often suppressed so that orthodoxy and catholicity are presented as homogeneous over against the relativist pluralisms of heterodoxy. Yet, even Nicene Christianity is pluralist and theological categories are elected (particularly *homoousios*) that one might describe as spacious.[30] A post-colonial church practice will shun any strategies or impulses to contract or centralize. The particularisms of, for example, provinces, dioceses, and parishes make up the story of the church. These along with the variant theological traditions and methodologies, apparently at odds with each other, are part of the spaciousness of God's grace grounded in church.

---

23. Hardt and Negri, *Empire*, xvi.
24. See Padilla and Scott, *Terrorism and the War in Iraq*.
25. See Rieger, *Christ and Empire*, 2–3, 276; Williams, R., "Kingdom and Empire."
26. Williams, R., *Arius: Heresy and Tradition*, loc. 3578.
27. Rieger, *Christ and Empire*, 96.
28. Williams, R., *Arius: Heresy and Tradition*, loc. 3578.
29. Ibid., loc. 3586.
30. See Ayres, *Nicea and its Legacy*, 98–100; Rieger, *Christ and Empire*, 94–95.

God and marginalization: Both Mbiti and Mugambi and the missionaries in East Africa they experienced, claim a christocentrism in thought and practice. It seems, however, that Christ reveals the power of divinity through marginalization. Divine power is met in the marginalization of the Son at the hands of imperialism. Caesar pushes Christ beyond the margins of empire and life only to find that, beyond death, Christ subverts and converts the margin into a threshold. The empire's marginalizing of God in Christ becomes the threshold for renewed life, renewed community, and the reign of God. Caesarian power is subverted by divine power from the margins. Cruciform power does not emanate from the center nor is it exercised from the top down. This liminal subversive power might be seen to have certain practical implications for a re-envisaged practice. Not least among such re-envisaged practice is a continued commitment to the margins and a practice of porosity because of the boundary crossing risen Christ. Christian churches, including the Anglicanism of Mbiti and Mugambi, can be particularly concerned with boundary or gate keeping. The danger here is that the bureaucratizing of center and margin stands in tension with a more christologically functioning center and margin. The center is Christ who needs no gatekeepers (John 10:9).

Instead of conceiving and practicing church in terms of covenant or confession, it is also possible to conceive and practice church as storied. Such communion would expect of believers and leaders regular testifying. At parish, diocesan, provincial, and international gatherings believers would be invited to testify to how their experiences and practices relate to biblical and Christian traditions. Testifying to how Christ is central to the practices of the church would then be the communion Christians share. Centering on Christ and Christ's mission, in the stories of scripture, tradition, and contemporary believers, turns the attention of Christians away from border-making to the threshold-creating Christ. Because Christ practices lordship on the margins, Christ is the center of the church. Centering on Christ means turning our backs on border policing while simultaneously being confronted by the margins of human experience in the broken body and poured out life of Christ. In the Spirit, Word and sacrament push believers to the experiential interface, where we are called to network ("from the bottom up") in missions of particularities and localisms. The extent to which such networks can exist will depend on, in large part, the recognition that ecclesiological boundaries are porous (mystical). The church is "mixed." It is hybridized fellowship.

God and hybridization: as has been seen, the primary characteristic of a post-colonial text is hybridity. For Kwok, "[t]he most hybridized concept in the Christian tradition is that of Jesus/Christ."[31] The attempt to fix the space between "Jesus" and "Christ" for systematic, missiological, or rationalistic reasons results, from this perspective, in a denial of the pluralist and hybrid contexts that shape gospel, and it simultaneously mollifies imperialism. It is because of the inherent hybrid nature of Jesus/Christ and the space ("contact zone" or "borderland") between Jesus and Christ, that marginal christologies exist.[32] It is the conviction that God has come to us in hybridity (God-human) that makes such commitment to Christ possible in the first place. In Christ, humanity is opened to divinity and divinity to humanity. When Christians are tempted toward boundary making or gate keeping, from a critically post-colonial perspective, there may be danger of solidifying boundaries which God in Christ makes porous.

As has been seen, hybridity in itself for itself does not necessarily hold theological value. Even cultural hybridity does not necessarily deliver transformative theological practice. For an emphasis on hybridity can disempower attempts at transformative action if it is assumed that all oppositional stances are now comprised of people and circumstances that are partly good and partly bad. Does not the message that, to some extent, we are all colonizers and colonized veil ongoing oppression? It is possible that such danger can be undercut if it is recognized that practices of hybridity are predicated on "differentials of power not just on difference in general." It is because of the differentials of power that the potentially revolutionary and decolonizing effects of hybridization exist. Hybridizing only has decolonizing and missional effect if powers are pushing for the erasure of local differences (see chapter 2) in favor of some kind of uniformity.[33]

Missiological Implications

Mbiti and Mugambi recognize an inherent power differential between creator and creature (see chapter 4). The danger is that this theological (ontological) power differential ultimately undermines all decolonizing action. Worse, the omnipotent lordship and sovereignty of God may, in the end, be accepted as justifiable theological ground for human empire building and expansionist mission practice. The mission Christianity experienced by Mbiti and Mugambi is expansionist. It is expansionist in that it has the capacity to justify the growth of the British empire in providential terms. It is expansionist in that it has the capacity to associate imperial expansion with

31. Kwok, *Postcolonial Imagination*, 171.
32. Ibid., 174–85.
33. Rieger, *Globalization and Theology*, 31.

missional opportunity and efficacy. It is expansionist in that it too often associates imperial culture with Christian discipleship.[34] Sugirtharajah argues that such "centre out" mission is intrinsically imperialist. Consequently, it is not by coincidence that evangelicals like William Carey re-discovered the "unfashionable" and "under-exegeted" command to preach to the world (Matt 28:19) at a time when Europe was pursuing expansionist policies.[35] Given the suffering that Mbiti and Mugambi bear witness to, a post-colonial missiology will not be expansionist. Rather, it will be, what might be termed, participationist.

Such emphasis on participation begins not with the idea of divine omnipotence or sovereignty. Rather, it begins with the practice of divine power revealed in the life of Jesus Christ. For a possible riposte to expansionist missiology might be to stress the kenotic exercise of divine power as both theologically well founded and practically decolonizing. However, some remedial work may be needed first. For the Christian tradition may obstruct a participatory missiology because of an Alexandrian understanding of *kenōsis*. Sarah Coakley observes that under the influence of Cyril of Alexander, *kenōsis* has become in no sense a loss of power. Contrary to the apparent plain meaning of the text of Philippians 2, *kenōsis* becomes "divine force that takes on humanity by controlling and partly *obliterating* it."[36]

Coakley deals with several Anglican scholars who seek to respond constructively to the problems of such an Alexandrian reading. For present purposes the approach of the missionary bishop of Zanzibar, Frank Weston, is of particular relevance because of his relationship to East Africa. Weston seeks to elucidate an incarnated power where Christ submits voluntarily to the "law of self-restraint."[37] Christ is like St. Francis de Sales acting "merely" as confessor to his parents and relating to them as their son. Christ is a defeated African leader made "a king in slavery." Christ is a favorite son of an officer transferred to his father's regiment. The son possesses both "self-consciousness" as a son and, now, "limited consciousness" as a subordinate rank.[38] Two of the analogies emerge directly from the crucible of colonization. Further, the African king alone suffers not so much from self-limitation but from forced limitation. The white priest and, it might be assumed, the white soldier have the freedom to abandon their limitations through resigning from holy and military orders. However, even viewed christologi-

---

34. See Warren, *Caesar, the Beloved Enemy*, 30–41.
35. Sugirtharajah, *Postcolonial Reconfigurations*, 21, 17–36.
36. Coakley, *Powers and Submissions*, 15–16.
37. Weston, *One Christ*, 149–53.
38. Ibid., 166–72.

cally, the emancipation of an African is unlikely. Decolonization, it appears, is not served by this type of kenoticism.

Coakley argues that true divine "empowerment" may occur "most unimpededly in the context of a *special* form of human 'vulnerability.'" Her proposal assumes an understanding of *kenōsis* that means choosing never to have "worldly" (colonizing) forms of power. Responding to the God who does not compete for space, believers make space for God in "defenceless" and "wordless" prayer.[39] Such worship is displacement. It is de-centering discipleship. It is human kenoticism in response to divine kenoticism. However, there is danger that such practice will be seized as a female and/or "non-Western" and/or lay "complement" in defining the roles and power of legions of male deacons, priests, and bishops.[40] Yet, the interstices between this space-making prayer and space-making God are sacred. It is not possible to occupy potentiality. Consequently, this discipleship of vulnerability (*askēsis*) is never an invitation or opportunity to be battered or silenced.[41] It is a call to be remade. In the current context, it is the Holy Spirit's call to participate in a re-envisaged, vulnerable, and dangerous mission within a vulnerable fellowship and world. A re-envisaged mission practice is not the expansion of projects or rationalities from the North. A re-envisaged mission practice resists top-down globalization. This is done not least in developing missional practices that are shaped not by center-out theorizing, but shaped, and constantly reformed, by relationships in networks of grassroots practice.

Pedagogical Implications

Given the present study, mission theology cannot be taught independent of the critique of those who have been the recipients of mission Christianity. Indeed, I argue that theologies of mission taught in both Northern and Southern academies should begin with criticism of mission practice. For such critique, arising from the particular and the experiential, begins not with past or present thought on mission but on the practice of mission. Missiology courses then will not begin with the Bible or with the history of mission but with the literature and critique emerging from the particular.[42] History, Bible, and theology are analyzed, therefore, not as ideas that

39. Coakley, *Powers and Submissions*, 31–34.
40. See Said, *Orientalism*, 96, 105–10; Oduyoye, *Daughters of Anowa*, 190–91.
41. Coakley, *Powers and Submissions*, 35.
42. This is in distinction, for example, to the major modern work on mission. See Bosch, *Transforming Mission*.

may or may not cohere and may or may not motivate mission. Rather, how missionaries act and how recipients reflect on such action becomes the site for the analysis of how mission Christianity understands history, Bible, and theology. To begin with the counter-discourse, it is submitted, is a post-colonial move, and one that Mbiti and Mugambi exhibit and can provide.

As has been seen, it is the transformative (decolonizing) intent in situations of coloniality and its social, cultural, political, and theological effects that ultimately define the "post-colonial" even if the authors of such material do not view themselves in such terms.[43] For that reason it has been argued that the ongoing significance of Mbiti's and Mugambi's writing is found in relation to the broad field of post-colonial literature and as part of a movement for decolonization.[44] The present study of these writings, it is hoped, will encourage theologians and especially post-colonial theologians to attend to those writers who have experienced historic colonialism. In the emerging field of post-colonial theology it is not uncommon for academics to complain about the lack of work done previously.[45] It is acknowledged that biblical studies has been more willing to engage with European colonialism but that theological studies has, until very recently, been largely untouched by the concerns of post-colonialism. Such a complaint, however, can only be made if the theologizing being done beyond the North Atlantic academies is marginalized. This is the very thing that post-colonial theology purports to overcome. As is seen in this study, it is not the case that theology ignored the issues of coloniality until recent times. Theologians such as Mbiti and Mugambi, who begin their formal theological work in the 1960s, are concerned with the domineering and hegemonic intent of European expansionism in Africa. They were raising such concerns forty years before post-colonial theology began to emerge. Despite this, not one of the contributors in Keller, Nausner, and Rivera's *Postcolonial Theologies* (2004) comes from Africa or engages with African theology.[46]

When voices from Africa and post-colonial concerns in broader theology and curricula are excluded, any claim to such theologizing being

---

43. See Ashcroft, et al., *Empire Writes Back*, 197.

44. That is to say, it is possible to understand it as post-colonial literature in the more technical sense of displaying themes present in other writings well established as post-colonial literature. It is, of course, uncontroversial to refer to African theology as post-colonial literature in the sense that much of it was produced in the era of Independence.

45. See the introduction in Keller, et al., *Postcolonial Theologies*.

46. The same can be said for Rieger, *Christ and Empire*, see 51–53, 140–47, 159–322; Rivera, *Touch of Transcendence*.

"critical" is undermined.[47] Consequently, with the continued justifications of Euro-American Christian expansionism by missiologists, mission historians, and foreign missionaries there remains much work to be done uncovering how imperialism and colonialism has often influenced Western theology.[48] As is already seen, the existence of this lacuna undermines the ongoing claim that the pedagogy of the traditional colonial centers is, in practice, critical. In practical terms, responding to coloniality and contributing to a decolonizing critique will therefore mean, at the very least, an engagement with marginalized theology and theologians.[49] For marginalized voices to interrupt or intervene in Eurocentric theology already redefines the discipline. For, as has been seen, no longer can coherency be a chief aim of the theological task. Instead, some sort of liberative or transformative practice will be the end goal for theology.[50] Such reflections underline the concern that some within the movement have that abstract and abstruse theorizing, while important and potentially transformative, can too easily lead the field away from the concrete, historical, practical theologizing that has been going on in particular contexts and particular experiences for many years. It is hoped that a critical engagement with the writings of Mbiti and Mugambi, taking into account both weaknesses and possible constructive moves that their work evokes, begins to disrupt such abstractionism and abstruseness.

Conclusion

This book begins with mention of conversations among Anglican students and faculty in East Africa. The present author has lived and worked in an East African Anglican university and now works in an American Episcopalian seminary with strong historic and contemporary links throughout the Anglican Communion. Many more conversations on how apparently disparate experiences, opinions, feelings, and theologizing in colonial and post-colonial East Africa might be seen as theologically significant have

---

47. Sugirtharajah, *Postcolonial Criticism*, 25, 28. See Porter, *Religion versus Empire*, 1–11; Metz, "Religion and Society," 507. See Sugirtharajah, *Postcolonial Criticism*, 2, 117–22; Graham, *Transforming Practice*, 130–41.

48. For a recent attempt at this, see Rieger, *Christ and Empire*. See also Douglas and Kwok, *Beyond Colonial Anglicanism*; Keller, et al., *Postcolonial Theologies*; Kwok, *Postcolonial Imagination*; Rivera, *Touch of Transcendence*.

49. Sugirtharajah, *Postcolonial Criticism*, 201.

50. For the possible indebtedness Post-Colonial Theology might have to Liberation theology, see the introduction to Keller, et al., *Postcolonial Theologies*, 1–19. See Mugambi, *FLTR*, 160–80.

been had. In reflecting and responding to such conversations, this book provides the first study of Kenya's two most innovative Anglican theologians together. It identifies, for the first time, a methodological shift that has repercussions for both writers and potentially for others also. It provides a new perspective on the writings of Mbiti and Mugambi within the broad field of post-colonialism, thus bringing them into relationship with a long tradition of resistance against imperialisms and identifies them as important antecedents to more recently emerging post-colonial theology.

The significance of this study, however, is not found simply in an academic reappraisal of the writings of Mbiti and Mugambi, nor does the significance end with suggestions for reformed or decolonizing practices of theology, mission, and pedagogy. For there is also existential significance as the author continues to share and discuss his findings with students and faculty in East Africa. For from a post-colonial reappraisal comes the realization that such members of the "old guard" embody very similar experiences, opinions, frustrations, and commitments to the Christian faith that new generations of East African Christians possess. This connection between new generations of African Christians and such theologians who lived at the time of a brutal colonial regime in Kenya is significant. For it gives a sense of continuity and solidarity with theologians who struggle to set an agenda not defined primarily by the North, but by Africa also. It is also significant that, even in experiencing coloniality, Mbiti and Mugambi do not allow suppression and oppression to rob them of hope or prevent them from making a theologically constructive contribution. Such contribution is significant for those from beyond Africa, as the hopeful theologizing of Mbiti and Mugambi judges so-called Western practices and, by implication, demands a more critical theology and contextualism that is decolonizing. Consequently, it is judgment and it is hope that emerges from the present study. Indeed, both continue to be needed as networks of theologians, within and without Africa, continue to seek to resist the powers that continue to globalize hegemonic intent. Again the vision of the God who comes to us from the margins to subvert caesarian power and bring abundant life is needed. It is needed not only for those who struggle to have their voice heard, it is needed also for those who remain in danger of associating their own voice with the voice of God.

> My soul magnifies the Lord,
> and my spirit rejoices in God my Savior . . .
> The Lord has brought down the powerful from their thrones,
> and lifted up the lowly . . . (Luke 1:46–47, 52)

Bibliography

Published Works by Mbiti

Mbiti, John S. "An African Answer." In *Why Did God Make Me?* edited by Hans Küng and Jürgen Moltmann, 88–90. New York: Seabury, 1978.

———. "African Christians and the Jewish Religion." *Christian Attitudes on Jews and Judaism: A Bimonthly Documentary Survey* 56 (October 1977) 1–4.

———. "African Concept of Sin." *Frontier* 3:7 (1964) 182–84.

———. "African Concept of Time." *African Theological Journal* 1 (1968) 8–20.

———. "African Concepts of Human Relations." *Ministry: Theological Review* 9 (1969) 158–84.

———. "African Concepts of Time, History and Death." *Afrika: German Review of Political, Economic and Cultural Affairs in Africa and Madagascar* 3:2 (1967) 33–38.

———. "African Indigenous Culture in Relation to Evangelism and Church Development." In *The Gospel and Frontier Peoples*, edited by R. Pierce Beaver, 79–95. Pasadena: Willam Carey Library, 1973.

———. "African Names of God." *Orita* 6:1 (1972) 3–14.

———. "African Religion." In *The Study of Spirituality*, edited by Cheslyn Jones et al., 513–16. New York: Oxford University Press, 1986.

———. "African Religion and its Contribution to World Order." In *The Whole Earth Papers* no. 16, edited by Pat Mische, 27–31. New Jersey: Global Education Associates, 1982.

———. "African Religion and World Order." In *Towards a Global Civilization? The Contribution of Religions*, edited by Patricia M. Mische and Melissa Merkling, 361–70. New York: Peter Lang, 2001.

———. *African Religions and Philosophy*. Garden City: Anchor, [1969] 1970.

———. *African Religions and Philosophy*. 2nd ed. Oxford: Heinemann, 1989.

———. "African Theology." In *Initiation into Theology: The Rich Variety of Theology and Hermeneutics*, edited by Simon Maimela and Adrio König, 141–57. Pretoria: J. L. Schaik, 1998.

———. "African Theology." *Worldview* 16 (1973) 33–39.

———. "African Traditional Architecture." *Africa Theological Journal* 8:2 (1979) 66–68.

BIBLIOGRAPHY

———. "African Traditional Medicine and its Relevance for Christian Work." In *So Sende Ich Euch: Festschrift für Dr. Martin Pörksen*, edited by O. Waack et al., 310-18. Kontal bei Stuttgart: Evangelischer Missionsverlag, 1973.

———. "An African views American Black Theology." In *Black Theology*, edited by Gayraud Wilmore and James H. Cone, 477-82. Maryknoll: Orbis, 1979.

———. "An African views American Black Theology." *Worldview* 17:8 (1974) 41-44.

———. "Afrikanische Beiträge zur Christologie." In *Theologische Stimmen aus Asien, Afrika und Lateinamerika*, vol. 3, edited by P. Beyerhaus et al., 72-85. Munich: Chr. Kaiser Verlag, 1968.

———. "Afrikanische Theologie: Hintergrunde, Schwerpunkte, Folgen." In *Herausforderung: Die Dritte Welt und die Christen Europas*, edited by Castillo Fernando et al., 65-78. Regensburg: Verlag Friedrich Pustet, 1980.

———. "Afrikanisches Verständnis der Geister im Lichte des Neuen Testamentes." In *Theologische Stimmen aus Asien, Afrika und Lateinamerika*, vol. 2, edited by G. Rosenkranz, 130-47. München: C. Kaiser Verlag, 1967.

———. *Akamba Stories*. Oxford: Clarendon, 1966.

———. "Asian and African Voices on the Uniqueness of Jesus." In *The Uniqueness of Jesus: A Dialogue with Paul F. Knitter*, edited by Leonard J. Swidler and Paul Mojzes, 100-106. Maryknoll: Orbis, 1997.

———. *Bible and Theology in African Christianity*. Nairobi: Oxford University Press, 1986.

———. "The Bible in African Culture." In *Paths of African Theology*, edited by Rosino Gibellini, 27-39. London: SCM, 1994.

———. "The Biblical Basis for Present Trends in African Theology." *Occasional Bulletin of Missionary Research* 4:3 (1980) 119-24. Also in *African Theology En Route*, edited by Kofi Appiah-Kubi and Sergio Torres, 83-94. Maryknoll: Orbis, 1979.

———. "The Biblical Basis in Present Trends of African Theology." *Africa Theology Journal* 7:1 (1978) 72-85.

———. "Blessed are Those who Mourn, for They shall be Comforted." In *. . . And Yet Happy: The Beatitudes Revisited*, edited by Emidio Campi, 29-32. Geneva: World Student Christian Federation, 1981.

———. "The Capture of the Sun." In *Modern Science and Moral Values: Proceedings of the Second International Conference on the Unity of the Sciences, Tokyo, November 18-21, 1973*, 191-98. Tarrytown: International Cultural Foundation, 1973.

———. "Cattle are Born with Ears, Their Horns Grow Later: Towards an Appreciation of African Oral Theology." *Africa Theological Journal* 8:1 (1979) 15-25.

———. "Challenges Facing Religious Education and Research in Africa: The Case of Dialogue Between Christianity and African Religion." *Religion and Theology* 3:2 (1996) 170-79.

———. "A Change of the African Concept of Man Through Christian Influence." In *For the Sake of the Gospel: Essays in Honour of Samuel Amirtham*, edited by Gnana Robinson, 54-63. Arasaradi, Madurai: TTS Publications, 1980.

———. "Christianity and African Culture." In *Border Regions of Faith: An Anthology of Religion and Social Change*, edited by Kenneth Aman, 387-99. Maryknoll: Orbis, 1987.

———. "Christianity and African Culture." *Journal of Theology for Southern Africa* 20 (1977) 26-40.

———. "Christianity and East African Culture and Religion." *Dini na Mila: Revealed Religion and Traditional Custom* 3:1 (1968) 1-6.

———. "Christianity and Traditional Religions in Africa." In *Crucial Issues in Missions Tomorrow*, edited by Donald McGarvan, 144-58. Chicago: Moody, 1972.

———. "Christianity and Traditional Religions in Africa." *International Review of Mission* 59 (1970) 430-40.

———. "Christianity in Independent Africa." *International Review of Mission* 70 (1981) 76-78.

———. "Christianity Tilts to the South: A New Challenge for Christian Ministry and Theological Education." *Indian Journal of Theology* 33 (January 1984) 1-9.

———. "Church and State: A Neglected Element of Christianity in Contemporary Africa." *Africa Theological Journal* 5 (December 1972) 31-45.

———. "The Concept of God in Jewish and African Traditions." In *Christian-Jewish Relations in Ecumenical Perspective: With Special Reference to Africa*, edited by Franz von Hammerstein, 53-61. Geneva: World Council of Churches, 1978.

———. *Concepts of God in Africa*. London: SPCK, 1970.

———. "Confessing Christ in a Multi-Faith Context, with two Examples from Africa." *Metanoia* 4:3-4 (1994) 138-45.

———. "Creation in African Religion." *Christian Jewish Relations* 20:1 (1987) 31-43.

———. "Creation in African Religion." In *Worlds of Memory and Wisdom: Encounters of Jews and African Christians*, edited by Jean Halpérin and Hans Ucko, 57-68. Geneva: World Council of Churches, 2005.

———. *Crisis of Mission in Africa*. Mukono: Uganda Church, 1971.

———. *Death and the Hereafter in the Light of Christianity and African Religion: An Inaugural Lecture*. Kampala: Makerere University, 1974.

———. "Dialogue between EATWOT and Western Theologians: A Comment on the 6th EATWOT Conference in Geneva 1983." In *Fullness of Life for All: Challenges for Mission in Early 21st Century*, edited by Inus Daneel et al., 91-104. Amsterdam: Rodopi, 2003.

———. "Do You Understand What You Are Reading? The Bible in African Homes, Schools and Churches." *Missionalia* 33:2 (2005) 234-48.

———. "Dreams as a Point of Theological Dialogue between Christianity and African Religion." *Missionalia* 25:4 (1997) 511-22.

———. "The Encounter between Christianity and African Religion." *Temenos: Studies in Comparative Religion* 12 (1976) 125-35.

———. "The Encounter of Christian Faith and African Religion." *Christian Century* 97:27 (1980) 817-20.

———. "The Encounter of Christian Faith and African Religion." In *Theologians in Transition: The Christian Century*, edited by James M. Wall, 54-59. New York: Crossroad, 1981.

———. "Eschatology." In *Biblical Revelation and African Beliefs*, edited by Kwesi Dickson and Paul Ellingworth, 159-84. London: Luterworth, 1969.

———. "The Ethical Nature of God in African Religion as Expressed in African Proverbs." In *Embracing the Baobab Tree: The African Proverb in the 21st Century*, edited by Willem Saayman, 139-62. Pretoria: University of South Africa Press, 1997.

———. "Eucharistie, Koinonia und Gemeinschaft in der Afrikanischen Christenheit." *Zeitschrift für Mission* 16:3 (1990) 149-54.

———. "Faith, Hope and Love in the African Independent Church Movement: An Ecumenical Discussion with John Mbiti, E. Schweizer, and others." *Study Encounter* 0:3 (1974) 1–19.

———. "Flowers in the Garden: The Role of Women in African Religion." In *African Traditional Religions in Contemporary Society*, edited by Jacob K. Olupona, 59–72. New York: Paragon, 1991.

———. "Flowers in the Garden: The Role of Women in African Religion." *Cahiers Des Religions Africaines* 22:43–44 (1986) 69–82.

———. "'For Now we See in a Glass Darkly . . .' The Emerging Faces of Jesus Christ in Africa." In *Cristologia e Missione Oggi*, edited by G. Colzani et al., 143–64. Vatican: Urbaniana University Press, 2001.

———. "From Africa." *Risk* 1:2 (1965) 14–19.

———. "The Future of Christianity in Africa." *Cross Currents* 28:4 (1978–79) 387–94.

———. "The Future of Christianity in Africa (1970–2000)." *Communio Viatorum* 13 (1970) 19–38.

———. "God, Dreams and African Militancy." In *Religion in a Pluralistic Society: Essays Presented to Professor C. G. Baëta*, edited by J. S. Pobee, 38–47. Leiden: E. J. Brill, 1976.

———. "God, Sin, and Salvation in African Religion." In *Constructive Christian Theology in the Worldwide Church*, edited by William R. Barr, 162–67. Grand Rapids / Cambridge: Eerdmans, 1997.

———. "God, Sin, and Salvation in African Religion." *The Journal of the Interdenominational Theological Center* 16:1–2 (1988–89) 59–68.

———. "The Gospel in the African Cultural Context: Theology Reflection Out of Africa." In *Toward Theology in an Australian Context*, edited by Victor C. Hayes, 18–26. Bedford Park: Australian Association for the Study of Religion, 1979.

———. "The Growing Respectability of African Traditional Religion." *Lutheran World* 19:1 (1972) 54–58.

———. "Harmony, Happiness and Morality in African Religion." *The Drew Gateway: A Journal of Comment and Criticism* 43:2 (1973) 108–15.

———. "He who has Never Traveled Thinks that his Mother is the Best Cook in the World." In *Indigenous Theology and the Universal Church: Report of Colloquium held at the Ecumenical Institute, Bossey, Geneva, Switzerland, June 16th–22nd, 1978*, edited by John S. Mbiti, 3–5.

———. "'Hearts Cannot be Lent!' In Search of Peace and Reconciliation in African Traditional Society." *The Princeton Seminary Bulletin* 20:1 (1999) 1–12.

———. "'The Hen knows when it is Dawn, but leaves the Crowing to the Cock': African religion looks at Islam." In *Religions view Religions: Explorations in Pursuit of Understanding*, edited by Jerald D. Gort et al., 151–76. Amsterdam / New York: Rodopi, 2006.

———. "The Holy Spirit in African Independent Churches." Essay contributed to the Festschrift for Professor Dr. Günter Wagner, Baptist Theological Seminary Rüschlikon, May 1993, 1–12.

———. "The Holy Spirit in African Independent Churches." In *Festschrift Günther Wagner*, edited by Faculty of Baptist Theological Seminary Rüschliken, 101–11. New York: Peter Lang, 1994.

———. "Hope, Time and Christian Hope." *Lumen Vitae* 30:1 (1975) 93–104.

———. *Introduction to African Religion*. London: Heinemann, 1975.

———. *Introduction to African Religion*. 2nd ed. Oxford: Heinemann, 1991.
———. "Is God a Hindrance to Intellectual Development?" *Présence* 4:1 (1970) 26–32.
———. "Is Jesus Christ in African Religion?" In *Exploring Afro-Christianity*, edited by John Samuel Pobee, 21–29. Bern / New York: Peter Lang, 1992.
———. "*Kwambaza*: An African Prayer for Help." *Dialogue and Alliance* 3:4 (1989–90) 14–17.
———. "Literature and the Oral Tradition." In *African Humanism—Scandinavian Culture: A Dialogue*, edited by Torben Lundbæk, 89–95. Copenhagen: Danish International Development Agency, 1970.
———. *Love and Marriage in Africa*. London: Longman, 1973.
———. "Man in Africa." In *Africa and the West: Legacies of Empire*, edited by Isaac James Mowoe and Richard Bjornson, 55–67. New York: Greenwood, 1986.
———. "Mission Outreach in African Theology." In *Christian Theology and Strategy for Mission*, edited by Rebecca Schmutz, 172–98. Geneva: The Lutheran World Federation, 1980.
———. "The Nature of God." In *Black Experience in Religion*, edited by C. Eric Lincoln, 274–85. Garden City: Anchor, 1974.
———. "New Testament Eschatology and the Akamba of Kenya." In *African Initiatives in Religion*, edited by D. B. Barrett, 17–28. Nairobi: East African, 1971.
———. *New Testament Eschatology in an African Background*. London: Oxford University Press, 1971.
———. "New Testament Eschatology in an African Background." In *Readings in Dynamic Indigeneity*, edited by Charles H. Kraft and Tom N. Wisley, 455–64. Pasadena: William Carey Library, 1979.
———. "On the Article of John W. Kinney: A Comment." *Occasional Bulletin of Missionary Research* 3:2 (1979) 68.
———. "Peace and Reconciliation in African Religion and Christianity." *Dialogue and Alliance* 7:1 (1993) 17–32.
———. *The People of God*. Geneva: World Student Christian Federation, 1962.
———. "'A Person Who Eats Alone Dies Alone': Death as a Point of Dialogue Between African Religion and Christiainity." In *Crises of Life in African Religion and Christianity*, edited by Hance A. O. Mwakabane, 83–106. Geneva: LWF Studies, 2002.
———. *Poems of Nature and Faith*. Nairobi: East African, 1969.
———. "Prayer and Spirituality in African Religion." Bedford Park: Australian Association for the Study of Religions for the Charles Strong Trust, 1978.
———. *The Prayers of African Religion*. London: SPCK, 1975.
———. "Resources for Worship." In *The Local Church in a Global Era*, edited by M. L. Stackhouse et al., 86–96. Grand Rapids: Eerdmans, 2000.
———. "The Role of the Jewish Bible in African Independent Churches." *International Review of Mission* 93:369 (2004) 219–37.
———. "ὁ σωτηρ ἡμῶν as an African Experience." In *Christ and Spirit in the New Testament*, edited by Barnabas Lindars and Stephen S. Smalley, 397–414. Cambridge: Cambridge University Press, 1973.
———. "Some African Concepts of Christology." In *Christ and the Younger Churches: Theological Contributions from Asia, Africa, and Latin America*, edited by Georg F. Vicedom, 51–62. London: SPCK, 1972.

———. "Some Current Concerns of African Theology." In *African and Asian Contributions to Contemporary Theology: Report of a Consultation held at the Ecumenical Institute, Bossey, 8-14 June, 1976*, edited by John S. Mbiti, 12-17. Céligny: World Council of Churches Ecumenical Institute, 1977.

———. "Some Reflections on African Experience of Salvation Today." In *Living Faiths and Ultimate Goals: A Continuing Dialogue*, edited by S. J. Samartha, 108-19. Maryknoll: Orbis, 1974.

———. "The South African Theology of Liberation: Appreciation and Evaluation." In *A Vision for Man: Essays in Honour of Joshua Russell Chandran*, edited by Samuel Amirtham, 348-58. Madras: The Christian Literature Society, 1978.

———. "Theological Impotence and the Universality of the Church." *Lutheran World* 21:3 (1974) 251-60.

———. "Theologische Zusammenarbeit zwischen dem Norden und dem Süden: Realität, Traum oder Hoffnung?" In *Weisheit in Vielfalt: Afrikanisches und Westliches Denken im Dialog*, edited by Claudius Luterbacher-Maineri and Stephanie Lehr-Rosenberg, 129-42. Fribourg: Academic, 2006.

———. "Theology of the New World: Some Current Concerns of African Theology." *The Expository Times* 87 (1976) 164-68.

———. "Traditional Religions in Africa." In *Historical Atlas of the Religions of the World*, edited by Isma'il Rāgī al Fārūqī, 61-68. New York: Macmillan, 1974.

———. *The Voice of Nine Bible Trees*. Mukono-Kampala: Church of Uganda, 1972.

———. "Wandlungen des Afrikanischen Menschenbildes durch den Einfluss des Christentums." In *Das Menschenbild unserer Zeit*, edited by Bernhard Mensen, 65-74. St. Augustine: Akademie Völker und Kulturen, 1978.

———. "The Ways and Means of Communicating the Gospel." In *Christianity in Tropical Africa*, edited by C. G. Baëta, 329-50. London: Oxford University Press, 1968.

———. "What God is Saying Through the African Independent Churches to the Western Churches." *Risk* 7:3 (1971) 56-58.

———. "'When the Right Hand Washes the Left Hand and the Left Hand Washes the Right Hand, the Two will be Clean.' Some Thoughts on Justice and Christian Mission in Africa." In *Festschrift für Horst Bürkle zum 75. Geburtstag (2000)*, edited by Klaus Krämer and Ansgar Paus, 433-64. Herausgeber: Die Weitte des Mysteriums. Christliche Identität im Dialog. Freiburg / Basel / Wien: Herder, 2000.

———. "Where African Religion is Found." In *Readings in African Traditional Religion*, edited by E. M. Uka, 69-75. Bern: Peter Lang, 1991.

———, ed. *African and Asian Contributions to Contemporary Theology: Report of consultation held at the World Council of Churches, June 8-14, 1976*. Céligny: Ecumenical Institute, Bossey, 1976.

———, ed. *Christian and Jewish dialogue on Man: Report of the Jewish and Christian Study Seminar at the Ecumenical Institute Bossey, March 12-16, 1978*. Céligny: Ecumenical Institute Bossey, 1980.

———, ed. *Confessing Christ in Different Cultures*. Céligny: Ecumenical Institute, Château de Bossey, 1977.

———, ed. *Indigenous Theology and the Universal Church*. Céligny: Ecumenical Institute, Bossey, 1978.

———, series ed. *African Proverbs Series*. Five Volumes. Pretoria: University of South Africa Press, 1997.

BIBLIOGRAPHY

Unpublished Works by Mbiti

Mbiti, John S. "'Affirmations and Differences: African Religion and Christianity.' Notes prepared for the Lutheran World Federation Working Group on African Religion and Christianity, Meeting in Nairobi, August 3–7, 1995." TMs. Burgdorf, 1995.

———. "'African Culture, Traditions, and Habits.' Answers to questions raised by RETURN Committee in Burgerhaus, Bern, March 9, 1994." TMs. Bern, 1994.

———. "'African Religion.' Article for the *Encyclopedia of Bioethics*, rev. ed. Schedule A. New York by John S. Mbiti, Burgdorf, Switzerland, March 1992 and January 1993." TMs. Burgdorf, March 1992, revised January 1993.

———. "'African Theology: Its Makers and Its Contents.' Lecture given in absentia by the Revd. Professor John Mbiti, at the Course for Theological Students and Young Pastors on: 'Theologies in Dialogue,' at the Ecumenical Institute, Bossey (Geneva), July 19–29, 1988." TMs. Bossey, 1988.

———. "Afrikanisches Zeitverständnis aus Christlicher Sicht." Unpublished TMs. Luzern, January 17, 1995.

———. "'Axes Carried in the Same Bag Cannot Avoid Rattling: Reflections on the Holy Spirit and Spirits in African Religious Experience.' Lecture at the All Africa Conference of Churches, Nairobi, Kenya, August 4, 1995." TMs. Burgdorf, 1995.

———. "Bibel und Bibelübersetzung." TMs, 1–8. Burgdorf, August 19, 1985.

———. "The Bible and God's Revelation in the World." Unpublished Lecture, TMs, 1–9. WCC Ecumenical Institute, Bossey, February 6, 1984.

———. "'The Biblical Basis in Present Trends of African Theology.' Paper presented at the Consultation of African Theologians on 'The Christian Commitment in African Today: Concerns of Emerging Christian African Theologies,' University of Ghana, Legon, Ghana, December 17–24, 1977." TMs. Legon, 1977.

———. "'Challenges Facing Religious Education and Research in Africa: The Case of Dialogue Between Christianity and African Religion.' Some thoughts presented at the Theological Faculty Day, University of South Africa (UNISA)." TMs. Pretoria, September 29, 1995.

———. "Children Confer Glory on Home. Introduction to The African Series." TMs. Burgdorf, October 21, 1995.

———. "Christian Eschatology in Relation to Evangelization of Tribal Africa." PhD diss., Cambridge University, 1963.

———. "Christusbekenntnis im Kontext Afrikanischer Religion." TMs, 1–12. University of Basel, June 25, 1997.

———. "Convergence and Divergence in the Concepts of God in African Religion and Christianity." TMs, 1–12. 1988.

———. "'Ethical Concepts of God in African Proverbs.' Paper presented at the 44th Graduate School of Ecumenical Studies, Ecumenical Institute, Bossey, Switzerland, on: 'Theology For Life,' January 8, 1996." TMs. Burgdorf, 1996.

———. "'The Eyes of the Frog in the Pool Cannot Stop the Giraffe from Drinking Water: Witnessing to the Gospel in Africa.' Summary of lecture by Prof. John Mbiti at the John Knox International Reformed Centre, Geneva, June 30, 1986." TMs. Geneva, 1986.

———. "Good, but are they all Liberation Theologians?" TMs. Burgdorf, 1988.

———. "'The Gospel and African Culture: Use and Unuse of Proverbs in African Theology.' Paper presented at the Missiological Consultation on African Proverbs and Christianity, Maputo, Mozambique, March 27–31, 1995." TMs. Burgdorf, 1995.

———. "The Gospel and Culture: A Living Issue." TMs, 1–4. Burgdorf, 1981.

———. "'The Gospel and Culture: A Living Issue.' Originally written for the Reformed Press Service of the World Alliance of Reformed Churches, Geneva, September 1979." TMs. Burgdorf, 1985.

———. "Hand to Mouth: Towards the Genesis of African Theology." TMs, outline of a lecture delivered at the Graduate School of Ecumenical Studies, 1–6. Ecumenical Institute, Bossey, January 23, 1986.

———. "Interreligious Dialogue and Cooperation: Focus on Africa: Peace and Reconciliation in African Religion and Christianity." TMs, Assembly of the World's Religions. Seoul, Korea, August 24–31, 1992.

———. "Kosmologie und Menschenbild." TMs. St. Gallen, November 10, 1982.

———. "Simbabwe: Ein Persönlicher Bericht." Unpublished MS, 1–10. Burgdorf, December 3, 1981.

———. "Spirituality in African Religion: Some Observations." TMs, 1–5. Burgdorf, Switzerland, 1981.

———. "When the Right Hand Washes the Left Hand and the Left Hand Washes the Right Hand, the Two will be Clean: Some Thoughts on Justice and Christian Mission in Africa (and Madagascar)." TMs, paper presented at the Conference on Justice and Global Witness: A Biblical Foundation for Action, 1–21. Washington DC, July 8–10, 1999.

Mbiti, John S. Interview by Robert S. Heaney. Audio recording. Burgdorf, Switzerland, April 7, 2009.

Mbiti, John S. Interview by Robert S. Heaney. Audio recording. Burgdorf, Switzerland, April 8, 2009.

Mbiti, John S. Interview by Robert S. Heaney. Audio recording. Burgdorf, Switzerland, April 9, 2009.

Published Works by Mugambi

Mugambi, J. N. K. "Africa and the Old Testament." In *Interpreting the Old Testament in Africa*, edited by Mary Getui et al. Nairobi: Acton, 2001.

———. *African Christian Theology: An Introduction*. Kenya: Heinemann, 1989.

———. "African Christian Theology: A Reflection." In *Salaam: Journal of the National Association of R. E. Teachers*. Nairobi, April 1981.

———. "African Churches in Social Transformation." *Journal of International Affairs* 50:1 (1996) 194–220.

———. "African Churches in Social Transformation." In *Democracy and Development in Africa: The Role of the Churches*, edited by J. N. K. Mugambi, 1–36. Nairobi: AACC, 1997.

———. "The African Experience of God." *Africa: Thought and Practice* 1:1 (1974) 49–58.

———. *African Heritage and Contemporary Christianity*. Nairobi: Longman, 1989. (Also published as *Christianity and African Culture*. Nairobi: Acton, 2002.)

———. "The African Heritage: Change and Continuity." In *The S. M. Otieno Case: Death and Burial in Modern Kenya*, edited by J. B. Ojwang and J. N. K. Mugambi, 165–79. Nairobi: Nairobi University Press, 1989.

———. "Applied Ethics and Globalization: An African Perspective." *All African Journal of Theology* (March 2005).

———. "The Bible and Ecumenism in African Christianity." In *The Bible in African Christianity: Essays in Biblical Theology*, edited by H. W. Kinoti and J. M. Waliggo, 68–85. Nairobi: Acton, 1997.

———. "The Biblical Basis for Evangelization." In *The Biblical Basis for Evangelization: Report of the AACC Consultation*. Nairobi: AACC, November 1978.

———. *The Biblical Basis of Evangelization: Theological Reflections Based on an African Experience*. Nairobi: Oxford University Press, 1989.

———. *Carry it Home*. Nairobi: East African Literature Bureau, 1974.

———. "Challenges to African Scholars in Biblical Hermeneutics." In *Text and Context in New Testament Hermeneutics*, edited by Johannes A. Smit and J. N. K. Mugambi, 6–21. Nairobi: Acton, 2004.

———. "The Christian Ideal of Peace and Political Reality in Africa." In *From Violence to Peace: A Challenge for African Christianity*, 2nd ed., edited by Mary N. Getui and Peter Kanyandago, 70–96. Nairobi: Acton, 2003.

———. *Christian Mission and Social Transformation*. Nairobi: Acton, 2003.

———. "Christian Mission and Social Transformation After the Cold War." *Journal of Constructive Theology* 4:2 (1998) 65–86.

———. "Christian Mission in the Context of Urbanization and Industrialization in Africa." In *Mission in African Christianity: Critical Essays in Missiology*, edited by A. Nasimiyu-Wasike and D. W. Waruta, 67–88. Nairobi: Uzima, 1993.

———. *Christian Religious Education, Book 1*. Nairobi: Longman, 1986.

———. "Christian Responses in Dehumanizing Situations." In *The Churches Responding to Racism in the 1980s: Report of the AACC Consultation*. Nairobi: AACC, 1980.

———. *Christian Theology and Social Reconstruction*. Nairobi: Acton, 2003.

———. "Christianity and the African Cultural Heritage." In *African Christianity: An African Story*, edited by Ogbu Kalu, 516–42. Pretoria: Department of Church History, 2005.

———. "Christological Paradigms in African Christianity." In *Jesus in African Christianity*, edited by J. N. K. Mugambi and Laurenti Magesa, 136–61. Nairobi: Initiatives, 1989.

———. "Churches and the Reconstruction of Society and Democracy: Some Reflections from the African Heritage." In *Peacemaking and Democratization in Africa*, edited by Hizkias Assefa and George Wachira, 34–41. Nairobi: East African Education, 1996.

———. *Critiques of Christianity in African Literature, with Particular Reference to the East Africa Context*. Nairobi: East African Education, 1992.

———. "Ecumenical Initiatives in African Christianity." In *The Church in African Christianity: Innovative Essays in Ecclesiology*, edited by J. N. K. Mugambi and Laurenti Magesa, 5–28. Nairobi: Initiatives, 1990.

———. "The Ecumenical Movement and the Future of the Church in Africa." In *The Church in African Christianity: Innovative Essays in Ecclesiology*, 2nd ed., edited by, J. N. K. Mugambi and Laurenti Magesa, 5–28. Nairobi: Acton, 1998.

———. "Environment/Ecology." In *Dictionary of the Ecumenical Movement*. Grand Rapids: Eerdmans, 1991.

———. "Evangelistic and Charismatic Initiatives in Post-Colonial Africa." In *Charismatic Renewal in Africa: A Challenge for African Christianity*, edited by Mika Vähäkangas and Andrew Kyomo, 111–44. Nairobi: Acton, 2003.

———. Foreword to *Responsible Church Leadership*, D. M. Gitari. Nairobi: Acton, 2005.

———. Foreword to *Theology of Reconstruction: Exploratory Essays*, edited by Mary N. Getui and Emmanuel A. Obeng. Nairobi: Acton, 1999.

———. Foreword to *Theology of Reconstruction: Exploratory Essays*, 2nd ed., edited by M. N. Getui and E. A. Obeng. Nairobi: Acton, 2003.

———. "Foundations for an African Approach to Biblical Hermeneutics." In *Interpreting the New Testament in Africa*, edited by Mary N. Getui et al., 9–29. Nairobi: Acton, 2001.

———. "A Fresh Look at Evangelism in Africa." *International Review of Mission* 87 (1998) 342–60.

———. "A Fresh Look at Evangelism in Africa." In *The Study of Evangelism: Exploring a Missional Practice of the Church*, edited by Paul W. Chilcote and Laceye C. Warner, 352–73. Grand Rapids / Cambridge: Eerdmans, 2008.

———. *From Liberation to Reconstruction: African Christian Theology After the Cold War*. Nairobi: East African, 1995.

———. "The Future of Religion." In *A Comparative Study of Religions*, edited by J. N. K. Mugambi, 291–96. Nairobi: Nairobi University Press, 1990.

———. "The Future of the Church and the Church of the Future in Africa." In *The Church in Africa: Towards a Theology of Reconstruction*, edited by José B. Chipenda et al., 29–50. Nairobi: All Africa Conference of Churches, 1991.

———. "God, Humanity and Nature in Ecumenical Discussion." In *Church and Society Report, Potsdam, July 1986*. Geneva: WCC, 1986.

———. *God, Humanity and Nature in Relation to Justice and Peace*. Geneva: WCC, 1987.

———. "A History of the Church in East Africa with Special Reference to Kenya." In *Towards a History of the Church in the Third World: Papers and Report of a Consultation on The Issue of Periodisation Convened by the Working Commission on Church History of the Ecumenical Association of Third World Theology (July 17–21, 1983, Geneva)*, edited by Lukas Visher, 40–52. Bern: Evangelische Arbeitssteile Okumene Schweiz, 1985.

———. Introduction to *Christian Presence Amid African Religion*, edited by J. V. Taylor. Nairobi: Acton, 2001.

———. Introduction to *Development and the Church in Angola: Chipenda the Trailblazer*, edited by Lawrence Henderson. Nairobi: Acton, 2000.

———. Introduction to *Philosophy of Religion: A Textbook*. Nairobi: University of Nairobi College of Education, 1988.

———. "Justice, Peace and Integrity of Creation in the Ecumenical Agenda." In *Church and Society Report, Potsdam, July 1986*. Geneva: WCC, 1986.

———. "Liberation and Theology." *WSCF Dossier* 5 (1974) 33–49.

———. "Missiological Research in the Context of Globalization." *Swedish Missiological Themes* 86:4 (1998) 541–79.

———. "Muhammad as the Founder of Islam." In *A Comparative Study of Religions*, edited by J. N. K. Mugambi, 213–18. Nairobi: Nairobi University Press, 1990.

———. "New Frontiers of Christian Mission in Kenya." In *Together in Hope: The Official Report of the Mission Conference 1989*, edited by Samuel Kobia and Godffrey P. Ngumi, 95–101. Nairobi: National Council of Churches of Kenya, 1991.

———. "Pastoral Care for Youth and Students." In *Pastoral Care in African Christianity*, edited by Douglas W. Waruta and Hannah W. Kinoti, 148–64. Nairobi: Acton, 1994.

———. "The Place of African Religion and Culture in Kenya's Education." *Quarterly Review of Religious Studies* 1:4 (1987).

———. "The Present State of Religion in the Contemporary World." In *A Comparative Study of Religions*, edited by J. N. K. Mugambi, 285–90. Nairobi: Nairobi University Press, 1990.

———. "Principles and Methods of Teaching the African Heritage." *Quarterly Review of Religious Studies* 1:2 (1986).

———. "Problems and Promises of the Church in Africa." In *The Church and the Future in Africa*, edited by J. N. K. Mugambi, 41–64. Nairobi: AACC, 1997.

———. "Problems of Meaning in Discourse with Reference to Religion." PhD diss., University of Nairobi, 1983.

———. "The Problems of Teaching Ethics in African Christianity." In *Moral and Ethical Issues in African Christianity*, edited by J. N. K. Mugambi and Anne Nasimiyu-Wasike, 11–28. Nairobi: Acton, 2003.

———. "Procedure of C. R. E. Curriculum Development in Kenya." *Quarterly Review of Religious Studies* 1:1 (1985).

———. *Religion and Social Construction of Reality: Inaugural Lecture delivered before the University of Nairobi on September 26, 1996*. Nairobi: Nairobi University Press, 1996.

———. "Religion and Social Reconstruction in Post-Colonial Africa." In *Church-State Relations: A Challenge for African Christianity*, edited by J. N. K. Mugambi and Frank Küshner-Pelkmann, 13–34. Nairobi: Acton, 2004.

———. "Religion in the Social Transformation of Africa." In *Democracy and Reconciliation: A Challenge for African Christianity*, edited by Laurenti Magesa and Zablon Nthamburi, 73–97. Nairobi: Acton, 1999.

———. "Religions in East Africa in the Context of Globalization." In *Religions in Eastern Africa in the Context of Globalization*, edited by J. N. K. Mugambi and Mary N. Getui, 3–29. Nairobi: Acton, 2004.

———. "The Religious Heritage of Arabia Before and During Muhammad's Time." In *A Comparative Study of Religions*, edited by J. N. K. Mugambi, 207–12. Nairobi: Nairobi University Press, 1990.

———. "Report of the Consultation on African and Black Theology, Greenhill, Accra, Ghana, Dec. 28–31, 1974." *The Journal of Religious Thought* 33:2 (1975).

———. "Research in the African Religious Heritage." *Orientation: Journal of Religious Studies* 1:1 (1975).

———. "Responsible Leadership in Education and Development." In *Responsible Leadership: Global and Contextual Ethical Perspectives*, edited by Christoph Stückelberger and J. N. K. Mugambi, 79–96. Nairobi: Action / Geneva: WCC, 2005.

———. "Rites of Passage and Human Sexuality in Tropical Africa Today." In *Marriage and Family in African Christianity*, edited by Andrew A. Kyomo and Sahaya G. Slevan, 228–45. Nairobi: Acton, 2007.

———. "The Role of Religion in Public Life." *Bulletin for Contextual Theology in Africa* 6:1 (1999).

———. "The Social Context of Christianity in Colonial and Post-Colonial Africa." *Quarterly Review of Religious Studies* 3:1–2 (1988).

BIBLIOGRAPHY

———. "Social Reconstruction of Africa: The Role of Churches." In *The Church and Reconstruction of Africa: Theological Considerations*, edited by J. N. K. Mugambi, 1–25. Nairobi: AACC, 1997.

———. "Some Lessons from a Century of Ecumenism in Africa." In *Visions of Authenticity: The Assemblies of the AACC 1963–1992*, edited by Efiong Utuk. Nairobi: AACC, 1997.

———. "Theological Method in African Christianity." In *Theological Method and Aspects of Worship in African Christianity*, edited by Mary N. Getui, 5–40. Nairobi: Acton, 1998.

———. "Theology of Reconstruction." In *African Theology on the Way*, edited by Diane Stinton, 139–49. London: SPCK, 2010.

———. "Towards Ecumenical Consensus on Baptism, Eucharist and Ministry." In *Christian Mission and Social Transformation*, J. N. K. Mugambi, 107–17. Nairobi: Initiatives, 1989.

———. "Traditional Religion of the Embu People." *Dini na Mila* 5:1 (1971) 1–58.

———. "Vision of the African Church in Mission." *Missionalia* 24:2 (1996) 233–48.

———, ed. *Christian Mission and Social Transformation*. Nairobi: National Council of Churches, 1989.

———, ed. *Christian Mission and Social Transformation: A Kenyan Perspective*. Nairobi: NCCK, 1989.

———, ed. *The Church in African Christianity*. Nairobi: Initiatives, 1990.

———, ed. *A Comparative Study of Religions*. Nairobi: Nairobi University Press, 1990.

Mugambi, J. N. K., and Anne Nasimiyu-Wasike, eds. *Moral and Ethical Issues in African Christianity*. 3rd ed. Nairobi: Acton, 2003.

Mugambi, J. N. K., and Frank Küschner-Pelkmann. *Church-State Relations: A Challenge for African Christianity*. Nairobi: Acton, 2004.

Mugambi, J. N. K., and J. B. Ojwang, eds. *The S. M. Otieno Case: Death and Burial in Modern Kenya*. Nairobi: Nairobi University Press, 1989.

Mugambi, J. N. K., and Johannes A. Smit, eds. *Text and Context in New Testament Hermeneutics*. Nairobi: Acton, 2004.

Mugambi, J. N. K., et al. *Ecumenical Initiatives in Eastern Africa: Final Report of the Joint Research Project of the All Africa Conference of Churches (AACC) and the Association of Member Episcopal Conferences of Eastern Africa (AMECEA), 1976–1981*. Nairobi: AACC / AMECEA, 1982.

Mugambi, J. N. K., and Kofi Appiah-Kubi. *Africa and Evangelization Today: Report of a Consultation on Indigenous African Christian Churches*. Nairobi: AACC, 1975.

Mugambi, J. N. K., and Laurenti Magesa, eds. *Jesus in African Christianity: Experimentation and Diversity in African Christianity*. Nairobi: Initiatives, 1989.

Mugambi, J. N. K., and Michael R. Guy. *Contextual Theology Across Cultures*. Nairobi: Acton, 2009.

Mugambi, J. N. K., and Mika Vähäkangas, eds. *Christian Theology and Environmental Responsibility*. Nairobi: Acton, 2001.

Mugambi, J. N. K., and Nicodemus Kirima. *The African Religious Heritage: A Textbook based on Syllabus 228 of the Kenya Certificate of Education*. Rev. ed. Nairobi: Oxford University Press, 1982.

BIBLIOGRAPHY

Unpublished Works by Mugambi

Mugambi, J. N. K. E-mail correspondence to Robert Heaney: October 17, 2007; March 1, 2008; September 23, 2008; February 11, 22, and 23, 2009; December 31, 2009; April 7, 2010; March 28, 2011; April 26 and 27, 2011.
———. "Problems of Meaning in Discourse with Reference to Religion." PhD diss., University of Nairobi, 1983.
———. "Some Perspectives of Christianity in the Context of the Modern Missionary Enterprise in East Africa with Special Reference to Kenya." MA diss., University of Nairobi, 1977.

Other Works

Abble, Albert, et al. *Des Prêtres Noirs s'Interrogent*. Paris: Les Éditions du Cerf, 1956.
Abraham, Susan. *Identity, Ethics, and Nonviolence in Postcolonial Theory: A Rahnerian Theological Assessment*. New York: Palgrave Macmillan, 2007.
Adar, Korwa G. "Assessing Democratisation Trends in Kenya: A Post-Mortem of the Moi Regime." *Commonwealth and Comparative Politics* 38:3 (2000) 103–30.
Adogame, Afe. "The Berlin-Congo Conference 1884: The Partition of Africa and Implications for Christian Mission Today." *Journal of Religion in Africa* 34:1–2 (2004) 186–90.
Agorsah, E. Kofi. *Religion, Ritual and African Tradition: African Foundations*. Bloomington: Author House, 2010.
Aguilar, Mario I. "The Communion, and Ancestry in African Biblical Interpretation: A Contextual Note on 1 Maccabees 2:49–70." *Biblical Theology Bulletin* 32:3 (August 2002) 129–44.
———. "Postcolonial African Theology in Kabasele Lumbala." *Theological Studies* 63 (2002) 302–23.
Ahluwalia, Pal D. *Politics and Post-Colonial Theory: African Reflections*. London: Routledge, 2000.
———. *Post-Colonialism and the Politics of Kenya*. New York: Nova Science, 1996.
Ahmad, Aijaz. *In Theory: Classes, Nations, Literatures*. London: Verso, 1992.
Akper, Godwin. "The Person of Jesus Christ in Contemporary African Christological Discourse." *Religion and Theology* 14:3–4 (2007) 224–43.
Althaus-Reid, Marcella. *Indecent Theology: Theological Perversions in Sex, Gender and Politics*. London / New York: Routledge, 2000.
Altick, Richard D. *Victorian People and Ideas*. London: Norton, 1973.
Alves, Rubem. *A Theology of Human Hope*. Washington DC: Corpus, 1969.
Ambler, Charles H. *Kenyan Communities in the Age of Imperialism: The Central Region in the Late Nineteenth Century*. New Haven / London: Yale University Press, 1988.
Amuta, Chidi. *The Theory of African Literature: Implications for Practical Criticism*. London: Zed, 1989.
Anderson, Benedict. *Imagined Communities: Reflections on the Origin and Spread of Nationalism*, rev. ed. London: Verso, 1991.
Anderson, David. *Histories of the Hanged: Britain's Dirty War in Kenya and the End of Empire*. London: Weidenfeld & Nicholson, 2005.

BIBLIOGRAPHY

Anderson, David M., and Douglas H. Johnson, eds. *Revealing Prophets: Prophecy in Eastern African History*. London: Currey, 1995.

Anderson, David M., and Richard Rathbone, eds. *Africa's Urban Past*. Oxford: James Currey, 2000.

Anderson, Dick. *We Felt like Grasshoppers: The Story of the Africa Inland Mission*. Nottingham: Crossway, 1994.

Anderson, John E. *The Struggle for the School*. London: Longman, 1970.

Anderson, Ross. *The Forgotten Front: The East Africa Campaign 1914-1918*. Stroud: Tempus, 2004.

Anderson, William B. *The Church in East Africa, 1840-1974*. Dodoma: Central Tanganyika, 1977.

Aniagolu, Chichi. "The First African Womanist Workshop." *Agenda* 37 (1998) 96-100.

Appiah, Kwame Anthony. *Cosmopolitanism: Ethics in a World of Strangers*. New York: W. W. Norton, 2006.

———. *The Ethics of Identity*. Princeton: Princeton University Press, 2005.

———. *In My Father's House: Africa in the Philosophy of Culture*. London: Methuen, 1992.

———. "Is the *Post-* in Postmodernism the *Post-* in Postcolonial?" *Critical Inquiry* 17 (Winter 1991) 336-57.

———. "Pan-Africanism." In *Africana: The Encyclopedia of the African and African American Experience*, edited by Kwame Anthony Appiah and Henry Louis Gates, 1484-86. New York: Basic Civitas, 1999.

Appiah-Kubi, Kofi, and Sergio Torres. *African Theology en Route: Papers from the Pan African Conference of Third World Theologians, December 17-23, 1977, Accra, Ghana*. Maryknoll: Orbis, 1979.

Arden, Donald S. "Out of Africa Something New." *Anglican Theological Review* 6 (1976) 17-36.

Aseka, Eric Masinde. "The Post-Colonial State and the Colonial Legacy." In *Kenya: The Making of a Nation*, edited by Bethwell A. Ogot and W. R. Ochieng', 92-105. Maseno: IRPS, 2000.

Ashcroft, Bill. *Post-Colonial Transformation*. London / New York: Routledge, 2001.

Ashcroft, Bill, et al., eds. *The Empire Writes Back: Theory and Practice in Post-colonial Literatures*. 2nd ed. London / New York: Routledge, 2002.

———. *The Post-Colonial Studies Reader*. London / New York: Routledge, 1995.

Atieno-Odhiambo, E. S. "Mungo's Prophesy." In *Kenya: The Making of a Nation*, edited by Bethwell A. Ogot and W. R. Ochieng', 5-15. Maseno: IRPS, 2000.

———. "A Portrait of the Missionaries in Kenya Before 1939." *Kenya Historical Review* 1:1 (1973) 1-14.

———. "Some Reflections on African Initiative in Early Colonial Kenya." *East African Journal* 8:6 (1971) 30-36.

Aulén, Gustaf. *Christus Victor: An Historical Study of the Three Main Types of the Idea of the Atonement*. London: SPCK, [1931] 2010.

Austen, Ralph A., and Woodruff D. Smith. "Images of Africa and British Slave-Trade Abolition: The Transition to an Imperialist Ideology, 1787-1807." *African Historical Studies* 2:1 (1969) 69-83.

Avis, Paul. *The Identity of Anglicanism: Essentials of Anglican Ecclesiology*. London: T & T Clark, 2008.

Ayres, Lewis. *Nicea and its Legacy: An Approach to Fourth-Century Trinitarian Theology*. Oxford: Oxford University Press, 2004.

BIBLIOGRAPHY

Baëta, Christian G. "Conflict in Mission: Historical and Separatist Churches." In *The Theology of the Christian Mission*, edited by Gerald H. Anderson, 290-99. London: SCM, 1961.

Baëta, Christian G., ed. *Christianity in Tropical Africa*. London: Oxford University Press, 1968.

Bahemuka, Judith M. "The Hidden Christ in African Traditional Religion." In *Jesus in African Christianity: Experimentation and Diversity in African Christology*, edited by J. N. K. Mugambi and Laurenti Magesa, 1-16. Nairobi: Initiatives, 1989.

Baillie, John. *What is Christian Civilisation?* London: Oxford University Press, 1945.

Bakhtin, M. M. *The Dialogic Imagination: Four Essays*. Austin: University of Texas Press, 1981.

Barclay, William. *Christian Ethics for Today*. San Francisco: Harper & Row, 1984.

Barker, John. "Where the Missionary Frontier Ran Ahead of Empire." In *Missions and Empire*, edited by Norman Etherington, 86-106. Oxford: Oxford University Press, 2005.

Barr, James. *Biblical Words for Time*. London: SCM, 1962.

Barrett, David B. *Schism and Renewal in Africa: An Analysis of Six Thousand Contemporary Religious Movements*. Nairobi: Oxford University Press, 1968.

Battiste, Marie. *Reclaiming Indigenous Voice and Vision*. Vancouver: UBC Press, 2000.

Bauckham, Richard. "Emerging Issues in Eschatology in the Twenty-First Century." In *The Oxford Handbook of Eschatology*, edited by Jerry L. Walls, 671-90. Oxford: Oxford University Press, 2008.

———. *Moltmann: Messianic Theology in the Making*. Basingstoke: Marshall Pickering, 1987.

———. "Moltmann's Theology of Hope Revisited." *Scottish Journal of Theology* 42:2 (1989) 199-214.

Bayer, Oswald. "Tillich as Systematic Theologian." In *The Cambridge Companion to Paul Tillich*, edited by Russell Re Manning, 18-36. Cambridge / New York: Cambridge University Press, 2009.

Bediako, Kwame. "African Theology." In *The Modern Theologians: An Introduction to Christian Theology in the Twentieth Century*, 2nd ed., edited by David F. Ford, 426-44. Oxford: Blackwell, 1997.

———. "Biblical Christologies in the Context of African Traditional Religions." In *Sharing Jesus in the Two Thirds World: Evangelical Christologies from the Contexts of Poverty, Powerlessness and Religious Pluralism: The Papers of the First Conference of Evangelical Mission Theologians from the Two Thirds World, Bangkok, Thailand, March 22-25, 1982*, edited by Vinay Samuel and Chris Sugden, 115-75. Bangalore: Partnership in Mission-Asia; Grand Rapids: Eerdmans, 1984.

———. *Christianity in Africa: The Renewal of a Non-Western Religion*. Maryknoll: Orbis, 1995.

———. *Jesus in Africa: The Christian Gospel in African History and Experience*. Oxford: Regnum, 2000.

———. "Jesus in African Culture." *Evangelical Review of Theology* 17:1 (1993) 54-64.

———. "John Mbiti's Contribution to African Theology." In *Religious Plurality in Africa: Essays in Honour of John S. Mbiti*, edited by Jacob K. Olupona and Sulayman S. Nyang, 367-90. Berlin / New York: Mouton de Gruyter, 1993.

———. "The Roots of African Theology." *International Bulletin of Missionary Research* 13:2 (1989) 58-65.

BIBLIOGRAPHY

———. *Theology and Identity: The Impact of Culture upon Christian Thought in the Second Century and in Modern Africa*. Oxford: Regnum, 1992.

———. "Understanding African Theology in the Twentieth Century." *Bulletin for Contextual Theology* 3:2 (1996) 1–11.

Beidelman, T. O. "Kaguru Time Reckoning: An Aspect of the Cosmology of an East African People." *Southwestern Journal of Anthropology* 19 (1963) 9–20.

Bennett, Norman R. "The Church Missionary Society at Mombasa, 1874–1894." *Boston University Papers on African History* 1 (1964) 159–94.

———, ed. *Leadership in Eastern Africa*. Boston: Boston University Press, 1968.

Bennett, Zoë. "'Action is the Life of All': The Praxis-based Epistemology of Liberation Theology." In *The Cambridge Companion to Liberation Theology*, 2nd ed., edited by Christopher Rowland, 39–54. Cambridge: Cambridge University Press, 2007.

Benson, Eugene, and L. W. Conolly. *Encyclopedia of Post-Colonial Literatures in English*. London: Routledge, 1994.

Benson, G. P. "Ideological Politics versus Biblical Hermeneutics: Kenya's Protestant Churches and the Nyayo State." In *Religion and Politics in East Africa*, edited by Holger Bernt Hansen and Michael Twaddle, 177–99. London: Currey, 1995.

Berman, Bruce. *Control and Crisis in Colonial Kenya: The Dialectic of Domination*. London: Currey, 1990.

Berman, Bruce J., et al. "Patrons, Clients, and Constitutions: Ethnic Politics and Political Reform in Kenya." *Canadian Journal of African Studies/La Revue Canadienne des Études Africaines* 43:3 (2009) 462–506.

Bernel, Martin. *Black Athena: The Afroasiatic Roots of Classical Civilization*. Vol. 1, *The Fabrication of Ancient Greece 1785–1985*. London: Free Association, 1987.

Bery, Ashok, and Patricia Murray, eds. *Comparing Postcolonial Literatures*. London: Macmillan, 2000.

Beti, Mongo. *The Poor Christ of Bomba*. Translated by Gerald Moore. London: Heinemann, 1971.

Beyaraza, Ernest K. *The African Concept of Time: A Comparative Study of Various Theories*. Vol. 2. Kampala: Makerere University Press, 2004.

Bhabha, Homi K. *The Location of Culture*. London / New York: Routledge, 1994.

———. "Of Mimicry and Man: The Ambivalence of Colonial Discourse." *October* 28 (Spring 1984) 125–33.

———. "The Third Space." In *Identity: Community, Culture, Difference*, edited by Jonathan Rutherford, 207–21. London: Lawrence & Wishart, 1990.

Biko, Steve. "Black Consciousness and the Quest for a True Humanity." In *Black Theology: The South African Voice*, edited by Basil Moore, 36–47. London: C. Hurst, [1972] 1973.

Birch, Charles. "Nature, Humanity and God in Ecological Perspective." In *Faith and Science in an Unjust World*. Vol. 1. Geneva: World Council of Churches, 1980.

Blyden, Edward Wilmot. *Christianity, Islam and the Negro Race*. London: W. B. Whittingham, 1887.

Boahen, A. Adu. "Africa and the Colonial Challenge." In *Africa under Colonial Domination 1880–1935*, edited by A. Adu Boahen, 1–18. London: Heinemann; Berkeley: University of California Press, 1985.

———. *African Perspectives on Colonialism*. Baltimore: Johns Hopkins University Press, 1987.

BIBLIOGRAPHY

Boesak, Allan A. *Farewell to Innocence: A Social-Ethical Study of Black Theology and Black Power.* Johannesburg: Ravan, 1976.

Boesak, Allan, and Alan Brews. "The Black Struggle for Liberation: A Reluctant Road to Liberation." In *Theology and Violence: The South African Debate*, edited by Charles Villa-Vicencio, 51-68. Grand Rapids: Eerdmans, 1988.

Boff, Leonardo, and Clodovis Boff. *Salvation and Liberation.* Maryknoll: Orbis, 1984.

Bohannan, Paul. "Concepts of Time among the Tiv of Nigeria." In *Myth and Cosmos: Readings in Mythology and Symbolism,* edited by John Middleton, 315-30. Garden City: Natural History, 1967.

Bolt, Christine. *Victorian Attitudes to Race.* London: Routledge, 1971.

Bonganjalo, Goba. "Corporate Personality: Ancient Israel and Africa." In *Black Theology: The South African Voice*, edited by Basil Moore, 65-73. London: C. Hurst, [1972] 1973.

Bonino, J. M. "Oikoumene and Anti-oikoumene." In *Whither Ecumenism? A Dialogue in the Transit Lounge of the Ecumenical Movement,* edited by Thomas Wieser, 26-31. Geneva: WCC, 1986.

Booth, Newell S. "Time and African Beliefs Revisited." In *Religious Plurality in Africa: Essays in Honour of John S. Mbiti,* edited by Jacob K. Olupona and Sulayman S. Nyang, 83-94. Berlin / New York: Mouton de Gruyter, 1993.

———. "Time and Change in African Traditional Thought." *Journal of Religion in Africa* 7:2 (1975) 81-91.

———. "Tradition and Community in African Religion." *Journal of Religion in Africa* 9:2 (1978) 81-94.

Bosch, David J. *Transforming Mission: Paradigm Shifts in Theology of Mission.* Maryknoll: Orbis, 2004.

Bouverie, Frank. "Christians Against the Mau Mau." *Church Quarterly Review* 156 (1955) 295-300.

Brown, Leslie. "Anglican Episcopacy in Africa." In *Bishops, But What Kind?* edited by Peter Moore, 135-48. London: SPCK, 1982.

Brydon, Diana, ed. *Postcolonialism: Critical Concepts in Literary and Cultural Studies.* London / New York: Routledge, 2000.

Bujo, Benezet. *African Christian Morality at the Age of Inculturation.* Nairobi: St. Paul, 1990.

———. *African Theology in its Social Context.* Nairobi: Paulines, 1999.

Buthelezi, Manas. "Toward Indigenous Theology in South Africa." In *The Emergent Gospel: Theology from the Developing World: Papers from the Ecumenical Dialogue of Third World Theologians, Dar es Salaam, August 5-12, 1976,* edited by Sergio Torres and Virginia Fabella, 56-75. London: Geoffrey Chapman, 1987.

Butler, Jon. *Awash in a Sea of Faith: Christianizing the American People.* Cambridge / London: Harvard University Press, 1990.

Byaruhanga, Christopher. *Bishop Alfred Tucker: And the Establishment of the African Anglican Church.* Nairobi: WordAlive, 2008.

———. "The Legacy of Bishop Frank Weston of Zanzibar 1871-1924 in the Global South Anglicanism." *Exchange* 35:3 (2006) 255-69.

Byaruhanga-Akiiki, A. B. T. "Africa and Christianity: Domestication of Christian Values in the African Church." In *Religious Plurality in Africa: Essays in Honour of John S. Mbiti,* edited by Jacob K. Olupona and Sulayman S. Nyang, 179-95. Berlin / New York: Mouton de Gruyter, 1993.

———. "The Luo Philosophy of Time." *African Ecclesial Review* 24:3 (1982) 164–70.

———. "The Philosophy and Theology of Time in Africa: The Bantu Case." *African Ecclesial Review* 22:6 (1980) 357–69.

Byron, William. *The Causes of World Hunger*. New York: Paulist, 1983.

Cabral, Amilcar. *Revolution in Guinea: An African People's Struggle*. London: Stage 1, 1969.

Cameron, Bruce J. R. "The Historical Problem in Paul Tillich's Christology." *Scottish Journal of Theology* 18:3 (1965) 257–72.

Césaire, Aimé. *Discourse on Colonialism*. Translated by Joan Pinkham. New York: Monthly Review, [1972] 2000. Kindle Edition.

Chakrabarty, Dipesh. "Postcoloniality and the Artifice of History." *Representations* 37 (Winter 1992) 1–26.

Chatterjee, Partha. *The Nation and its Fragments: Colonial and Postcolonial Histories*. Princeton: Princeton University Press, 1993.

Chesworth, John A. "Anglican Liturgical Reform in Kenya." *Encounter* 2 (2002) 9–18.

Chopp, Rebecca S. "Latin American Liberation Theology." In *The Modern Theologians: An Introduction to Christian Theology in the Twentieth Century*, 2nd ed., edited by David F. Ford, 409–25. Oxford: Blackwell, 1997.

Clark, Adam. "Against Invisibility: Negritude and the Awakening of the African Voice in Theology." *Studies in World Christianity* 19:1 (2013) 71–92.

Clark, J. C. D. "The Failure of a 'Grand Narrative.'" *The Historical Journal* 55:1 (2012) 161–94.

Clayton, John Powell. "Is Jesus Necessary for Christology? An Antinomy in Tillich's Theological Method." In *Christ, Faith and History*, edited by S. W. Sykes and J. P. Clayton, 147–63. Cambridge: Cambridge University Press, 1972.

Coakley, Sarah. *Powers and Submissions: Spirituality, Philosophy and Gender*. Oxford: Blackwell, 2002.

Cobain, Ian. "Mau Mau Veterans Launch Second Round of Legal Action." *The Guardian*. http://www.theguardian.com/world/2012/jul/16/mau-mau-veterans-secret-documents.

Cobain, Ian, and Jessica Hatcher. "Kenyan Mau Mau Victims in Talks with UK Government over Legal Settlement." *The Guardian*. http://www.theguardian.com/world/2013/may/05/mau-mau-victims-kenya-settlement.

Cobb, John B. Jr., "Beyond Pluralism." In *Christian Uniqueness Reconsidered*, edited by G. D. D'Costa, 84. Maryknoll: Orbis, 1990.

Collingwood, R. G. *The Idea of History*. London: Oxford University Press, 1961.

Comaroff, Jean, and John L. Comaroff. *Of Revelation and Revolution: Christianity, Colonialism, and Consciousness in South Africa*. Vol. 1. Chicago / London: University of Chicago Press, 1991.

———. *Of Revelation and Revolution: Christianity, Colonialism, and Consciousness in South Africa*. Vol. 2. Chicago / London: University of Chicago Press, 1997.

Comaroff, John L. "Images of Empire, Contests of Conscience: Models of Colonial Domination in South Africa." In *Tensions of Empire: Colonial Cultures in a Bourgeois World*, edited by Frederick Cooper and Ann Laura Stoler, 163–97. Berkeley: University of California Press, 1997.

Cone, James H. *Black Theology and Black Power*. New York: Seabury, 1969.

———. *A Black Theology of Liberation*. Philadelphia: Lippincott, 1970.

———. *For My People: Black Theology and the Black Church*. Maryknoll: Orbis, 1984.

BIBLIOGRAPHY

Cooper, Frederick. *Africa since 1940: The Past of the Present.* Cambridge: Cambridge University Press, 2002.

———. *Colonialism in Question: Theory, Knowledge, History.* Berkeley: University of California Press, 2005.

———. "Conflict and Connection: Rethinking Colonial African History." *American Historical Review* 99:5 (1994) 1516–45.

———. "Empire Multiplied." *Comparative Studies in Society and History* 46 (2004) 247–72.

———. *On the African Waterfront: Urban Disorder and the Transformation of Work in Colonial Mombasa.* New Haven: Yale University Press, 1987.

Cox, James L. *Rational Ancestors: Scientific Rationality and African Indigenous Religions.* Cardiff: Cardiff Academic, 1988.

Craffert, Pieter F. *The Life of a Galilean Shaman: Jesus of Nazareth in Anthropological-Historical Perspective.* Cambridge: James Clark, 2008.

Crummell, Alexander. *The Future of Africa: Addresses, Sermons, Etc., Etc., Delivered in the Republic of Liberia.* New York: Charles Scribner, 1862.

Curry, James A., and Richard B. Riley. "Notes on Church-State Affairs." *Journal of Church and State* 25:1 (1983) 181–202.

———. "Notes on Church-State Affairs." *Journal of Church and State* 26 (1984) 147–50.

Davidson, A. B. "African Resistance and Rebellion against the Imposition of Colonial Rule." In *Emerging Themes of African History*, edited by T. O. Ranger, 177–88. Nairobi: East African, 1968.

Davidson, Basil. *The Black Man's Burden: Africa and the Curse of the Nation-State.* New York: Times, 1992.

Dedji, Valentin. *Reconstruction and Renewal in African Christian Theology.* Nairobi: Acton, 2004.

Devarajan, Shantayanan, et al., eds. *Aid and Reform in Africa.* Washington: The World Bank, 2001.

Diagne, Souleymane Bachir. "On Prospective Development and a Political Culture of Time." *African Development* 29:1 (2004) 62.

Dickson, Kwesi A. "The African Theological Task." In *The Emergent Gospel: Theology from the Developing World: Papers from the Ecumenical Dialogue of Third World Theologians, Dar es Salaam, August 5–12, 1976*, edited by Sergio Torres and Virginia Fabella, 46–49. London: Geoffrey Chapman, 1978.

———. *Theology in Africa.* London: Darton, Longman & Todd, 1984.

Dickson, Kwesi, and Paul Ellingworth, eds. *Biblical Revelation and African Beliefs.* Maryknoll: Orbis, 1969.

Douglas, Ian T., and Kwok Pui-lan, eds. *Beyond Colonial Anglicanism.* New York: Church, 2001.

Dube, Musa W. *Postcolonial Feminist Interpretation of the Bible.* St. Louis: Chalice, 2000.

———. "Reading for Decolonization: John 4:1–42." *Semeia* 75:1 (1996) 37–59.

Duggan, Joseph. "'I Found Space for My Voice.'" *Journal of Anglican Studies* 7:1 (2009) 5–11.

Eagleton, Terry. "Postcolonialism and 'postcolonialism.'" *Interventions: International Journal of Postcolonial Studies* 1:1 (1998) 24–26.

Eagleton, Terry, et al. *Nationalism, Colonialism, and Literature.* London: University of Minnesota Press, 1990.

Edelman, Marc, and Angelique Haugerud, eds. *The Anthropology of Development and Globalization: From Classical Political Economy to Contemporary*. Malden: Blackwell, 2005.

Edgerton, Robert B. *Mau Mau: An African Crucible*. London: I. B. Tauris., 1990.

Edwards, David. "Mad Mullahs and Englishmen: Discourse in the Colonial Encounter." *Comparative Studies in Society and History* 31 (1989) 649–70.

Ela, Jean-Marc. "The Memory of the African People and the Cross of Christ." In *The Scandal of a Crucified World: Perspectives on the Cross and Suffering*, edited by Yacob Tesfai, 17–35. Maryknoll: Orbis, 1994.

———. *My Faith as an African*. Maryknoll: Orbis, 1988.

Elbourne, Elizabeth. "The Foundation of the Church Missionary Society: The Anglican Missionary Impulse." In *The Church of England c.1689–c.1833: From Toleration to Tractarianism*, edited by John Walsh et al., 247–64. Cambridge: Cambridge University Press, 1993.

Eliade, Mircea. *Myth of the Eternal Return*. 2nd ed. Princeton: Princeton University Press, [1965] 1971.

———. *Patterns in Comparative Religion*. London: Sheed & Ward, [1958] 1979.

Eliot, T. S. *The Idea of a Christian Society*. London: Faber, 1939.

Elkins, Caroline. *Britain's Gulag*. London: Pimlico, 2005.

Ellingworth, Paul. "Renewal and Advance: An African Reaction." *Frontier* 4:7 (Winter 1964) 284–86.

Erikson, Erik H. *Gandhi's Truth*. New York: W. W. Norton, 1969.

Escobar, Arturo. *Encountering Development: The Making and Unmaking of the Third World*. Princeton / Oxford: Princeton University Press, 1996.

Etherington, Norman. "Education and Medicine." In *Missions and Empire*, edited by Norman Etherington, 261–84. Oxford: Oxford University Press, 2005.

———. "Missionaries and the Intellectual History of Africa: A Historical Survey." *Itinerario* 7:2 (1983) 116–43.

———, ed. *Missions and Empire*. Oxford: Oxford University Press, 2005.

Evans-Pritchard, E. E. *The Nuer: A Description of the Modes of Livelihood and Political Institutions of a Nilotic People*. Oxford: Clarendon, 1940.

———. *Theories of Primitive Religion*. Oxford: Clarendon, [1965] 1982.

Ewechue, Ralph, ed. *Makers of Modern Africa*. 2nd ed. London: Africa, 1991.

Eze, Emmanuel Chukwudi, ed. *Postcolonial African Philosophy*. Oxford: Blackwell, 1997.

Ezigbo, Victor I., and Reggie L. Williams. "Converting a Colonialist Christ: Toward an African Postcolonial Christology." In *Evangelical Postcolonial Conversations: Great Awakenings in Theology and Praxis*, edited by Kathryn Smith et al., 88–101. Downers Grove: InterVarsity, 2014.

Fanon, Frantz. *The Wretched of the Earth*. Translated by Constance Farrington. New York: Grove, [1963] 1965.

Farisani, Elelwani. "The Use of Ezra-Nehemiah in a Quest for an African Theology of Reconstruction." *Journal of Theology for Southern Africa* 116 (2003) 27–50.

Fasholé-Luke, Edward W. "The Quest for an African Christian Theology." *The Ecumenical Review* 27:3 (1975) 259–69.

———. "The Quest for an African Christian Theology." In *Mission as Liberation: Third World Theologies*, edited by M. L. Daneel and J. N. J. Kritzinger, 1–11. Pretoria: Unisa, 1989.

Fasholé-Luke, Edward W., et al., eds. *Christianity in Independent Africa*. London: Rex Collings, 1978.
Fiddes, Paul. *Participating in God: A Pastoral Doctrine of the Trinity*. London: Darton, Longman & Todd, 2000.
Forrester, Duncan B. *Beliefs, Values and Policies*. Oxford: Clarendon, 1989.
———. "The Scope of Public Theology." *Studies in Christian Ethics* 17:5 (2004) 5–19.
Forsyth, Andrew C. "The Implications for Christology of David Tracy's Theological Epistemology." *Scottish Journal of Theology* 63:3 (2010) 302–17.
Freire, Paulo. *Pedagogy of the Oppressed*. London: Penguin, [1970] 1996.
Frere, Bartle. *Eastern Africa as a Field for Missionary Labour: Four Letters to His Grace the Archbishop of Canterbury*. London: John Murray, 1874.
Frieder, Ludwig, and Afe Adogame, eds. *European Traditions of the Study of Religion in Africa*. Wiesbaden: Harrassowitz Verlag, 2004.
Fueter, Paul D. "A Christian Council in Action: The Christian Council of Kenya." *International Review of Missions* 49 (1960) 291–300.
———. "Theological Education in Africa." *International Review of Missions* 27 (1956) 377–95.
Gale, Richard M. "Time, Temporality, and Paradox." In *The Blackwell Guide to Metaphysics*, edited by Richard M. Gale, 66–86. Oxford: Blackwell, 2002.
Gandhi, M. K. *The Bhagavad Gita*. New Delhi: Orient Paperback / Vision, 1926.
Gathogo, Julius. *Liberation and Reconstruction in Africa: A Critical Analysis in the Works of J. N. K. Mugambi*. Saarbrücken: LAP Lambert Academic, 2011.
Gebe, Boni Yao. "The Quest for a Union Government of Africa: Reflections on the Vision and the Realities of Political Integration." *South African Journal of International Affairs* 15:1 (2008) 41–53.
Geertz, Clifford. *Available Light: Anthropological Reflections on Philosophical Topics*. New ed. Princeton: Princeton University Press, 2001.
———. *The Interpretation of Culture*. New ed. New York: Basic, [1973] 2000.
Gehman, Richard. "The African Inland Mission: Aspects of Its Early History." *African Journal of Evangelical Theology* 23:2 (2004) 115–44.
———. "The East African Revival." *East African Journal of Evangelical Theology* 5 (1986) 36–56.
Ghai, Dharam, ed., *Renewing Social and Economic Progress in Africa*. London: Macmillan, 2000.
Gibellini, Rosino. "African Theologians Wonder . . . and Make Some Proposals." In *Paths of African Theology*, edited by Rosino Gibellini, 1–7. London: SCM, 1994.
———, ed. *Frontiers of Theology in Latin America*. New York: Orbis, 1979.
Gifford, Paul. *African Christianity: Its Public Role*. London: C. Hurst, 1998.
———. "Some Recent Developments in African Christianity." *African Affairs* 93:373 (October 1994) 513–34.
———, ed. *The Christian Churches and the Democratisation of Africa*. Leiden: E. J. Brill, 1995.
Gillies, Francis. "The Bantu Concept of Time." *Religion* 10 (1980) 16–29.
Gitari, David. "Church and Politics." *Evangelical Review of Theology* 28:3 (2004) 220–31.
Githiga, Gideon Gichuhi. *The Church as the Bulwark against Authoritarianism: Development of Church and State Relations in Kenya with Particular Reference to the Years after Political Independence 1963–1992*. Oxford / Irving: Regnum, 2001.

BIBLIOGRAPHY

Godia, George I. *Understanding Nyayo: Principles and Policies in Contemporary Kenya.* Nairobi: Transafrica, 1984.

Graham, Elaine L. *Transforming Practice: Pastoral Theology in an Age of Uncertainty.* London: Mowbray, 1996.

Graham, Elaine L., and Esther D. Reed, eds. *The Future of Christian Social Ethics: Essays on the Work of Ronald H. Preston, 1913–2001.* London: Continuum, 2004.

Gray, Richard. *Black Christians and White Missionaries.* New Haven / London: Yale University Press, 1990.

Gray, Robert F. *The Sonjo of Tanganyika: An Anthropological Study of an Irrigation-Based Society.* London: Oxford University Press, 1963.

Grillo, Laura S. "Divination: Epistemology, Agency, and Identity in Contemporary Urban West Africa." *Religion Compass* 3:6 (2009) 921–934.

Gugelberger, Georg M., and Diana Brydon. "Postcolonial Cultural Studies." In *The Johns Hopkins Guide to Literary Theory and Criticism,* 2nd ed., edited by Michael Groden et al., 756–68. Baltimore / London: The Johns Hopkins University Press, 2005.

Gurr, Andrew, and Pio Zirimu, eds. *Black Aesthetics: Papers from a Colloquium held at The University of Nairobi, June 1971.* Nairobi: East African Literature Bureau, 1973.

Gutiérrez, Gustavo. *A Theology of Liberation.* Rev. ed. Translated by Caridad Inda and John Eagleson. London: SCM, 1988.

Gyekye, Kwame. *An Essay on African Philosophical Thought: The Akan Conceptual Scheme.* Rev. ed. Philadelphia: Temple University Press, 1995.

Haight, Roger. *Jesus, Symbol of God.* Orbis: Maryknoll, 1999.

Hall, Catherine. *Civilising Subjects: Metropole and Colony in the English Imagination, 1830–1867.* Cambridge: Polity, 2002.

Hall, Stuart. "When was 'the Postcolonial'? Thinking at the Limit." In *The Postcolonial Question: Common Skies, Divided Horizons,* edited by Iain Chambers and Lidia Curti, 242–58. New York: Routledge, 1996.

Hamelink, Cees J. *Cultural Autonomy in Global Communications: Planning National Information Policy.* New York / London: Longman, 1983.

Hamilton, Michael P., ed. *Anglicanism: Present and Future.* Washington, DC: Washington National Cathedral, 1992.

Hardt, Michael, and Antonio Negri. *Empire.* Cambridge / London: Harvard University Press, 2000.

Haselbarth, Hans. *Christian Ethics in the African Context.* Nairobi: Uzima, 1976.

Hastings, Adrian. *African Christianity: An Essay in Interpretation.* London: Geoffrey Chapman, 1976.

———. *A History of African Christianity 1950–75.* Cambridge: Cambridge University Press, 1979.

Heaney, Robert S. "Coloniality and Theological Method in Africa." *Journal of Anglican Studies* 71:1 (2009) 55–65.

———. "Conversion to Coloniality: Avoiding the Colonization of Method." *International Review of Mission* 97:384–85 (April 2008) 65–77.

———. "Moral Scepticism and Education: Approaching Integrative Education in a Christian University." *Journal of Education and Christian Belief* (forthcoming).

———. "Prospects and Problems for Evangelicalisms and Post-colonialisms." In *Evangelical Postcolonial Conversations: Global Awakenings in Theology and Praxis,* edited by Kay Higuera Smith et al., 29–43. Downers Grove: IVP Academic, 2014.

———. "Towards the Possibility of Impassibilist Pastoral Care." *Heythrop Journal* 48 (2007) 171–86.

———. "Views of Colonization Across the Anglican Communion." In *The Wiley-Blackwell Companion to the Anglican Communion*, edited by Ian S. Markham et al., 726–38. Chichester: Wiley-Blackwell, 2013.

Held, David. "The Development of the Modern State." In *Formations of Modernity*, edited by Stuart Hall and Bram Gieben, 71–119. Cambridge: Polity, 1992.

Hick, John. *God and the Universe of Faiths: Essays in the Philosophy of Religion*. London: Macmillan, 1973.

———. *God Has Many Names*. Philadelphia: Westminster, 1982.

Hobley, Charles W. *Ethnology of A-Kamba and other East African Tribes*. Cambridge: Cambridge University Press, 1910.

Holger, Bernt Hansen. *Mission Church and State in a Colonial Setting: Uganda 1890–1925*. London: Heinemann, 1984.

Hopkins, Dwight N. "A Transatlantic Comparison of a Black Theology of Liberation." In *Freedom's Distant Shores: American Protestants and Post-colonial Alliances with Africa*, edited by R. Drew Smith, 83–109. Waco: Baylor University Press, 2006.

Horton, James Africanus Beale. *West African Countries and Peoples: A Vindication of the African Race*. Cambridge: Cambridge University Press, [1868] 2011.

Horton, Robin. "African Conversion." *Africa: Journal of the International African Institute* 41:2 (1971) 85–108.

Hountondji, Paulin J. *African Philosophy: Myth and Reality*. 2nd ed. Translated by Henri Evans with the collaboration of Jonathan Rée. Bloomington / Indianapolis: Indiana University Press, 1996.

Hulburt, C. E. "Star-Points in Africa's Darkness: Survey of the Year." *Inland Africa* 4:16 (1923) 27–32.

Hulme, Peter. *Colonial Encounters: Europe and the Native Caribbean, 1492–1797*. London: Methuen, 1986.

———. "Including America." *Ariel* 26:1 (1995) 117–23.

Idowu, Bolaji E. *African Traditional Religion: A Definition*. London: SCM, 1973.

———. *Olodumare: God in Yorùbá Belief*. Ikeja: Longman, 1962.

———. *Towards an Indigenous Church*. London: Oxford University Press, 1965.

Ilo, Stan Chu. *The Church and Development in Africa: Aid and Development from the Perspective of Catholic Social Ethics*. Eugene: Pickwick, 2011. Kindle Edition.

Isichei, Elizabeth. *A History of Christianity in Africa: From Antiquity to the Present*. London: SPCK, 1995.

Jaspers, Karl. "Myth and Religion." In *Kerygma and Myth: A Theological Debate*, vol. 2, edited by Hans-Werner Bartsch, 133–80. London: SPCK, 1972.

Jenkins, David. *The Contradiction of Christianity*. London: SCM, 1977.

Jenson, Robert. *Systematic Theology*. Vol. 1, *The Triune God*. Oxford: Oxford University Press, [1997] 2001.

Joh, Wonhee Anne. *Heart of the Cross*. Louisville / London: Westminster John Knox, 2006.

———. "The Transgressive Power of Jeong." In *Postcolonial Theologies: Divinity and Empire*, edited by Catherine Keller et al., 149–63. St. Louis: Chalice, 2004.

Johnson, Aaron P. *Ethnicity and Argument in Eusebius' Praeparatio Evangelica*. Oxford: Oxford University Press, 2006.

Kalu, Ogbu U. *African Pentecostalism: An Introduction*. Oxford: Oxford University Press, 2008.

BIBLIOGRAPHY

———. "*Sankofa*: Pentecostalism and African Cultural Heritage." In *The Spirit in the World: Emerging Pentecostal Theologies in Global Contexts*, edited by Veli-Matti Kärkkäinen, 135–52. Grand Rapids / Cambridge: Eerdmans, 2009.

Karanja, John K. "The Biblical Prophetic Ministries of Henry Okullu and David Gitari." *Anglican and Episcopal History* 75:4 (2006) 580–604.

Karotemprel, Sebastian. "Introduction: Christology and Mission Today." In *Christologia e Missione Oggi*, edited by G. Colzani et al., 15–31. Rome: Urbaniana University Press.

Kasibante, Amos. "The Ugandan Diaspora in Britain and Their Quest for Cultural Expression within the Church of England." *Journal of Anglican Studies* 7:1 (2009) 79–86.

Kato, Byang H. "Black Theology and African Theology." *Perception* 6 (October 1976) 1–8.

———. "Christianity as an African Religion." *Perception* 16 (May 1979) 1–8.

———. "A Critique of Incipient Universalism in Tropical Africa." *International Journal of Theology and Philosophy in Africa* 1:1 (1989) 55–84.

———. "Eschatology in Africa: Problems of Hermeneutics." In *Readings in Dynamic Indigeneity*, edited by Charles H. Kraft and Tom N. Wisley, 467–99. Pasadena: William Carey Library, 1979.

———. *Theological Pitfalls in Africa*. Kisumu: Evangel, 1975.

———. "Theological Trends in Africa Today." *Theological News Monograph* 6 (1973) 1–9.

Keller, Catherine, et al., eds. *Postcolonial Theologies: Divinity and Empire*. St. Louis: Chalice, 2004.

Kelsey, David H. *The Fabric of Paul Tillich's Theology*. New Haven: Yale University Press, 1967.

———. "Paul Tillich." In *The Modern Theologians: An Introduction to Christian Theology in the Twentieth Century*, edited by David Ford, 87–102. Oxford: Blackwell, 1997.

Kenyatta, Jomo. *Facing Mount Kenya: The Traditional Life of the Gikuyu*. London: Secker & Warburg, 1938.

———. *Harambee: The Prime Minister of Kenya's Speeches, 1963-1964*. Nairobi: Oxford University Press, 1964.

———. *My People of the Kikuyu and The Life of Chief Wangombe*. Nairobi: Oxford University Press, 1966.

Kibicho, John. "The Continuity of the African Concept of God into and through Christianity: A Kikuyu Case-Study." In *Christianity in Independent Africa*, edited by E. Fasholé-Luke et al., 370–88. London: Collings, 1978.

Kim, Kirsteen. *Concepts of Development in the Christian Traditions*. Birmingham: International Development Department, 2007.

———. *The Holy Spirit in the World: A Global Conversation*. London: SPCK, 2007.

Kim, Uriah Y. *Decolonizing Josiah: Toward a Postcolonial Reading of the Deuteronomistic History*. Sheffield: Sheffield Phoenix, 2005.

King, Kenneth J. *Pan-Africanism and Education*. Oxford: Clarendon, 1971.

King, Richard. *Orientalism and Religion: Postcolonial Theory, India and the Mystic East*. London: Routledge, 1999.

Kinghorn, Johann. "The Theology of Separate Equality: A Critical Outline of the DRC's Position on Apartheid." In *Christianity Amidst Apartheid: Selected Perspectives on the Church in South Africa*, edited by Martin Prozesky, 57–80. Houndmills: Macmillan, 1990.

Kings, Graham. *Christianity Connected: Hindus, Muslims and the World in the Letters of Max Warren and Roger Hooker*. Zoetermeer: Boekencentrum, 2002.

———. "Proverbial, Intrinsic, and Dynamic Authorities: A Case Study on Scripture and Mission in the Dioceses of Mount Kenya East and Kirinyaga." *Missiology* 24:4 (1996) 493–501.
Kings, Graham, and Geoff Morgan. *Offerings from Kenya to Anglicanism: Liturgical Texts and Contexts Including a Kenyan Service of Holy Communion*. Cambridge: Grove, 2001.
Kinkupu, Léonard S., et al., eds. *Des Prêtres Noirs s'Interrogent: Cinquante ans Après*. Paris: Karthala / Présence Africaine, 2006.
Kinney, John W. "The Theology of John Mbiti: His Sources, Norms, and Method." *Occasional Bulletin of Missionary Research* 3:2 (1979) 65–68.
Kirigia, Joyce Karuri. "Liturgical Developments in the Anglican Church of Kenya." *Encounter* 2 (2002) 1–8.
Koestler, Arthur. *The Sleepwalkers*. London: Hutchinson, 1959.
Krapf, J. L. *Travels, Researchers and Missionary Labours*. London: Trübner, 1860.
———. *Vocabulary of Six East-African Languages*. Tübingen: Lud. Friedr. Fues., 1850.
Kundu, Nyukuri Barasa. "Ethnicity and the Challenge of Nationhood in Kenya." In *Kenya: The Making of a Nation*, edited by Bethwell A. Ogot and W. R. Ochieng', 171–86. Maseno: IRPS, 2000.
Kwanya, Charles Odira. *Debate on African Concept of Time: Analysis of its Missionary Consequence on the Pluralistic Society*. Roma: Pontificia Universitas Urbaniana, Facultas Missiologiae, 2009.
———. "Time and Not the Other Time in Africa: On Ernest Beyaraza: The African Concept of Time: A Comparative Study of Various Theories." *Forum for Intercultural Philosophy* 3 (2001) http://lit.polylog.org/3/rsd-en.htm.
Kwok, Pui-lan. *Discovering the Bible in the non-biblical World*. Maryknoll: Orbis, 1995.
———. "The Legacy of Cultural Hegemony in the Anglican Church." In *Beyond Colonial Anglicanism: The Anglican Communion in the Twentieth-First Century*, edited by Ian T. Douglas and Kwok Pui-lan, 47–70. New York: Church, 2001.
———. "Mercy Amba Oduyoye and African Women's Theology." *Journal of Feminist Studies in Religion* 20:1 (2004) 7–22.
———. *Postcolonial Imagination and Feminist Theology*. London: SCM, 2004.
Kyle, Keith. *The Politics of the Independence of Kenya*. London: Macmillan, 1999.
Landau, Paul. "Language." In *Missions and Empire*, edited by Norman Etherington, 194–215. Oxford: Oxford University Press, 2005.
Landsberg, Chris. "Reflections on the African Union after Decade One: Looking Back in Order to Look Forward." *Africa Insight* 42:3 (2010) 1–12.
Lartey, Emmanuel Yartekwei. *Postcolonializing God: An African Practical Theology*. London: SCM, 2013.
Lindblom, Gerhard. *The Akamba in British East Africa: An Ethnological Monograph*. 2nd ed. Uppsala: Appelbergs Boktryckeri, 1920.
Lonergan, Bernard. *Method in Theology*. London: Darton, Longman & Todd, 1971.
Lonsdale, John. "The European Scramble and Conquest in African History." In *Cambridge History of Africa*, vol. 6: *From 1870–1905*, edited by Roland Oliver and G. N. Sanderson, 680–766. Cambridge: Cambridge University Press, 1985.
———. "States and Social Processes in Africa: A Historiographical Survey." *African Studies Review* 24:2–3 (1981) 139–225.
Loomba, Ania. *Colonialism/Postcolonialism*. 2nd ed. London / New York: Routledge, 2005.

Loux, Michael J. "Time: The A-Theory and the B-Theory." In *Metaphysics: Contemporary Readings*, 2nd ed., edited by Michael J. Loux, 251–59. London / New York: Routledge, 2001.

Lowe, E. J. "The Indexical Fallacy in McTaggart's Proof of the Unreality of Time." *Mind* 96:381 (1987) 62–70.

Lowe, Lisa. *Critical Terrains: French and British Orientalism.* Ithaca: Cornell University Press, 1991.

Lyons, C. H. *To Wash an Aethiop White: British Ideas about Black African Educability, 1530–1960.* New York: Teachers College, 1975.

MacGaffey, Wyatt. "Kimbanguism and the Question of Syncretism in Zaïre." In *Religion in Africa: Experience and Expression*, edited by Thomas D. Blakely et al., 241–56. London: James Currey, 1994.

Macquarrie, John. *A Guide to the Sacraments.* London: SCM, 1997.

———. *Twentieth Century Religious Thought.* London: SCM, 1963.

Maddox, Gregory H. "African Theology and the Search for the Universal." In *East African Expressions of Christianity*, edited by Thomas T. Spear and Isaria N. Kimambo, 25–36 London: James Currey, 1999.

Magaga, Gordon Obote. "The African Dream: 1920–63." In *Kenya: The Making of a Nation*, edited by Bethwell A. Ogot and W. R. Ochieng', 79–90. Maseno: IRPS, 2000.

Magesa, Laurenti. "The Church in Eastern Africa: Retrospect and Prospects." *Journal of Inculturation Theology* 1 (1994) 88–102.

Malina, Bruce J. *The Social World of Jesus and the Gospels.* London / New York: Routledge, 1996.

Maluleke, Tinyiko Sam. "Black and African Theologies in the New World Order: A Time to Drink from our Own Wells." *Journal of Theology for Southern Africa* 96:1 (1996) 3–19.

———. "Half a Century of African Christian Theologies." In *The Church and Reconstruction of Africa: Theological Considerations*, edited by J. N. K. Mugambi, 84–114. Nairobi: All Africa Conference of Churches, 1997.

Mamdani, Mahmood. *Citizen and Subject: Contemporary Africa and the Legacy of Late Colonialism.* London: James Currey, 1996.

Manus, Ukachukwu Chris. *Intercultural Hermeneutics in Africa.* Nairobi: Acton, 2003.

Markham, Ian S. *A Theology of Engagement.* Oxford: Blackwell, 2003.

Marsh, Zoe, and George Kingsnorth. *An Introduction to the History of East Africa.* Cambridge: Cambridge University Press, 1961.

Martey, Emmanuel. *African Theology: Inculturation and Liberation.* Maryknoll: Orbis, 1993.

Matonya, Moses. *Real Power.* Wheaton: Oasis International, 2008.

Maxon, R. M. "The Colonial and Foreign Offices: Policy and Control." In *Kenya: The Making of a Nation*, edited by Bethwell A. Ogot and W. R. Ochieng', 33–48. Maseno: IRPS, 2000.

———. *Struggle for Kenya: The Loss and Reassertion of Imperial Initiative 1912–1923.* Rutherford: Farleigh Dickson, 1993.

Mazrui, Alamin M. "Aesthetic Dualism and Creative Literature in East Africa." In *Black Aesthetics*, edited by Andrew Gurr and Pio Zirimu, 32–51. Nairobi: East African Literature Bureau, 1973.

———. "Cultural (Re)Construction and Nation Building in Kenya: 1963–1970." In *Kenya: The Making of a Nation*, edited by Bethwell A. Ogot and W. R. Ochieng', 118–31. Maseno: IRPS, 2000.
Mbeki, Thabo. "The African Union at Ten Years Old: A Dream Deferred!" *Africa Insight* 42:3 (2010) 13–24.
McCarthy, Thomas. *Race, Empire, and the Idea of Human Development*. Cambridge: Cambridge University Press, 2009.
McClintock, Anne. "The Angel of Progress: Pitfalls of the Term Post-colonialism." *Social Text* 31–32 (1992) 84–98.
———. *Imperial Leather: Race, Gender and Sexuality in the Colonial Context*. New York: Routledge, 1995.
McCormack, Bruce L. *Karl Barth's Critical Realistic Dialectical Theology: Its Genesis and Development 1909–1936*. Oxford: Oxford University Press, 1997.
McTaggart, Ellis. "The Unreality of Time." *Mind* 17:68 (1908) 457–74.
McVeigh, Malcolm. *God in Africa: Conceptions of God in African Traditional Religion and Christianity*. Cape Cod: Claude Stark, 1974.
Metz, Johannes Baptist. "Religion and Society in the Light of a Political Theology." *Harvard Theological Review* 61:4 (1968) 507–23.
———. *Theology of the World*. London: Burns & Oates, 1969.
Middleton, John. "Kenya." In *History of East Africa*, vol. 2, edited by Vincent Harlow et al., 386–87. Oxford: Oxford University Press, 1965.
———. *The Kikuyu and the Kamba of Kenya*. London: International African Institute, 1953.
Mitchell, W. J. T. "Postcolonial Culture, Postimperial Criticism." *Transition* 56 (1992) 11–19.
Mkandawire, P. Thandika, and Charles Soludo. *African Voices on Structural Adjustment*. Trenton: Africa World; London: Turnaround, 2003.
Mofokeng, Takatso. "Black Theology in South Africa: Achievements, Problems and Prospects." In *Christianity Amidst Apartheid: Selected Perspectives on the Church in South Africa*, edited by Martin Prozesky, 37–54. Houndmills: Macmillan, 1990.
Moi, Daniel Arap. *Kenya African Nationalism: Nyayo Philosophy and Principles*. London / Basingstoke: Macmillan, 1986.
Moltmann, Jürgen. *The Crucified God*. London: SCM, 1974.
———. "The Liberation of the Future and its Anticipations in History." In *God Will Be All in All: The Eschatology of Jürgen Moltmann*, edited by Richard Bauckham, 265–89. Edinburgh: T & T Clark, 1999.
———. *Religion, Revolution, and the Future*. Translated by M. Douglas Meeks. New York: Charles Scribner's Sons, 1969.
———. *The Spirit of Life*. London: SCM, 1992.
———. *Theology of Hope*. London: SCM, 1967.
———. "The World in God or God in the World?" In *God Will Be All in All: The Eschatology of Jürgen Moltmann*, edited by Richard Bauckham, 35–41. Edinburgh: T & T Clark, 2005.
Mombo, Esther. "Missiological Challenges in the HIV/AIDS Era: Kenya." *Theology Today* (2005) 58–66.
———. "Theological Education in Africa." In *Voices from Africa: Transforming Mission in a Context of Marginalization: An Anthology*, edited by Andrew Wheeler, 127–33. London: Church, 2002.

BIBLIOGRAPHY

———. "Why Women Bishops are Still on the Waiting-List in Africa." In *Call for Women Bishops*, edited by Jane Shaw and Harriet Harris, 163–67. London: SPCK, 2004.

———. "The Windsor Report: A Paradigm Shift for Anglicanism." *Anglican Theological Review* 89:1 (2007) 69–78.

Moore, Basil, ed. *Black Theology: The South African Voice*. London: C. Hurst, [1972] 1973.

Moore-Gilbert, Bart. "Postcolonial Cultural Studies and Imperial Historiography: Problems of Interdisciplinarity." *Interventions: International Journal of Postcolonial Studies* 1:3 (1999) 397–411.

———. *Postcolonial Theory: Contexts, Practices, Politics*. London: Verso, 1997.

———. "Spivak and Bhabha." In *A Companion to Postcolonial Studies*, edited by Henry Schwarz and Sangeeta Ray, 451–66. Malden: Blackwell, 2005.

Morgan, Robert. "Rudolf Bultmann." In *The Modern Theologians: An Introduction to Christian Theology in the Twentieth Century*, 2nd ed., edited by David F. Ford, 68–86. Oxford: Blackwell, 1997.

Morris, Jeremy. "Secularization and Religious Experience: Arguments in the Historiography of Modern British Religion." *The Historical Journal* 55:1 (2012) 195–219.

Mosha, R. Sambuli. *The Heartbeat of Indigenous Africa: A Study of Chaga Educational System*. New York: Garland, 2000.

Moule, C. F. D. *The Origin of Christology*. Cambridge: Cambridge University Press, 1977.

Muck, Terry C. "Theology of Religions after Knitter and Hick: Beyond the Paradigm." *Interpretation* 61:1 (2007) 7–22.

Mudimbe, Valentin Yves. *The Invention of Africa: Gnosis, Philosophy, and Other Knowledge*. Bloomington: Indiana University Press; London: Currey, 1988.

Muller, Herbert J. *The Uses of the Past: Profiles of Former Societies*. New York: Oxford University Press, 1952.

Muller, Louise. "A Thematic Comparison Between Four African Scholars: Idowu, Mbiti, Okot p'Bitek and Appiah." *Quest: An African Journal of Philosophy* 18 (1995) 109–24.

Munro, H. D. "Culture." In *A Dictionary of Sociology*, edited by G. D. Mitchell. London: Routledge / Kegan Paul, 1968.

Musopole, Augustine C. *Being Human in Africa*. New York: Peter Lang, 1994.

Mutiso-Mbinda, John. "Ecumenical Challenges of Small Christian Communities and the African Synod of Bishops." In *How Local is the Local Church? Small Christian Communities in Eastern Africa*, edited by A. Radoli, 120–35. Eldoret: AMECEA, 1993.

———. "Towards a Theology of Harambee." *African Ecclesiastical Review* 20:5 (1978) 287–95.

Muzorewa, Gwinyai H. *An African Theology of Mission*. Lewiston / Lampeter: Mellen, 1990.

———. *The Origins and Development of African Theology*. Markyknoll: Orbis, 1985.

Mwase, Isaac M. T. "Kuona, An African Perspective on Religions: J. N. K. Mugambi's Contribution." *Paideia*. www.bu.edu/wcp/Papers/Reli/ReliMwas.htm, accessed October 16, 2007.

———. Review of *From Liberation to Reconstruction: African Christian Theology after the Cold War* by J. N. K. Mugambi, *Journal of the American Academy of Religion* 65:4 (1997) 909–11.

Mwase, Isaac M. T., and Eunice Kamaara, eds. *Theologies of Liberation and Reconstruction*. Nairobi: Acton, 2012.

BIBLIOGRAPHY

Nandy, Ashis. *The Intimate Enemy: Loss and Recovery of Self under Colonialism*. Delhi: Oxford University Press, 1988.

Naugle, David K. *Worldview: The History of a Concept*. Grand Rapids / Cambridge: Eerdmans, 2002.

Neale, Caroline. *Writing "Independent" History: African Historiography 1960-1980*. Westport: Greenwood, 1985.

Neill, Stephen. *Colonialism and Christian Missions*. New York: McGraw Hill, 1966.

Neill, Stephen C., et al., eds. *Concise Dictionary of the Christian World Mission*. London: United Society for Christian Literature, 1971.

Ng'eny, Samuel A. Arap. *Rabai to Mumias: A Short History of the Church of the Province of Kenya 1844 to 1994*. Nairobi: Provincial Unit of Research Church of the Province of Kenya / Uzima, 1994.

Nkrumah, Kwame. *Consciencism: Philosophy and Ideology for De-colonization*. New York: Monthly Review, [1964] 2009.

———. *I Speak of Freedom: A Statement of African Ideology*. New York: Frederick A. Praeger, 1962.

———. *Neo-Colonialism*. London: Heinemann, 1965.

———. *Towards Colonial Freedom: Africa in the Struggle against World Imperialisms*. London: Panaf, 1973.

Nugent, Paul. *Africa Since Independence: A Comparative History*. Houndmills: Palgrave Macmillan, 2004.

Nwatu, Felix. "'Colonial' Christianity in Post-Colonial Africa?" *Ecumenical Review* 46:3 (1994) 352–60.

Nyamiti, Charles. "African Christologies Today." In *Faces of Jesus in Africa*, edited by Robert J. Schreiter, 3–23. Maryknoll: Orbis, 2005.

———. *African Theology: Its Nature, Problems and Methods*. Kampala: Gaba, 1971.

———. *Christ as Our Ancestor: Christology from an African Perspective*. Gweru: Mambo, 1984.

———. *The Scope of African Theology*. Kampala: Gaba, 1973.

———. *Studies in African Theology*. Vol. 1, *Jesus Christ, the Ancestor of Humankind: Methodological and Trinitarian Foundations*. Nairobi: The Catholic University of Eastern Africa, 2005.

Nyerere, Julius. *Ujamaa: Essays on Socialism*. Dar es Salaam: Oxford University Press, 1968.

Oborji, Francis Anekwe. "In Dialogue with African Traditional Religion: New Horizons." *Mission Studies* 19:1 (2002) 13–35.

Odhiambo, E. S. Atieno. "Ethnic Cleansing and Civil Society in Kenya 1969–1992." *Journal of Contemporary African Studies* 22:1 (2004) 29–42.

Odhiambo, E. S. Atieno, and John Lonsdale, eds. *Mau Mau and Nationhood: Arms, Authority and Narration*. Oxford: James Currey, 2003.

O'Donovan, Oliver. *The Desire of the Nations: Rediscovering the Roots of Political Theology*. Cambridge: Cambridge University Press, 1999.

———. "Political Theology, Tradition and Modernity." In *The Cambridge Companion to Liberation Theology*, 2nd ed., edited by Christopher Rowland, 265–77. Cambridge: Cambridge University Press, 2007.

Oduyoye, Mercy Amba. "A Coming Home to Myself: The Childless Woman in the West African Space." In *Liberating Eschatology: Essays in Honor of Letty M. Russell*, edited by Margaret A. Farley and Serene Jones, 105–22. Kentucky: Westminster John Knox, 1999.

———. "A Critique of John Mbiti's View on Love and Marriage in Africa." In *Religious Plurality in Africa: Essays in Honour of John S. Mbiti*, edited by Jacob K. Olupona and Sulayman S. Nyang, 341–65. Berlin / New York: Mouton de Gruyter, 1993.

———. *Daughters of Anowa: African Women and Patriarchy*. Maryknoll: Orbis, 1998.

———. "Feminist Theology in an African Perspective." In *Paths of African Theology*, edited by Rosino Gibellini, 166–81. London: SCM, 1994.

———. *Hearing and Knowing: Theological Reflections on Christianity in Africa*. Maryknoll: Orbis, 1986.

———. *Introducing African Women's Theology*. Sheffield: Sheffield Academic, 2001.

Ogden, Steven. "In the Spirit of Tillich: A Postmodern Christology based on the Theology of Paul Tillich." *International Yearbook of Tillich Research* 6 (2011) 187–220.

Ogot, Bethwell A. "Boundary Changes and the Invention of 'Tribes.'" In *Kenya: The Making of a Nation*, edited by Bethwell A. Ogot and W. R. Ochieng', 16–31. Maseno: IRPS, 2000.

———. *Historical Dictionary of Kenya*. Metuchen / London: Scarecrow, 1981.

———. "Introduction." In *Kenya: The Making of a Nation*, edited by Bethwell A. Ogot and W. R. Ochieng', 1–3. Maseno: IRPS, 2000.

———. "A Man More Sinned Against Than Sinning—The African Writer's View of Himself." In *Black Aesthetics*, edited by Andrew Gurr and Pio Zirimu, 20–31. Nairobi: East African Literature Bureau, 1973.

———. "The Settler Dream for a White Dominion." In *Kenya: The Making of a Nation*, edited by Bethwell A. Ogot and W. R. Ochieng', 49–69. Maseno: IRPS, 2000.

Ogot, Bethwell A., and W. R. Ochieng', eds. *Decolonization and Independence in Kenya, 1940–1993*. London: Currey, 1995.

———, eds. *Kenya: The Making of a Nation: A Hundred Years of Kenya's History, 1895–1995*. Maseno: Institute of Research and Postgraduate Studies, Maseno University, 2000.

Òkè, Moses. "From an African Ontology to an African Epistemology: A Critique of J. S. Mbiti on the Time Conception of Africans." *Quest: Philosophical Discussions: An International African Journal of Philosophy* 18:1–2 (2004) 25–36.

Okorocha, Cyril C. "African Social History and the Christian Mission in Africa: Implications and Challenges for the Afro-Anglicanism Movement." *Anglican Theological Review* 77:4 (1995) 480–96.

Okullu, Henry. *Church and Politics in East Africa*. Nairobi: Uzima, 1974.

O'Leary, Michael. *The Kitui Akamba: Economic and Social Change in Semi-Arid Kenya*. Nairobi: Heinemann Educational, 1984.

———. "Population, Economy and Domestic Groups—The Kitui Case." *Africa: Journal of the International African Institute* 53:1 (1983) 64–76.

Oliver, Roland. *The Missionary Factor in East Africa*. London: Longmans, Green, 1952.

Oliver, Roland, and Gervase Mathew, eds. *History of East Africa*. Vol. 1. Oxford: Clarendon, 1963.

Olupona, Jacob K. "A Biographical Sketch." In *Religious Plurality in Africa: Essays in Honour of John S. Mbiti*, edited by Jacob K. Olupona and Sulayman S. Nyang, 1–9. Berlin / New York: Mouton de Gruyter, 1993.

Olupona, Jacob K., and Sulayman S. Nyang, eds. *Religious Plurality in Africa: Essays in Honour of John S. Mbiti*. Berlin / New York: Mouton de Gruyter, 1993.

Opoku, Kofi Asare. "Introduction." In *Worlds of Memory and Wisdom: Encounters of Jews and African Christians*, edited by Jean Halpérin and Hans Ucko, 9-14. Geneva: World Council of Churches, 2005.

Osborn, H. H. *Pioneers in the East African Revival*. Winchester: Apologia, 2000.

Padilla, C. René, and Lindy Scott. *Terrorism and the War in Iraq: A Christian Word from Latin America*. Buenos Aires: Kairos Ediciones, 2004.

Parratt, John. "African Theology and African Socialism." *Africa Theological Journal* 17:3 (1988) 247-54.

———. "African Theology and Biblical Hermeneutics." *Africa Theological Journal* 12:2 (1983) 88-94.

———. *Reinventing Christianity: African Theology Today*. Grand Rapids / Cambridge: Eerdmans; Trenton: African World, 1995.

———. "Time in Traditional African Thought." *Religion* 7 (1977) 117-26.

———, ed. *An Introduction to Third World Theologies*. Cambridge: Cambridge University Press, 2004.

———, ed. *The Practice of Presence: Shorter Writings of Harry Sawyerr*. Grand Rapids: Eerdmans, 1996.

———, ed. *A Reader in African Christian Theology*. London: SPCK, 1987.

Parrinder, Geoffrey. *African Mythology*. Rev. ed. London: Hamlyn, 1982.

———. *Religion in Africa*. Harmondsworth: Penguin, 1969.

Parry, Benita. "Problems in Current Theories of Colonial Discourse." *Oxford Literary Review* 9:1-2 (1987) 34.

P'Bitek, Okot. *African Religions in Western Scholarship*. Nairobi: East African Literature Bureau, 1970.

———. "Reflect, Reject, Recreate." *East Africa Journal* 9:4 (1972) 28-31.

———. *Song of Lawino and Song of Ocol*. Nairobi: East African, 1966.

Peel, John D. Y. *Aladura: A Religious Movement Among the Yoruba*. London: Oxford University Press, 1968.

———. *Religious Encounter and the Making of the Yoruba*. Bloomington / Indianapolis: Indiana University Press, 2000.

Perkinson, James W. "John S. Mbiti." In *Empire and the Christian Tradition: New Readings of Classical Theologians*, edited by Kwok Pui-lan et al., 455-69. Minneapolis: Fortress, 2007.

Petrella, Ivan. *Beyond Liberation Theology: A Polemic*. London: SCM, 2008.

———. *The Future of Liberation Theology: An Argument and Manifesto*. London: SCM, 2006.

Phiri, Isabel Apawo, and Sarojini Nadar, eds. *African Women, Religion, and Health: Essays in Honor of Mercy Amba Ewudziwa Oduyoye*. Maryknoll: Orbis, 2006.

Pike, Kenneth L. *Language in Relation to a Unified Theory of the Structure of Human Behaivour*. 2nd rev. ed. The Hague: Mouton, 1967.

———. "On the Emics and Etics of Pike and Harris." In *Emics and Etics: The Insider/Outsider Debate*, edited by Thomas N. Headland et al., 28-47. London: Sage, 1990.

Platvoet, Jan. "From Object to Subject: A History of the Study of the Religions in Africa." In *The Study of Religions in Africa: Past, Present and Prospects*, edited by Jan Platvoet et al., 105-38. Cambridge: Roots & Branches, 1996.

Pobee, John S. "African Theology Revisited." In *Religious Plurality in Africa: Essays in Honour of John S. Mbiti*, edited by Jacob K. Olupona and Sulayman S. Nyang, 135-43. Berlin: Mouton de Gruyter, 1993.

———. "Contextuality and Universality in Theological Education." In *Variations in Christian Theology in Africa*, edited by John S. Pobee and Carl F. Hallencreutz, 1–13. Nairobi: Uzima, 1986.

Pollock, Sheldon. "Deep Orientalism? Notes on Sanskrit and Power Beyond the Raj." In *Orientalism and the Post-colonial Predicament*, edited by Carol A. Breckenridge and Peter van der Veers, 76–133. Philadelphia: University of Pennsylvania Press, 1993.

Porter, Andrew. "An Overview, 1700–1914." In *Missions and Empire*, edited by Norman Etherington, 40–63. Oxford: Oxford University Press, 2005.

———. *Religion versus Empire? British Protestant Missionaries and Overseas Expansion, 1700–1914*. Manchester / New York: Manchester University Press, 2004.

Posnansky, Merrick. "Archaeology, Ritual and Religion." In *The Historical Study of African Religion: With Special Reference to East and Central Africa*, edited by T. O. Ranger and I. N. Kimambo, 29–44. London: Heinemann, 1972.

Radhakrishnan, S. *Recovery of Faith*. New Delhi: Orient, [1955] 1967.

Radin, Paul. *Primitive Religion: Its Nature and Origin*. London: Hamish Hamilton, 1938.

Raiser, Konrad. *Ecumenism in Transition*. Geneva: WCC, 1991.

Ranger, Terence O. "Connexions between 'Primary Resistance' Movements and Modern Mass Nationalism in East and Central Africa: Part 1." *Journal of African History* 9:3 (1968) 437–53.

———. "Connexions between 'Primary Resistance' Movements and Modern Mass Nationalism in East and Central Africa: Part 2." *Journal of African History* 9:4 (1968) 631–41.

———. *Emerging Themes of African History*. Nairobi: East African, 1968.

Ranger, Terence O., and I. Kimambo. *The Historical Study of African Religion*. London: Heinemann, 1972.

Ray, Benjamin C. *African Religions: Symbol, Ritual, and Community*. 2nd ed. Upper Saddle River: Prentice Hall, 2000.

Reed, Colin. *Founded in Faith: The Early Years of the Anglican Church in Kenya*. Nairobi: Uzima, 2003.

———. *Pastors, Partners, and Paternalists: African Church Leaders and Western Missionaries in the Anglican Church in Kenya, 1850–1900*. Leiden / New York: E. J. Brill, 1997.

Reijnen, Anne Marie. "Tillich's Christology." In *The Cambridge Companion to Paul Tillich*, edited by Russell Re Manning, 56–73. Cambridge / New York: Cambridge University Press, 2009.

Richardson, Kenneth. *Garden of Miracles*. London: Africa Inland Mission, 1976.

Rieger, Joerg. *Christ and Empire: From Paul to Postcolonial Times*. Minneapolis: Fortress, 2007.

———. "Christian Theology and Empires." In *Empire and The Christian Tradition: New Readings of Classical Theologians*, edited by Kwok Pui-lan et al., 1–13. Minneapolis: Fortress, 2007.

———. *Globalization and Theology*. Nashville: Abingdon, 2010.

———. *Remember the Poor: The Challenge to Theology in the Twenty-First Century*. Harrisburg: Trinity International, 1998.

———. "Between Accommodation and Resistance: Theology in a Globalizing World." *Soma: An International Journal of Theological Discourses and Counter-Discourses* (2011) 1–21. www.sjut.org/journals/ojs/index.php/soma/article/view/1, accessed April 20, 2013.

BIBLIOGRAPHY

Rivera, Mayra. *The Touch of Transcendence: A Postcolonial Theology of God.* Louisville: Westminster John Knox, 2007.

Robinson, Cedric J. *Black Marxism: The Making of the Black Radical Tradition.* London: Zed, 1983.

Rooney, David. *Kwame Nkrumah: Vision and Tragedy.* Accra: Sub-Saharan, [1988] 2007.

Rowland, Christopher. "In Dialogue with Itumeleng Mosala: A Contribution to Liberation Exegesis." *Journal for the Study of the New Testament* 50 (1993) 43–57.

———. "Render to God What Belongs to God." *New Blackfriars* 70:830 (2007) 365–71.

———. *Revelation.* London: Epworth, 1993.

Rowland, Christopher, and Mark Corner. *Liberating Exegesis: The Challenge of Liberation Theology to Biblical Studies.* London: SPCK, 1990.

Ruether, Rosemary Radford. "Feminist Theology: Where is it Going?" *International Journal of Public Theology* 4 (2010) 5–20.

Russell, Bertrand. *History of Western Philosophy.* 2nd ed. London: Allen & Unwin, 1901.

Russell, William P. *Church, State and Society in Kenya: From Mediation to Opposition, 1963-1993.* Portland: Frank Cass, 2002.

———. "Time Also Moves Backwards: John Mbiti's Traditional Concept of Time and the Future of World Christianity." *Studies in World Christianity* 9:1 (2003) 88–102.

Sabar-Friedman, Galia. "Church and State in Kenya, 1986–1992." *African Affairs* 96 (1997) 25–52.

———. *Church, State and Society in Kenya.* Portland: Frank Cass, 2002.

———. "The Power of the Familiar: Everyday Practices in the Anglican Church of Kenya (CPK)." *Journal of Church and State* 38 (1996) 377–95.

Said, Edward W. *Culture and Imperialism.* London: Vantage, 1994.

———. *Orientalism.* London: Penguin, [1978] 2003.

Sandgren, David P. *Christianity and the Kikuyu: Religious Divisions and Social Conflict.* New York: Peter Lang, 1989.

———. "Kamba Christianity: From Africa Inland Mission to African Brotherhood Church." In *East African Expressions of Christianity*, edited by Thomas Spear and Isaria N. Kimambo, 169–95. Oxford: James Currey, 1999.

Sanneh, Lamin. "Translatability in Islam and Christianity in Africa: A Thematic Approach." In *Religion in Africa: Experience and Expression*, edited by Thomas D. Blakely et al., 23–45. London: James Currey, 1994.

———. *Whose Religion is Christianity? The Gospel Beyond the West.* Grand Rapids / Cambridge: Eerdmans, 2003.

Sawyerr, Harry. "The Basis of a Theology for Africa." *International Review of Mission* 52:207 (1963) 266–78.

———. *Creative Evangelism: Towards a New Christian Encounter with Africa.* London: Lutterworth, 1968.

Schreiter, Robert J. *Constructing Local Theologies.* Maryknoll: Orbis, 1985.

———. *The New Catholicity: Theology between the Global and the Local.* Maryknoll: Orbis, 1997.

———, ed. *Faces of Jesus in Africa.* Maryknoll: Orbis, 1991.

Schweiker, William. "Theology of Culture and its Future." In *The Cambridge Companion to Paul Tillich*, edited by Russell Re Manning, 138–51. Cambridge / New York: Cambridge University Press, 2009.

Schydlowsky, Daniel, ed. *Structural Adjustment: Retrospect and Prospect.* Westport: Praeger, 1995.

Sebastian, Mrinalini. "Mission without History? Some Ideas for Decolonizing Mission." *International Review of Mission* 93:368 (2004) 75–97.

Segovia, Fernando. *Decolonizing Biblical Studies: A View from the Margins*. Maryknoll: Orbis, 2000.

———. *Interpreting Beyond Borders*. Sheffield: Sheffield Academic, 2000.

Senghor, Léopold Sédar. *Fondements de l'Africanité ou Négritude et Arabité*. Paris: Présence Africaine, 1967.

Serequeberhan, Tsenay. "The Critique of Eurocentrism and the Practice of African Philosophy." In *Postcolonial African Philosophy: A Critical Reader*, edited by Emmanuel Chukwudi Eze, 141–61. Oxford: Blackwell, 1997.

Setiloane, Gabriel M. "I am an African." In *Mission Trends*, no. 3, edited by G. H. Anderson and T. F. Stransky, 128–31. New York: Paulist, 1976.

Sharma, C. A. *Critical Survey of Indian Philosophy*. Delhi: Motilal Banarsidass, 1976.

Shaw, Rosalind. "The Invention of 'African Traditional Religion.'" *Religion* 20:4 (1990) 339–54.

———. "'Traditional' African Religions." In *Turning Points in Religious Studies: Essays in Honour of Geoffrey Parrinder*, edited by Ursula King, 181–91. Edinburgh: T & T Clark, 1990.

Shepperson, George, and Thomas Price. *Independent Africa*. Edinburgh: Edinburgh University Press, 1958.

Shoemaker, Sydney. "Time Without Change." In *The Philosophy of Time*, edited by Robin Le Poidevin and Murray MacBeath, 68–79. Oxford: Oxford University Press, 1993.

Shohat, Ella. "Notes on the Postcolonial." *Social Text* 31–32 (1992) 99–113.

Shohat, Ella, and Robert Stam. *Unthinking Eurocentrism: Multiculturalism and the Media*. London / New York: Routledge, 1994.

Shorter, Aylward. *African Christian Theology—Adaptation or Incarnation?* London: Geoffrey Chapman, 1975.

———. "African Traditional Religion: Its Relevance in the Contemporary World." *Cross Currents* 28:4 (1978–79) 421–31.

———. *Toward a Theology of Inculturation*. London: Geoffrey Chapman, 1988.

Shorter, Aylward, and Eugene Kataza, eds. *Missionaries to Yourselves*. London: Geoffrey Chapman, 1972.

Slemon, Stephen. "Post-colonial Critical Theories." In *New National and Post-Colonial Literatures*, edited by Bruce King, 178–97. Oxford: Clarendon, 1996.

———. "The Scramble for Post-colonialism." In *De-scribing Empire: Post-colonialism and Textuality*, edited by Chris Tiffin and Alan Lawson, 15–32. London: Routledge, 1994.

Smart, Ninian. *Dimensions of the Sacred*. Glasgow: Collins, 1997.

Smith, Anthony D. *State and Nation in the Third World: The Western State and African Nationalism*. Brighton: Wheatsheaf, 1983.

Smith, Daniel. "Time and Not the Other Time in Africa: On Ernest Beyaraza: The African Concept of Time: A Comparative Study of Various Theories." *Forum for Intercultural Philosophy* 3 (2001) http://lit.polylog.org/3/rsd-en.htm.

Smith, Edwin W. "The Whole Subject in Perspective." In *African Ideas of God: A Symposium*, edited by Edwin W. Smith, 1–35. London: Edinburgh, 1950.

———, ed. *African Ideas of God: A Symposium*. London: Edinburgh, 1950.

Smith, Kay Higuera, et al., eds. *Evangelical Postcolonial Conversations: Global Awakenings in Theology and Praxis*. Downers Grove: IVP Academic, 2014.

Smith, Linda Tuhiwai. *Decolonising Methodologies: Research and Indigenous Peoples.* 2nd ed. London: Zed, 1999. Kindle Edition.
Somé, Magloire, and Cecily Bennett. "Christian Base Communities in Burkina Faso: Between Church and Politics." *Journal of Religion in Africa* 31:3 (2001) 275–304.
Song, C. S. *The Compassionate God: An Exercise in the Theology of Transposition.* London: SCM; New York: Orbis, 1982.
———. *Jesus, the Crucified People.* Minneapolis: Fortress, 1996.
Soyinka, Wole. *Myth, Literature and the African World.* Cambridge: Cambridge University Press, 1976.
Spear, Thomas. "Towards the History of African Christianity." In *East African Expressions of Christianity*, edited by Thomas Spear and Isaria N. Kimambo, 3–24. Oxford: James Currey, 1999.
Spear, Thomas, and Isaria N. Kimambo, eds. *East African Expressions of Christianity.* Oxford: James Currey, 1999.
Spivak, Gayatri Chakravorty. *A Critique of Postcolonial Reason: Toward a History of the Vanishing Present.* Cambridge / London: Harvard University Press, 1999.
Stanley, Brian. *The Bible and the Flag: Protestant Missions and British Imperialism in the Nineteenth and Twentieth Centuries.* Leicester: Apollos, 1990.
———. "Conversion to Christianity: The Colonization of the Mind?" *International Review of Mission* 92:366 (2003) 315–31.
———. "The Future in the Past: Eschatological Vision in British and American Protestant Missionary History." *Tyndale Bulletin* 51:1 (2000) 101–20.
———, ed. *Missions, Nationalism, and the End of Empire.* Cambridge: Eerdmans, 2003.
Stinton, Diane. "Africa, East and West." In *An Introduction to Third World Theologians*, edited by John Parratt, 105–36. Cambridge: Cambridge University Press, 2004.
———. "African Christianity." In *Jesus in History, Thought, and Culture: An Encyclopedia*, edited by J. L. Houlden, 3–14. Santa Barbara: ABC-CLIO, 2003.
———. *Jesus of Africa: Voices of Contemporary African Christology.* Maryknoll: Orbis, 2006.
———, ed. *African Theology on the Way.* London: SPCK, 2010.
Strayer, Robert W. *Kenya: Focus on Nationalism.* New Jersey: Prentice-Hall, 1975.
———. *The Making of Mission Communities in East Africa: Anglicans and Africans in Colonial Kenya, 1875–1935.* London: Heinemann; New York: State University of New York, 1978.
———. "Mission History in Africa: New Perspectives on an Encounter." *African Studies Review* 19:1 (1976) 1–15.
———. "Missions and African Protest." *Protest Movements in colonial East Africa.* New York: Syracuse University, 1973.
Strong, Rowan. *Anglicanism and the British Empire: c.1700–1850.* Oxford: Oxford University Press, 2007.
Stückelberger, Christoph. *Global Trade Ethic.* Geneva: WCC, 2002.
Stückelberger, Christoph, and J. N. K. Mugambi, eds. *Responsible Leadership: Global and Contextual Ethical Perspectives.* Nairobi: Action / Geneva: WCC, 2005.
Stumpf, Hulda J. "How Dark is Their Darkness?" *Inland Africa* 9:12 (British ed. Dec. 1925) 10–11.
Sugden, Chris, and Vinay Samuel, eds. *Anglican Life and Witness: A Reader for the Lambeth Conference of Bishops, 1998.* London: SPCK, 1998.

Sugirtharajah, R. S. *Asian Biblical Hermeneutics and Postcolonialism: Contesting the Interpretations*. Maryknoll: Orbis, 1988.

———. *The Bible and Empire: Postcolonial Explorations*. Cambridge: Cambridge University Press, 2005.

———. *The Bible and the Third World: Precolonial, Colonial and Postcolonial Encounters*. Cambridge: Cambridge University Press, 2001.

———. *Postcolonial Criticism and Biblical Interpretation*. Oxford: Oxford University, 2002.

———. *Postcolonial Reconfigurations: An Alternative Way of Reading and Doing Theology*. London: SCM, 2003.

———. *Still at the Margins: Biblical Scholarship Fifteen Years After the Voices from the Margins*. Edinburgh: T & T Clark, 2007.

———, ed. *The Postcolonial Bible*. Sheffield: Sheffield Academic, 1998.

———, ed. *The Postcolonial Biblical Reader*. Oxford: Blackwell, 2006.

Sundkler, Bengt. *Bantu Prophets in South Africa*. 2nd ed. London: Oxford University Press, 1961.

Sundkler, Bengt, and Christopher Steed. *A History of the Church in Africa*. Cambridge: Cambridge University Press, 2000.

Sykes, Stephen. *Unashamed Anglicanism*. Nashville: Abingdon, 1995.

Taylor, John V. *The Growth of the Church in Buganda*. London: SCM, 1958.

———. *The Primal Vision: Christian Presence amid African Religion*. London: SCM, [1963] 2001.

Taylor, Mark Lewis. "Spirit and Liberation: Achieving Postcolonial Theology in the United States." In *Postcolonial Theologies: Divinity and Empire*, edited by Catherine Keller et al., 39–55. St. Louis: Chalice, 2004.

Taylor, Michael. *Not Angels but Agencies*. London: SCM, 1995.

Temu, Arnold J. *British Protestant Missions*. London: Longman, 1972.

Temu, Arnold, and Bonaventure Swai. *Historians and Africanist History: A Critique: Post-Colonial Historiography Examined*. London: Zed, 1981.

Thiselton, Anthony C. "Biblical Theology and Hermeneutics." In *The Modern Theologians: An Introduction to Christian Theology in the Twentieth Century*. 2nd ed., edited by David F. Ford, 520–37. Oxford: Blackwell, 1997.

Thompson, V. B. *Africa and Unity*. London: Longman, 1969.

Throup, David. "Render unto Caesar the Things that are Caesar's: The Politics of Church-State Conflict in Kenya, 1978–1990." In *Religion and Politics in East Africa*, edited by B. Hansen and M. Twaddle, 143–76. London: James Currey, 1995.

Throup, David, and Charles Hornsby. *Economic and Social Origins of Mau Mau 1945–53*. London: Currey, 1987.

———. *Multi-Party Politics in Kenya: The Kenyatta and Moi States and the Triumph of the System in the 1992 Election*. London: James Currey, 1998.

Tiffin, Helen. "Plato's Cave: Educational and Critical Practices." In *New National and Post-Colonial Literatures: An Introduction*, edited by B. King, 143–63. Oxford: Clarendon, 1996.

Tillich, Paul. *The Shaking of the Foundations*. New York: Scribner, 1948.

———. *Systematic Theology*. Vol. 1. Chicago: University of Chicago Press, [1951] 1963.

———. "Theologian (Part 3)." In *The Shaking of the Foundations*, 129–32. New York: Scribner, 1948.

Tinker, George E. *Spirit and Resistance: Political Theology and American Indian Liberation*. Minneapolis: Fortress, 2004.
Torrey, R. A., and Charles E. Hurlburt. *What We Stand For*. Brooklyn: Africa Inland Mission, n.d.
Tovey, Philip. *Inculturation of Christian Worship: Exploring the Eucharist*. Aldershot: Ashgate, 2004.
Tracy, David. *The Analogical Imagination: Christian Theology and the Culture of Pluralism*. New York: Crossroad, 1981.
———. *Blessed Rage for Order*. New ed. Chicago: University of Chicago Press, 1996.
Turley, David. *The Culture of English Antislavery, 1780–1860*. London: Routledge, 1991.
Turner, Harold W. *African Independent Church: The Life and Faith of the Church of the Lord (Aladura)*. Vol. 2. Oxford: Clarendon, 1967.
———. *History of an African Independent Church: The Church of the Lord (Aladura)*. Vol. 1. Oxford: Clarendon, 1967.
Tylor, Edward B. *Primitive Culture*. New York: Harper, [1871] 1958.
Utuk, Efiong, ed. *Visions of Authenticity: The Assemblies of the AACC 1963–1992*. Nairobi: AACC, 1997.
Van Beek, Walter E. A. "The Innocent Sorcerer: Coping with Evil in Two African Societies (Kapsiki and Dogon)." In *Religion in Africa: Experience and Expression*, edited by Thomas D. Blakely et al., 196–228. London: James Currey; Portsmouth: Heinemann, 1994.
Van Der Veer, Peter, ed. *Conversion to Modernities: The Globalization of Christianity*. New York: Routledge, 1996.
Villa-Vicencio, Charles. "South African Civil Religion: An Introduction." *Journal of Theology for Southern Africa* 19 (June 1977) 5–15.
———. *A Theology of Reconstruction: Nation-building and Human Rights*. Cambridge: Cambridge University Press, 1992.
Visser't Hooft, W. A., and J. J. Oldham. *The Church and Its Function in Society*. London: Allen & Unwin, 1937.
Wainwright, Geoffrey. *Lesslie Newbigin: A Theological Life*. New York: Oxford University Press, 2000.
Waller, Richard. "They Do the Dictating and We must Submit: The African Inland Mission in Maasailand." In *East African Expressions of Christianity*, edited by Thomas Spear and Isaria N. Kimambo, 83–126. Oxford: James Currey; Athens / Ohio: Ohio University Press, 1999.
Ward, Kevin, and Emma Wild-Wood, eds. *The East African Revival: History and Legacies*. Farnham: Ashgate, 2012.
Warren, Max. *Caesar, The Beloved Enemy: Three Studies in the Relation of Church and State*. London: SCM, 1955.
Wa Thiong'o, Ngũgĩ. *Barrel of a Pen—Resistance to Repression in Neo-Colonial Kenya*. Trenton: African World, 1983.
———. *Decolonising the Mind: The Politics of Language in African Literature*. London: James Curry, 1986.
———. *Moving the Centre: The Struggle for Cultural Freedoms*. London: J. Currey / Portsmouth: Heinemann, 1993.
———. *Something Torn and New: An African Renaissance*. New York: Basic Civitas, 2009.
Welbourn, Frederick B. *East African Christian*. London: Oxford University Press, 1965.
———. *East African Rebels: A Study of Some Independent Churches*. London: SCM, 1961.

BIBLIOGRAPHY

Welbourn, Frederick B., and B. A. Ogot. *A Place to Feel at Home: A Study of Two Independent Churches in Western Kenya.* London: Oxford University Press, 1966.

West, Gerald O. *The Academy of the Poor: Towards a Dialogical Reading of the Bible.* Sheffield: Sheffield Academic, 1999.

———. *Biblical Hermeneutics of Liberation: Models of Reading the Bible in the South African Context.* Pietermaritzburg: Cluster, 1991.

———. "Mapping African Biblical Interpretation: A Tentative Sketch." In *The Bible in Africa: Transactions, Trajectories, and Trends,* edited by Gerald O. West and Musa W. Dube, 29–53. Leiden: Brill, 2000.

———, ed. *Reading Other-wise: Socially Engaged Biblical Scholars Reading with Their Local Communities.* Leiden: Brill, 2007.

Weston, Frank. *The One Christ: An Enquiry into the Manner of the Incarnation.* Rev. ed. London: Longmans, Green, 1914.

Wevers, John William. *New Century Bible Commentary: Ezekiel.* London: Nelson, 1969.

White, Evan. "Kwame Nkrumah: Cold War Modernity, Pan-African Ideology and the Geopolitics of Development." *Geopolitics* 8:2 (2003) 99–124.

Williams, Chancellor. *The Destruction of Black Civilization: Great Issues of a Race from 4500 B.C. to 2000 A.D.* Rev. ed. Chicago: Third World, 1974.

Williams, Joseph J. *Hebrewism of West Africa: From Nile to Niger with the Jews.* London: Allen & Unwin, 1930.

Williams, Rowan. *Arius: Heresy and Tradition.* 2nd ed. Grand Rapids: Eerdmans, 2002. Kindle Edition.

———. "Kingdom and Empire: A Biblical Orientation." *Soma: An International Journal of Theological Discourses and Counter-Discourses* (2011) www.sjut.org/journals/ojs/index.php/soma/article/viewFile/2/pdf_4.

Wilmore, Gayraud S. *Pragmatic Spirituality: The Christian Faith Through an Africentric Lens.* New York: New York University Press, 2004.

Wood, David. *Bishop John V. Taylor: Poet, Priest and Prophet.* London: Churches Together in Britain and Ireland, 2002.

Wood, Nicholas. *Faiths and Faithfulness: Pluralism, Dialogue and Mission in the Work of Kenneth Cragg and Lesslie Newbigin.* Bletchley: Paternoster, 2009.

Woods, Ngaire. *The Globalizers: The IMF, the World Bank, and their Borrowers.* Ithaca: Cornell University Press, 2006.

Yates, T. E. *Christian Mission in the Twentieth Century.* Cambridge: Cambridge University Press, 1996.

Yeğenoğlu, Meyda. *Colonial Fantasies: Towards a Feminist Reading of Orientalism.* Cambridge: Cambridge University Press, 1998.

Young, Josiah U. *African Theology: A Critical Analysis and Annotated Bibliography.* Westport: Greenwood, 1993.

Young, Robert J. *Colonial Desire: Hybridity in Theory, Culture and Race.* London / New York: Routledge, 1995.

———. "Ideologies of the Postcolonial." *Interventions: International Journal of Postcolonial Studies* 1:1 (1998) 4–8.

———. *Postcolonialism: An Historical Introduction.* Oxford: Blackwell, 2001.

———. *Postcolonialism: A Very Short Introduction.* Oxford: Oxford University Press, 2003.

———. *White Mythologies: Writing History and the West.* London: Routledge, 1990.

Zack-Williams, Alfred. "Five Decades On: Some Reflections on 50 Years of Africa's Independence." *Review of African Political Economy* 39:131 (2012) 1–10.

Zondi, Siphamandla. "The African Union and the State of Continental Integration." *South African Journal of International Affairs* 15:1 (2008) 25–41.

Other Sources

Alagoa, E. J. "The Ijaw as a Moral Community: Levels of Awareness." Unpublished paper presented to the African History and Politics Seminar. University of Oxford, January 23, 2006.

Arsen, E. H. "The Africa Inland Mission in Kenya Turns Over." TMs, 1–6. Col. 81, AIM/ABGC. Kijabe, Kenya: African Inland Mission, 1972.

Barnett, Eric S. "Acceptance of Negro Missionaries from USA to Kenya Field." TL. Col. 81, AIM/ABGC. April 1951.

———. "Kenya Field Director, to Ralph T. Davis." TL. Col. 81, AIM/ABGC. June 22, 1951.

Board of Directors of the Africa Inland Mission Incorporated. "Minutes of the Meeting of the Saturday, Sept. 6, 1919." TMs. AIM/ABGC. September 6, 1919.

Burleson, Blake Wiley. "John Mbiti: The Dialogue of an African Theologian with African Traditional Religion (Time)." PhD diss., Baylor University, 1986.

The Church Missionary Gleaner. Vol. 2, 1875.

The Church Missionary Gleaner. Vol. 3, 1876.

Davis, Ralph T. "General Secretary AIM, to Members of the AIM." TL. Col. 81, AIM/ABGC. December 7, 1951.

Dayton, Robert, narrator, with comments by Ralph Davis. "Kenya Calls." Film 4. Pre-1956 filmstrip, audio only. Col. 81, AIM/ABGC. n.d.

DePue, Miriam, et al. "How Do 'You' Fit In? Missionary Orientation Handbook." Section 4. 39/16 Col. 81, AIM/ABGC. May 1963.

Editorial. "Kenya: Evil and the Empire." *The Guardian.* http://www.theguardian.com/commentisfree/2013/may/05/kenya-evil-empire-editorial?INTCMP=SRCH.

Eusebius of Caesarea. *Praeparatio Evangelica.* www.earlychristianwritings.com/jackson2/04_eus.html.

Farisani, Elelwani. "Theology of Reconstruction." PhD diss., University of Natal, 1999–2001.

Ferrin, Howard W. "To Ralph T. Davis, September 15, 1955." TL. 1/12 Col. 81, AIM/ABGC.

Ferrin, Howard W. "To Ralph T. Davis, September 22, 1955." TL. 1/12 Col. 81, AIM/ABGC.

Gration, John Alexander. "The Relationship of the Africa Inland Mission and its National Church in Kenya between 1895 and 1971." PhD diss., New York University, 1974.

Kibicho, S. G. "The Kikuyu Concept of God, its Continuity into the Christian Era and the Question it raises for the Christian Idea of Revelation." PhD diss., Vanderbilt University, 1972.

Kioko, Samuel M., General Secretary, AIC. "Africa Inland Church Memorandum to the AIM Home Council at Limuru, 10th June, 1968." TL. Col. 81, AIM/ABGC. June 10th, 1968.

BIBLIOGRAPHY

Koopman, Nico. "Churches and Public Policy Discourses in South Africa." Unpublished paper, http://www.csu.edu.au/__data/assets/word_doc/0020/51617/Churches-and-public-policy-discourses-in-South-Africa.doc.

Morad, Stephen D., and Shelley Arensen. "The Spreading Tree: A History of the Africa Inland Church in Kenya: 1895-1995." TMs. AIM/ABGC. n.d.

Mwase, Isaac M. T. "A Critical Evaluation of J. N. K. Mugambi's Correlation of Christianity with the African Heritage: An Apologetic Perspective." PhD diss., Southwestern Baptist Theological Seminary, 1993.

N.a. "Extension of the Reformed Catholic Church." *Colonial Church Chronicle* 1 (July 1847–June 1848) 3–5.

N.a. "Rise and Progress of the Colonial Episcopate." *Colonial Church Chronicle* 1 (July 1847–June 1848) 6–11.

N.a. "Crisis of Church Leadership in Africa: Scott Theological College, Machakos, Kenya, East Africa (circa 1971), 1." TMs. AIM/ABGC. n.d.

Ranger, Terence O. "Religion in Africa: A Series of Three Lectures, Lecture Two: Mission Christianity." Unpublished paper, presented to the Oxford Center for Mission Studies, 1–16. October 4, 2005.

Ritchie, Ian. "African Theology and Social Change: An Anthropological Approach." PhD diss., McGill University, 1993.

Stauffacher, John. "History of the Africa Inland Mission." TMs. AIM/ABGC. c. 1915.

Taylor, Clyde. "Conference on Evangelical Fellowship and Ecumenicity, Held at the Africa Inland Mission Station of Machakos, Kenya, February 16–18, 1962." TMs. 11/32 Col. 81, AIM/ABGC. February 16–18, 1962.

Website. *United Nations Development Programme.* http://hdr.undp.org/en/.

Wolfe, Ray. "Random Thoughts on Theological Education." TMs. 39/16 Col. 81, AIM/ABGC. n.d.

Woodward, Josh. "The Cost of Credit: The Ascent of State-Directed Entrepreneurship in Sub-Saharan Africa." MPhil diss., Oxford University, 2009.

Young, Robert J. C. "What is the Postcolonial? Anglican Identities and the Postcolonial." Unpublished paper, 1–8. Lambeth Conference, July 21, 2008.

Index

Africa Inland Mission (AIM)
　history, 39, 40, 47, 48, 64–65
　teaching, 44, 61, 48, 50, 63, 65, 67–76, 78–79, 84, 89
　critiques, of, 35, 39, 44, 63, 65–74, 76, 79, 81, 89–92, 184, 197, 203
　legacy, 35, 45
Africa Inland Church, 40, 64, 67n20
African Initiated Churches (AICs), 1, 2, 26, 37, 46, 57–58, 66–67, 96, 137n56, 194
African Theology, 2, 3–9, 23, 25–26, 31–33, 39, 42–43, 46, 50, 62, 64, 65, 67n20, 74, 77–78, 86, 93, 96, 106–7, 110, 112, 119–21, 125, 127, 146–48, 149, 153, 156–57, 159, 172, 176–77, 180, 186, 199–204, 206–9, 216
　definition, 51, 150, 191
　themes, 50–55, 57–61, 99, 131–32, 139–40, 151
African Traditional Religion(s), 8–9, 33, 50, 52, 54, 58, 64, 93, 94–96, 98–99, 102, 104–9, 118–25, 127, 129–30, 132, 137, 141–44, 146–47, 180, 181n188, 186, 194, 197, 201–3
Agency, 12, 14–16, 19n41, 21, 99, 183
　theological, 8, 11, 18, 27–28, 30, 31, 40, 45, 50, 55, 59–61, 85–86, 88, 123, 131, 138, 141–42, 155, 169, 172, 184–87, 189, 193–94, 196–99, 204–5, 209

Akamba, 44, 61, 62–64, 66–85, 87–93, 96, 147, 173, 176, 184, 186, 196–98, 202–4
Anglican/Anglicanism, 3, 4, 6, 8, 29, 34n14, 37, 41, 45, 46, 48, 51, 65, 136, 141, 192, 208, 210, 212, 214, 217–18

Barth, Karl, 107, 111, 171
Bhabha, Homi, 15, 152n16, 183n4
Bultmann, Rudolf, 111–14, 171

Catholicity, 58, 126, 131–33, 145–46, 211
Colonialism, 12, 15, 17, 20, 23, 115, 173, 183, 194–95, 206, 217
　and foreign missions/missionaries, 26, 31, 36–39, 50–51, 109, 122, 127, 146, 157, 183, 190, 196
　British, 31
　definition of, 13–14
　experiences of, 1, 2, 6–7, 11, 17, 29, 46, 216
　history of, 46, 99, 206n1
　neo-colonialism, 13, 29, 41, 52, 118, 151, 155n34, 195
　See also Coloniality, Post-colonialism, Decolonization
Christology, 7–9, 28, 67, 89, 91–93, 124–27, 130–33, 139–46, 148, 183, 190–91, 201–2, 204
Christopraxis, 7, 9, 126–27, 141–42, 144–47, 197, 200, 202, 204

259

INDEX

Church Missionary Society (CMS), 34n16, 35n25, 36

Coloniality, 2, 7–10, 11–12, 14–15, 17, 19–22, 27, 29–30, 42, 92–93, 129–31, 138, 145–46, 148, 149–50, 156, 177, 180, 182–83, 185–86, 189–90, 192–93, 196, 198–205, 207, 216–18

Contextual/Contextualization/Inculturation, 2–3, 7–10, 46, 53, 58, 59–62, 66, 68, 73–74, 79, 81, 89, 91–93, 103, 105–6, 112, 115n122, 118, 120, 122–25, 127–28, 131, 133–35, 139, 141–42, 146–48, 149, 155–56, 171, 176–77, 184, 189–91, 193–97, 200–204, 206–7, 210, 218

Culture(s), 2, 8n18, 14, 17n36, 20, 22, 29, 34n15, 37, 40, 42–45, 52, 54, 56–59, 72, 84–86, 94, 97, 107–9, 115–18, 121–23, 126–33, 135, 137, 141, 150, 152–53, 156–57, 162–64, 167, 169, 171, 173–74, 177, 188–89, 194, 207, 210, 214

Decolonization, 2, 7, 10, 11–13, 17–21, 23–27, 29–30, 51, 86n106, 116, 152n16, 175, 183, 186, 190–95, 198–99, 205, 209–10, 213–18

Dedji, Valentin, 113, 114n115, 155, 175, 177, 178n176

Denominations/Denominationalism, 31, 40, 46–47, 50, 57, 61, 64, 132, 136, 169–70, 183, 191

Dialogue, 7, 9–10, 46, 62, 96, 112, 122–25, 132, 143–44, 178, 185, 197, 200, 202–3

Ecclesiology/Ecclesial, 25, 29, 113, 131, 140, 144, 149, 153, 157n48, 164–67, 169–70, 180–81, 198, 212
See also Denominations/Denominationalism; Ecumenism/Ecumenical

Ecumenism/Ecumenical, 4–5, 46–48, 57, 59, 61, 151, 157, 164–65, 169–71, 173, 175–76, 180, 195

Empire(s)/Imperialism(s), 1, 12–13, 15, 17, 20, 23–29, 31, 33–34, 36–41, 50, 53, 98, 107, 113, 116, 128, 133, 135–36, 139–40, 143, 145–47, 150, 169, 183, 186, 188, 191–92, 194–95, 200, 203, 206, 210–14, 217–18

Eschatology, 3, 7–8, 33, 53, 61, 62–75, 77, 79–84, 89, 91–93, 121, 125, 128, 148, 164, 180, 183, 186, 193, 198, 201–4

Exodus, 54, 56, 87, 101, 150, 152, 160, 166, 174, 180, 192

Expansionism, 1, 34, 48, 216–17

Fanon, Frantz, 21

Gillies, Francis, 64, 79–84, 87–88

Globalization, 29, 38, 113n112, 117, 146, 158, 177, 192, 198n57, 215

God, 2, 7, 27, 34, 37–39, 41, 44, 49, 56, 59, 91–93, 95–97, 119, 126–27, 129–30, 132–42, 144, 150, 153–54, 168, 173, 186–87, 190–91, 195, 210–13, 215, 218
attributes of, 29, 32, 53, 58, 68, 101–2, 120, 197
in Traditional African Religion, 4, 9, 54–55, 69, 72, 75, 77–78, 94, 96–106, 108, 116, 121–22, 138, 142, 147, 197, 204

Hegemony, 8, 11–12, 15, 17, 19, 21, 29–30, 37, 107, 158, 193, 195, 199, 205, 208

Hybridity/Hybridization, 12, 16–19, 21, 27–29, 109n94, 183, 186–87, 189, 193, 195, 197, 205–7, 209–10, 212–13

Idowu, Bolaji, 5, 76n72, 98n28

Kato, Byang, 181n188

Kenya, 2–4, 6–9, 13, 19n41, 33, 34n18, 35, 36, 38–39, 40–43, 45–48, 50, 60, 64–65, 74n58, 86–87, 93, 102, 109–10, 116, 126, 131, 136, 140–41, 145, 147, 148, 151, 157–59,

INDEX

161, 164, 168, 174, 178n177, 179, 181, 183n4, 189–90, 193, 196–98, 201, 203, 207, 218
Kenyatta, Jomo, 207
Krapf, Ludwig, 34n17, 34n18, 64–65

Liberation, 35, 36, 53, 57, 120, 129, 131, 138, 140, 150, 152–56, 166, 172, 178
Liberation theology, 19, 27, 37, 39, 60, 139, 146, 151, 155, 174, 176, 178, 192, 209
  critiques of, 26, 51, 52, 155, 156, 166, 174, 181, 187, 189, 206
Liturgy, 73, 139n68, 141, 143

Mbiti
  African Tradtional Religion, 8, 42–46, 49, 54–58, 63, 75, 76, 82, 85–88, 94–125, 130, 138, 143, 144
  Akamba, 44, 61, 62–93, 96, 147, 173, 176, 184, 186, 196–98, 202–4
  Christ, 9, 36, 55, 65–70, 73, 77, 78, 80, 84, 91, 92, 95, 107, 108, 123, 124, 126–48, 153, 180, 183, 186, 190, 191, 195, 199, 204, 212–14
  eschatology, 33, 40, 41, 44, 45, 49, 50, 53, 55, 61, 62–84, 89, 91–93, 121, 125, 128, 148, 164, 180, 183, 186, 193, 198, 201–4
  missionaries, 31–61, 64–75, 83, 89, 91, 92, 94, 95, 99, 104–8, 128, 131, 134, 141, 145, 183, 184, 186, 187, 196, 203, 205, 216
  Praeparatio Evangelica, 36, 94, 105–7, 138, 142, 194
  temporality, 8, 50, 61, 62–93, 125, 148, 180, 193, 194, 198, 201, 203
  sacraments, 68, 70, 72–74, 103, 104
  salvation, 52, 54n152, 56, 65, 78, 96, 126, 134, 136–38, 141, 144, 156
Mission, 3, 7, 8, 30, 31–58, 60–70, 74, 77, 80, 81, 95, 97, 99, 125, 129, 136, 137, 147, 150, 152, 158, 164, 165, 168, 173, 175, 179, 183, 184, 187, 189, 191, 194, 200, 201, 210, 214–18
Missiology, 185, 214, 215

Modern Missionary Movement
  history of, 31, 40, 46, 187, 199
  themes, 187, 192
  critique of, 2, 32, 33, 35, 39–41, 46
Moltmann, Jürgen, 38, 72n46, 80,
Moule, C.F.D, 69n33,
Mugambi
  African Traditional Heritage, 4, 41, 45, 59, 94–96, 98, 99, 105, 108–10, 113, 115, 117, 118, 121, 125, 129, 136, 139, 177, 199, 210, 203–5
  Christ, 9, 36, 55, 61, 67, 69, 108, 123, 124, 126–48, 153, 154, 180, 186, 190, 191, 199, 204, 205, 212–16
  empire, 36, 133, 146, 188, 191, 214
  globalization, 38, 117, 146, 158, 177, 192
  imperialism, 36, 37, 41, 50, 53, 116, 140, 169, 195, 206, 211, 212
  indigenous theology, 14, 58, 108n88, 186, 205
  missionaries, 14, 33, 35–42, 45–56, 61–69, 85, 94–99, 104, 105, 107, 109, 128, 131, 139, 141, 145, 169, 179–84, 187, 191, 196, 205, 210, 216
  myth, 113, 120, 168, 171, 177
  reconstruction, theology of, 4, 6, 9, 54, 94, 109–13, 118, 140, 148, 182, 183, 188, 192, 195, 196, 198, 202, 205
  re-mythologization, 94, 106, 108–20, 125, 153, 167, 168, 177, 203
  salvation, 52, 53, 126, 136, 137, 141, 154–56, 178
Mwase, Isaac, 32n5

Négritude, 177
Nkrumah, Kwame, 160, 207

Oduyoye, Mercy, 121, 181n187

Pedagogy, x, 217, 218
Post-Colonialism, 11–30
  theology, 1, 2, 5, 7–9, 11–30, 37, 93, 135, 139–41, 182–85, 189–99, 200, 205, 206, 210, 213–18

Mbiti and Mugambi, 98, 145, 148, 202, 203, 205, 206–10, 214–18
Power analysis, 7, 10, 18, 19n41, 145, 148, 178, 182, 184, 193, 196–200, 202, 204–5
Praeparatio Evangelica, 94, 105–7, 138, 142, 147, 194

Reconstruction, theology of, 4, 6, 7, 9, 54, 94, 109–11, 113, 114n115, 115, 118, 130, 140, 148, 149–57, 165–67, 168, 172–81, 182, 183, 192, 195, 196, 198, 201, 202, 205,
Resurrection, 70, 74, 77–80, 100

Sacraments, 68, 70, 72–74, 103–4
Said, Edward, 14n18, 15, 17n36, 20, 85n102, 152n16, 183n4,
Salvation, 52–56, 65, 78, 96, 126, 134–38, 141–44, 154–56, 178
Song, C.S., 188
Stinton, Diane, 127, 128, 135, 173,
Sugirtharajah, R.S, 12, 23, 24, 207, 214

Symbol, x, 7, 9, 24, 54, 65–69, 72, 102, 111–13, 116, 124–26, 133, 140–44, 153, 171, 197, 202, 204

Taylor, John, 32–33, 48, 66, 98, 104
Temporality
African, 61, 62, 64, 69, 70, 72, 79–93, 125, 148, 180, 193, 194, 198, 201, 203
mission, 50, 64, 67n21, 82, 93
western, 50, 70, 79, 84, 93, 203
Tillich, Paul, 97n18, 100n39, 114, 115n119-n120, 116, 142–43, 152, 167, 171, 177

Villa-Vicencio, Charles, 174, 175n165, 178n176, 179

War, World Wars, 33, 34, 175
World Council of Churches, 4, 5, 6, 45, 124n165, 175, 176

Young, Robert, 14n18, 15, 21, 22, 23, 25, 183, 184n4, 185, 206

www.ingramcontent.com/pod-product-compliance
Lightning Source LLC
Chambersburg PA
CBHW071245230426
43668CB00011B/1597